Research in Comparative and Global Social Policy

Series Editors: **Heejung Chung**, University of Kent, UK,
Alexandra Kaasch, Bielefeld University, Germany and
Stefan Kühner, Lingnan University, Hong Kong

Through a unique combination of comparative and global social
perspectives, this series questions how nation states and
transnational policy actors deal with globally shared challenges.

Also available

Varieties of Precarity
Melting Labour and the Failure to Protect Workers in the Korean Welfare State
By **Sophia Seung-yoon Lee**

Women, Welfare and Productivism in East Asia and Europe
By **Ruby Chau** and **Sam Yu**

Compulsory Income Management in Australia and New Zealand
More Harm than Good?
By **Greg Marston, Louise Humpage, Michelle Peterie, Philip
Mendes, Shelley Bielefeld** and **Zoe Staines**

Welfare Reform and Social Investment Policy in Europe and East Asia
International Lessons and Policy Implications
Edited by **Young Jun Choi, Timo Fleckenstein** and
Soohyun Lee

Minimum Income Standards and Reference Budgets
International and Comparative Policy Perspectives
Edited by **Christopher Deeming**

Find out more

policy.bristoluniversitypress.co.uk/
research-in-comparative-and-global-social-policy

Coming soon

Welfare Attitudes in East Asia
The Case of Beijing and Singapore
By **Trude Sundberg**

Editorial advisory board

Find out more

policy.bristoluniversitypress.co.uk/
research-in-comparative-and-global-social-policy

EMERGING TRENDS IN SOCIAL POLICY FROM THE SOUTH

Challenges and Innovations in Emerging Economies

Edited by
Ilcheong Yi, Alexandra Kaasch and Kelly Stetter

P

First published in Great Britain in 2024 by

Policy Press, an imprint of
Bristol University Press
University of Bristol
1–9 Old Park Hill
Bristol
BS2 8BB
UK
t: +44 (0)117 374 6645
e: bup-info@bristol.ac.uk

Details of international sales and distribution partners are available at
policy.bristoluniversitypress.co.uk

© Bristol University Press 2024

British Library Cataloguing in Publication Data
A catalogue record for this book is available from the British Library

ISBN 978-1-4473-6790-1 hardcover
ISBN 978-1-4473-6791-8 ePub
ISBN 978-1-4473-6792-5 ePdf

FSC
www.fsc.org
MIX
Paper | Supporting
responsible forestry
FSC® C013604

Contents

Series Editors' Preface

Heejung Chung (University of Kent, UK)
Alexandra Kaasch (Bielefeld University, Germany)
Stefan Kühner (Lingnan University, Hong Kong)

In a world that is rapidly changing, increasingly connected and uncertain, there is a need to develop a shared applied policy analysis of welfare regimes around the globe. *Research in Comparative and Global Social Policy* is a series of books that addresses broad questions around how nation states and transnational policy actors manage globally shared challenges. In so doing, the book series includes a wide array of contributions, which discuss comparative social policy history, development and reform within a broad international context. The book series invites innovative research by leading experts on all world-regions and global social policy actors and aims to fulfil the following objectives: it encourages cross-disciplinary approaches that develop theoretical frameworks reaching across individual world-regions and global actors; it seeks to provide evidence-based good practice examples that cross the bridge between academic research and practice; not least, it aims to provide a platform in which a wide range of innovative methodological approaches, may it be national case studies, larger-N comparative studies, or global social policy studies can be introduced to aid the evaluation, design and implementation of future social policies.

The edited collection by Ilcheong Yi, Alexandra Kaasch and Kelly Stetter makes an excellent contribution to our series. It sheds light on innovative solutions, new approaches and novel experiences in the Global South – while posing the question what it means to be *novel* or *transformative*. More specifically, this book asks where to look for new inspiration in social policy making, and what actors or factors to study. The selection of case studies reflects an encompassing take on social problems and global crises to which social policies respond using a wide range of different countries in different world-regions that are not frequently explored in the study of social policy. Taken together, these case studies, as well as the more conceptual chapters, allow for a truly new and global perspective on what can be studied and learned from countries of the Global South that goes way beyond "South-to-South" learning and exchange.

The researchers and authors involved in this volume are heterogeneous and spread across the globe. They are all renowned social policy scholars and experts on various aspects of social policy development and they bring unique insights in their specific country cases. In highlighting six specific trends, the contributors to this volume seek out innovative approaches by not just looking for and commenting on common categories in social policy research, but looking at countries of the Global South with interest and curiosity in what new phenomena can be and must be observed, especially when we go beyond the traditional Western-centric approaches of the welfare state analysis. Through such perspectives the key roles of non-state actors, the meanings of supranational social policies, and the active roles of informal workers in shaping social policies, among other findings, are revealed. There is also a close connection between public policies, development policies and social policies explored in some of the chapters that give an idea about alternative ways of studying and understanding contemporary social policies.

Another speciality of this book is how it connects the worlds of international organizations with those of university researchers. In that way, the contextualization and questions provided in this volume are closely connected to the agendas of international social and development policies, while drawing also on the conceptual and theoretical knowledge of researchers from academia. On that basis, the conclusions drawn here are also able to connect issues of promising social policy reform (connected to policy advice) with more nuanced ways to do research on social policies in a global context. Finally, this book contributes to one of our book series' goals of decolonizing academia by going beyond the stories and perspectives of the Global North and Western European countries. This edition provides more evidence to show how providing space and elevating diverse voices and cases in the study of social policy allows us a better understanding of global challenges and potential solutions, enhancing academic knowledge overall.

We are very pleased to have this book in our series, and we hope you enjoy reading it.

List of Figures and Tables

Figures

Tables

Notes on Contributors

Rina Agarwala is Professor of Sociology at Johns Hopkins University. She is the author of the award-winning *Migration-Development Regime: How Class Shapes Indian Emigration* (2022) and *Informal Labor, Formal Politics and Dignified Discontent in India* (2013). Agarwala has worked at the United Nations Development Programme, Self-Employed Women's Association, and Women's World Banking. She holds a PhD in Sociology and Demography from Princeton University, USA.

Linda J. Cook is Professor Emerita of Political Science and Slavic Studies, Brown University, USA. She has authored *The Soviet Social Contract*, *Postcommunist Welfare States* and many other publications. Her book, *Welfare Nationalism in Europe and Russia: The Politics of Exclusionary and Inclusionary Migration*s, is forthcoming from Cambridge University Press.

Lijie Fang is Professor at Renmin University, China. She specializes in health policy, elderly care and community development. Serving as the Director of RUC's Social Policy Project, she consults for China's central ministries and has collaborated with the United Nations Research Institute for Social Development (UNRISD) and the London School of Economics. Involved in international projects and community initiatives, she is a pivotal voice in China's welfare studies.

Louise Haagh is Professor in Politics at the University of York, UK. A long-standing consultant in global development, she is a standing expert to the World Health Organization and Chair Emeritus of the Basic Income Earth Network (BIEN). Her recent book *The Case for Universal Basic Income* (2019) was showcased in US *Orion Magazine* and the *Stanford Social Innovation Review*.

Yara A. Halasa–Rappel is a health services researcher and Assistant Professor in the Department of Population and Quantitative Health Sciences at the University of Massachusetts Medical School, USA. Her research includes economic cost and cost effectiveness analysis and behavioural interventions in areas including oral health and healthcare delivery-related projects.

Bo Hu is Assistant Professorial Research Fellow at the Care Policy and Evaluation Centre, London School of Economics (LSE). With doctoral degrees from Nankai University (China) and LSE, his focus includes long-term care, dementia care, unmet needs and healthy ageing, using mixed methods.

Elena Iarskaia-Smirnova is Professor of Sociology at the Higher School of Economics (Moscow, Russia) and the European Humanities University (Vilnius, Lithuania). She serves as Head of the International Laboratory of Social Integration Research and Editor-in-Chief of the *Journal of Social Policy and Gender Studies*. Her research interests include sociology of welfare policy, social work, gender, disability, professions, family and childhood.

Alexandra Kaasch is Professor in German and Transnational Social Policy at Bielefeld University, Germany, and holds a PhD from the University of Sheffield, UK. She is Lead Editor of the journal *Global Social Policy* and has published widely on issues of global and comparative social policies.

Amna Khan holds a Master's Degree in Public Affairs from the University of Texas at Austin, USA. She has over a decade of experience across six countries, focusing primarily on human development, system strengthening and public policy advice. At the time of collaboration, she was an independent researcher.

Roosa Lambin is a visiting Research Fellow at The Open University, UK. Her work is focused on social policy developments in the sub-Saharan African region, and the role and functions of philanthropic donor agencies in development, particularly in the area of health policy.

Bingqin Li is Professor at the University of New South Wales, Australia. Her research examines social inclusion, governance and urban dynamics in China and Australia, emphasizing state–market–society relations in social service delivery. She is frequently a consultant for UN agencies, governments and NGOs.

Milla Nyyssölä is Chief Researcher at the Labour Institute for Economic Research (Labore) in Helsinki, Finland. She works on labour economics and demography, as well as gender, poverty, vulnerability and sustainable development. Before joining Labore, she was the research focal point for UNU-WIDER's country programme on Tanzania, "Sustainable development solutions for Tanzania—strengthening research to achieve SDGs".

Sophie Plagerson is Visiting Associate Professor at the Centre for Social Development in Africa, University of Johannesburg, South Africa. She is currently based in the Netherlands and working as an independent consultant. She holds a PhD in Epidemiology from the London School of Hygiene and Tropical Medicine. She is interested in the intersection between disciplines and policy fields, and in how a social justice lens frames approaches to social policy and social protection.

Heath J. Prince is a research scientist, quantitative analyst, lecturer and Director of the Ray Marshall Center at the LBJ School of Public Affairs, University of Texas at Austin, USA. His work focuses on conducting impact evaluations of employment policies and programmes in the MENA region, sub-Saharan Africa, Central America and Nepal.

Sanjay Ruparelia is Associate Professor of Politics and the Jarislowsky Democracy Chair at Toronto Metropolitan University, Canada. His major publications include *Divided We Govern: Coalition Politics in Modern India* (2015); *The Indian Ideology: Three Responses to Perry Anderson* (edited; 2015); and *Understanding India's New Political Economy: A Great Transformation?* (co-edited; 2011).

Smita Srinivas (Technological Change Lab) specializes in economic development, innovation and industrial policy, with experience in health and social policy analysis. She has served as co-chair or member on several expert task forces on global health, urbanization, sustainability and higher education programmes. Srinivas was recognized as the 2021 AFEE Clarence E. Ayres Scholar in institutional economics, and was awarded the 2015 EAEPE Joan Robinson Prize in evolutionary political economy.

Kelly Stetter is Technical Officer in Social Security at the International Social Security Association.[1] She has previously held positions with the United Nations Economic Commission for Europe, the United Nations Environment Programme, UNICEF and UNRISD. Her work focuses on social and sustainable development, including in humanitarian contexts.

Lauren Stuart is a post-doctoral fellow at the Centre of Excellence for Human Development at the University of the Witwatersrand, South Africa. Prior to this, she worked at the Centre for Social Development in Africa. She has co-authored several research reports and journal articles, and her areas of interest are unemployment, education, social policy, social protection as well as methods of monitoring and evaluation.

Jing Wang is Associate Professor at the Chinese Academy of Social Sciences, where she directs the Department of Social Work and Welfare Sociology.

---

[1] The statements and opinions expressed in this volume should not be attributed to the International Social Security Association.

A key figure in the Chinese Sociological Association, she has been a Visiting Scholar at Harvard University, USA, and the University of Mannheim, Germany. Her research centres on social policy, elderly services and social security in China. Key works include *Bring the Family Back*.

Brooke Wilmsen is Senior Lecturer in Development Studies in the School of Humanities and Social Sciences, La Trobe University, Australia. She holds a PhD in Geography from the University of Melbourne, Australia. Brooke is author of many works critically examining the impacts of displacement that have been published, for example, in *Global Environmental Change*, *World Development*, *Development and Change*, *Geoforum*, *Progress in Human Geography* and *Asia Pacific Viewpoint*.

Nicola Yeates is Professor and Chair of Social Policy at The Open University, UK. She specializes in global social policy, with particular reference to labour, health and social protection. Further information about her research publications is available at: https://oro.open.ac.uk/view/person/ny265.html.

Ilcheong Yi is Senior Research Coordinator at UNRISD in Geneva, Switzerland. He has been researching various issues of alternative economies, international development cooperation, the Social and Solidarity Economy (SSE), measurement of sustainable development performance, and transformative social policy.

Introduction: New Social Policy Trends and Innovations

Ilcheong Yi, Alexandra Kaasch and Kelly Stetter

Attaining the ambitious, transformative visions and goals of the 2030 Agenda for Sustainable Development requires a radical departure from business as usual in designing and implementing strategies, policies and action plans. An innovative approach is needed more than ever in the social policy sector since new and significant challenges and risks have, albeit at different speeds, started to raise questions on the validity of existing policy tools.

Climate change poses some of the greatest economic, social, and sometimes political challenges of the twenty-first century. Global carbon dioxide (CO_2) emissions will accelerate climate change and threaten the lives and well-being of present and future generations and the planet itself (UNDESA 2019). Climate change causes significant negative consequences in terms of production, particularly in the sectors of agriculture, coastal resources, energy, forestry, water and tourism, which are major industries of many developing countries. Inequality has increased in almost all countries since the 1980s, which marks the end of a postwar egalitarian regime. The level of inequality in terms of income accounted for by the nation's top 10 per cent earners is particularly high (more than 50 per cent of national income) in many developing countries in Central and Latin America, the Middle East, Southeast Asia, sub-Saharan Africa and India (Chancel et al 2021). The latest estimates hint at the COVID-19 crisis further reinforcing these trends, not only in terms of financial inequalities, but even regarding gender, formal and informal workers, and marginalized racial and ethnic groups, among others. Extreme poverty remains entrenched in many parts of the world.

The rapidly changing demographic structure over the past two decades has had, and will continue to have, a significant impact on political, social and economic structures, and the environment. At global level, the lower-end estimate of the United Nations (UN) in 1999 was that by 2050, the population would have reached 7.3 billion people. This figure was exceeded in 2015 (Sardak et al 2018). Population growth, combined with the increased flow of migrants, has brought about changes in the age, religious, cultural and socioeconomic structures of the population with different impacts across countries. The formation of a new demographic structure will lead to radical change and demand a new mechanism for development in society. Decreases in regular employment levels and increased uncertainty over global economic

1

governance, food security, shelter, health and energy pose questions on the validity of postwar public policies, in particular social policies that have been considered means to mitigate risks and insecurities in our lives. We must examine whether and how to adapt postwar social policies to new social risks, and how to make social policies to serve new risk groups that do not fit into the previously defined categories of the postwar welfare state (Bonoli 2006; Swank 2020).

To draw insights for retrofitting or forward fitting social policy, policy makers are increasingly paying attention to innovative solutions to social, economic and environmental problems such as inequality, sustainable growth and climate change. They search for examples of good practice in policy and institutional innovations from not only the global North but also the global South. Innovations, particularly those from developing countries, attract attention, as we can see in the extensive discussions on South–South cooperation in academia and practitioners' communities for international development cooperation. Assumptions that rich Western countries know best, and that knowledge, technology and expertise are transferred from developed to developing countries, have also been gradually debunked as policy makers begin to realize that "ideas drawn from organizations of, or working in, the poorest countries also help to improve the work of human service organizations in the wealthier countries of the world" (Lewis 2017:327).

What innovations and reforms have been made in the global South over the past decades? How have they affected people, planet and prosperity? Are these innovations and reforms transformative in the sense that they contribute to restructuring the underlying economic, political and social structures that produce and entrench social injustice, changing norms and institutions that generate inequality and poverty, and rebalancing the asymmetry of power relations? Ultimately, can they contribute to realizing the transformative visions and goals of the 2030 Agenda?

New and innovative social policy reforms in developing countries are so numerous that one book cannot possibly cover them all. The authors in this book took the approach of selecting trends in reforms and zooming in on specific countries with notable changes in social policy sectors to evaluate them. Six trends in reforms and innovations that could significantly affect the realization of the transformative vision of the 2030 Agenda in both developing and developed countries have been selected. They are: a rights-based approach to social welfare; integration of social policy into other public policies; the newly assumed role of civil society organizations (CSOs) in delivering social services in transition economies; the emergence of supranational-level social policy; informal workers shaping the system of social policy programmes; and national ownership of social policy in the context of development cooperation.

Diverse Understandings of Social Policy

The first step of enquiry in any studies about reforms or innovations is to clearly delineate the scope of what is to be reformed or innovated. Understandings or conceptualizations of social policy vary immensely across contexts and are shaped by factors such as socioeconomic and political conditions, social questions or problems, and political ideologies dominating and shaping policy discourse and implementation. The concept of social policy is socially constructed and its scope, subjects and objectives are politically determined by the interactions between ideas, motivations, beliefs and values, resources and practices employed by different groups in society.

Despite differences in the perceptions of social policy, all these concepts attach one of two notions of "social" to social policies: something related to the quality of caring/sharing or something to do with society as a whole. Although these two notions are compatible, they do not always go together in policy terms. Social policy with the former as a defining quality is primarily geared toward promoting individual well-being. The British understanding of social policy based on the Titmuss tradition falls into this category of social policy, which meets "social needs" arising out of the nature of society and being beyond the individual's capacity to resolve without outside help (Titmuss 1968). Consequently, social protection above a universal minimum is the responsibility of the individual, as the Beveridgean universal model shows. Such a social policy will consequently contribute to increasing the benefits of society as a whole, but individual welfare is the primary concern in this kind of social policy (Jones 1985).

The German concept of *sozialpolitik*, which is the first example of the usage of the social policy concept in printed materials, however, implies a different ordering of priorities. In the document where the concept was originated, *sozialpolitik* meant "social action directed towards problems affecting society as a whole and the continued attainment of society's goals" (Cahnman and Schmitt 1979:47). The goal of *sozialpolitik* was to promote the long-term interests of society as a whole. Of course, factors influencing individual or family well-being, such as health, job/income security, education and housing, can be promoted in this kind of social policy. However, individual or family well-being is not the ultimate goal, and if there is any conflict between individual well-being and long-term societal enhancement, this type of social policy opts for the long-term interest of society at the expense of individual well-being. Incorporating status-preserving benefits into public schemes was one example of the state prioritizing the long-term interest of society, that is, stability. In a way, the German concept of social policy is more indicative of collective well-being than individual welfare (Jones 1985; Hagen 2001).

3

The Scandinavian concept of social policy is a mixture of these two categories with unique characteristics such as an emphasis on the equality achieved by state institutions and democratic decision making on the scope and quality of social services. Social policy in Scandinavia denotes an array of redistributive, egalitarian and comprehensive state actions aiming at promoting economic efficiency, improving the ability of society to solve its problems, and enriching and equalizing the living conditions of all citizens based on universalism (Erikson et al 1987; Hagen 2001; Kuhnle and Hort 2004). The characteristics of the Scandinavian welfare state, such as high tax, high levels of employment, universalism and a large public social service sector, are all considered the elements constituting the unique notion of "the social" attached to Scandinavian social policy.

Social policy with these different objectives and motivations can have a broad range of policy tools or activities in different national contexts. Any collective action to address social issues to affect individual well-being or society's long-term benefits can be considered social policy. Therefore, as Jones describes:

> Social policy per se signifies interference (or a public attempt to interfere) in a given social order. It does not of itself outline what sort of interference is entailed and to what end. ... Components of social policy have, therefore to be deduced (e.g., what counts as "social expenditure"?) rather than simply noted down. (Jones 1985:15)

Evolution of Social Policy in the Global South

Social policy after independence

In many countries of the global South that became independent over the three decades after the Second World War, social policy was understood as a means to facilitate development. Understanding what was meant by development in these countries is critical to comprehend how social policy was understood in these newly independent countries. Development seemed to have been understood as a process consisting of two dynamic functions: state-building and nation-building. All these countries inherited colonial institutions—the civil service, army and social services if there were any—which were often destroyed by a *coup d'état*, conflicts with neighbouring countries, or both. State-building involved the creation of a viable formal structure, political apparatus and institutions of the government that would replace the inherited, often precarious ones. It meant a process to give substance through reforms to reflect the realities of independent nations. Nation-building as a process of consolidating national identity involved the formulation of a national moral or political code, or at least a general acceptance of basic rules of social and political procedures. Maintaining the territory of the state, infrastructure of the state and the level of modernity that had been achieved, which we could call state-preserving, was a precondition for these state-building and nation-building processes. Although the rulers of many of these countries, be they in uniform or not, were mostly autocratic, if not despotic, narrowly based and prone to corruption, they were all involved in these processes of state-preserving, state-building and nation-building in one way or another (Jacobson 1964; Sens 1968; Jeffrey 1987; Oliver and Atmore 2005; Yi 2015).

In these processes, social policy, be it for individual welfare or long-term social benefits, was naturally integrated into development policies. Various social policy or social policy equivalents, ranging from a radical redistributive policy such as land reform to basic social services such as education, health and emergency relief, were implemented to mobilize support for the government from the core groups, enhance the legitimacy of the government or facilitate industrialization (Chang 2004; Estevez-Ave 2008). Integration of, or the attempt to integrate, social policy into the development process was clearly shown in the national slogans of these newly independent countries of the global South, such as "education for self-reliance" (Nyerere 1968:44). The government policy aimed at transforming the inherited colonial education system to "inculcate the values of the colonial society and train individuals for the service of the colonial state" to one that would "prepare young people for the service of their own country" (Nyerere 1968:47; see also Livingstone 1969; Obanya 1999; Cheng and Townsend 2000; Tilak 2000). The intention of most governments to domesticate their administration also played a significant role in rapid education policy reform. The inadequacies of the inherited colonial system, as evidenced by lack of universal access, inappropriate orientation and content, and inappropriate skills for nation-building, were pointed out and promised to be addressed. From independence to the mid-1980s, in Africa, for instance, schools were opened up to a wider section of the populace and access improved considerably. Free, compulsory primary education was also tried in some countries, such as Nigeria and Tanzania. Schools of all categories increased in numbers, and one commentator, albeit describing the low quality of education and lack of secondary and post-secondary school reform, even talked of a schooling boom in Africa (Chazan et al 1992; Obanya 1999).

The governments of newly independent countries with rapid population growth but without industries to absorb the increased labour force were interested in land or agrarian reform. Foreign aid agencies often urged, supported, advised and financed land reforms in those countries too (USAID 1970; Montgomery 1972; Bernstein 2002). Some countries in Asia had a successful land reform, which contributed to the long-term benefits of society in terms of increased productivity and provision of educated labour to the manufacturing industries (Kwon and Yi 2010; Chung 2014; Yi 2015;

Yi et al 2018). In many countries in sub-Saharan Africa, governments did not effect land reform but instead implemented agricultural policies to boost agricultural production, such as input and credit subsidies, social expenditure, infrastructure and extension services. The aversion of the governments to land reform was partly due to the fear of conflict, often in violent forms, which could be caused by the existence of multiple collective landholding groups such as the territorial authority, the clan, the lineage or production unit. To the governments that prioritized mineral rents for revenue and did not expect substantial surpluses from the agricultural sector, agricultural policies were more or less redistributive measures for the tillers (Mkandawire and Soludo 1998; Mafeje 2003).

Social policy reforms during structural adjustment

While welfare states or social policy programmes of the global North began their retrenchment within the neoliberal policy framework in existence since the late 1970s, social policy reforms also took place in the global South. Two changes in social policies are particularly notable: the dismantling of publicly provided social services in the 1980s and the so-called social turn in the 1990s.

In the 1970s, many developing countries, in particular sub-Saharan African countries, had a significant deficit in both the state budget and the balance of payment. External factors such as oil shocks and a fall in international commodity prices had a significant impact on their economies. The capacity for import and production was significantly reduced. Inefficient use of foreign exchange inflows was also one of the causes of these financial imbalances. Even though there was the political will to use financial resources efficiently, the ongoing projects to establish the infrastructural and institutional conditions needed to ensure the efficient use of foreign exchanges had yet to create real gains (Mkandawire and Soludo 1998; Meilink 2003).

Structural Adjustment Programmes (SAPs), a package of policies to address macroeconomic instability, first provided by the Bretton Woods Institutions (namely, the International Monetary Fund and the World Bank), and followed by other donors, had a significant impact on social policies in many developing countries, in particular those on the African continent. Addressing the balance of payment problems, deficits in the government budget and inflation control through demand restraint were the objectives of the SAPs (Meilink 2003). The prescriptions within the framework of the SAPs included as a condition of the loans a clause stating that government budgets should be significantly reduced. While the amount of reduction varied across sectors, budgets for public services were particularly affected, which in turn had a devastating impact on social services, and by extension, on society as a whole.

Many aid-dependent countries adopted SAPs that pursued stabilization and liberalization measures of economy and public policy. Governments that pursued these neoliberal policies fared no better. Economic reforms often resulted in the stagnation of economic growth, and the safety net programmes that made up part of the structural adjustment increased poverty, political discontent and debilitation of democracy (Bresser-Pereira et al 1994; Mkandawire and Soludo 1998; Bangura 2006).

Some developing countries and regions, however, and in particular those in East Asia, including South Korea, Taiwan, Singapore and Hong Kong, fared better in terms of the development of social policies from the late 1970s. With common characteristics such as low social expenditure, the state as a regulator rather than a provider, residual welfare policies, emphasis on productive aspect and self-reliance, and mobilization of non-governmental resources such as enterprises, communities and families, these countries' social policies were well incorporated into their economic growth and political legitimization strategies (Jones 1990; Kwon 1997, 2005; White and Goodman 1998; Holliday 2000; Jacobs 2000). Despite their similar characteristics, each country developed a social policy system that reflected unique situational factors such as colonial legacies, geopolitical size and location, and migration (Walker and Wong 2005).

As the number of working poor, particularly one-parent households in poverty, and people who are at risk of exclusion in multiple dimensions increased in advanced welfare states in the early 1990s, poverty and social exclusion became a key concern on the agenda of the rich Organisation for Economic Co-operation and Development (OECD) countries (Vanhercke 2012). Social policy in Europe, for instance, rather than dealing with the root causes of poverty and inequality such as employment insecurity caused by the flexible labour market and changes in family structure and the traditional breadwinner model, started focusing on anti-poverty and social cohesion measures. Since the early 1990s, European countries have paid more attention to economic distributional issues and the "well-being of a social group defined by reference to their conditions of life rather than their relationship to the labour market," which is often pointed out as "the limit of the existing mandate of the European institutions in social policy" (Room 2010:9; see also Madanipour et al 2015). In parallel with this policy trend, academic research and discussions in the social policy field also focused on individualization of poverty and the groups of people at risk of social exclusion (Madanipour et al 2015).

The emphasis on the anti-poverty aspect of social policy was already materialized and transferred in the forms of aid policies to developing countries when the advanced welfare states and international organizations started to influence the shape and scope of social policy in developing countries. This coincided with the renewed interest in poverty and the

7

signal of the shift of international development policy in the 1990s, which is called the "social turn," after more than a decade of policy prescriptions within the context of SAPs in developing countries (UNDP 1990; Lipton and Maxwell 1992). The poor performance of these policies in terms of economic and social development during the period of extensive SAPs led the international donors to introduce social policy programmes which again focused on poverty alleviation. These social policy programmes were often lumped together under the term "social protection." The social protection programmes implemented in developing countries had a strong connotation of a minimum standard and "safety nets" that would play a limited role in protecting vulnerable or poor people from the removal of previous public supports and the higher risks associated with markets. The shift of the emphasis to anti-poverty or social protection was accompanied by an emphasis on minimizing the coverage and service delivery costs and, in policy terms, targeting mechanisms and non-governmental organizations as key service providers, often bypassing the government (Ellis et al 2009). From the mid-1980s to the 1990s, social protection became the key terminology replacing social policy in developing countries. Its flagship programme was conditional cash transfer, which became widespread in the global South, particularly after the Asian Financial Crisis in the late 1990s (Holzmann and Jorgensen 2001; Sugiyama 2011).

Although the provision of care has always been an important subject in social studies and public policies in advanced welfare states, until the 1980s it was considered a women-specific concept and was mostly discussed by the feminist literature. The focus of discourse on care was to identify the specific or unique features of care provision as an unpaid and informal activity and explain the characteristic of women's living conditions. Care provision as a social issue became a key subject of social policy discourse around the 1990s when scholars working on advanced welfare states started to argue that social care should become a key analytical concept of social policy studies, in particular comparative welfare regime or social policy studies (Daly and Lewis 2000; Razavi 1999). In OECD countries, discussions on care policies often took place in the context of child poverty, work–life balance, pension reform and financing health care. They reflected the changes in the conditions of the male-breadwinner model such as increases in women's involvement in the labour market, divorce/separation, and single parenthood and the prospect of the ageing baby boomers. Child poverty and social investment ideas, in particular in Latin America, also strongly influenced the shape and nature of policy discourse and design associated with care provision (Dobrowolsky 2002; Cohen et al. 2004; Jenson 2010).

In developing countries, care provision was also tightly connected to the anti-poverty aspect of social policy and human capital investment. Care policy programmes in developing countries, especially those heavily dependent upon aid, were often designed to connect the areas of child health care. In addition, conditional cash transfers, often with a focus on education and health, became a major tool of social protection across almost all developing countries, particularly after the mid-1990s.

A Broad Concept of Social Policy

The diverse understandings in the evolution of social policy described earlier demonstrate that the conceptualization of social policy has been a process of distinctive discursive response to social problems or questions constructed in each society. Specific aspects or elements of social policy addressing specific social problems have been emphasized in the discourse on social policy and had more weight than did other aspects or elements. The changing discourse in advanced welfare states or OECD countries had a strong influence on the design and implementation of social policies in developing countries or aid recipient countries.

To consider these features found in the evolution in the understanding of social policy, it may be better to define social policy in terms of its properties rather than listing all the social policy programmes or stipulative meanings of social policy. By providing a list of properties rather than tools of social policy, we would be in a better position to identify the changes or, more specifically, innovations in social policy tools and programmes.

One of the attempts to conceptualize social policy in this line is that in Thandika Mkandawire's social policy, which is defined as collective interventions in the economy to influence the access to and the incidence of adequate and secure livelihoods and income. Focusing on the historical role of social policy in transformation or development of society, he listed key properties or functions of social policies, such as protection, production, redistribution and reproduction, which had differing influences across countries and within countries over time (Mkandawire 2004).

This approach makes the concept of social policy broad enough to include various publicly provided services responding to social questions or problems (Yi 2010). It allows us to include in the scope of social policy analysis even those policies conventionally categorized as economic or labour policies. For instance, those policies formed to respond to environmental degradation or climate change can be defined as social policy as long as they directly address social questions or problems that affect individual well-being or long-term societal benefits through their impacts on production, protection, redistribution or reproduction. As such, discussions on the interactions between social and environmental issues and policies such as eco-social-growth trilemma, triple bottom line, planetary boundaries, green growth, degrowth, post growth, and just transition or "well-being transition" have become the discussions of or on social policy, which has received new names such as eco-social policy or green social policy (Fitzpatrick and Cahill 2002; Mandelli 2022).

Employing an intentionally broad definition of social policy also has advantages in identifying "functional equivalents of social policy" or social policy by other means, which are often prevalent in the countries where social policy system-building is in its early stages (Estevez-Abe 2008:3). Various forms of policies to address the living conditions of people in the states emerged from civil war or violence and the beginning of state-building can be a case in point.

A narrow definition of social policy often tends to conflate social policy with social welfare assistance or similar kinds of programmes that serve low-income persons. Consequently, it ignores its linkages with diverse areas such as asset development, family policy, housing, juvenile and criminal justice, public transportation, community and economic development, environmental protection and energy assistance. A broad definition, however, is helpful in identifying the interfaces of social policies with other public policies. Social policy is closely intertwined with and constitutive of the broader policy institutions of rights, citizenship and political economy configuration.

In this volume, the chapter authors share this broad conceptual approach. It helps them to identify and explain what new or emerging social problems and questions social policy needs to address, what specific purpose and functions in social policy are designed to fulfil, and how those services are linked with other public policies (Kwon 2005; Mkandawire 2014; Yi 2015).

Novelty and Innovations in Social Policy

To explore new social policies or new directions in social policy, we need to identify what policies are new, and in particular, whether and how these policies can be distinguished from the old policies. In policy discourse, the terms "new" and "innovative" have been used interchangeably in innovation and diffusion studies in political science since the 1960s. There has been revived interest in innovation, especially since the 1980s when the public sector's adoption of the modus operandi of the private sector in the delivery of public services became increasingly common. In the 1990s, when it became a key part of the "reinventing government" debate and initiatives, innovation became a kind of mantra of public sector reform (Osborne and Gaebler 1993; Cabinet Office 2003; Black 2005). The term "new" or "innovative" attached to a policy carries at least two connotations: change and novelty. These two connotations can be interpreted differently. Identifying change often means spotting a movement from a state of being x to a state of being y. But the meanings of this movement vary, ranging from successive improvements on existing products, processes and services to radical, systematic or transformative changes that cause substantial shifts in organizational, social and cultural arrangements (Black 2005).

Novelty can have both positive and negative meanings. In the context of the neoliberal type of new public management discourse, innovations mean making bureaucracies as entrepreneurial as their private-sector counterparts. In this context, the policies to make bureaucracies entrepreneurial are considered innovative when they explicitly embrace competition, measure outputs rather than inputs or processes and strengthen accountability (Triantafillou 2017). For some, however, these innovative policies may be interpreted as the "treatment which causes its own disease" (Black 2005:1) or "fiasco" (Moran 2003:26). Therefore, defining "new" or "innovative" policies is often an exercise in choosing a normative position about the nature of policy changes and their direction. And this normative overtone may hinder the discussion on the substance and nature of the new and innovative social policy.

To address questions and problems that potentially delay or even hinder our exploration of social policy, in this volume we understand policies as new or innovative when they meet the following specific conditions for change and novelty. Novelty is assessed in the context of a geographical area (that is, the case countries), a policy domain (namely, aid policy and care provision), unit of analysis (community, and civil society organization) or some combinations of the three. As long as policies are new to the case countries, policy domains or units of analysis that adopt them, it does not matter how old the programmes are or how many other geographical areas, policy domains or units of analysis may have already adopted them (Walker 1969; Black 2005). We will consider them new or innovative.

Second, changes take place in many dimensions of policies. They include but are not limited to the methods or the process of provision of inputs, resources needed for producing output, and organization of policy design and implementation. Implementation processes of policies can also be redesigned to realize intended changes. Changes are qualified as new and innovative when, in the design and implementation of policies, they remove existing rules and introduce new ones; introduce new rules on top of or alongside existing ones; introduce new actors or establish new relations between actors and change the impact of existing rules and relations by changing the institutional and policy environment; and reinterpret and enact the existing rules in new ways (Mahoney and Thelen 2010).

Third, policies are understood as innovative or new when they deal with both old and new problems with new solutions. Expanded old solutions to address old problems, however successful they are, are not understood as new or innovative social policies in this volume.

What Makes Social Policy Transformative?

If we are to be able to say whether or not the new or innovative social policies are transformative, we need some criteria against which to assess their potential or capacity to transform the economy and society. The exercise to come up with the criteria necessitates operationalizing two of the most important and elusive terms in the vocabulary of the current social science: structure and transformation itself.

"Structure" constitutes one pillar of various conceptual dichotomies, such as "actors and structure," "individual and society," "part and whole," "individualism and holism," "micro and macro," "voluntarism and determinism," "subjectivism and objectivism," and so forth, all of which are considered central problems in social and political theory. There has been a convergence in understanding that two elements are not antagonistic but interrelated in the sense that structures shape actors or agents (individuals or collective, but most often the former), but are also constituted and reproduced by actors or agents (Bourdieu 1977; Giddens 1986; Carlsnaes 1992). Another convergence is that neither structures nor actors remain constant over time. They are mutable in the sense that they are changing through the inextricably intertwined process where the two are in interaction. In this process, neither determines the other. They are both independent variables (Cerny 1990; Carlsnaes 1992). In this line of understanding, policies are understood as choices made by collective actors who are constrained and enabled by social structures and also create and shape those structures (Carlsnaes 1992).

Transformation, or similar concepts such as deep change and revolution, in the context of social science connotes episodic, discontinuous and intermittent as opposed to continuous, evolving and incremental changes in the way society is organized. Adopting this dichotomy of change, we may interpret transformation as a departure from the continuous processes of incremental social change that are at work, which involves major shifts in the dominant cultural, economic, political and social patterns or structures (Castles 2010). This interpretation can also be applied to social policy discourse. Although changes occur along a continuum from incremental to radical in policy reform, we may be able to identify whether those changes are architectural, that is, changes within a policy regime or paradigm, or transformative or revolutionary, that is, the changes or transition from one policy regime or paradigm to another (Dewar and Dutton 1986; Dosi 1988). The transition from one policy regime to another means the departure from a dominant structure in social policy reform. In current terms, the transition or departure from the dominant structure may mean "attacking the root causes of the current structure that generate and reproduce economic, social, political and environmental problems and inequities, not merely their symptoms" or addressing the practices generating inequalities and injustice (UNRISD 2016:3).

Practices generating and reproducing inequality and injustice occur in many distinct levels and dimensions of the interplay between structures and actors, both individual and collective. They operate in different modalities and are supported by widely varying types and quantities of resources. They have different logics and dynamics. They are sometimes coherent within a certain area of practice, such as geographical area or policy dimension, but also have sharply conflicting claims and empowerments (Sewell 1996, 2005). Therefore, social policy as a means of transformation needs to engage with various levels and dimensions of interplay between structure and actors to dismantle the structures (for example, institutions, norms, ideologies and culture) that generate and reproduce inequality and injustice on the one hand, and on the other hand empower agents to create and reproduce capacity to change unequal and unjust structures, in order to rebalance the power asymmetry. The United Nations Research Institute for Social Development (UNRISD) in its Flagship Report, suggests various pathways to transformation in policy terms that can also be used to identify the transformative character of social policies (UNRISD 2016). They include but are not limited to:

- reversing the dominant normative hierarchy in current policy making, such that social and ecological justice become the overriding concerns in all policy making and the hitherto prioritized objectives of economic growth and profit maximization are subordinated to those of social and environmental justice;
- overcoming patterns and processes of stratification (related, for example, to class, gender, ethnicity, religion and location) that perpetuate vulnerabilities and inequalities;
- strengthening universal and rights-based approaches;
- re-embedding economic policies and activities in social and environmental norms; and
- fostering truly participatory decision-making approaches involving all stakeholders in the transparent and democratic political processes.

New Directions in Social Policy in the Context of the 2030 Agenda

The 2030 Agenda for Sustainable Development emphasizes the departure from business as usual to realize the vision of transformation. For instance, it highlights the need to develop new institutions and policies to realize multiple goals of economic, social, environmental and governance dimensions, that is, a balanced and integrated approach to addressing multiple Sustainable Development Goals. Social policy is also in need of reform to create complementarity or synergies with other policy sectors. In particular, given the importance of goals associated with climate change and the environment, it is essential to find a way to incorporate concerns about climate change into the design and implementation of social policy. With "leaving no one behind" as a key principle, the 2030 Agenda also demands that social policy set inequality reduction, as well as poverty eradication, as a central objective. Its emphasis on universalism in receiving the benefits and gains of development reconfirms the importance of universal social service provisions.

As we have explained earlier, the trajectory of social policy development in the global South has been shaped by various internal and external factors. Since the social turn of the 1990s, facing the challenges of regional- and global-level economic crisis and taking advantage of changes in global discourse and practices for development, many developing countries have designed and implemented various new and innovative social policies. New forms and contents of social policy programmes and innovative ways of designing and implementing social policy have been created in these countries. New actors or new roles of actors have also emerged in the implementation of these social policy programmes. The following chapters in this volume are primarily concerned with significant changes in the social policy sector that have occurred in developing countries since the turn of the millennium. Have the needs and problems that social policy aims to address been changed and, if so, how? What are the newly emerging ideas and principles by which social policy allocates resources and provides social services? What are the purposes and functions social policies have been designed to fulfil? What are the consequences of new trends and innovations in social policy, particularly in terms of their impacts on structures and actors? How have the changes in social policies taken place under various political, economic, social and ecological circumstances? And, ultimately, are these changes in social policies transformative? In addressing these questions, this volume has a particular focus on the following themes associated with the global South in which we can observe the innovations of theoretical and analytical frameworks and practices of social policy:

- rights-based approach to social welfare;
- integrated and balanced approach to social policy;
- CSOs in transition economies;
- emergence of regional social policy;
- informal workers shaping the system of social policy programmes; and
- strengthening social policy ownership in the context of official development assistance.

The chapters explain key issues and topics of these themes through discussions on theoretical or analytical frameworks or case country studies around these themes. Chapters 1, 2, 3 and 4 introduce new explanatory and analytical frameworks which help to identify and deepen our understanding of newly emerging actors, institutions and processes in the global South. Chapters 5, 6, 7, 8, 9, 10 and 11 examine innovations in the design and implementation of social policy in countries and regions of the global South such as South Africa, India, Tanzania, and Middle East and North Africa countries, Indonesia, China and Russia.

References

Bangura, Y. 2006. "Fiscal and Capacity-Building Reform." In *Public Sector Reform in Developing Countries: Capacity Challenges to Improve Services*, edited by Y. Bangura and G. A. Larbi, 131–160. Geneva: United Nations Research Institute for Social Development and Palgrave Macmillan.

Bernstein, Henry. 2002. "Land Reform: Taking a Long(er) View." *Journal of Agrarian Change*, 2(4):433–463.

Black, Julia. 2005. "What Is Regulatory Innovation?" In *Regulatory Innovation: A Comparative Analysis*, edited by Julia Black, Martin Lodge and Mark Thatcher, 1–15. Cheltenham and Northampton, MA: Edward Elgar.

Bonoli, Giuliano. 2006. "New Social Risks and the Politics of Post-Industrial Social Policies." In *The Politics of Post-Industrial Welfare States*, edited by Klaus Armingeon and Giuliano Bonoli, 3–26. London and New York: Routledge.

Bourdieu, Pierre. 1977. *Outline of a Theory of Practice*. Cambridge: Cambridge University Press.

Bresser-Pereira, Luiz Carlos, Jose Maria Maravall and Adam Przeworski. 1994. "Economic Reforms in New Democracies: A Social Democratic Approach." In *Theoretical and Comparative Perspective for the 1990s*, edited by William C. Smith, Carlos H. Acuna and Eduardo Gamarra, 181–212. New Brunswick: Transaction Books.

Cabinet Office. 2003. *Innovation in the Public Sector*. London: Her Majesty's Stationery Office.

Cahnman, W. and C. Schmitt. 1979. "The Concept of Social Policy (Sozialpolitik)." *Journal of Social Policy*, 8(1): 47–59.

Carlsnaes, Walter. 1992. "The Agency-Structure Problem in Foreign Policy Analysis." *International Studies Quarterly*, 36(3):245–270.

Castles, Stephen. 2010. "Understanding Global Migration: A Social Transformation Perspective." *Journal of Ethnic and Migration Studies*, 36(10):1565–1586.

Cerny, P. G. 1990. *The Changing Architecture of Politics*. London: Sage Publications.

Chancel, L., T. Piketty, E. Saez and G. Zucman. 2021. *World Inequality Report 2022*. Paris: World Inequality Lab.

Chang, Hj. 2004. "The Role of Social Policy in Economic Development: Some Theoretical Reflections and Lessons from East Asia." In *Social Policy in a Development Context*, edited by T. Mkandawire, 246–261. London: Palgrave Macmillan.

Chazan, Naomi, Robert Mortimer, John Ravenhill and Donald Rothchild. 1992. *Politics and Society in Contemporary Africa*. Boulder: Lynne Rienner.

Cheng, Y. S. and T. Townsend (eds). 2000. *Educational Change and Development in the Asia Pacific Region: Challenges for the Future*. Exton: Swets & Zeitlinger.

Chung, M. 2014. "The Development of Transformative Social Policy in South Korea: Lessons from the Korean Experience." In *Learning from the South Korean Developmental Success*, edited by I. Yi and T. Mkandawire, 108–135. Basingstoke and New York: Palgrave Macmillan.

Cohen, B., P. Moss, P. Petrie and J. Wallace. 2004. *A New Deal for Children? Reforming Education and Care in England, Scotland and Sweden*. Bristol: The Policy Press.

Daly, M. and J. Lewis. 2000. "The Concept of Social Care and the Analysis of Contemporary Welfare States." *British Journal of Sociology*, 51(2):281–298.

Dewar, Robert and Jane Dutton. 1986. "The Adoption of Radical and Incremental Innovations: An Empirical Analysis." *Management Science*, 32:1422–1433.

Dobrowolsky, A. 2002. "Rhetoric versus Reality: The Figure of the Child and New Labour's Strategic 'social investment state'." *Studies in Political Economy*, 69:43–73.

Dosi, Giovanni. 1988. "Sources, Procedures, and Microeconomic Effects of Innovation." *Journal of Economic Literature*, 26(3): 1120–1171.

Ellis, Frank, Stephen Devereux and Philip White. 2009. *Social Protection in Africa*. Cheltenham and Northampton: Edward Elgar.

Erikson, R., E. J. Hansen, S. Ringen and H. Uusitalo. 1987. *The Scandinavian Model: Welfare States and Welfare Research*. Armonk: M.E. Sharpe.

Estevez-Abe, M. 2008. *Welfare and Capitalism in Postwar Japan: Party, Bureaucracy, and Business* (Cambridge Studies in Comparative Politics). Cambridge: Cambridge University Press.

Fitzpatrick, T. and M. Cahill. 2002. *Environment and Welfare: Towards a Green Social Policy*. London: Palgrave Macmillan.

Giddens, Anthony. 1986. *The Constitution of Society: Outline of the Theory of Structuration*. Berkeley: University of California Press.

Hagen, Kåre. 2001. "Towards a Europeanisation of Social Policies? A Scandinavian Perspective." *Politique européenne*, 1(2):67–86.

Holliday, I. 2000. "Productivist Welfare Capitalism: Social Policy in East Asia." *Political Studies*, 48(4):706–723.

Holzmann, Robert and Steen Jorgensen. 2001. "Social Risk Management: A New Conceptual Framework for Social Protection, and Beyond." *International Tax and Public Finance*, 8:529–556.

Jacobs, D. 2000. "Low Public Expenditure on Social Welfare: Do East Asian Countries Have a Secret?" *International Journal of Social Welfare*, 9(1):2–16.

Jacobson, Harold K. 1964. "Onuc's Civilian Operations: State-Preserving and State-Building." *World Politics*, 17(1):75–107.

Jeffrey, Robin. 1987. "Introduction: The Setting for Independence." In *Asia—The Winning of Independence*, edited by Robin Jeffrey, 1–22. Basingstoke: Macmillan Education.

Jenson, Jane. 2010. "Diffusing Ideas for After Neoliberalism: The Social Investment Perspective in Europe and Latin America." *Global Social Policy*, 10(1):59–84.

Jones, Catherine. 1990. "Hong Kong, Singapore, South Korea and Taiwan: Oikonomic Welfare States." *Government and Opposition*, 25(4):447–462.

Jones, Catherine. 1985. *Patterns of Social Policy: An Introduction to Comparative Analysis*. London and New York: Tavistock Publications.

Kuhnle, Stein and Sven E. O. Hort. 2004. *The Developmental Welfare State in Scandinavia: Lessons for the Developing World*. Social Policy and Development Programme Paper No. 17. Geneva: United Nations Research Institute for Social Development.

Kwon, Huck-Ju. 2005. "Transforming the Developmental Welfare State in East Asia." *Development and Change*, 36(3):477–497.

Kwon, Huck-Ju. 1997. "Beyond European Welfare Regimes: Comparative Perspectives on East Asian Welfare Systems." *Journal of Social Policy*, 26(4):467–484.

Kwon, Huck-Ju and Ilcheong Yi. 2010. "Economic Development and Poverty Reduction in Korea: Governing Multifunctional Institutions." *Development and Change*, 40(4):769–792. doi:10.1111/j.1467-7660.2009.01571.x.

Lewis, David. 2017. "Should We Pay More Attention to South-North Learning?" *Human Service Organizations: Management, Leadership & Governance*, 41(4):327–331.

Lipton, M. and S. Maxwell. 1992. *The New Poverty Agenda: An Overview*. IDS Discussion Paper 306. Brighton: Institute of Development Studies.

Livingstone, Arthur. 1969. *Social Policy in Developing Countries*. London: Routledge.

Madanipour, Ali, Mark Shucksmith and Hilary Talbot. 2015. "Concepts of Poverty and Social Exclusion in Europe." *Local Economy*, 30(7):1–21.

Mafeje, Archie. 2003. *The Agrarian Question, Access to Land, and Peasant Responses in Sub-Saharan Africa*. Civil Society and Social Movements Programme Paper. Geneva: United Nations Research Institute for Social Development.

Mahoney, James and Kathleen Thelen. 2010. "A Theory of Gradual Institutional Change." *Explaining Institutional Change*, 2010:1–37.

Mandelli, Matteo. 2022. "Understanding Eco-Social Policies: A Proposed Definition and Typology." *Transfer: European Review of Labour and Research*, 28(3):333–348.

Meilink, H. 2003. *Structural Adjustment Programmes on the African Continent.* ASC Working Paper No. 53. Leiden: African Studies Centre.

Mkandawire, Thandika 2014. "Lessons from the Social Policy Development of South Korea: An Interrogation." In *Learning from the South Korean Developmental Success*, edited by Ilcheong Yi and Thandika Mkandawire, 11–30. Basingstoke and New York: Palgrave Macmillan.

Mkandawire, T. 2004. "Social Policy in a Development Context: Introduction." In *Social Policy in a Development Context*, edited by Thandika Mkandawire, 1–33. New York: United Nations Research Institute for Social Development and Palgrave Macmillan.

Mkandawire, Thandika and Charles C. Soludo. 1998. *Our Continent Our Future.* Dakar: Council for the Development of Social Science Research in Africa.

Montgomery, John D. 1972. "Allocation of Authority in Land Reform Programs: A Comparative Study of Administrative Processes and Outputs." *Administrative Science Quarterly*, 17(1):62–75.

Moran, Michael. 2003. *The British Regulatory State: High Modernism and Hyper Innovation.* Oxford: Oxford University Press.

Nyerere, Julius K. 1968. *Ujama: Essays on Socialism.* Dar es Salaam, Nairobi, London and New York: Oxford University Press.

Obanya, P. 1999. *The Dilemma of Education in Africa.* Dakar: United Nations Educational, Scientific and Cultural Organization Regional Bureau for Education in Africa.

Oliver, Roland and Anthony Atmore. 2005. *Africa Since 1800.* Cambridge: Cambridge University Press.

Osborne, D. and T. Gaebler. 1993. *Reinventing Government.* New York: Plume.

Razavi, S. 1999. "Gendered Poverty and Well-being: Introduction." *Development and Change*, 30(3):409–433.

Room, G. 2010. "The Path to Lisbon: The European Anti-Poverty Programmes from the 1970s to the 1990s." *Kurswechsel*, 3:9–18.

Sardak, S., M. Korneyev, V. Dzhyndzhoian, T. Fedotova and O. Tryfonova. 2018. "Current Trends in Global Demographic Processes." *Problems and Perspectives in Management*, 16(1):48–57.

Sens, Andrew D. 1968. "The Newly Independent States, the United Nations, and Some Thoughts on the Nature of the Development Process." *Journal of Politics*, 30(1):114–136.

Sewell, Jr, William H. 2005. *Logics of History: Social Theory and Social Transformation.* Chicago and London: The University of Chicago Press.

Sewell, Jr, William H. 1996. "Historical Events as Transformations of Structure: Inventing Revolution at the Bastille." *Theory and Society*, 25(6):841–881.

Sugiyama, Natasha Borges. 2011. "The Diffusion of Conditional Cash Transfer Programs in the Americas." *Global Social Policy*, 11(2–3):250–278.

Swank, D. 2020. "The Partisan Politics of New Social Risks in Advanced Postindustrial Democracies: Social Protection for Labour Market Outsiders." In *The European Social Model under Pressure*, edited by R. Careja, P. Emmenegger and N. Giger, 139–157. Wiesbaden: Springer.

Tilak, J. 2000. *Education and Development: Lessons from Asian Experience.* New Delhi: National Institute of Educational Planning and Administration.

Titmuss, R. 1968. *Commitment to Welfare.* London: Allen and Unwin.

Triantafillou, P. 2017. *Neoliberal Power and Public Management Reforms.* Manchester: Manchester University Press.

UNDP (United Nations Development Programme). 1990. *Human Development Report 1990.* New York and Oxford: UNDP.

UNDESA (United Nations Department of Economic and Social Affairs). 2019. *Sustainable Development Outlook 2019.* New York: UNDESA.

UNRISD (United Nations Research Institute for Social Development). 2016. "Policy Innovations for Transformative Change." UNRISD Flagship Report. Geneva: UNRISD.

USAID. 1970. *A.I.D. Spring Review of Land Reform.* Washington, DC: US Agency for International Development.

Vanhercke, Bart. 2012. *Social Policy at EU Level: From the Anti-Poverty Programmes to Europe 2020.* European Social Observatory Deliverable: Background Paper. Brussels: European Social Observatory.

Walker, Alan and Chack-kie Wong. 2005. "Conclusion: From Confucianism to Globalization." In *East Asian Welfare Regimes in Transition: From Confucianism to Globalization*, edited by Alan Walker and Chack-kie Wong, 213–224. Bristol: The Policy Press.

Walker, Jack L. 1969. "The Diffusion of Innovations among the American States." *American Political Science Review*, 63(3): 880–899.

White, Gordon and Roger Goodman. 1998. "Welfare Orientalism and the Search for an East Asian Welfare Model." In *The East Asian Welfare Model: Welfare Orientalism and the State*, edited by Roger Goodman, Gordon White and Huck-ju Kwon, 3–24. London: Routledge.

Yi, Ilcheong. 2015. "Diversity Moving Towards Integrated, Coordinated and Equitable Social Protection Systems: Experiences of Japan, the Republic of Korea, and Taiwan, Province of China." In *Prepared for the UNDP Project on Establishing an Integrated, Equitable and Inclusive Social Welfare System in China*, edited by UNRISD/UNDP China. Geneva: UNRISD/UNDP China.

Yi, Ilcheong. 2010. "Social Protection, Social Security and Social Service in a Development Context: Transformative Social Policy Approach." *Journal of International Development Cooperation*, 4:57–84.

Yi, Ilcheong, Jiyoung Kim and Hyuk-Sang Sohn. 2018. "Aid Effectiveness and Institutional Complementarity." *Korean Journal of Area Studies*, 36(2):255–284.

The Globalizing Dynamics of Social Policy: A Transnational Analytics of and for Southern Social Policy

Nicola Yeates

Introduction

A perennial research interest among scholars of social policy is how contemporary globalizing dynamics are (re)shaping the social organization and relations of welfare.[1] In this, a substantially new analytical framework of enquiry into the contemporary dynamics of welfare and social change has placed at its centre transborder exchanges, links and ties that entwine populations, economies and polities—and, crucially, welfare systems— in webs of interconnectedness and interdependence spanning multiple territories around the world. Illustratively, these include cross-border flows of capital, goods and services; cross-border flows of images, information, cultural modes and sociopolitical ideas; cross-border movements of people; and cross-border sites and spaces of political engagement and action. Such cross-border processes have long historical antecedents, often linked to histories of colonialism and liberation movements. They are in any case a structural feature of contemporary societies, "woven" into the heart of the social fabric and integral to older and newer welfare histories.

If, as Khagram and Levitt (2005:1) argue, "social life crosses, connects, underlies, alters, transcends and even transforms boundaries and borders, as well as structures, processes and agents ostensibly contained in them," then we need good analytical approaches capable of comprehending these global dynamics *concretely* in relation to social policy, and moving beyond and behind the broad abstractions with which this chapter has, of necessity, begun. This chapter has two such concretizing objectives. First, it aims to unpack some key features of a global analytics of social policy through the lens of transnational actors, structures, sites, spheres, processes and ideas.

---

[1] Use of the concept "global" and "globalizing" does not signal uncomplicated or wholesale acceptance of the strong "globalization thesis" (Yeates, 1999).

Second, it aims to illustrate these transnational analytics through concrete, contextualized examples. The geopolitical focus of the chapter lies with the global South. This is a constructed, contested category encompassing countries with markedly different circumstances, resources, histories and social policies. Pragmatically, it is broadly operationalized as non-Organisation for Economic Co-operation and Development (OECD) middle- and low-income countries. These are territories where some of the most radical and innovative sources of social policy reform to address "intractable" health and welfare issues are to be found. They are concrete sites of contestation to shape new horizons for social policy and are generative of innovations not just receptors of them.

The examples selected from the social protection sector and from world-regional social policy illustrate these points as well as helping to elucidate the broader question inspiring this chapter: can social policy be understood any longer as the outcome of sociopolitical forces rooted in domestic spheres of governance and playing out solely through them? Posed as a different question, this asks: can social policy be studied in isolation from its embeddedness in an international society of nations, away from the border-spanning institutions, actors, policies and practices that shape that international society and the governance of territories, populations and their health and welfare? Despite the reflex negative answer both may incline to invoke, these are not "straw men" questions. They point to deep-rooted, methodological issues relating to the analysis of social policy. The delineation of transnationalisms raises fundamental questions regarding received knowledge about the nation-state, sovereignty and territorial autonomy embedded in "methodologically nationalist" modes of social policy analysis that privilege social processes and forms of social organization occurring *within* countries at the expense of those that cut across them, together with the ways in which social policies are *co-produced* in practice by interactions of national and transnational forces.

Analytical Perspectives

At the heart of global approaches to social policy lie a set of concerns with: (i) how social policy issues are increasingly being perceived and understood as being cross-border in scope, cause and impact; (ii) how cross-border flows of people, goods, services, ideas and finance relate to the course of social policy development (as process, in content or as outcome); (iii) the emergence of transnational forms of collective action, including the development of multilateral and cross-border modes of social governance and policy; and (iv) how cross-border modes of governance and policy making impact on social policies at country level. Elements of these can be traced to before "globalization" entered the mainstream conceptual grammar of social policy in the 1990s, but the past two decades have seen a substantial interest in these matters because they address large-scale shifts in welfare systems that explanations wholly directed toward social structures and interactions within domestic spheres of governance do not adequately capture.

Understandably, perhaps, much of the research effort has been directed toward the impacts of neoliberalism and economic liberalization on the content and direction of social policies. Rapidly changing social structures, and sites and modes of social organization in the world economy, politics, and in cultural and social reproduction, were linked to transformations in the conditions of welfare institution-building, the structures of social funding, regulation and provision (including the mix of public, commercial, voluntary and informal sectors), the dynamics of policy making, and welfare and wider development outcomes. Scenarios of rising social polarization, inequality and poverty within and between countries, the wholescale retrenchment of public welfare, the lowering of social, health, labour and environmental standards, and the resurgence of welfare markets and private (commercial, corporate) welfare provision, and the diminution in the quality of social rights (to name but a few) have all been foremost issues for the global North *and* South.

Initially, these welfare change scenarios were largely read off from economic (and labour market) changes that were attributed to the centralization of economic power and the emergence of transnational economic spaces dominated by neoliberal allies among state and capital. As more diverse forms of globalizing dynamics and forces were "found," welcome nuance and complexity entered the discussion. Key here is the insight that "local" and regional factors play a decisive role in determining the pace, timing and outcomes of global restructuring in context-specific ways (Mittelman 1995; Yeates 1999, 2002, 2014a, 2014b; Yeates and Holden 2022), such that "national institutional, cultural and political differences are likely to prevail rather than be eliminated under the weight of global, 'external' forces" (Yeates 1999:373). Variegated and path-dependent patterns of development (or underdevelopment) across different zones and territories of the world continue to exist, despite the supposed "levelling" impacts of unifying and converging forces (Abu Sharkh and Gough 2010; Mishra 1999). Distinctively different institutional formations of welfare remain even within supposed "convergence clubs" in the global North (see, for example, Achterberg and Yerkes 2009; Paetzold 2013; Schmitt and Starke 2011) and global South (Palan et al 1996; Stallings 1992). More generally, strategic responses by states to economic internationalization processes reflect their particular histories, factor endowments and capacities, as well as their position in the international political system (Palan et al 1996).

Nevertheless, considerable contestation remains as to the onset and timing of social policy change, its causes and expressions, and its significance and effects. A key axis of this contestation is between those who regard transnationalization processes as integral to social structures (including transnational actors as having a significant level of autonomy from states) (for example, Deacon et al 1997, 2007; Orenstein 2005) and those who see these processes and actors as dependent on states and who attribute the principal drivers of national social policy change to countries' own social, demographic and economic structures (for example, Pierson 1998).

Pluralistic analyses of global dynamics have attracted an increasingly significant share of interest. These recognize multiplicities (of process, institutions, actors, ideas, outcomes and impacts), context specificity, contingent factors and countervailing forces, not only in domestic spheres of governance but also in cross-border ones. The strength of countervailing or moderating forces, the implications of continued fragmentation *and* rescaling of political and social spheres, and the emergence of new political spaces within and across states, are recognized as significant features that need to be taken account of, not least because of their power to expand social policy "horizons" in ways supportive of welfare universalism or other progressive forms of social policy. Relatedly, this has opened up the prospect of greater attention to how power and influence flow *multidirectionally* among a wider range of social policy actors, institutions and sites, rather than just from "the top down" (as in from intergovernmental organizations [IGOs] to nations) or (crucially, given the focus of this chapter) from the global North to global South.

At the same time, a wider range of "everyday" border-spanning, transnationalizing processes than corporate structures and activities and capital accumulation have surfaced. These include political and community activism and advocacy campaigns; communities, epistemic and diasporic; households, families and parenting; migration; and professions.[2] Such perspectives accord greater weight to agency and to interactions among diverse social actors than "strong" globalization literatures. In turn, they have lent substantial credence to a complex and interesting picture of how globalizing forces and structures are variously enabled, governed, regulated and opposed by a wide range of national and transnational actors working (often in conjunction with and/or in opposition to each other) in defined institutional contexts, within and across myriad domestic and cross-border spheres of governance (Yeates 2002, 2014a, 2014b; Yeates and Holden 2022).

---

[2] For the relevant literature on these issues, see Yeates 2018.

Transnational Social Policy

Who are transnational social actors and what are transnational social institutions? Broadly defined, transnational actors are "organizations (multilateral state, or non-state) or individuals that seek to develop and advocate well-elaborated policy proposals in multiple national contexts" (Orenstein 2008b:1; see also Béland and Orenstein 2009). A narrower definition—and arguably a more easily operationalized one—restricts transnational social policy actors to "elite" global institutions and actors, notably IGOs (Deacon et al 1997:195). In any case, transnational policy actors are "proposal actors" not just "veto players" (Orenstein 2008b): they have control over their own policy agendas (ideas and proposals), and pursue influence over the framing, making and enactment of policy through advocacy initiatives and policy reform campaigns directed at more than one country (Orenstein 2008b). In this view, what distinguishes transnational from national actors is not so much the sphere of governance (multilateral versus domestic) that they operate in, but that they seek to influence the course of events across *many* countries. Transnational social policy actors include IGOs, international non-governmental organizations (NGOs), transnational activist networks, epistemic communities, expert networks and policy entrepreneurs, all of which are leading sources of policy norms and ideas in countries worldwide (Orenstein 2008b:6). They can also include governments to the extent that these exert influence on policy and provision in many other countries' social policies through domestic policy (for example, recruitment of overseas labour, migration regimes) and foreign policy (on development, trade and aid) pursued through multilateral forums as well as bilaterally (often serially) with selected countries (Yeates, Macovei and Langenhove 2010; Yeates and Pillinger 2018, 2019).

This broader understanding of who are transnational policy actors has unfolded alongside recognition of the *multiple* socio-spatial sites, levels and scales of social policy formation. This has directed attention to additional institutions and actors not otherwise captured by a focus on IGOs. For example, subglobal transnational regional and continental groups of countries (for example, Association of Southeast Asian Nations, Southern African Development Community, and African Union) are important sites of global social policy contestation and many have a high degree of "global actorness," structuring policy norms and projecting power and influence "outwards" in, for example, global fora as well as "inwards" to member states. This broader understanding has also directed attention toward "non-elite" transnational social policy actors. Migrants and their families, for example, are emblematic of transnationalized connectedness in the social organization and relations of social welfare and policy. Their international state border and cultural crossings, propelled and sustained by transnational networks that mobilize and channel their movement and settlement, structure their social relations of participation, belonging and integration across more than one (and sometimes multiple) countries. Social and financial remittances to sustain human welfare and support social and community development in the source country are sent and received through these networks. Such is the volume of financial remittances, their low level of attrition over time and their significance as a source of income for recipients, that Yeates and Owusu-Sekyere (2019) designated them as an informal transnational social protection system. Such systems and their function within "national" social policy systems are invariably missed by analytical gazes confined to IGOs or to "bounded" national welfare systems.[3]

What we are moving toward, then, emphasizes an "embedded transnationalism" that recognizes the existence of transnational spaces within nation-states and the playing out of transnational processes *within* national territories *as well as* across them in the more visible border-spanning structures and "high-level" forums and processes (Yeates 2008, citing Clarke 2005). Embedded transnationalism includes the "globalizing" strategies of a wide range of social policy actors that impact on the social organization and relations of welfare and their outcomes (see Yeates 2018:Table 1). We might also invoke "national" policy makers and officials applying "world society" ideas on human rights, social justice and equality in domestic legislatures (see Chapter 6). Attention to the myriad "bottom-up," informal transnationalizations as well as top-down and highly institutionalized ones usefully foregrounds how social relations of power and authority, of connectedness and responsibility, are structured across distant and proximate geographies. Such a perspective underlines the point that boundaries between national and transnational social policy are more blurred in practice than in theory.

Conditional Cash Transfers

Conditional cash transfers (CCTs) are the first policy area I have selected to illustrate these propositions. The speed and rate of the adoption of CCTs internationally is remarkable, and has occurred to a degree that could only be explained by a transnational process with considerable reach worldwide. Across highly divergent political, demographic and welfare regimes, over the space of a decade (1997–2007) some 30 countries across Latin America, Africa and Asia developed CCT programmes (Fiszbein and Schady 2009). As of 2018, more than 80 countries have at least one type of CCT (Parker

---

[3] For the typology of transnational entities and their relevance for social policy, see Table 1 in Yeates 2018.

and Vogl 2018). These programmes are concentrated in low- and middle-income countries on all continents, and their size in terms of spending and coverage has also grown. The remarkable degree of similarity across CCT programmes of the world suggests the existence of a standard model—even if different local expressions are evident.

In many ways, the spread of CCTs seems to be a classic case of the influence of the most visible and global of transnational policy actors—international organizations—on national policy development. Indeed, a key factor in the rise of the CCT as a policy model for addressing poverty is the high degree of support and consensus it rapidly commanded among international organizations. The degree of unity among them cut across institutions holding markedly different interpretive frameworks on poverty, social policy and development. Alongside the World Bank, four United Nations social agencies (United Nations Children's Fund, United Nations Educational, Scientific and Cultural Organization, the Food and Agriculture Organization of the United Nations, and the International Labour Organization) and regional development banks (in Latin America, the Inter-American Development Bank, IDB) supported the CCT policy model.

> These agencies reach a consensus during the 1990s over what the WB called a two-pronged approach to social protection: economic growth combined with investment in poor people's human capital, which would be expanded through investments in basic health care and primary education—well-targeted safety nets provided by the state. (Fenwick 2013:147)

The new interpretive framework used to understand poverty has nevertheless been one of "social safety nets" and residual social provision for the poorest, and in this respect it aligned well with the World Bank's social protection policy. However, and crucially, because CCTs were framed in terms of rights-based social justice they appealed to a far wider constituency than might otherwise have been expected. This new framing also helped decontextualize the policy model from neoliberal World Bank social policy (Ancelovici and Jenson 2013; Fenwick 2013).

With the exception of the earliest programmes, international funders have been core promoters and subsidizers of CCTs—in particular the World Bank IDB in Latin America, and various European foreign aid agencies working in Africa, notably the UK, Denmark, Ireland, Germany, Norway and Sweden (Ancelovici and Jenson 2013:305). In low-income (especially African) countries, the composition of transnational social policy actors has differed. There, CCT policy promulgation also involved aid agencies, particularly from Europe, working in tandem with other international and multilateral actors (for example, regional development banks). As with the pensions case (Orenstein 2008a), international supporters offered technical assistance and financial support for governments willing to introduce CCT programmes. Foli's (2015) study of Ghana's adoption of a CCT programme (LEAP) clearly shows the existence of transnational policy networks at work and the multiple development aid agencies (bilateral, multilateral and national) involved. This was, from the outset, a transnational policy campaign process spanning three continents (South America, Europe and Africa), becoming adapted to specific regional and national circumstances before it was institutionalized through LEAP.

Ideational consensus is clearly important in transnational policy reform campaigns, but so too are structural features. The degree of leverage powers that IGOs can exert are not the only explanator of successful "take-up" of CCT programmes. In Latin America, where nearly every country[4] adopted a CCT programme, IGOs were involved in some way[5] but there were also obvious countervailing sources mitigating their influence. The debt crisis had long passed, and increased private capital flows had removed the need to borrow from international financial institutions that would have embedded policy reform obligations as a condition of lending. The neoliberal economics propounded so strongly by international lending institutions was losing credibility, as was their accompanying policy reform advice (Teichman 2007:558). Expert-driven international ideas penetrated the domestic policy process irrespective of domestic regime and circumstances, yet national context and specific characteristics were also significant. Thus, designation of CCTs as social policy rather than as aid or emergency relief (even if they were still financed by international banks, aid agencies or NGOs) (Ancelovici and Jenson 2013) created political space for national actors to own the model and to adapt it to local circumstances and preferences.

The history of partnering between international organizations and governments is also known to be important (see Chapters 8 and 9). This shapes the degree of openness or closure to international policy prescriptions, the dynamics of the policy development process and the characteristics of the programme itself. Again, in the Latin American context, the IDB has enjoyed "a closer and more cooperative relationship with the governments of Latin America than has been the case for the World Bank" (Teichman 2007:560). This is attributed to a shared "cultural understanding" and to the

---

[4] The exception was Costa Rica, which remained closed to international influence (Franzoni and Voorend 2011).

[5] The World Bank and the IDB were consistent partners in these reforms though the United Nations Development Programme was also a significant actor (especially in an early adopter country, Brazil) (Ancelovici and Jenson 2013:306; Fenwick 2013; Franzoni and Voorend 2011; Sugiyama 2011; Teichman 2007).

fact that IDB's borrower members are also majority shareholders (Teichman 2007). The closeness of IDB to governments in the region meant that it did not push civil society participation on reluctant governments through its loan facilities. In contrast, the World Bank, which is more autonomous from Latin American governments, has been more intensively engaged with civil society organizations in the region (Teichman 2007). Other factors are also important, because the degree of openness or closure to international influence on this matter has varied within the region. In Mexico, the transnational policy network is tightly knit and highly integrated, involving a high degree of trust and personalized friendships; it involved the IDB, a large overseas consultancy, the International Food Policy Research Institute (IFPRI) and Mexican government officials. In Chile, the transnational policy network was institutionally based and less tightly integrated; personal relationships did not play an important role. And, while the World Bank had a less important impact there, it was nonetheless significant in insisting upon civil society involvement in policy making and expressed a lower level of reticence about pushing borrowing on governments on this issue (Teichman 2007:561). For Costa Rica, El Salvador and Chile, Franzoni and Voorend (2011) point to other sources of structural differentiation in the degree to which IGOs influence the course of domestic social policy:

> Welfare regimes seem correlated with a larger or smaller role of technocracies in adopting international policy prescriptions ... the more informal the country's welfare regime, the more reliant it is on either international technocracies or lesson drawing from countries with different welfare regimes. Under both state welfare regimes [considered in the study] domestic factors played a larger role in filtering international policy prescriptions. (Franzoni and Voorend 2011:291)

CCTs occupy a significant role in Southern social policy not only for the extent of take-up of the policy model, but also because they are a flashpoint over whether they constitute a "new" pathway toward welfare universalism or not. One concern here is that the (geographic and income) targeting methods embedded by CCTs risk recalibrating currently more universalistic systems toward more residualist ones. Over time, structured divergence can be expected:

> As the range of countries running CCT programmes diversifies, we would expect their targeting mechanisms, and possibly the outcomes from them, to diversify as well. Some countries may choose universalism over targeting, as Bolivia has done in the Juancito Pinto programme for all first-grade students. Eastern European countries that already have established means testing systems may use those;

community-based targeting may play a larger role in Africa and Asia than in Latin America. Moreover, the results that reasonably can be achieved will vary, depending on such context and design features as the range of ages covered by the programme. (Fiszbein and Schady 2009:80)

Such scenarios "speak" to the continued relevance of the divergence/convergence debate, and indicate a fruitful field for future research. Here, the co-production of ostensibly "national" provision by alliances of transnational and national actors (and the conflicts between them) in all its stages of development and over the long term (following "implantation") would be an important way of further developing transnational analytics in comparative (intra- or cross-regional) context.

World-Regional Social Policy

World-regionalism is integral to contemporary globalization strategies, the rescaling of social governance and the emergence of "new" political spaces and institutions at subglobal level. It has taken hold as a major focal point of ideational and political struggle to define how social, political and economic relations among peoples and territories are to be organized in an increasingly interconnected world economy. Social policy has been a central feature of these struggles, with "new," larger integrative scales of social governance emerging on a regional scale. Regional social policy is broadly defined as cross-border public interventions on a regional scale that directly affect social welfare, social institutions and social relations. It involves overarching concerns with redistribution, regulation, production and reproduction, protection and social rights within and among participating countries (Yeates 2018).

Over the past two decades, international momentum has grown around the possibilities afforded by a stronger regional approach to social policy and development. The resurgence of world-regionalist development strategies pursued by state and non-state actors to "lock in" internationalizing flows of trade and investment on a regional basis among groups of "most favoured nations" has invariably been enabled by "new" regional institutions to strengthen links, ties and exchanges between member countries. These regional projects, and the regionalizing processes that they engender and further mobilize, shape the conditions of social development but have tended to take on regional social policy mandates with identifiable regional goals, funding sources and programmes of social provision, including (sometimes) regional social rights with legal entitlements for citizens of member states to challenge their governments' perceived failures to uphold these rights (Deacon et al 2010; Mackinder et al 2022).

Most attention in this area has focused on Northern world-regionalisms (notably the European Union, EU) but there is growing interest in Southern ones (Yeates 2014b, 2014c; Yeates and Rigirozzi 2015). One aspect of enquiry concerns how regional integration affects national social policies, and specifically whether membership of a regional grouping induces welfare convergence. Comparative studies that incorporate the global South are rare at the best of times, but that by Madeira (2014) is a notable exception in a field that has tended to "look North." Madeira's analysis of the influence of regional integration on government social spending measured the degree to which countries are integrated into regional economic and political organizations. Her study spanned eight such organizations having at least a free trade area—besides the EU, the European Free Trade Association and the North American Free Trade Agreement, she included five in the global South—four of which were in Central or South America (the Southern Cone Common Market [Mercosur], the Central American Common Market [CACM], the Andean Common Market [ANCOM], the Caribbean Community [CARICOM]), and one in Asia (the Association of South-East Asian Nations, ASEAN). The study's results showed that "greater regionalisation is associated with higher levels of social spending," in all except (perhaps surprisingly) the EU, and support the welfare divergence hypothesis rather than the "race to the bottom" welfare convergence one. This, she argues, is not explained by trade openness, but more by the degree to which countries are more broadly integrated into the regional institutions. Key components of this integration include the degree of labour mobility, which, she posits, may counterbalance "race to the bottom" competitive pressures.

This raises a question about the relationship between "deeper" forms of regional integration (that is, beyond trade openness) and regional social policy. How are regional institutions and actors tackling the relationship between trade, labour and social standards? And how are they maintaining fiscal capacity and social solidarity in the face of international competition? Madeira's study did not examine this, but social policy research has shown that across diverse development contexts worldwide, collective action on a world-regional scale is widely seen as a compelling means of tackling the cross-border nature of many social policy challenges, especially those that arise from greater cross-border connectivity and interdependence. World-regional social policy can enable a more effective set of responses to pressing social policy issues than governments acting unilaterally or bilaterally. Equally, world-regional-level collective action can be easier to negotiate and conclude among a more restricted set of international partners (usually dozens regionally compared with hundreds in global organizations). It can also sustain the interest of prospective partners within and outside the region (Yeates 2014b; Yeates 2017; Yeates, Moeti and Luwabelwa 2019).

Cutting across ideational struggles about what kinds of social policy for what kind of regional integration are a range of "practical" policy issues regarding whether social policy is to remain a sovereign matter or whether it is to evolve over larger integrative scales. How far is the strategic ambition of regional social policy confined to minimal interstate coordination necessary to promote labour mobility and address the most palpable cross-border harms? And how far is it founded upon "thicker" principles of social inclusivity, equality and democracy that imply greater levels of coordination and, indeed, of integration? The forms that world-regional social policy take may be a defining element of the character of regional integration—indeed, of "regionness" (Hettne and Söderbaum 2000) itself. In other words, the kinds of regional social policies emerging reveal much about nascent societal models underpinning world-regional projects, such as whether priority is to be given to market integration (with freedom of movement of capital and business needs given priority over labour and wider welfare issues) or whether human welfare in all its forms is incorporated into the regional project in a multidimensional, integrated and balanced way.

In practice, Southern world-regional social policy as a set of political (usually governmental) practices takes many different forms. First, the sectoral scope is diverse. World-regional action on health and disease control has become a significant area as public health threats from communicable diseases, pollution and antibiotic resistance, for example, cannot be addressed by countries working alone in an increasingly interconnected world. World-regional initiatives are also increasingly embracing diverse other areas from professional qualifications and food security to child trafficking, expanding to regional "road maps" for social development more generally (Table 1.1). Some kinds of world-regional social policies are more aligned than others to the ambitious goal of social transformation. Second, world-regional institutions use diverse instruments to develop and realize regional social policy mandates and objectives (Table 1.1).

Most regional groupings are IGOs with low levels of sovereignty sharing; they are, moreover, primarily regional economic groupings in which social policy may have a high profile in terms of mandate but be reliant on "weaker" forms of regional instruments designed to promote information sharing and mutual education. There are, however, important exceptions to this, as Table 1.1 shows (for example, the Economic Community of West African States' [ECOWAS] regional labour court with rights of redress, the Andean Community's [CAN] regional social fund; ASEAN's regional human rights body). The Southern African Development Community (SADC) has developed an infrastructure and capacity for regional cooperation on issues of child labour, communicable diseases and the referral of patients between member states. Notably, in 2017 it established a regional monitoring and evaluation system against which member states assess their achievement

Table 1.1: Regional social policy instruments and examples from five continents

Instrument	Functions to ...	Instances
Regional forum	Share information for mutual education, analysis and debate; promote shared analyses and create epistemic communities and networks that can inform policy debate and provide a platform for collaboration.	Capacity building and communicable diseases: CARICOM Regional Compact (for example, peer review mechanisms for country development plans): PIF Cross-border information exchange: SAARC Regional health think tank: UNASUR
Social standard-setting	Define international social standards and common frameworks for social policy (for example, human rights charters, labour, social protection and health conventions).	Social Charter: SAARC Constitutional Treaty enshrining common normative framework: UNASUR Development Goals regional roadmap: ASEAN Regional framework on people trafficking: ASEAN
Resource mobilization and allocation	Provide resources supporting policy development and provision (for example, stimulus finance, technical assistance, policy advice and expertise).	Regional Social Humanitarian Fund: CAN Anti-poverty projects, social and solidarity economy trading schemes: ALBA Food security schemes: ASEAN, SAARC Regionally funded health think tank delivering institutional reform, professionalization and capacity-building programmes: UNASUR
Regulation	Regulate in the interests of health and social protection. Regulatory instruments and reform affect entitlements and access to social provision.	Regional court of justice adjudicating on labour rights: ECOWAS, EU Social Charter: EU, SAARC Removal of work visa requirements for migrant workers from other member states: CARICOM, ECOWAS, EU, SAARC, SADC Mutual recognition agreements (of professional and educational qualifications and educational institutions): ASEAN, CAN, EU, Mercosur Social security portability entitlements: EU, Gulf Cooperation Council, Mercosur, CARICOM, ANZCERTA, SADC

Source: author's own, drawing on Deacon et al (2010) and Yeates (2014b, 2017). ALBA, Bolivarian Alternative for the Americas; ANZCERTA, Australia-New Zealand Closer Economic Relations Trade Agreement; ASEAN, Association of South-East Asian Nations; CAN, Andean Community; CARICOM, Caribbean Community; ECOWAS, Economic Community of West African States; EU, European Union; GCC, Gulf Cooperation Council; Mercosur, Southern Cone Common Market; PIF, Pacific Islands Forum; SAARC, South Asian Association for Regional Cooperation; SADC, Southern African Development Community; UNASUR, Union of South American Nations.

of regional goals (Yeates et al 2019). Mercosur has established regional harmonization of pharmaceutical regulation under its access to medicines initiative. The South Asian Association for Regional Cooperation's (SAARC) Social Charter enshrines entitlements to basic services and development goals in poverty alleviation, education, health and the environment (Deacon et al 2010, passim). These are all important developments that demonstrate new sources of collective action and capability. In practice, though, the "strongest" regulatory measures tend to be reserved for social policies directly related to the construction of regional labour markets (for example, removal of work visa requirements, mutual recognition agreements for educational and professional qualifications, and social security portability agreements) (Table 1.1). This is not dissimilar to Northern world-regionalisms, notably the EU, which has a far longer history than many (but by no means all) Southern world-regionalisms (Yeates 2014b).

This consideration of regional social policy elucidates the realities of complex multilateralism that social actors (whether national or transnational) must navigate and negotiate. The kinds of regional economic groupings considered here are just one multilateral institution among many bearing on social policy development. In addition to regional development banks, the UN system has its own distinct regional structure, in the form of UN Regional Commissions and regional offices of UN agencies (for example, World Health Organization regional health organizations such as the Pan-American Health Organization (PAHO), or the ILO regional offices). These are also transnational regional social policy actors and institutions, each with varied social policy mandates and objectives, and regulatory and resourcing structures, along with distinct policy communities. Complicating this, from a country perspective, is that country membership of these myriad organizations tends to differ. For example, country membership of the West African Health Organization is not co-terminous with that of ECOWAS. In addition, countries can be members of more than one regional economic and political institution, as is the case in parts of Africa (Yeates and Surender 2021) and South America (Yeates 2014b).

The multitude of regional institutions and actors means that there is not just one regional social policy in any region, but many. This diversity can greatly compound complexity in national as well as in regional policy making (and attempts to strengthen it). Another way of looking at this is that it can also generate welcome policy debate. Different policy models promulgated through regional fora and by regional organizations can stimulate vibrant discussion (and real alternatives) about what kind of development is desirable, the basis on which it is built and how it can be realized through context-specific responses. These induce ideational and policy diversity and "competition" among international donors and agencies. Further research is needed into whether and how these burgeoning regional institutions with their expanding social policy agendas alongside their embrace of trade openness are tangibly impacting upon the formation of social policy in the global South. Again, the prospects for using comparative social policy methods to investigate this promise to be productive.

Conclusions and Future Lines for Research

For all the methodological and theoretical difficulties that globalizations raise for social policy analytics, they open up an intriguing set of discussions about the myriad ways in which social policies are embroiled in cross-border relations and structures of interconnectedness and interdependence. Theoretical and methodological constructs gravitating around "container" notions of nation-states are no longer sufficient, if they ever were. The border-spanning, transnational exchanges and connections surveyed in this chapter have helped prise open "settled" questions about the determinants and directions of social policy: in a globalizing world, who, where and what are the key drivers and sites of social policy and development? In this, transnational analytics has highlighted that domestic spheres of governance institutions, actors and ideas shaping social policy can no longer be studied in isolation from their embeddedness in transnational social, economic and political institutions—if they ever could be. Transnational policy formation and social provision are major features of contemporary social policy in the global South.[6] Country-level welfare systems are interconnected and interdependent; they are embroiled in globalizing dynamics in complex ways—both propagating and impacted by them. These transnational relations of welfare are dynamic: they generate new social risks at the same time as they generate new forms of collective action, actors and institutions. The manifestations of these relations are context specific. They vary between place and over time. They are pluralistic in the ways they unfold and diverse in their impacts.

A key objective of this chapter has been to open up a dialogue between methodologically nationalist and methodologically transnationalist approaches. These two analytical methods coexist within social policy research, yet they rarely converse in any meaningful way. To this end, the chapter has sought to find points of contact and dialogue. While making the case for far greater emphasis on research strategies that foreground transnationalization processes, I do not advocate a totalizing approach to the subject. Nor do I argue that country-based studies should be dispensed with or be displaced or superseded by a focus on transnational processes.

---

[6] The historical dimensions of this mode of policy formation is outside the scope of this chapter.

Rather, better conceptual, theoretical and methodological tools are urgently needed to understand how national and transnational structures of power and authority are configured and distributed within and across countries, and how the course of social policy making and its outcomes are impacted by these.

The evidence from both national and transnational social policy research points to three shared principal conclusions. First, that variegated and path-dependent patterns of development and "underdevelopment" across different territories of the world continue to exist, despite unifying and converging forces. Second, transnational actors, institutions and processes matter in the determination of social policy, but they do not all matter equally in all contexts all of the time. Sometimes they have little discernible influence at all. Third, a multiplicity of institutions and actors are at work in different constellations (in alliance as well as in opposition with each other) at different points in time, on different issues, in different settings. This holds true as much at the level of global policy and international organizations as it does at the national level; at both levels we see fractions and divisions within and between them.

It is clear that some ideas, actors and institutions attain more power and influence over the content and direction of social policy than others. Pensions and cash transfer policies are all high-profile examples of transnational actor influence. At the same time, it is far from clear that transnational forces are always significant or determining in the pace, timing and content of policy change—not least because we do not yet have enough research in this area. However, findings from this area suggest that transnational and national actors work closely with one another, within and across multiple venues and sites of policy making. They reciprocally interact with, and influence, one another to structure each other's agendas. The question has been—and remains—what constellation of which actors under what conditions are able to produce "new" directions and settlements in social policy?

Research strategies open to the diverse border-spanning activities, exchanges, links and connections are a vital, indeed essential, feature of contemporary social policy research, both in its "landscape" and "portrait" versions. Such strategies can help better situate and understand the dynamics of social policy formation, and the intersecting forces combining to shape the social organization and relations of welfare within and between countries. They are capable of revealing sources and drivers of new social policy agendas and the arenas in which they are generated, progressed and contested. More high-quality research evidence is needed. Global policy making and policy diffusion studies have tended to focus on high-visibility cases involving high-profile global institutions (particularly those associated with neoliberal, and neoliberal-inspired, policy agendas) and/or "dramatic" events such as crises or where tidal waves of policy reform in many countries have occurred. Greater attention to a wider range of sectors and intersectoral issues, institutional sites and actors, and to "undramatic" events and failed transnational policy campaigns is needed. We need good, in-depth, country-focused comparative studies to understand the myriad ways in which different social policies are structured and produced by transnational forces, within and between different parts of the world. We also sorely need more in-depth studies of the intersections between multiple spheres (subnational, national, cross-border; bilateral, trilateral, regional and multilateral), levels (micro, meso and macro), sites (between different institutions and policy domains), processes (economic, political, social and cultural) in the production of social policies and their outcomes.

This chapter has argued that a transnational analytics of social policy can productively illuminate the contemporary dynamics of social policy. Analytically, this is not business as usual. Globalizing processes and influences need to be integrated into research design from the outset. Case studies need to go beyond the "single societies" approach to examine other sites, forums and dynamics. In this, the transnational connections between higher-income and lower-income territories and zones of the world need to be kept to the foreground, as well as between and among lower-income ones. In a similar vein, the ways in which certain Southern actors are developing capabilities of their own to shape norms and policies within their own "neighbourhoods" and beyond also constitutes a vital topic (Yeates 2014b, 2014c, 2017). More cases from other sectors and fields of social policy using comparative methods would help better elucidate how actors and networks are differentially structured within and between different policy arenas, and what the effects of this are on the course of social policy reform. This could usefully incorporate a wider range of obvious "success" cases of rapidly spreading policy models, but also of stalled or "failed" policy models.

Comparative methods are essential to this analytical endeavour. Indeed, the empirical questions to be addressed are essentially comparative in nature: how are social provision and policy structured by different kinds of transnational forces? Under what conditions and circumstances do transnational agendas influence the course of social policy change, and with what effects? In turn, studies of transnational social policy need to account more systematically for variation over time, issue/policy area and place. Context-specific factors—history and geography, institutions and politics—remain of immense importance in mediating social policy change. If the lessons from the early globalization literatures are to be carried over to this new research agenda, then it is vital to recognize that the transnational social relations and organization of welfare are as incomplete and contested as they are varied in their manifestations and impacts. In short, greater attention is needed to the ways in which national and transnational processes combine to *co-produce* social policy change in defined diverse contexts. Finally, I reiterate the importance of the methodological tools of comparative analysis in post-national social politics and policy research. A clearer focus on the *co-production* of social policy using *comparative* methods is critical to the twin challenges of strengthening the evidence base and theory-building about the sources, drivers, processes, effects and outcomes of contemporary welfare restructuring and social policy change across the global South, including how policies "travel" to and are embedded in the welfare institutions of the global North.

References

Abu Sharkh, Miriam and Ian Gough. 2010. "Global Welfare Regimes: A Cluster Analysis." *Global Social Policy*, 10(1):27–58.

Achterberg, Peter and Mara Yerkes. 2009. "One Welfare State Emerging? Convergence Versus Divergence in 16 Western Countries." *Journal of Comparative Social Welfare*, 25(3):189–201.

Ancelovici, Marcos and Jane Jenson. 2013. "Standardization for Transnational Diffusion: The Case of Truth Commissions and Conditional Cash Transfers." *International Political Sociology*, 7: 294–312.

Béland, Daniel and Mitchell Orenstein. 2009. "How Do Transnational Policy Actors Matter?" Paper presented to Annual Conference of the Research Committee on Poverty, Social Welfare and Social Policy (RC19) of the International Sociological Association, Montreal, 20–22 August.

Clarke, J. 2005. "Welfare States as Nation States: Some Conceptual reflections". *Social Policy and Society*, 4(4): 1–9.

Deacon, Bob. 2007. *Global Social Governance and Policy*. London: Sage.

Deacon, Bob, Michelle Hulse and Paul Stubbs. 1997. *Global Social Policy: International Organisations and the Future of Welfare*. London: Sage.

Deacon, Bob, Luk van Langenhove, Maria Macovei and Nicola Yeates (eds). 2010. *World-Regional Social Policy and Global Governance: New Research and Policy Agendas in Africa, Asia, Europe and Latin America*. London: Routledge.

Fenwick, Tracy B. 2013. "Stuck between the Past and the Future: Conditional Cash Transfer Programme Development and Policy Feedbacks in Brazil and Argentina." *Global Social Policy*, 13(2):144–167.

Fiszbein, Ariel and Norbert Schady with Francisco Ferreira, Margaret Grish, Niall Keleher, Pedro Olinto and Emmanuel Skoufi. 2009. *Conditional Cash Transfers: Reducing Present and Future Poverty*. Washington, DC: The World Bank.

Foli, Rosina. 2015. "Transnational Actors and Policymaking in Ghana: The Case of the Livelihood Empowerment Against Poverty." *Global Social Policy*, 16(3):268–286.

Franzoni, Juliana M. and Koen Voorend. 2011. "Actors and Ideas behind CCTs in Chile, Costa Rica and El Salvador." *Global Social Policy*, 11(2–3):279–298.

Hettne, Björn and Fredrik Söderbaum. 2000. "Theorising the Rise of Regionness." *New Political Economy*, 5(3):457–473.

Khagram, Sanjeev and Peggy Levitt. 2005. *Towards a Field of Transnational Studies and a Sociological Transnationalism Research Program*. Hauser Center for Non-Profit Organizations Working Paper No. 24. Cambridge, MA: Harvard University.

Mackinder, Sophie, Chris Holden and Nicola Yeates. 2022. "Global and Regional Social Governance." In *Understanding Global Social Policy* (3rd edition), edited by Nicola Yeates and Chris Holden, 25–46. Bristol: The Policy Press.

Madeira, Mary-Ann. 2014. "Regional Integration and National Social Policies." *Research and Politics*, October–December:1–9.

Mishra, Ramesh 1999. *Globalisation and the Welfare State*. Cheltenham: Edward Elgar.

Mittelman, James. 1995. "Rethinking the International Division of Labour in the Context of Globalisation." *Third World Quarterly*, 16(2):273–295.

Orenstein, Mitchell. A. 2008a. "Global Pensions Policy." In *Understanding Global Social Policy*, edited by N. Yeates, 207–227. Bristol: Policy Press.

Orenstein, Mitchell. A. 2008b. *Privatizing Pensions: The Transnational Campaign for Social Security Reform*. Princeton: Princeton University Press.

Orenstein, Mitchell. A. 2005. "The New Pension Reform as Global Policy." *Global Social Policy*, 5(2):175–202.

Paetzold, Jörg. 2013. "The Convergence of Welfare State Indicators in Europe: Evidence from Panel Data." *European Journal of Social Security*, 15(1):28–54.

Palan, Ronan, Jason Abbott and Phil Deans. 1996. *State Strategies in the Global Political Economy*. London: Pinter.

Parker, Susan and Tom Vogl. 2018. *Do Conditional Cash Transfers Improve Economic Outcomes in the Next Generation? Evidence from Mexico*. Cambridge, MA: NBER Working Paper.

Pierson, Paul. 1998. "Irresistible Forces, Immovable Objects: Post-Industrial Welfare States Confront Permanent Austerity." *Journal of European Public Policy*, 5(4):539–560.

Schmitt, Carina and Peter Starke. 2011. "Explaining the Convergence of OECD Welfare States: A Conditional Approach." *Journal of European Social Policy*, 21(2):120–135.

Stallings, Barbara. 1992. "International Influence on Economic Policy: Debt, Stabilization and Structural Reform." In *The Politics of Economic Adjustment*, edited by Stephan Haggard and Robert. R. Kaufman, 41–88. Princeton: Princeton University Press.

Sugiyama, Natasha B. 2011. "The Diffusion of Conditional Cash Transfer Programs in the Americas." *Global Social Policy*, 11(2–3):250–278.

Teichman, Judith. 2007. "Multilateral Lending Institutions and Transnational Policy Networks in Mexico and Chile." *Global Governance*, 13:557–573.

Yeates, Nicola. 2018. *Global Approaches to Social Policy: A Survey of Analytical Methods*. United Nations Research Institute for Social Development Thematic Paper, New Directions in Social Policy Series. WP 2018-2. Geneva: UNRISD.

Yeates, Nicola. 2017. *Southern Regionalisms, Global Agendas: Innovating Inclusive Access to Health, Medicines and Social Protection in a Context of Social Inequity*. PRARI Policy Brief No. 8. Milton Keynes: The Open University. Accessed 28 June 2022. http://www.open.ac.uk/socialsciences/prari/com munications-outputs/index.php?lang=en#policy_briefs.

Yeates, Nicola (ed.). 2014a. *Understanding Global Social Policy* (2nd edition). Bristol: Policy Press.

Yeates, Nicola. 2014b. "The Socialisation of Regionalism and the Regionalisation of Social Policy: Contexts, Imperatives and Challenges." In *Transformations in Global and Regional Social Policies*, edited by A. Kaasch and P. Stubbs, 17–43. Basingstoke: Palgrave Macmillan.

Yeates, Nicola. 2014c. *Global Poverty Reduction: What Can Regional Organisations Do?* PRARI Policy Brief No. 3. Milton Keynes: The Open University, Milton Keynes. Accessed 28 June 2022. http://www.open. ac.uk/socialsciences/prari/communications-outputs/index.php?lang= en#policy_briefs.

Yeates, Nicola (ed.). 2008. *Understanding Global Social Policy*. Bristol: Policy Press.

Yeates, Nicola. 2002. "Globalization and Social Policy: From Global Neoliberal Hegemony to Global Political Pluralism." *Global Social Policy*, 2(1):69–91.

Yeates, Nicola. 1999. "Social Politics and Policy in an Era of Globalisation." *Social Policy and Administration*, 33(4):372–393.

Yeates, Nicola and Chris Holden (eds). 2022. *Understanding Global Social Policy* (3rd edition). Bristol: Policy Press.

Yeates, Nicola and Freda Owusu-Sekyere. 2019. "The Financialisation of Transnational Family Care: A Study of UK-Based Senders of Remittances to Ghana and Nigeria." *Journal of International and Comparative Social Policy*, 35(2):137–156.

Yeates, Nicola and Jane Pillinger. 2019. *International Health Worker Migration and Recruitment: Global Governance, Politics and Policy*. London: Routledge.

Yeates, Nicola and Jane Pillinger. 2018. "International Healthcare Worker Migration in Asia Pacific: International Policy Responses." *Asia Pacific Viewpoint*, 59(1):92–106.

Yeates, Nicola and Pia Rigirozzi (eds). 2015. Special issue of *Global Social Policy on Southern Social Policy World-regionalisms*, 15(3).

Yeates, Nicola and Rebecca Surender. 2021. "Southern Social World-Regionalisms: The Place of Health in Nine African Regional Economic Communities." *Global Social Policy*, 21(2):191–214.

Yeates, Nicola, Maria Macovei and Luk van Langenhove. 2010. "The Evolving Context of World-Regional Social Policy: Bilateralism and Trans-Regionalism". In *World-Regional Social Policy and Global Governance: New Research and Policy Agendas in Africa, Asia, Europe and Latin America*, edited by B. Deacon, L. van Langenhove, M. Macovei and N. Yeates, 191–212. London: Routledge.

Yeates, Nicola, Themba Moeti and Mubita Luwabelwa. 2019. "Regional Research—Policy Partnerships for Health Equity and Inclusive Development: Reflections on Opportunities and Challenges from a Southern African Perspective." *IDS Bulletin*, 50(1):121–142.

2

Institutional–Evolutionary Analysis and Industry-Based Methods in Social Policy

Smita Srinivas

Introduction: New Approaches to Social Policy Analysis

There is no shared "global" social policy history that exists. Social policy has geographic, historic and economic features. Its history depends in large part on the nature of economic activity and industries in a specific region or country and existing technological capabilities. Benefits such as disability coverage, funeral expenses, health insurance, education, or for specific groups (veterans, civil servants, factory workers, teachers, 'informal' workers) have distinct histories and national features. The technological capabilities that develop define not merely who is vulnerable and their representation or eligibility for benefits, but also how the products, services and constitutional or other guarantees can be identified and administered. Health policy in most countries today comprises, with pensions (where they exist), the most expensive portion of social policy outlays. And health policy and public health strategies have their own unique scientific, industrial, technological, and in some cases, colonial and regressive features (such as segregation). In this sense, an analysis of health policy with a focus on its use of health technologies and the wider health industry that generates its products and services, offers important insights for future direction of social policy analysis which has to deal with both old and newly emerging industrial and technological issues directly related to various welfare services and benefits.

Technological advances in general, and especially the production of medical technology, are dramatically affecting a range of health care system challenges. These challenges include but are not limited to cost to patient, pricing, state procurement, reimbursements, generics availability and prescription choices. The technological advances determine the scope and quality of treatments and diagnostic tests that are advised, insurance offerings and priorities for managed care. In other words, institutional variety of health care systems is closely linked to technological transformations.

Examining the national histories of the health industry is crucial to understanding institutional variety within its industrial organization and embeds industrial policy design in the actual, practical problems of knowledge use and geography-specific industrial and labour history (Srinivas 2012, 2019a). This co-evolutionary, combinatorial approach can be explored through specific industrial problems such as the "informal economy," industrial sub-sector growth, or "sustainability" (Srinivas 2021a, 2021b). In the health sector, new institutional arrangements may come into being to propel scientific and technological discoveries or to curtail costs through the development of institutions such as public sector firms, procurement and social insurance. Different countries have developed a variety of legal, technical and customary institutions that often delineate the roles of the state in health to manage such institutional variety and new arrangements. The fact that health policy is not a simple subset of social policy and technology but plays a central role in the design and implementation of health policy has been well recognized. Moran (2000), for example, states very clearly that the modern welfare state cannot be understood without understanding health care, nor is health care a simple subset of the welfare state because health care institutions have dynamics of their own.

This chapter aims to introduce and explain some core arguments for a new approach to social policy analysis from the perspective of an industry-focused co-evolutionary framework which was invited by UNRISD and based on a prior UNRISD working paper (Srinivas 2019a; see also Srinivas 2021a, 2021b, 2023). COVID-19 has shown us that not only do dynamic industry frameworks matter to global health but they are peculiar to how countries build and manage their technological capabilities for social policy (Albuquerque 2007; Fransen et al 2021; Srinivas 2012; Sutz and Arocena 2006).

Industry-Based Institutional–Evolutionary Analysis

New social policies and programmes emerge across the global South, which create first steps toward more ambitious welfare states. However, framing social protection as an antithesis to markets makes it difficult to analyse variations in social policy programmes in industrializing countries, which have extremely diverse institutions and organized and disparate actors involved in their industrialization processes. The framework that pits social policies against markets is based on Polanyi's influential twentieth-century analysis of the Poor Laws in England. In his powerful analysis, social protections—through specific public policies and programmes—offered liberation from the slavery of waged labour and the state's complicity in forcing people into this dependence.

In such classical political economies, especially originating in the analysis of England and the European continent, Adam Smith, much earlier than

Polanyi but arguing from different observations and political philosophy, posed markets as largely counter to the state but also not necessarily aligned with social protections. This arguably allowed later representations of Smith's writing presenting the market as a dynamic, liberating mechanism to provide for equality, and which could demolish class structures that the state itself supports. The market thus seen institutes various types of equality through harsh competition, the doing away of monopolies and protectionism, allowing citizens more direct freedoms to pursue their welfare (for example, Smith 1961/1776:232–236).

Equally critical of the state, but vastly more critical of capitalist investment in creating markets, and pitting manager and capitalist against workers, Marxian thinking further emphasized the politics of large-scale industrial transformation. Rather than the market, social mobilization and class pressures would force the financial powers and propertied classes to redistribute. Emancipation would emerge from class friction and social mobilization seeking recognition of the centrality of labour to the industrial process (see Esping-Andersen 1990:10–11; see also Mesa-Lago 1978; Wood and Gough 2006).

Other frameworks, however, exist in the industrial landscape. Schumpeter's entrepreneur plays a unique role, distinct from the financier or factory worker in Marxian industrial transformation, managing uncertainty in economic development. Own-account workers, for example, may be exploited in the Marxian world or must make do in the informal economy, but the Schumpeterian assumptions of risk, entrepreneurship and access to capital or rents allow for some possibility through economic dynamism for the own-account worker to be a successful entrepreneur.

Finally, although less democratically aligned, "benign" power such as monarchies and dictatorships could, in principle, offer a similar resolution of redistribution by a promise of class benefits and social welfare, and a broader claim to social stability. This coincides with the historical fact that many of Europe's welfare states were seeded at the height of fascism and other non-democratic movements.

Industrial dynamics' diverse protagonists, therefore, deserve closer inspection. Labour has often been a fulcrum around which arguments for linking social policy and the economy are established. Marx saw labour power as the mechanism through which a challenge to the propertied classes could create redistributive measures of capital to society, through the destruction of class differences. In a similar vein, but with important differences, Karl Polanyi argued that the commodification of labour lay at the heart of capitalism's crisis. By pushing for labour commodification, capitalism was unable to resolve how to prevent its own destruction. British income security measures, in fact, prevented the full commodification of labour, because, without them, landless workers would have been forced to move in much more considerable measure to urban mills (Polanyi 1944). The combination of wage employment and substantial income insecurity embedded in and compounded by feudal relations ensured that workers remained tied to a land system that had little future for them, unable to fully transition to an existence where wage income alone could provide full support. In the absence of a welfare state system or personal property (land), workers had to make difficult, life-threatening choices about the extent to which to behave as a commodity and move to urban manufacturing centres. As many have commented, Adam Smith in contrast (and depending on the analysis) saw markets and moral ties as central to individual action, propping up a liberal society in which shared values, trust or supports might be required as a basis for markets to exert their full advantages, while providing their own emancipation from class identities and state complicity, and permitting workers to learn, specialize and benefit from opportunities offered by these markets. Schumpeter had other concerns of economic development's dynamics (and solutions) in mind. Veblen, Ayres and other institutionalists took this further, situating industrial transformation beyond class concerns in the realm of wider institutional frameworks—meaning, social norms, habits and customs.

Moving Beyond Classical Political Economy

The persuasiveness of classical political economy is the drama of land, labour and capital, and the fights and resolutions between the three. This drama is not for the faint-hearted. Who could argue with the grand stage, the actors, the battles and historical outcomes? How could there be any doubt that what we see is some embattled outcome of contestation or cooperation between these three elements? Yet there is quite a body of evidence—both in new programmes and consolidation of old ones, as well as a messy reality in terms of labour regulation and analysis—to indicate that we cannot close the book on social policy theorizing just yet.

If markets and how they function are less clear in the realm of social protection, then at least it is clearer from policy trends that framers and implementers are more sceptical of market fundamentalism as a cure-all solution for complex social vulnerabilities (UNRISD 2014). Nevertheless, there are considerable uncertainties about how to frame and manage disparate social programmes, many of which—driven by the market-friendliness of earlier years—provide at best minimal benefits, overdependent on the social safety net model. There is, therefore, a move away from markets as a cure-all solution on the one hand, and, on the other, continued reliance on residual types of market-based systems.

It is clear that positioning markets as the other end of the pendulum swing from social protections hides various nuances of technological advances in certain industry sectors.

Therefore, precisely because these diverse "industrial" perspectives allude to but do not specify the detailed technological transformations under way, there is an opportunity for an evolutionary–institutional approach rooted in the meso- and micro-technological dynamism of industry sectors. Notably, not all industry analysis is necessarily either institutional or evolutionary. Analysis merely using the terms industries or production can be based on equilibrium analysis, or more narrowly market analysis alone, and may push technological dynamism to the background. Foregrounding industry analysis allows for a deliberate understanding of dynamism within sectors, rather than as a generalized framework of industrial development more common in social policy analysis. Dynamism is not incidental but vital to the understanding of work, tasks, products, process generation, business cycles and a more visible role of entrepreneurs, small firms and financiers. For example, the political economy of the innovation process in the specific industry allows us a view of the conditions under which the state crowds in or crowds out entrepreneurs (innovators) and financiers in the pursuit of public benefits (Courvisanos 2009). It may underscore the hard slog to building self-sufficiency or sufficient autonomy over health products (Fransen et al 2021; Mackintosh et al. 2016). Therefore, in stark contrast to a Marxian or a liberal political economy, we see that the evolutionary character of technological advancement does not necessarily have a given bias in favour of class, religion, age or other social characteristics. That is not to say that inequalities, exploitation and exclusion do not exist, such as the inability to access health innovations. But, as Ayres and others have emphasized, price signals alone may not be drivers of change nor of such exclusions. Other opportunities to expand access may increase if one acknowledges the specifics of the existing technological capabilities or of global disparities in trade. Indeed, rather than overt bias, capital's availability, combined with state efforts, can lead to unpredictable outcomes, resulting in a politics that is technologically contingent to some degree. From a more deterministic viewpoint of social policy evolution alongside industrial development or, even more narrowly, manufacturing, this uncertainty might be deeply dissatisfying because it provides no easy pointers to labour or other solidarity. Instead, the evolutionary–institutional approach allows us to have specific domains of social policy design such as health care that are technologically deeply contingent, from antibiotics to COVID-19 diagnostics.

It is increasingly common to see technologically advanced nations with health industries, yet substantial pockets of health deprivation alongside (Fransen et al 2021; Srinivas 2012). In essence, by foregrounding industry analysis, we move beyond viewing sectors primarily through a labour lens but can draw on histories of products or processes, their financing, their timeline of dynamism, their mechanisms for responding to demand and so forth. This approach is much more amenable to both understanding economic dynamism and acknowledging the burst in organizational variety through which new social programmes, actors and institutions come about. Industry sectors, subsectors and specific technological advance details matter.

Industry Analysis: Variety and Co-evolution at Micro-Levels

Institutions do not simply evolve separately, rather they *co-evolve*. Institutional change is a combinatorial problem, where some institutional combinations ("complementarities" when compatible) dominate societies (Amable 2000; Srinivas 2012).[1] The dynamism of labour markets forms the major theoretical fulcrum around which we have come to see industrial entitlements and the spatial and institutional manifestations of how and where people work. However, if we assume that the labour market, for instance, factory labour, is only one such strand even of labour history, at least three distinct evolutionary strands can be discerned as we can see in Table 2.1 (Srinivas 2010, 2015). This taxonomy helps us to differentiate one European historical trajectory from another (for example, England, Germany and the Netherlands) and better understand the evolution of subnational elements of an industrializing nation such as India, where distinct social programmes were built in former royal states such as Mysore (Srinivas 2010, 2015).

This taxonomy helps us to see that several institutional permutations exist around social insurance systems and associated health care provisions. Some people may access health care through Work-, Workplace- and Place-based systems at different times, and other than through a national vocabulary, every actual programme is located in the realities of where people live and work, and thus has distinct institutional combinations and spatial features. This is consistent with the programmatic challenge involved in rolling out social programmes. Noteworthy Asian cases include the Self-Employed Women's Association (SEWA) health insurance programme, and the Philippines' Social Health Insurance-Networking and Empowerment (SHINE). Similarly, established state-led and/or centralized entitlements for the military, civil service or union-led public services (for example, schoolteachers) may stall in expansion and lose legitimacy across the country (many cases from Latin America have been well documented in Mesa-Lago (1978)), or too many

---

[1] This point of co-evolution and dominance of some institutions over others in the evolution of institutions has been especially well recognized by several original institutional economists ("American Institutionalism" and wider explorations between philosophy, economics and other social sciences). Questions directly relevant to assets, austerity, financialization and industries and specialization and labour are increasingly visible in the rejuvenated evolutionary political economy debates.

Table 2.1: A triad framework of institutional bases of labour entitlements

Institutional basis (definition)	Description
Place (location of residence)	Residence (Place) may be the worksite (Workplace), but not always. This may vary across industrial sectors, seasons, work hours, days per week, type of task, livelihood portfolio by sector, by gender or other factors such as telework arrangements during the COVID-19 pandemic.
Work (labour status often defined by national labour law)	Labour status (Work) or work-based identity is rarely without spatial character and invariably relates to benefits. The rise of organizations representing informal workers has demonstrated that traditional labour-organizing strategies at workplaces and the nationally defined labour status, for example, do not serve the bulk of the working population well. These strategies and status invariably neglect women or those whose Place (residence) may define their working activity. White-collar telecommuting has not necessarily improved the recognition of other lower-income groups.
Workplace (location of work, institutional recognition of industry)	The Workplace is distinct from Place (settlement/residence), although occasionally it may overlap in some instances (for example, home-based workers, telecommuters, itinerant workers, and so on). Historically, factories (Workplace) defined much of the scope of the Work (labour status) and social policy design. Workplace may require formal recognition by the state to act as the basis for eligibility and disbursement of social benefits. Although rights to work may be constitutionally embedded, the rights to places to work may not.

Source: adapted from Srinivas (2010, 2015)

entitlements under the umbrella of "benefits" may raise the question of whether social policy design even exists.

This scrutiny of change in different groups and industries usefully reinforces the reality of a complex, dynamic, three-dimensional world of living and working instead of a less precise national social policy language and national economic growth. It may provide a bridge between practical arrangements of industrial associations or specific regional industry clusters and state government strategies to manage direct cash benefits or service and infrastructure (including digital services) to residents of the area. It also allows us a new approach to current debates on welfare states and immigration. For instance, the immigration debate is often discussed in terms of citizenship-based or residence-based entitlements. The taxonomy presents the opportunity to discuss anew the relevance of Place and its unique industrial and community dynamics in spatial analytical terms.

Work-, Workplace- and Place-based benefits provide three such evolutionary strands of institutional and spatial features to social programmes (Srinivas 2010, 2015). Once this is recognized, labour entitlements can be analysed further in their specific industry and technology contexts. Digital transformations in banking and mobile payments from India, for example, have permitted a significant consolidation of residence, income- or identity-based quotas. India now has the largest welfare spending programmes rolled out across the last eight years under the Bharatiya Janata Party government. In some cases, these build on prior programmes but include ambitious new digital access, basic food and hygiene services, and financial inclusion programmes: the world's largest publicly funded health programme by numbers targeted, including a health insurance programme (of up to Rs 500,000 per family per year on a family floater basis[2]) and 150,000 health and wellness centres for primary health aim toward Universal Health Coverage ("Ayushman Bharat"),[3] and Jan Aushadi centres for low-cost medicines, devices and diagnostics, plus sanitary pads.[4] Furthermore, significant digitalization of personal identity cards (*Aadhaar*) and a new Digital Health Mission,[5] have created the convergence of technology with financial assets and essential services, with direct cash transfers to new bank accounts such as the central scheme of the Jan Dhan programme and free food rations during the COVID-19 pandemic for the indigent in state-level programmes in health. These have been combined with identification of areas within states that are excluded and lacking in services and infrastructure, creating pressures for higher roll-out of complementary, location-based supports such as dry rations, cooking gas, toilet construction to enable women's health and safety, electrification and easy access to tap water. These are not traditional labour-based benefits such as the cash for labour in public works (Mahatma Gandhi Rural Employment Guarantee Scheme, MNREGA), but are better analysed by spatial spread and social groups, with strong benefits for women and girls. The eventual national form of such policies remains

---

[2] A family floater is coverage for a family (not individual) up to a cap of the amount stated. See "Benefit Cover Under PM-JAY", https://nha.gov.in/PM-JAY, last accessed 16 November 2023.

[3] https://pmjay.gov.in/, and https://www.nhp.gov.in/ayushman-bharat-yojana_pg.

[4] http://janaushadhi.gov.in/pmjy.aspx.

[5] https://www.nhp.gov.in/national-digital-health-mission-(ndhm)_pg.

quite open-ended, leaving plenty of room for contestation and consolidation of specific benefits (for example, housing, education, health and disability) and mechanisms of disbursements (received via workplace, through place of settlement, ward-level officials or health clinics, or perhaps through work-based schemes accessed through national worker identity cards). There may be controversies around measurement and evaluation, or of lack of incentives to get off benefits for "graduation" or too many receiving benefits.[6] Seasonal work such as farming, or cyclical industrial work such as construction, may involve people holding multiple jobs, including those in factory settings and migrant employment. This means that the traditional Workplace-based social policy programmes face serious challenges in their current form.

As Table 2.1 has laid out and Figure 2.1 indicates, the informal economy has traditionally involved a range of non-factory work, and multiple institutional and spatial categories. Theoretically, too, it features challenges such as differences between entrepreneurs in the Schumpeterian schema and own-account workers or owner-managers in the Marxian tradition. Be it Polanyian, Smithian, Marxian or other, the conditions of workers in such an economic status might be victims, beneficiaries or other participants in a dynamic economy. Arguably, social policy analysis has been dominated by Marxian analysis or by class distinctions rather than other approaches to economic activity. The functions of "workers" and the "system" they inhabit are often parsed understandably in terms of the difficult contexts of economic participation and deprivation: benefiting or not from capital investment, government regulation, business costs, police harassment and difficulties in accessing credit and training. This leads to structural growth categories for micro-enterprises drawn from Marxian analysis: "residual" or "exploited" versus those types of analysis (innovation, neoliberal or other) interested in "flexible" or "agile" dynamism and less in redistribution. Consequently, the informal economy has become a complex political arena in framing the issue of policy design as well as revealing the theoretical assumptions of dynamism and variety it represents (a new effort to understanding the informal economy in these terms is described in Srinivas 2021a). The workers who constitute the informal economy in any country are classified in ways that underscore the continuum to waged work that was especially a European transition to social policy analysis.

The informal economy is a clumsy hold-all term for a range of labour types, and is thus clumsy in the design of social benefits. Some "informal" workers who work in the putting-out system of the garment industry may never enter the factory gates, but they remain essential to the industry's

---

[6] Likely to be debated on Indian data and poverty measurement "smell tests": Bhalla et al (2022), much debated and challenged.

Figure 2.1: The modified triad with spatial–institutional–evolutionary features

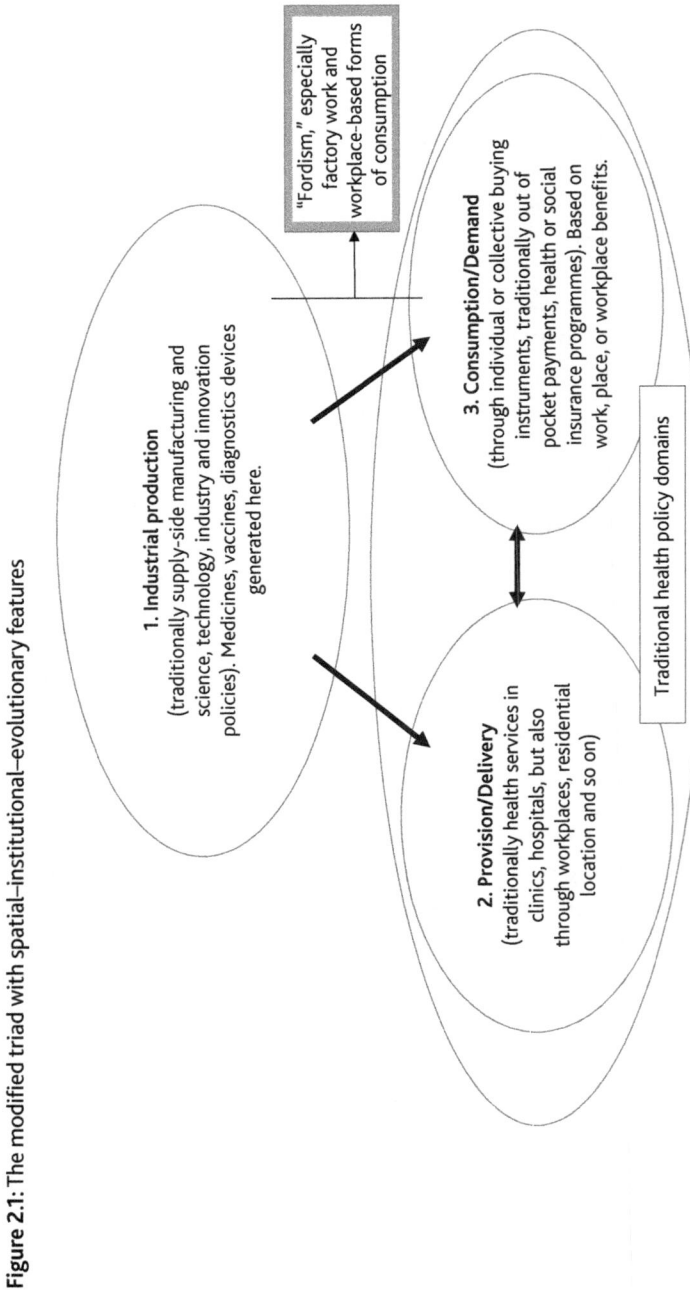

Source: adapted from Srinivas (2012:8)

dynamics and its evolution. Similarly, construction workers may remain within construction more days than usual or become more attuned to seeking and finding work in a range of geographically contiguous sectors.

Toward Industry Methods in Evolutionary Political Economy

Neo-Schumpeterian advances in thinking about evolution and dynamism have led to increasing recognition that institutional change is highly varied and stochastic, especially when considering industrial development. While patterns do emerge in this stochastic process, evolutionary trends imply a time element for different populations (people, firms, products). Patterns are time-bound and reveal multiple institutional combinations. First, neither institutions nor institutional processes progress singly; they *co-evolve*. This co-evolution of institutions allows institutions to permute in myriad ways. Thus, within co-evolution, one might study phenomena such as institutional synergy, complementarity, path dependency and the hierarchy of some institutions, actors and others, while keeping track of the timeline of such evolution. Importantly, in the neo-Schumpeterian language, co-evolution provides a way to capture specific and dynamic growth arenas (see, for example, Nelson 1994).

In this vein, the industry-based analysis, in addition to the taxonomy described earlier, offers a distinct methodological choice about how to view social policy. The focus on industrial features of construction workers, garment workers or some IT workers helps us to understand how Work-based mechanisms interact with industry-specific features. The industry-based analysis may also help us to improve or revise Workplace-based mechanisms of social policy benefits, since construction workers who shift from site to site may require a Place-based approach to social benefits (as indeed, many programmes have recognized with mobile nurseries and schools). For instance, urban planning remains a spatial and institutional gap in thinking of provision: South Africa has experimented for some time with mobile vans that disburse pensions at various sites on market days (Lund 1993; Lund and Srinivas 2000; Proudlock 2011). Industry-based analysis, therefore, attunes us to the institutional and spatial characteristics of the work and workers. Furthermore, it shifts us away from labour status- (Work-) based views alone to understand technological dynamism in the industry sectors as foreground, not the backdrop. It may reveal where any solidarity other than Work- or Workplace-based solidarity can emerge. This helps us move beyond the more restrictive categorizations of workers by production type, that is, primary, secondary and tertiary production, that has plagued social programmes and labour market reforms of many industrializing countries. The industry-based analysis suggests that labour market dynamics alone neither present consistent cross-national trends that make much sense in the context of lower- and middle-income nations currently industrializing, nor do they necessarily provide the only interesting barometer of economic dynamism. Technology and subsectors matter.

While it is common to view economic and social policies as separate spheres of life and policy making, the evidence is pushing us to reconsider this. Market failures are not enough to explain the presence of social policy. Rather, social policy studies should move beyond market failure arguments by identifying positive integration of both market and non-market institutions from an evolutionary perspective. A framework of a triad of institutions (Srinivas 2012:8) shown in Figure 2.1 proposes that we understand social service sectors as consisting of three primary institutional dynamics: industrial production, provision of service and the consumption (demand) of service. Focusing on the dynamism of institutional variety through an evolutionary lens helps to understand institutional variety, ways to manage the variety and the conditions (perhaps limited) under which the institutional and organizational variety offers a way to bind economic and social policies together.

The three realms of production, provision and consumption immediately make it more evident that health policy is normally concerned with spheres 2 and 3, and industrial/innovation, and science and technology policies primarily with sphere 1. This demarcation would be sufficient in a more static analysis where other spheres were being held constantly and, therefore, were absent their own dynamism and effects. As Table 2.1 indicates, Work, Place, and Workplace define the spatial and institutional context in which the spheres of health policy (spheres 2 and 3) are defined.

For instance, during the COVID-19 pandemic, vaccines were available for everybody or for free in many contexts, but testing was not. Medicines and food supplies or reimbursements were available to some types of workers or workplaces, while in other countries they were given by subnational region or district or province. People migrated to avoid shutdowns or to access food, and schooling in classrooms or independent of place (by internet access) was highly variable across regions and countries. In fact, innovation depended on this upending of spatial and social institutions. The reworking of the institutional triad's domains of production, demand and delivery, combined with new spatial realities of Place, Work and Workplace, generated new technological solutions to old problems: telemedicine; tele-education; rapid testing for diseases; digital payment systems, cash benefits; new delivery, logistics and warehousing; miniaturization and self-use of medical devices and test kits and so on. In other words, the production domain of sphere 1 was changing on a very short timescale. Therefore, one must take this technological dynamism seriously to appreciate how much social policy change is possible in short- and long-term timelines, and which are governed by new social norms and laws. This requires attention to the evolutionary trends in these spheres, their co-evolving attributes and institutional variety. While it is impossible to track all institutional permutations at the same time, an attempt at enumeration can give rise to new political strategies, bureaucratic challenges, industrial phasing, technological choices and ethical/value propositions in health care decisions. As such, this allows us a way in which to think of social policies as existing in multiple spheres of policies and programmes and not neatly positioned against the dynamic of "the market," but rather a "market menagerie" where markets exist in all these three realms and their interconnected institutional spheres (Srinivas 2012:163–185). Institutional variety matters and has especially mattered in different forms in the health industry during COVID-19 (Srinivas 2021b).

Late industrial and Schumpeterian-inspired analysis, for example, has emphasized repeatedly that industrial transformation involves changes across classical categories of the economy—agriculture, manufacturing and services. Furthermore, the transformation from learning and innovation is fundamental. A dynamic and evolutionary process emerges as firms or other organizations transform themselves, generating new knowledge which may be proprietary or applied in new ways. Learning by individuals and organizations, the use and generation of knowledge, and the development of new technologies, separates out different types of actors in the system and manifests at the micro-level the vitality or stagnation of firms: workers (whether employed or contracted), entrepreneurs, financiers, own-account, piece-, project-rate, or new types of "portfolio" careers and "gigs," across a spectrum from low to high incomes. Working from home and working remotely or across countries, now driven by accelerated technological changes and digital platforms, add to this rich spectrum of Place, Work and Workplace evolution and shifts in organization learning.

Beyond these considerations are critical comparative methodological features for social policy. While the late industrial and Schumpeterian literature offers a means to understand the dynamism and evolution of industrial development, these are predominantly supply-side analyses of industrial development. Amsden (2010), for example, emphasizes that supply-side policies in labour markets that focus on education policies and vocational training run the risk of underestimating demand for such educated and skilled workers. The Say's Law critique looking at unemployment rates among educated workers in Africa, for instance, demonstrates why a more microeconomic and dynamic approach may assist us in understanding the more macro, sectoral features of industrial development where some sectors are—because of their considerable dynamism or growth—able to absorb such workers while others are not (Amsden 2010).

The Health Industry in Late Industrial Economies

In this section, I draw extensively on industry analysis of the health sector in Srinivas's work (2012, 2016, 2019a), in particular of the conditions under which late industrial nations (especially democracies) with vibrant pharmaceutical and biotech sectors managed to resolve problems and succeed or falter in better health provisioning. The research focus is industry analysis—specifically production, process, technology platform and industry evolution in specific subsectors. Technological progress is essential to understanding how health goals are framed and evolve, and the sometimes contentious, sometimes more harmonious co-evolution of economic and social goals. As India became a "supplier to the world," the growth and availability of old and new medicines, vaccines, diagnostics and devices also emboldened health policy ambitions. This co-evolution, across supply, demand and delivery, seen in the institutional triad (see Figure 2.1) reveals the many dynamics in play of institutional change and expansion of social policy ambitions. The dynamism of many of the new social programmes of the Middle East and North Africa, South Asia, Southeast Asia and sub-Saharan Africa reveals that the programmes, agencies and actors are not evolving along predictable timelines, nor with correlates that are predictable by central ministry or labour strategy.

The framework of the institutional triad underscores how supply-side analyses alone offer biased perspectives on vital sectors such as health, employment and livelihood creation and sustenance, and especially how entitlements are formed to shape the benefits of industrial advancement through social policies and service delivery. Specifically, analysis of health policy is equally unbalanced because it sets aside the immense dynamism of the industrial elements of the sector, such as rapid technological advancement in all three domains of the triad, not production alone. The data are also supported by new evidence available on the importance of local industrial capabilities in the health sectors in several African countries, and the differing degrees to which industrial and health priorities can be politically phased and jointly instituted, with many failures of self-reliance or buying systems mixed in with improvements of domestic health systems (Fransen et al 2021; Mackintosh et al 2016).

Dynamism and evolution in an approach attentive to industrial micro-features and technological characteristics have a further benefit because they complement social policy approaches by helping them to recognize new actors, agencies, programmes and policy domains, including their changing and sometimes conflicting rules. For example, the rapid growth of the East Asian electronics and semi-conductor sectors was driven by ambitious and well-monitored industrial policies.

Moreover, health care involves governing consumption, provision and technology. According to Moran (2000) and Srinivas (2012), for instance, consumption and demand are closely aligned with distinctive high-technology, high-investment forms of research and development in medicine and pharmaceuticals, exemplified, of course, by the innovation but especially high costs of the US health industry. It is particularly notable that technological shifts are not only important, but offer multiple ways for evolution to occur within a sector, and often dramatically different policy domain and stakeholder platforms through which we might act. Specifically, health entitlements within social policy drawn from industry analysis show us that, in fact, nations cannot simply be compared along the production dimension, nor are those health outcomes necessarily assured in nations that might be highly successful in producing medicines and vaccines. Late industrial countries require a much closer, technologically contingent, social policy analysis. While the complexity confounds a simple catch-up in this sector, it offers in principle more policy handles for how to intervene and plan for health outcome-based industrial incentives, which might tighten the mechanisms through which we link health and industrial policies. The latter is clearly necessary.

Analytically, the institutional triad based on a co-evolutionary approach does not use a framework of market versus state. It is premised on the idea that the state's task is to create, legitimize, regulate and sometimes end multiple markets (the market menagerie, see Srinivas 2012). Very few nations, it turns out, do well on all dimensions or across time but the dramatic changes seen during the COVID-19 pandemic make it evident that, even in the health sphere, positive changes have occurred that enable rapid delivery under surging demand. Furthermore, industrial or technological sophistication on the supply side offers no guarantee of health access, and in some cases it can add complications.

As a method, therefore, the co-evolutionary–institutional triad in social policy sectors allows us more traction in considering the following (these points are elaborated in Srinivas 2019a):

- how, why and when nations may be more successful in one sector of social policies than another (variety of social policy institutions);
- why nations may be good at one dimension of the triad in one sector, but not so good in another dimension (institutional variety within sectors);
- why nations may be good for some time in some sectors or some triad elements of sectors but not for all time (institutional variety over time); and
- how global or exogenous factors affect the control of the national government over each dimension of the triad (institutional variety within and outside the nation-state).

According to this approach, India has done quite well in certain types of health policies (but not in education); Brazil has done much better in biotechnologies than in generics; and Cuba—although, not a democracy—has done quite abysmally on the economic front but very well on a wide range of diseases and their health-improvement plans. Moreover, local pharmaceutical or vaccine production is clearly a necessary but insufficient condition in most countries. The health industry, therefore, includes health policy and health programmes, but it also includes the wider dynamic economic arena where private and public firms compete and collaborate. Health policy-oriented programmes are either the subset or superset of the health industry system (Srinivas 2012, 2019a, 2019b).

The standard public and private distinction is rather simplistic. We know, for example, that private pharmacies are both a profitable store and a public venue for access to affordable medicines mandated by the welfare state. These sites within cities, towns and sometimes villages act as crossroads for multiple plans and policy interventions. Pharmacies constitute their own market and social protection spheres, as do health insurance firms. The health industry, therefore, has public and private firms, hybrid organizations, public institutes, non-profits, non-governmental organizations and a range of other organizations in practically every sphere of the triad. In this context, markets cannot be simply positioned against social protections and private, public or hybrid firms, and organizations play multiple roles in production, delivery and consumption. Seen thus, every dimension of the triad constitutes an institutional mix of markets, social protection systems and other ways of constituting the economy.

India and Cuba, for example, offer very different insights about dynamism and variety across the three dimensions of the institutional triad. Domestic demand through fragile or fragmented health policies and insurance systems in India, and its chemical capabilities, were in direct contrast to the effectiveness of rapid advances in, and the delivery of, COVID-19 vaccines and medicines under emergency conditions. Cuba prioritized industrial capabilities, though outside of a democratic framework, but was able to solve domestic health problems. As such, through the co-evolutionary framework, we see that production success is only a partial marker for health outcomes. It may be a necessary but vastly insufficient condition. This insufficiency is not an indictment of the firms, rather a recognition of the powerful incentives and limitations of welfare state markets. Better regulatory requirements, price controls where needed, more articulate domestic health priorities and routine design improvements of procurement systems, all offer clear incentives for private and public firms alike in improving health systems.

When health policy is further layered into the approach of Place, Work and Workplace histories, we begin to see how different entitlements might be spatially and institutionally circumscribed. This is visible in access debates on affordable medicines or urgent care, traditional therapies or increasing human rights concerns of pre-existing conditions, reproductive health or neo-natal emergency response. The three dimensions of Place, Work and Workplace affect all three dimensions of the institutional triad: that is, production, delivery and consumption. The Fordist approach, for example, focuses on Work and Workplace, primarily the production domain, but recognizes that Fordist workers are the audience for demand (consumption) and delivery. Furthermore, as specific diseases have proliferated, such as HIV–AIDs, Ebola and COVID-19, it has become clear that the global responses to coordinate and buy medicines have created skewed incentives for firms and have consequently affected production and delivery. A new economics is required for the health industry and health policy reform (Srinivas 2019a; Fransen et al 2021).

The conceptual terrain in the health sector clearly shows how theorizing in overly broad terms can drift away from some hard realities on the difficulties of having viable and responsible technological capabilities that solve specific social policy problems, but also that are vague about how these match up to specific programme interventions in practice. For instance, because of their widespread use, industrial-scale solutions in the health industry create health problems owing to the excessive use of chemicals and biologics affecting human health, food systems and water. Swine flu (H1N1) and new animal-health cross-over diseases such as COVID-19 show us the fragile, dangerous uncertainties in how industrialized dairy farms, piggeries and fisheries rely on antibiotic and vaccine use and abuse. This endangering of human and animal health alike creates skewed industry incentives for production (and overproduction), which in turn influence the design of demand systems, delivery systems and their safeguards in all three triad spheres. Finally, animal health and factory farming, combined with zoonoses concerns, demonstrate policy discrepancies in designing industrial incentives and health and environmental outcomes.

Conclusion: Policy Considerations

Low- and middle-income countries are witnessing a surge of new social programmes that are aligned neither with the linear narrative of a rise in social programmes alongside industrial development, nor with labour considerations. Micro-level industry dynamics are thus useful in understanding evolution and co-evolution in subsectors and should constitute an essential part of any social policy analysis.

New approaches to industry methods in social policy offer various benefits. First, we begin to see the sector's dynamics in more detail, which otherwise might have been obscured by the economy at large. As the triad and layered heuristic has shown, contrasting countries according to production capabilities alone is misleading. For instance, while India and Cuba have had strong industrial supply-side capabilities in health, the institutional triad demonstrates why their social policy record and the political context of provision and entitlement are vastly different. Foregrounding the nature of technological progress and its regulatory lessons in the analysis of social policy is necessary.

Second, industry subsectors reveal specific features of the state, businesses and stakeholders. Industry sectors are political economy domains of social policy in which technology features matter. This is not merely rates of return but the difficult collective or administrative decisions about why such investments were planned or legitimized in the first place.

Features of both sector dynamics, and of the politics of investment and redistribution, demand a further examination of markets versus social protection. The Schumpeterian perspective often focuses on the sector's business dynamics, which reveals the productive/innovative roles of the entrepreneur and financier. However, the Schumpeterian perspective is far less focused on the second dynamic within the sector, of the planning and iterative evaluative frameworks—which are different across the world—through which investment decisions must be filtered and evaluated.

Third, the role of firms becomes more evident in social policy. Highly technologically innovative firms may generate products or services that are not neatly aligned with single political paradigms of social policy. Artificial intelligence and automation are familiar examples. Less familiar are considerations of firms that produce highly toxic chemicals on the one hand, but also generate health care solutions on the other (sometimes unregulated cosmetics, household products, food and pesticide portfolios exist within "health care" firms). These various products produced by single firms differentially but directly affect health care outcomes. Public procurement rules may also lack clarity on regulation.

Fourth, an industry-specific and institutional–evolutionary analysis helps to examine what constitutes the notion of "community" and the practicalities of risk-pooling. Can private firms or hybrid arrangements play a role in resolving some of the more complex programmatic and moral questions of care? Extended producer responsibility frameworks for industries often mean programmes for take-back of products and waste, but could instead refer to hazardous waste and health care responsibility. Ironically, hospitals and clinics as a community may generate such unchecked hazardous waste.

Fifth, and finally, several practical considerations follow from an evolutionary perspective embedded in technological changes.

- There is no inevitability about a progressive or efficient social agenda as countries industrialize, or the idea that economic development and health improvements go hand in hand. All three domains of the institutional triad and further subdomains are stages of considerable industrial dynamism and political goals and leadership matters.

- Medical capabilities help health policy but are only one among several institutional features and market elements. Medical expertise cannot determine health care or the regulation of the health industry. History has shown that a broader perspective beyond biomedical and clinical is needed.
- Co-evolution increases the way the traditional welfare state regimes can be extended. Countries considered to have the same welfare regime may have different institutional arrangements for production and technology that significantly affect the design and implementation ("delivery in hand") of social policy.
- If co-evolution comprises both market and non-market institutions, we can no longer craft policies using the simple language of public, private or market systems. Multiple markets (the menagerie) exist as well. Furthermore, the co-evolution of three distinct spheres of production, delivery and consumption makes it more visible that state-led acts of social policy creation or propagation require committed bureaucratic/ administrative capacity in three distinct and integrative, dynamic ways.
- Welfare markets merge the simple distinction between welfare states and markets into useful firm-centric opportunities for profits and social ends. Innovation policies can thus centre (as they do to some extent already) on social policy goals. Welfare markets also reflect the reality that many firms in industrializing countries depend on the buying power of welfare states as critical export opportunities in other countries.
- Problem-solving and patient, long-term plans are essential for social policies. Building state capacity for problem solving in these domains is essential. It does no good to allow production capacity and vaccines to rot on shelves without disbursement or refrigeration infrastructure as we have seen in the cases of various mRNA-based COVID-19 vaccines (reliable electricity supplies are needed at the very least). Other types of supply chains for health care may be necessary, not necessarily focused on labour politics, for example, sustaining plant nurseries for traditional medicines is now urgent.
- The financial adaptation that accompanies industrial policies and procurement systems, or technical standardization such as safety standards, requires donors and governments, and for international foundations to coordinate their efforts and not skew social policy design to favour international harmonization over domestic goals for building or protecting technological capabilities toward the affordability of medicines.

This evolutionary perspective helps us to understand not only the trajectories of policy development and their variations across time (the business cycle perspective), but several markets and other institutions need constant attention: regulating the market menagerie as opposed to the market. Industry studies can do more than simply draw attention to the technological dynamism inherent in specific sectors. The fits and starts of social programmes, the stops and gaps, the fragmentation and coalescing are processes that can be seen to analytical advantage with new methods of approach. This pulls considerably away from traditional late industrial development scholarship focused on specific institutional choices: states versus markets, nation-states rather than subregional governance and industrial policy as the preferred pivot.

By embracing the fits and starts, fragmentation and otherwise partially disjointed social policy designs and welfare programmes, we can document and recognize the conditions under which social policy emerges and evolves.

References

Albuquerque, Eduardo da Motta E. 2007. "Inadequacy of Technology and Innovation Systems at the Periphery." *Cambridge Journal of Economics*, 31(5):669–690.

Amable, Bruno. 2000. "Institutional Complementarity and Diversity of Social Systems of Innovation and Production." *Review of International Political Economy*, 7(4):645–687.

Amsden, Alice H. 2010. "Say's Law, Poverty Persistence, and Employment Neglect." *Journal of Human Development and Capabilities*, 11(1):57–66.

Bhalla, Surjit, Karan Bhasin and Arvind Virmani. 2022. "Pandemic, Poverty, and Inequality: Evidence from India." Accessed 10 April 2022. https://www.imf.org/en/Publications/WP/Issues/2022/04/05/Pandemic-Poverty-and-Inequality-Evidence-from-India-516155.

Courvisanos, Jerry. 2009. "Political Aspects of Innovation." *Research Policy*, 38:1117–1124.

Esping-Andersen, Gøsta. 1990. *The Three Worlds of Welfare Capitalism*. Cambridge, UK: Polity Press.

Fransen, Lieve, John Nkengason, Smita Srinivas and Stefano Vella. 2021. *Boosting Equitable Access and Production of Diagnostics, Therapeutics and Vaccines to Confront Covid-19 on a Global Footing*. Policy Brief, Task Force 1 on Global Health and COVID-19. Accessed 2 May 2022. https://www.t20italy.org/2021/09/08/boosting-equitable-access-and-production-of-diagnostics-therapeutics-and-vaccines-to-confront-covid-19-on-a-global-footing/#.

Lund, Frances. 1993. "State Social Benefits in South Africa." *International Social Security Review*, 46(1):5–25.

Lund, Frances and Smita Srinivas. 2000. *Learning from Experience: A Gendered Approach to Social Protection for Workers in the Informal Economy*. Geneva: International Labour Organization.

Mackintosh, Maureen, Geoff Banda, Paula Tibandebage and Watu Wamae. 2016. *Making Medicines in Africa: The Political Economy of Industrializing for Local Health*. London: Palgrave Macmillan.

Mesa-Lago, Carmelo. 1978. *Social Security in Latin America: Pressure Groups, Stratification, and Inequality*. Pittsburgh, PA: University of Pittsburgh Press.

Moran, Michael. 2000. "Understanding the Welfare State: The Case of Health Care." *British Journal of Politics & International Relations*, 2(2):135–160.

Nelson, Richard R. 1994. "The Coevolution of Technologies and Institutions." In *Evolutionary Concepts in Contemporary Economics*, edited by R. W. England, 139–156. Ann Arbor: The University of Michigan Press.

Polanyi, Karl. 1944. *The Great Transformation: The Political and Economic Origins of Our Time*. Boston: Beacon Press.

Proudlock, Paula. 2011. "Lessons Learned from the Campaigns to Expand the Child Support Grant in South Africa." *Social Protection for Africa's Children*, 1:49–175.

Smith, Adam. 1961/1776. *The Wealth of Nations, Book I*. Chicago: University of Chicago Press.

Srinivas, Smita. 2023. "When is Industry 'Sustainable'? The Economics of Institutional Variety in a Pandemic." *Review of Evolutionary Political Economy*, 1–33.

Srinivas, Smita. 2021a. *Institutional Variety in the Informal Economy: Learning and Knowledge Systems for Theory and Policy*. Prepared for the ILO's research project on Assessing Social Capabilities for New Technologies, Innovation and Job Creation in South Africa. Geneva: International Labour Organization.

Srinivas, Smita. 2021b. *Institutional Variety and Sustainable Industrial Policy*. Background Paper BP13, prepared for the Industrial Development Report (IDR) 2022, Department of Policy, Research and Statistics Working Paper No. 20/2021. Vienna: United Nations Industrial Development Organization. Accessed 2 May 2022. https://www.unido.org/api/opent ext/documents/download/25405859/unido-file-25405859.

Srinivas, Smita. 2019a. *Institutional-Evolutionary Analysis and Industry-Based Methods in Social Policy*. UNRISD Working Paper. Geneva: United Nations Research Institute for Social Development.

Srinivas, S. 2019b. "A New Economics for Health." In *Health of the Nation: India*, edited by A. Mehdi and I. Rajan. New Delhi: Oxford University Press.

Srinivas, Smita. 2016. "Healthy Industries, Unhealthy Populations: Lessons from Indian Problem-solving." In *Making Medicines in Africa*, edited by M. Mackintosh, G. Banda, P. Tibandebage and W. Wamae, 183–199. Basingstoke: Palgrave Macmillan.

Srinivas, Smita. 2015. "Place, Work, Work-Place." Ford Foundation Urban Inclusion Project, IIHS Teaching Case, Bengaluru, India.

Srinivas, Smita. 2012. *Market Menagerie: Health and Development in Late Industrial States*. Stanford: Stanford University Press.

Srinivas, Smita. 2010. "Industrial Welfare and the State: Nation and City Reconsidered." *Theory and Society*, 39(3–4):451–470.

Sutz, Judith and Rodrigo Arocena. 2006. *Integrating Innovation Policies with Social Policies: A Strategy to Embed Science and Technology into Development Processes.* Strategic Commissioned Paper, IDRC Innovation, Policy and Science Program Area, International Development Research Centre, Canada. Accessed 1 March 2022. https://idl-bnc-idrc.dspacedirect.org/bitstream/handle/10625/33061/124734.pdf.

UNRISD (United Nations Research Institute for Social Development). 2014. "New Directions in Social Policy: Project Inception Workshop." Accessed 20 December 2018. http://www.unrisd.org/unrisd/website/events.nsf/(httpEvents)/8F2C57F7A9936CE5C1257C9E0054EE76?OpenDocument.

Wood, Geof and Ian Gough. 2006. "A Comparative Welfare Regime Approach to Global Social Policy." *World Development*, 34(10):1696–1712.

3

Incorporating Informal Workers in Twenty-First-Century Social Contracts

Rina Agarwala

Introduction

Amid widespread uncertainty, new social policies that promise to protect certain groups are emerging throughout the developing world. This is not surprising. History has shown that in times of crisis, discontent rises and government leaders make policy changes to retain their legitimacy and quell social discontent. Whether states enact transformative policy changes of redistribution and mass-based security or repress parts of the population alongside palliative efforts to attain consent (Arrighi 1978; Moore 1966; Riley and Desai 2007), a new social contract is often inaugurated. Welfare regimes thus emerge from conflict and collaboration between states and their societies.

Analyses of recent social policies, therefore, demand an examination of state forces from above *and* social movements pushing change from below. This chapter examines the changing relationship between states and their societies through the analysis of social agents that are sorely underexamined in contemporary research, that is, informal workers.

Through the comparative analysis of eight countries of the global North and South, this study offers an initial framework on contemporary trends in informal workers' movements. The findings of this chapter indicate that informal workers' alternative movements are spearheaded by workers of the global South (including those living in the South and those who have migrated to the North). Despite their geographic spread, these workers engage with remarkably similar types of work and struggles. Studies on contemporary social movements must, therefore, include new units of analysis that capture national-level sociopolitical contexts *and* transnational human mobility. Only then can we understand varieties and continuities in twenty-first-century social contracts across national contexts.

Shifting Our Gaze on Social Change

Before the spread of twentieth-century regulations formalizing labour rights, all labour was "informal" or unprotected and unregulated. This informal labour demanded, formulated and, in some cases, governed early to mid-twentieth-century welfare policies designed to recognize workers, regulate working conditions, mitigate exploitation and protect workers' dignity and rights (Thompson 1966). While countries varied in their levels of implementation of labour regulations during this period, they shared an expressed commitment to formally recognize labour under law, hold states responsible for the enforcement of labour protections, and ensure that capital de-commodifies workers' productive and reproductive labour through minimum wages, job security, work contracts, health care and old-age benefits (Esping-Anderson 1990). This commitment gave labour the power, confidence and legitimacy to make welfare demands vis-à-vis the state, employers and the public.

However, these "victories" for labour rights also forced scholars and activists examining social change to shift their focus to only one segment of the working class—that is, formal workers or those legally entitled to the protections and regulations that all labour fought to attain. Those who remained informal were no longer highlighted as change agents. Instead, they were (and still are) assumed to be unable to organize, since informal employment disperses the site of production through home-based work, complicates employer–employee relationships through multiple subcontracting arrangements and atomizes labour relationships by eliminating the daily shop floor gathering of workers (Berger and Piore 1989; Hyman 1992).

These assumptions that informal workers are unable to organize fly against the historical fact that it was informal workers who established the concept of "formal workers" by fighting for twentieth-century labour regulations (Thompson 1966). Moreover, we know that class politics must be examined as a dynamic social relationship (Agarwala 2006). In a system where capital and labour are bound to each other in a simultaneously co-dependent and competing relationship, both groups constantly innovate to protect their interests. Capital will find new ways to exclude or exploit labour to expand profits, while labour will fight deregulation and commodification to protect their rights (Marx 1976; Polanyi 2001). Given that informal labour is involved in capitalist production, there exists no theoretical basis for assuming that informal labour will not seek innovative sources of power to protect their humanity.

Omitting informal labour from analyses of social change also weakens our understanding of the historical relations between informal and formal labour in capitalist economies. Despite the labour movement's impressive strides in attaining labour regulations worldwide, the vast majority of the world's workers were always excluded from these regulations. This exclusion enabled capital to continue using flexible, low-cost, informal labour to subsidize the costs of employing a minority of protected workers (Lenin 1939; Luxemburg 1951). In addition, the exclusion enabled formal workers to access low-cost goods and services to meet the reproduction costs of food, clothing and other needs. Formal labour, informal labour and capital are thus embedded in a complicated social relationship of interdependence within capitalist production.

Finally, seeing formal workers as the only potential change agents among workers has forced a misreading of contemporary capitalism as devoid of class politics since the 1980s. Despite early development theories predicting an eventual fall in the share of informal workers and a concurrent rise in the share of formal workers (Lewis 1954), the share of informal, unprotected workers in developed and developing countries has risen since the 1980s (ILO-WIEGO 2013). Since informal workers are assumed to be unable to organize, their rising share has been equated to the demise of workers' movements. Many have mourned the loss of dignity among the world's workers (Davis 2006), highlighting the role that contemporary neoliberalism plays in exacerbating workers' poverty (Harvey 2005) and warning against potential dangers of a swelling, disorganized precariat (Standing 2011). Failure to examine informal workers as potential change agents has led to an incomplete analysis of processes through which new welfare regimes are forming to affect workers worldwide.

Instead of class, scholars since the 1980s have highlighted the rise of "new social movements" (NSM), featuring interest-based movements on (among others) environment and poverty and identity-based movements organized by gender, caste, religion or ethnicity (Touraine et al 1983). In recent years, scholars have depicted these movements in the global South as budding "counter-movements" of resistance to neoliberalism. Resurrecting a version of Karl Polanyi's (2001) predictions that market fundamentalism will catalyse people to protect themselves against commodification, scholars have showcased the rise of migrant protests for access to social rights in China (Friedman 2014), community protests for service delivery in South Africa (Hart 2002), caste-based movements for equality in India (Omvedt 1993), immigrant movements for new definitions of citizenship in the United States (Fine and Milkman 2013; Meyer and Fine 2017) and gender movements for democracy in Tunisia (Charrad 2001).[1]

---

[1] Few have examined Polanyi's prediction that counter-movements also include fascist movements.

While this recent literature has usefully illustrated the discontent expressed in the face of rising poverty under neoliberal, globalized production structures, it has been less helpful in providing a dynamic framework on class or illuminating informal workers as change agents. Often, these NSMs are analysed relative to formal workers' movements. Some celebrate the NSMs' ability to offer women and ethnic minorities a promising alternative to the workers' movements that grew but often excluded minority genders and races in the first half of the twentieth century (Charrad 2001). Others critique NSMs for being "alienated," "cellular" and "fragmented" (Chatterjee 2006; Friedman 2014). Even the media repeatedly notes the "limited" impact recent NSMs have had on policy (*The Economist* 2015). These critiques are sometimes posed in contrast to the more profound impacts of twentieth-century workers' movements and, other times, as consistent with the earlier movement's challenges.

In all cases, these analyses frame NSMs that resist deleterious forces of neoliberalism as distinct from class-based movements, despite the fact that NSMs are often spearheaded by poor, informally employed workers. Focusing exclusively on the non-class identities used to organize NSMs, the current literature ignores the central relationship of labour exploitation in modern neoliberal economies and omits an important segment of workers as potential contributors to transforming the contemporary social contract. Thus, we know surprisingly little about how poor workers are affecting change today. Additionally, assessments of NSMs' successes and failures are often made relative to formal workers' twentieth-century movements, which have had the advantage of over a century of experience. NSMs are thus often written off prematurely, and contemporary social contracts are misread as merely a product "from above."

To escape these traps in the current literature on social change, we must revisit the analytical boundaries around present definitions of class, identity and social movements. Only then, can we "see," let alone analyse, informal workers' movements from below and their impact on social policies from above.

Defining "Informal Work"

Scholars have long debated the meaning of informal work and the reasons for its existence (Bromley and Gerry 1979; Rakowski 1994). An attempt to distinguish the informal economy from the formal economy underlies such debates, which has come to typify advanced, industrial modernity (Agarwala 2009). It is thus unsurprising that definitional debates on informality are more advanced in the global South, where scholars, labour activists and policy makers have been grappling with the simultaneous presence of informal and formal labour as a central feature of their modern economies for decades.

In the global North, recent scholars have popularized the term precarious work. Some define "precarity" as a "continuum" comprising four criteria: the degree of certainty of continuing employment, control over the labour process, the degree of regulatory protection (though unions or laws) and income level (Cranford et al 2003). Guy Standing (2011) defined "the precariat" as a social category comprising people lacking seven forms of labour security: labour market security; employment security against arbitrary dismissal; job security and access to upward mobility; work security or protection against accidents, illnesses and arduous working conditions; skill reproduction security; income security; and representation security. While these definitions are useful in illustrating features of precarious work, they are too disparate to operationalize. Moreover, they do not embed the concept of precarity within larger socioeconomic structures, thus failing to explain *why* precarity exists in the first place.

In contrast, scholars drawing from the global South offer definitions that are more simple, operational and analytically rigorous. This scholarship has favoured the term informal work.[2] Since the 1980s, these scholars have highlighted the "social relationship" between labour, capital and the state, emphasizing the role of regulation. Portes, Castells and Benson (1989), for example, drew on the experiences of Latin America to define informal workers as those engaged in producing and providing legal goods and services, but who operate outside labour, health and financial regulation. Similarly, Jan Breman and Marcel van der Linden draw from the cases of South Asia to define informal work as "a type of waged employment thoroughly flexibilized and unregulated by public intervention," featuring part-time, flexible jobs; low wages and decreased secondary benefits; increased outsourcing and self-employment; irregular workdays (lengthened and shortened); and relaxed controls on work conditions (Breman and van der Linden 2014:926).

These regulation-based definitions enable us to analyse informal workers' relationships with other economic actors, such as the state, formal workers and employers. As Vladimir Lenin (1939) and Rosa Luxemburg (1951) illustrated, informal workers are not a remnant of a feudal past or a temporary step in the transition to a capitalist future. Rather, the informal economy has always fuelled modern, formal capitalist economic growth. Under imperialism, Europe drew on alternative modes of production (such as pre-capitalist, artisan, feudal and petty bourgeois) in colonies to secure raw materials for growing manufacturing structures. In addition, class struggles that increased

---

[2] There is little consensus on the distinctions between "precarious" and "informal." This chapter uses the terms interchangeably.

European wages forced European capitalists and formally protected workers to rely on the colonies' cheap, flexible, informal workforce for low-end manufactured goods and services. Following independence, political and social institutions in the developing world continued to ensure that informal workers absorbed the formal economy's cost of low-end production and labour reproduction by forsaking benefits or minimum wages. For instance, informal workers in Bogotá's shoe-making industry worked as subcontractors for formally regulated firms in Colombia (Peattie 1987). Working in the privacy of their homes or unregistered worksheds, they mitigated employers' overhead costs (Moser 1978) and helped states constrain the expansion of a costly formal working class (Portes and Walton 1981).

These insights explain why the informal economy has persisted even in the context of capitalist economic growth. Employers have avoided labour regulations against exploitation by hiring workers through unregulated subcontracting arrangements since the early 1900s when formal labour regulations were first born. Although the struggles and social contracts of the twentieth century did much to improve the lives of millions of workers, they failed to include the mass of workers capital employed outside the purview of labour laws, who in turn could subsidize the minority of protected formal workers.

To avoid existing labour laws, employers made use of its narrow confines to the "standard employment relationship" or SER, by hiding the employer–employee relationship in two ways. First, capital hired "contract" or "casual" workers, directly involved in capitalist production, but hired through subcontractors to avoid visibility, regulation and protection. Contract workers' principal employers can be small, unregulated enterprises or formally registered companies, such as Honda or H&M. These workers work in their homes, unregulated worksheds or on the factory floor next to formal workers.

Second, capital relied on "self-employed" workers—that is, owners of small, unregulated businesses that provide cheap inputs for capital production (such as autoparts, transport or products manufactured to order), and goods and services to capital owners (such as cleaning, elderly care, gardening and waste collection) and to low-wage workers (such as food, clothing and haircuts). Many countries define "formal" employment by enterprise size, thereby excluding from labour protection self-employed workers (who own small enterprises) and workers in small enterprises. In contexts where contract workers are protected under law, employers avoid regulation by claiming they "buy" their finished products from a self-employed worker, rather than a hired contract worker, though the product is ordered and designed by the employer. In these cases, self-employed workers resemble mislabelled contract workers. They work in their own homes, employers' homes or in public spaces like the street.

Together, contract and self-employed workers are referred to as "informal" or "precarious" workers. Both groups make legal goods and services, yet neither have a legal labour contract. Therefore, informality features non-standard employment relationships, which, by definition under most existing labour laws for those in SER, are unregulated and unprotected. Most informal workers operate in vulnerable working conditions with low incomes. Today, they can be found in all sectors of the economy, including agriculture, manufacturing, construction and services.

An important drawback to the regulation-based definition is that it does not accommodate contemporary informal workers' efforts to establish new regulations of protection. As detailed in this chapter, informal workers worldwide are launching alternative labour movements to demand protections. Yet, they are still identifying as informal in terms of their employment relationship. This chapter thus qualifies the regulation-based definition to specify that informal workers are those not regulated or protected by the SER defining formal workers' employment relationship (Agarwala 2013a). But informal workers may very well be regulated— sometimes punished, sometimes protected—by other state laws.

Since many workers simultaneously operate as formal workers and moonlight as informal workers, some might question the usefulness of the distinction. Why not simply speak of informal vs formal "work" or "sectors," rather than "workers"? Indeed, as is shown in the following section, early discussions did focus on "work," rather than "workers." However, the distinctions between informal and formal work were found to be as blurry as with workers, since so much informal work takes place alongside formal work, by the same employer, sometimes on the same shop floor. Moreover, informal workers are purposefully articulating their identity in contrast to formal workers. But by defining themselves as workers with diverse employment relationships, they are ultimately redefining the concept of *all* workers and may eventually erase the need for formal/informal worker distinction.

Operationalizing the Definition

In 1993, participants in the 15th International Conference of Labor Statisticians (ICLS) marked a historic turning point by agreeing that informal workers must be counted in labour force surveys to improve analyses of the modern global economy (ILO 1993). An internationally consistent, operational definition of the informal economy was viewed as a first step toward collecting and analysing data on the subject. The absence of such a definition until then had yielded case studies offering different, sometimes conflicting, conclusions about causes and effects of informal work (Rakowski 1994). To address this issue, ICLS participants drafted a definition that was subsequently incorporated into the 1993 System of National Accounts (SNA).[3]

The 1993 ICLS definition was limited by its underlying economic theorization of the informal economy that ignored its social and political relations with the formal economy. The ICLS defined informal economy as "enterprises" that have a low level of organization, little or no division between capital and labour as factors of production and, where labour relations consist of social relationships, not formal contracts. Under this definition, the informal economy comprised only unregistered or unincorporated enterprises owned by households producing goods and services to generate employment (ILO 1993).[4] This definition omitted, and thus undermined the ability to empirically examine other growing subsets of informal workers that are crucial to the neoliberal agenda. These include unregulated contractors working for formal companies; workers who move back and forth between, or work simultaneously in, informal and formal employment; and self-employed workers who work alone at home or in multiple locations on the street, whose workplaces are not counted as "enterprises" (Satpathy 2004).

Criticisms of the 1993 ICLS definition spawned a new operational definition of all informal workers in terms of their employment status (that is, casual, self-employed or regular worker) and the characteristics of their enterprises (legal status and/or size of the enterprise). Ralf Hussmanns (2002) of the International Labour Organization (ILO) outlined this broader definition that ensures the inclusion of informal workers in informal and formal enterprises and of regular workers in informal enterprises, thereby incorporating economic sociologists' relational definition of informal workers. Although this newer definition has not yet been incorporated into the SNA, in 2003, the 17th ICLS began using the term "informal economy," instead of "informal sector," to capture informal workers in both informal and formal enterprises.

Drawing on this definition of informal workers—that is, all those that are unregulated and unprotected by laws based on the SER—this chapter will now examine the changes experienced in informal work under neoliberalism and globalization.

---

[3] SNA sets the international statistical standard for measuring the market economy to ensure international comparability. It is published by the United Nations, the Commission of the European Communities, the International Monetary Fund, the Organisation for Economic Co-operation and Development and the World Bank. The first SNA was established in 1953.

[4] Production and household expenditures in these enterprises are usually combined and financial accounts are rarely maintained.

Informal Workers and Neoliberalism

As noted earlier, scholars of informality in the global South remind us that informal labour is neither a remnant of a feudal past, nor a new product of neoliberalism.

What is new under neoliberalism, however, is the increased growth of the relative share of informal workers globally. Particularly striking has been its growth in the global North (as well as the South). In South Asia, Southeast Asia and Africa (excluding South Africa), the informal workforce represents 60–80 per cent of the non-agricultural workforce; in Latin America, it represents 40–60 per cent (ILO-WIEGO 2013). Case studies from Japan, the United States, Canada and Europe illustrate similar trends of a swelling informal workforce, coupled with a shrinking formal workforce (Bakan and Stasiulis 1997; Boris and Klein 2012; Gottfried 2015; Wills 2009).

How can we explain this unpredicted global rise in informal work? Much has been written about the ideological forces of neoliberalism and globalization urging states worldwide to deregulate markets and absolve capital of any responsibility for labour's welfare (Harvey 2005). Firms claim that to remain competitive in an increasingly global market, they must hire additional informal workers unbound from legal recognition, labour benefits and job security. In response to these claims, governments have pulled away (to varying degrees) from their responsibility to enforce labour regulations and enfold all workers into the protected, regulated sphere. More so than before, the public, capital and states are overtly sanctioning informal labour, despite its operations outside state laws.

Within this framework of decreased restrictions on employers, employment has grown in the global South over the past two decades. East Asia and South Asia have lower unemployment levels (at 3–4 per cent) than the global average of 5–6 per cent.[5] Despite a slight increase after the 2008 crisis, unemployment levels are lower now than in 1991. In Latin America and sub-Saharan Africa, unemployment levels are higher than the global average—which is being pushed down by Asia—at 6–9 per cent; however, there has been a steady decline since 2000 in sub-Saharan Africa and since 2003 in Latin America.[6] Additionally, labour productivity throughout the global South has increased in the past two decades, especially in services (ILO 2013).

Poverty figures, however, suggest that expansion in work and improvements in labour productivity in the global South can be attributed to decreased real wages and worsened work conditions. Although the number of people living in extreme poverty (less than USD 1.25/per day) has dropped in recent

---

[5] Youth unemployment in these regions remains high.
[6] Although there was a brief increase in 2008, Latin America had a quick recovery.

decades—which is consistent with expanding employment—the number of people living in "near poverty" (between USD 2 and 4 per day) has increased by 142 million in the past decade, raising the total to 661 million people (ILO 2013). More of the world's workers are thus operating in degraded conditions, with little pay and visibility. Enabling this trend is a fading respect for the twentieth-century social contract, where even the expressed commitment to mitigate labour exploitation is waning. Herein lies the second failure in twentieth-century social contracts—they have proven to be unsustainable.

Therefore, even more important than the growth in relative size of the world's informal workforce in recent decades has been the decline in the relative *power* of the world's workers to protect themselves against labour appropriation. Neoliberalism has altered the politics around informal work. The challenges facing labour today have not squashed labour politics, rather they have altered worker organizations' terms, strategies and members.

In the following sections, I illustrate informal workers' organizing efforts, drawing on my own research in India and the initial findings of a comparative study conducted by a new global network of labour scholars and grassroots organizations studying informal and precarious worker organizing across Brazil, Canada, China, India, Mexico, South Africa, South Korea and the United States.[7] Indian informal workers have been organizing since the 1970s and thus provide an important lens into one set of fairly developed movements. However, we know that social movements are context specific; indeed, India's colonial history bred a powerful, anti-colonial movement among workers and its post-colonial commitment to democracy bred active civic engagement. The cross-country examination thus provides clues to the similarities and differences in informal workers' movements across country specifics.

Informal Workers' Organizations in India

Contrary to popular belief that informal production structures prevent labour organization, recent evidence has shown that informal workers are organizing to defend their humanity.

I have analysed elsewhere how informal workers in India are advancing their rights through alternative workers' struggles across diverse employment

---

[7] The Experiences Organizing Informal Workers (EOIW) is a global network of labour scholars and labour organizations that seek to expand knowledge of new organizing efforts taking place among informal and precarious workers around the world. The author is a founding member of EOIW.

relationships and sectors including construction, domestic work, garments, tobacco and waste collection (Agarwala 2013a, 2016; Agarwala and Saha 2018). Rather than fighting unregulated, flexible production structures and demanding traditional work benefits, such as minimum wages and job security, from employers, Indian informal workers are using their power as voters to also demand state responsibility for social consumption or reproductive needs, such as education, housing and health care.

To institutionalize this strategy, Indian informal workers are fighting to enact and implement an innovative institution called "welfare boards." These are tripartite institutions implemented by the state or central government and are funded by governments, taxes on employers and membership fees from workers. In return for being a member of a board, workers are entitled to a variety of welfare benefits. Currently, welfare boards in India are occupationally based; benefits differ according to trade. Welfare boards have become an increasingly popular protection mechanism among informal workers' organizations in India. Their success (which has been mixed) depends on the political and economic context in which they are implemented. Those operating under competitive populist parties aiming to implement neoliberalism have, ironically, been more successful than those operating under a single, hegemonic party rule, even when that party is left wing (Agarwala 2013a). In recent years, they have come under further attack from some political parties.

Despite the challenges, Indian informal workers are pulling the state into playing an even more central role than it did in formal workers' movements. Interestingly, doing so has not precluded Indian informal workers from also mobilizing at the transnational level. For instance, a leading informal workers' union in India, the Self-Employed Women's Association (SEWA), joined forces with a multilateral organization, the ILO, and the most legitimate producers of knowledge in the North, Harvard University, to define and operationalize the concept of informal work and revise national-level labour force surveys to better capture informal workers (Agarwala 2012).

Moreover, informal workers are forging a new class identity that connects them to the state through their social consumption needs (such as health care, education and housing). This strategy has enabled these workers to address their gendered productive and reproductive needs (Agarwala 2013b, 2018. This recognition comes in the form of a worker identity card that provides official state recognition for their work, even in the absence of employer recognition.

In addition to struggling for welfare boards, informal workers continue to struggle for reformed wage rules. For example, they have fought the state to alter minimum wages from time-based to piece-rate, and self-employed workers are forming their own cooperatives and companies to ensure the security of their livelihood (Agarwala 2016.

To attract the attention of elected state politicians to enact the welfare boards, identity cards and redefined minimum wages, informal workers utilize a rhetoric of "citizenship" rather than labour rights. These workers are organizing at the neighbourhood level, rather than on the shop floor, to mobilize the dispersed, unprotected workforce without disrupting production. Given the unregulated nature of their work, it may seem ironic that these workers are trying to strengthen their relations with the state. Yet this movement is developing across states and industries in India—thereby reflecting the state's interest in informal work. Furthermore, these movements reiterate that the definition of informal workers applies to the circumstances of their work, and not to their politics, which may indeed be "formal" or officially registered.

Informal Workers' Organizations Globally

Recent scholarly evidence has shown that Indian informal workers are not unique in organizing. Retail store workers in South Korea, street vendors in Mexico and restaurant workers in the United States are also launching alternative movements to challenge neoliberal policies (Chun 2009; Cross 1998; Fine 2006; Milkman and Ott 2014). These seemingly disparate case studies call on us to examine the themes and relationships that may be emerging among informal workers' movements across national contexts, to better examine how twenty-first-century social contracts will be shaped "from below."[8]

Informal workers are redefining the category of "workers"

Perhaps the most striking feature of current informal workers' struggles is that across countries, these workers are mobilizing groups previously excluded from formal workers' movements. Particularly, informal workers are organizing women and migrant workers—both of whom have long been deemed the most vulnerable and "unorganizable" workers. They are not being organized to the exclusion of men and/or native workers; indeed, men and native workers are growing in the informal sector. However, the fact that women and migrant workers are being included in, and even leading, informal workers' struggles implies that informal workers are expanding the categories of "work" and "workers," which has important implications for their demands and future social policies.

---

[8] The findings in this section draw from the following: Agarwala 2013a; Chun 2014; Fine and Milkman 2013; Garza 2013; Mosoetsa 2012; Ngai and Xin 2012; Salas and Kerr 2013; Vosko et al 2014.

Informal work has long been known to employ a disproportionate share of female workers. Therefore, by recruiting female members and leaders, informal workers' movements are challenging the use of gendered stereotypes to guarantee a "docile" workforce that is assumed not to need or demand job security or high wages. As a result of their focus on women workers' rights and their disproportionate share of women leaders, informal workers' struggles have organized workers in traditionally "feminized" occupations long unorganized. These include domestic work (United States, South Africa, China, Mexico, South Korea and India), street vending (South Africa and Mexico), homecare work (Canada and South Korea), and manufacturing in apparel and tobacco (Brazil and India). In some countries (China, South Korea, India and South Africa), women workers have developed networks and organizations designed exclusively to address women's issues; these include the Chinese Working Women Network (CWWN), the Korean Women's Trade Union (KWTU), SEWA in India and the South African Self-Employed Women's Association (SASEWA). CWWN and KWTU provide legal counselling services. CWWN, SEWA and SASEWA provide health services, training on occupational health and a women workers' cooperative. Moreover, SEWA provides micro-banking facilities, childcare services and a union for women workers in the informal economy. All four groups have emerged owing to the male domination found in traditional unions.

In addition to mobilizing previously excluded occupations, informal workers' focus on female workers and leaders has altered demands from those of the twentieth-century formal workers. Specifically, informal workers' struggles (across national and industry contexts) place a larger emphasis on reproductive rights. For instance, in India, South Korea and the United States, informal workers' struggles to decommodify the reproductive labour costs that women workers have disproportionately borne without compensation have resulted in health and education benefits, housing, childcare and assets directly in women's hands. (Agarwala 2018; Milkman and Terriquez 2012). Thus, informal workers are highlighting intersections of class and gender through means that formal workers' movements or feminist movements have not used previously.

Furthermore, informal workers have mobilized migrant workers. Increasingly, employers have turned to international and domestic migrants to staff informal jobs. As with women, migrant workers have long been considered unorganizable by labour activists. Informal workers, however, are challenging these notions by revising the meaning of "citizenship rights" to extend past passports. In the United States, Canada and South Africa, informal workers have fought for improved rights for immigrant workers by advocating to legalize undocumented workers, publicize all labour abuses and provide direct support services to immigrant workers, including legal aid, leadership training and popular education. In the

United States and Canada, these organizations usually operate under the worker centre model. Notably, in Canada, the United Food and Commercial Workers (UFCW) and the Agricultural Workers Alliance have created ten centres for migrant farmworkers, one of which has provided a path to permanent residency for temporary foreign workers in their collective agreement. In South Africa, these organizations are informal and unregistered, although they are often official members of international networks such as StreetNet.

In China, informal workers have actively fought for improved rights and recognition for rural–urban migrants from within China. Until 2003, these workers were excluded from China's only legal union, the All-China Federal Trade Union (ACFTU). By 2007, four years after the ACFTU opened its doors to migrants, 70 million migrant workers registered as union members. Additionally, migrant workers developed alternative organizations, such as the Migrant Worker Documentary Center (MWDC), which provides legal aid and counsel for labour disputes and overdue compensation, a cultural development centre, an occupational safety network, as well as monitors codes of conduct, collects data on labour conditions, and conducts workshops on local and international labour laws.

Informal workers are expanding the definition of work

Informal workers across country contexts are organizing occupational categories that have long been excluded from traditional workers' movements. Part of their success can be attributed to their ability to organize the types of workers that staff these occupational categories (that is, women and migrants). Additionally, informal workers are reorganizing occupational categories whose changing structures of production are demanding new forms of organization. At the comparative level, it is striking to note similarities in occupational sectors organizing across countries, despite variations in country contexts. Specifically, we find that organization occurs in domestic work, construction, manufacturing, street vending, transport and waste picking. Findings show that most informal workers' struggles are taking place in urban (or semi-urban), non-agricultural work.

This similarity across sectors in several countries suggests that structures of occupations, regardless of the country context, may play an important role in determining the forms, strategies and potential for informal workers' organizations. Moreover, it seems likely that parallel organization of particular occupations is promoted by regional and global occupation-specific networks, such as the International Domestic Workers Federation, HomeNet and StreetNet, along with some global unions, such as the Building and Wood Workers International, which work with construction workers worldwide.

Another notable trend across occupational categories is that informal workers' demands appear to be correlated with the geography of their workplace. Workers who operate in public spaces—street vendors, transport workers and waste pickers—are primarily constrained by antagonistic relations with local enforcement authorities, rather than traditional employers. Their efforts in these occupations thus focus on attaining state recognition for their work through identity cards, securing a right to work by attaining access to public space, and regulating the industry through licences and taxes to avoid police harassment. In doing so, informal workers are expanding the narrow definition of "exploitation," from employer to employee, ingrained in twentieth-century social contracts, to include additional axes of exploitation, such as from state to worker. For instance, in the case of waste picking, municipal governments profit from the underpaid work of informal trash collectors, while the police simultaneously profit from bribes collected from the very same informal trash collectors (Agarwala 2016).

In some contrast, workers operating in private spaces, such as homes, contractors' worksheds or employers' premises are constrained by the antagonistic relations with employers and are thus demanding economic and social benefits to improve their standard of living. These occupations include domestic workers, construction workers and manufacturing workers. In some cases, these informal workers call for improved wages and working conditions; in others, they call for welfare benefits. Across all occupational categories, informal workers' organizations supplement collective action strategies against the state and employers with direct services to members.

Furthermore, initial findings suggest that informal workers' organizing strategies may depend on their employment relationship—as a contract worker with a traditional (albeit unofficial and unrecognized) relationship with an employer or as a self-employed worker, who sits in a contradictory class position as simultaneously a capitalist owner and a labourer. Although both types of workers share several characteristics, namely that they are not protected or regulated by existing labour laws and live in daily precarity, the structures of their work and their employment relationships differ in ways significant for organizing (see Figure 3.1). This chapter suggests that contract workers (as in construction and garments) tend to fight for economic and social benefits, such as welfare boards and increased wages, to de-commodify their labour against market forces. Self-employed workers (such as street vendors and waste pickers, and rickshaw drivers), in contrast, fight to ensure their right to participate in the market of exchange without harassment from local authorities by demanding licences and taxes and access to work space. Some self-employed workers (such as *bidi*, or hand-rolled cigarette, manufacturers) are mislabelled as such and actually operate as disguised wage-workers; in these cases, they fight to redefine their buyers to whom they sell finished projects "on order,"

Figure 3.1: Informal workers' movements across employment relationships

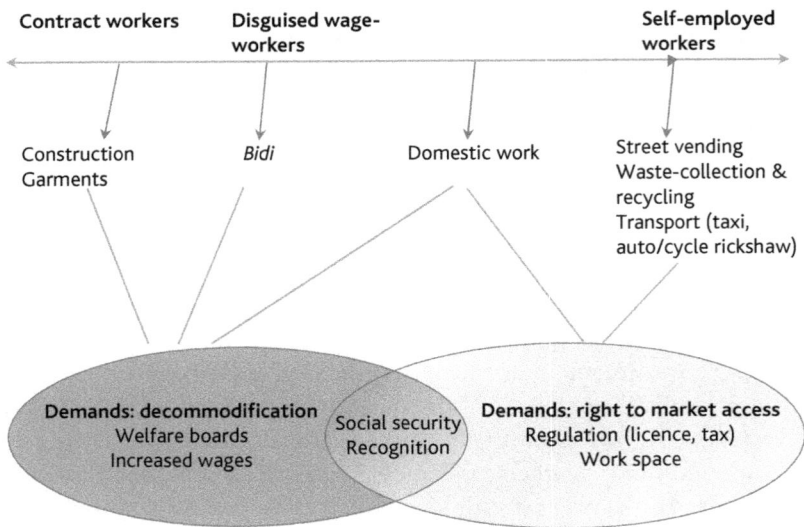

Figure 3.1: Informal workers' movements across employment relationships

as "employers," despite not having an employment contract and then echo contract workers' demands for decommodification. Others (such as domestic workers) operate in employment relationships that fall in the middle of the spectrum, and they tend to make both sets of demands. Across the spectrum of employment relationships, informal workers target their demands to the state, employers and, in some cases (such as with recyclers and transport workers), consumers.

Perhaps most significant, all organized informal workers across occupational categories and employment relations have demanded greater social security and share a "struggle for recognition" of themselves as workers and their occupations as legitimate categories of work. To attain such recognition, informal workers' organizations have educated workers to own and express their own identities as workers and advocated governments to alter their labour force surveys to better capture home-based and other informal work, to include more occupations within the jurisdiction of local labour laws and to issue worker identity cards to informal workers.

Informal workers are organizing through a variety of institutions

A striking feature of informal workers' struggles in the contemporary era is the variety of organization forms that informal workers have utilized to address their needs. These include unions, labour-based non-governmental organizations (NGOs), service NGOs, mutual aid societies, worker centres, community organizations and cooperatives.

Brazil deserves attention for its success in building cooperatives with government support; South Korea offers an interesting model of regional unions. The United States and Canada are notable for their worker centres, which fuse elements of labour NGOs, service NGOs and traditional unions. These organizations collaborate with traditional unions and provide services for informal workers and undocumented immigrants. South Korea's and China's examples of symbolic public dramas through crane protests are unique in an age where the world's workers—informal and formal—have made a more pragmatic turn out of fear of losing employment. Finally, India has been innovative in launching welfare boards.

Important questions remain as to when these varying forms of organizations can form coalitions versus when they compete for scarce resources, and how the organization type affects workers' success and failure. Further research must also examine whether the diversity of organization type is related to country contexts. For example, although Mexico displays similar political economic patterns to Brazil and India, it offers far fewer examples of informal workers' organizations.

Informal workers are formulating bridges with formal labour and other social movements

Another significant characteristic of informal workers' movements has been the innovative ways they establish bridges between labour movements and identity-based social movements (such as those around gender, race and caste). Part of this tendency is due to necessity—in many countries informal workers have no legal right to organize into unions, since they cannot prove their employment relationship. Therefore, they partner with other existing movements that organize around social identities in non-union organizational forms. However, some of this tendency can be attributed to a deliberate mobilization strategy. Informal workers organize marginalized populations who were often excluded from twentieth-century labour movements. Addressing their needs through identity-based movements that articulate gender and race-based identities has often resulted in higher mobilization rates than mobilizing them along class lines, especially in the current anti-labour era.

In several countries (the United States, Canada, South Africa and Mexico), informal workers have joined hands with immigrant and Indigenous rights movements. One interesting example is the US-based domestic workers' Caring Across Generations campaign, which links improving pay and working conditions for homecare workers with immigration reform, proposing the creation of special visas for homecare workers to meet the growing demand for homecare work. This campaign not only bridges efforts between informal workers and immigrant movements, it also includes the Service Employees International Union, the American Federation of State, County and Municipal Employees and the American Federation of Labor and Congress of Industrial Organizations (AFL-CIO). Among street vendors in the United States, VAMOS engages with the immigrant rights movement on behalf of its largely undocumented membership. Several US campaigns in New York, New Jersey and Texas have been initiated to help new immigrant workers in construction by establishing new union locals with worker centre representation in the leadership. Similarly, Mexican street vendors, from Mexico City's Alameda Central, have combined street vending rights with Indigenous rights and preservation of the cultural tradition of selling in public space. In South Africa, faith-based organizations have been assisting immigrants with job referrals and legal advice.

Faith-based organizations are particularly notable as a locus of partnerships in their own right, as are youth movements. US campaigns aiming to increase publicity on sweatshop conditions in the garment industry have appealed, with moderate success, to religious leaders. Similarly, in South Africa, faith-based associations in churches and mosques have achieved the greatest success in attracting support among subcontracted and home-based garment workers. Moreover, South Korea, the United States and China reflect interesting examples of informal workers partnering with student groups. Contrarily, informal workers in India and Brazil do not appear to be using bridges with social movements as a primary strategy. Rather, informal workers appear to be relying more on unions that expand their demands to include civic and community needs of citizenship, rather than partnering with another movement that is addressing civic, but not labour needs. Given this trend, an important area for future research will be to identify when and why informal workers choose to build or avoid a bridge or partnership with another social movement.

Conclusion

This chapter aimed to provide a theoretical framework for understanding the political economy of informal workers. Particularly, it offered a new definition of "informal workers" focusing on the mass of workers operating outside the narrow regulations of labour laws that protect those operating within the SER. Informal workers operate in non-standard employment relationships and are thus unprotected by most twentieth-century social contracts. However, they remain embedded in inter-dependent social relationships with formal workers, employers and states, and are clearly regulated, even punished, by other state laws.

Second, this chapter offered a historical and global framework to examine informal workers under neoliberalism. Informal work is not a product of neoliberalism—it has long existed to subsidize and boost capitalist growth, especially in developing countries. However, it has grown over recent years owing to the political framework guiding neoliberalism. In the process, informal workers have ironically become a driving force of counter-movements designed to reshape the contemporary welfare state. Findings from budding informal workers' movements in Brazil, Canada, China, India, Mexico, South Africa, South Korea and the United States suggest that the world's poorest workers may be mobilizing to catalyse a transformative social process that can potentially reshape twenty-first-century social contracts.

This chapter highlights informal workers' organizations and the laws, regulations and programmes affecting informal workers. Informal workers' movements show remarkable commonalities across national contexts. Rather than fighting to be formally recognized through a standard employment contract and protected by employers at the workplace (as they did at the turn of the twentieth century), informal workers today are fighting to redefine the categories of "workers" and "employers" to include a range of employer–employee relationships and workplaces. By expanding these definitions, these workers are increasing the numbers and diversity of potential beneficiaries of labour rights. Informal workers' movements include women, ethnic and racial minorities, and occupations often excluded from the definition of "workers" protected by twentieth-century social contracts. Redefining "work" to bring these groups into the fold of workers' movements is not part of an organizational strategy to achieve utopian democracy, as many scholars of "social movement unionism" have surmised; instead, it is a "mobilizational necessity" owing to the failures of twentieth-century social contracts.

References

Agarwala, Rina. 2018. "From Theory to Praxis and Back to Theory: Informal Workers' Struggles against Capitalism and Patriarchy in India." *Political Power and Social Theory*, 35: 29–57.

Agarwala, Rina. 2016. "Redefining Exploitation: Self-Employed Workers' Movements in India's Garments and Trash Collection Industries." *International Labor and Working Class History*, 89(Spring):107–130.

Agarwala, Rina. 2013a. *Informal Labor, Formal Politics and Dignified Discontent in India*. New York: Cambridge University Press.

Agarwala, Rina. 2013b. "A Second Marriage? An Intersection of Marxism and Feminism among India's Informal Workers." In *Handbook on Gender in South Asia*, edited by Leela Fernandes, 220–233. London: Routledge.

Agarwala, Rina. 2012. "The State and Labor in Transnational Activism: The Case of India." *Journal of Industrial Relations*, 54(4): 443–458.

Agarwala, Rina. 2009. "An Economic Sociology of Informal Work: The Case of India." *Research in the Sociology of Work*, 18:315–342.

Agarwala, Rina. 2006. "From Work to Welfare: A New Class Movement in India." *Critical Asian Studies*, 38(4):419–445.

Agarwala, Rina and Shiny Saha. 2018. "The Employment Relationship and Movement Strategies among Domestic Workers in India." *Critical Sociology*, 44(7/8):1207–1223.

Arrighi, Giovanni. 1978. "Towards a Theory of Capitalist Crisis." *New Left Review*, I(111):3–24.

Bakan, A. B. and D. Stasiulis. 1997. *Not One of the Family: Foreign Domestic Workers in Canada*. Toronto: University of Toronto Press.

Berger, Suzanne and Michael Piore. 1989. *Dualism and Discontinuity in Industrial Societies*. Cambridge: Cambridge University Press.

Boris, E. and J. Klein. 2012. *Caring for America: Home Health Workers in the Shadow of the Welfare State*. New York: Oxford University Press.

Breman, Jan and Marcel van der Linden. 2014. "Informalizing the Economy: The Return of the Social Question at a Global Level." *Development and Change*, 45:920–940.

Bromley, Ray and Chris Gerry. 1979. "Who are the Casual Poor?" In *Casual Work and Poverty in Third World Cities*, edited by Ray Bromley and Chris Gerry, 2–26. New York: Wiley.

Charrad, Mounira. 2001. *States and Women's Rights: The Making of Postcolonial Tunisia, Algeria, and Morocco*. Berkeley: University of California Press.

Chatterjee, Partha. 2006. *The Politics of the Governed: Reflections on Popular Politics in Most of the World*. New York: Columbia University Press.

Chun, Jennifer Jihye. 2014. *The Struggles of Irregularly-Employed Workers in South Korea, 1999–2012*. Unpublished Experiences Organizing Informal Workers Working Paper.

Chun, Jennifer Jihye. 2009. *Organizing at the Margins: The Symbolic Politics of Labor in South Korea and the United States*. Ithaca: Cornell University Press.

Cranford, Cynthia J., Leah F. Vosko and Nancy Zukewich. 2003. "Precarious Employment in the Canadian Labour Market: A Statistical Portrait." *Just Labour*, 3. https://doi.org/10.25071/1705-1436.164.

Cross, John. 1998. *Informal Politics: Street Vendors and the State in Mexico City*. Stanford: Stanford University Press.

Davis, Mike. 2006. *Planet of Slums*. New York: Verso.

Economist, The. 2015. "Advancing, Not Retreating: Forecasts of the Decline of Capitalism Are Premature." *The Economist*, 52.

Esping-Anderson, Gøsta. 1990. *The Three Worlds of Welfare Capitalism*. Princeton: Princeton University Press.

Fine, Janice. 2006. *Worker Centers: Organizing Communities at the Edge of the Dream*. Ithaca: Cornell University Press.

Fine, Janice and Ruth Milkman. 2013. *US Country Inventory of Informal Worker Organizing*. Unpublished Experiences Organizing Informal Workers Working Paper.

Friedman, Eli. 2014. "Alienated Politics: Labour Insurgency and the Paternalistic State in China." *Development and Change*, 45(5):1001–1018.

Garza, Enrique de la. 2013. *Mexico Informal Worker Organizing Inventory*. Unpublished Experiences Organizing Informal Workers Working Paper.

Gottfried, Heidi. 2015. *A Reproductive Bargain: Deciphering the Enigma of Japanese Capitalism*. Leiden: Brill.

Hart, Gillian. 2002. *Disabling Globalization: Places of Power in Post-Apartheid South Africa*. Berkeley: University of California Press.

Harvey, David. 2005. *A Brief History of Neoliberalism*. Oxford: Oxford University Press.

Hussmanns, Ralf. 2002. "A Labour Force Survey Module on Informal Employment: A Tool for Enhancing the International Comparability of Data." Paper presented at 6th Meeting of the Expert Group on Informal Sector Statistics (Delhi Group), Rio de Janeiro, 17 September.

Hyman, Richard. 1992. "Trade Unions and the Disaggregation for the Working Class." In *The Future of Labour Movements*, edited by M. Regini, 150–156. Newbury Park: Sage.

ILO (International Labour Organization). 2013. *Global Employment Trends 2013: Recovering from a Second Jobs Dip*. Geneva: ILO.

ILO (International Labour Organization). 1993. "Report of the 15th International Conference of Labour Statisticians." Presented at 15th International Conference of Labour Statisticians, Geneva, 19 January.

ILO-WIEGO (International Labour Organization–Women in Informal Employment: Globalizing and Organizing). 2013. *Women and Men in the Informal Economy: A Statistical Picture*. Geneva: ILO.

Lenin, V. I. 1939. *Imperialism, the Highest Stage of Capitalism*. New York: International Publishers.

Lewis, W. A. 1954. "Economic Development with Unlimited Supplies of Labour." Manchester: Manchester School, 22.

Luxemburg, Rosa. 1951. *The Accumulation of Capital*. London: Routledge and Kegan Paul.

Marx, Karl. 1976. *Capital*, vol. 1. London: Pelican Books.

Meyer, Rachel and Janice Fine. 2017. "Grassroots Citizenship at Multiple Scales: Rethinking Immigrant Civic Participation." *International Journal of Politics, Culture, and Society*, 30(4):323–348.

Milkman, Ruth and Ed Ott (eds). 2014. *New Labor in New York: Precarious Workers and the Future of the Labor Movement*. Ithaca: Cornell University Press.

Milkman, Ruth and Veronica Terriquez. 2012. "'We Are the Ones Who Are Out in Front': Women's Leadership in the Immigrant Rights Movement." *Feminist Studies*, 38(3):723–752.

Moore, Barrington. 1966. *Social Origins of Dictatorship and Democracy: Lord and Peasant in the Making of the Modern World*. Boston: Beacon.

Moser, Caroline. 1978. "Informal Sector or Petty Commodity Production: Dualism or Dependence in Urban Development?" *World Development*, 6(9/10):1041–1064.

Mosoetsa, Sarah. 2012. *The State of Informal Workers' Organisations in South Africa.* Unpublished Experiences Organizing Informal Workers Working Paper.

Ngai, Pun and Tong Xin. 2012. *China's Informal Labor and Labor Organizing.* Unpublished Experiences Organizing Informal Workers Working Paper.

Omvedt, Gail. 1993. *Reinventing Revolution: New Social Movements and the Socialist Tradition in India.* Armonk: M. E. Sharpe.

Peattie, Lisa R. 1987. "An Idea in Good Currency and How It Grew: The Informal Sector." *World Development,* 15(7):851–858.

Polanyi, Karl. 2001. *The Great Transformation.* Boston: Beacon Press.

Portes, Alejandro, Manuel Castells and Lauren A. Benton. 1989. *The Informal Economy: Studies in Advanced and Less Developed Countries.* Baltimore: Johns Hopkins University Press.

Portes, Alejandro and John Walton. 1981. *Labor, Class and the International System.* New York: Academic Press.

Rakowski, Cathy A. 1994. *Contrapunto: The Informal Sector Debate in Latin America.* Albany: State University of New York Press.

Riley, Dylan J. and Manali Desai. 2007. "The Passive Revolutionary Route to the Modern World: Italy and India in Comparative Perspective." *Comparative Studies in Society and History,* 49(4):815–847.

Salas, Carlos and Lucas Kerr. 2013. *Brazil: Country Literature Review.* Unpublished Experiences Organizing Informal Workers Working Paper.

Satpathy, Anoop. 2004. "Size, Composition and Characteristics of Informal Sector in India." *National Labor Institute Research Studies Series.* New Delhi: V.V. Giri National Labour Institute.

Standing, Guy. 2011. *The Precariat: The New Dangerous Classes.* Huntington: Bloomsbury.

Thompson, E. P. 1966. *The Making of the English Working Class.* New York: Vintage Books.

Touraine, Alain, François Dubet, Michel Wieviorka and Jan Strzelecki. 1983. *Solidarity: The Analysis of a Social Movement: Poland 1980–1981.* Cambridge: Cambridge University Press.

Vosko, Leah, Mark Thomas, Angela Hick and Jennifer Jihye Chun. 2014. *Organizing Precariously-Employed Workers in Canada.* Unpublished Experiences Organizing Informal Workers Working Paper.

Wills, Jane. 2009. "Subcontracted Employment and Its Challenge to Labor." *Labor Studies Journal,* 34(4):441–460.

4

Universal Welfare Design in a New Age: Equality versus Equity in the Debate about Universal Basic Income Policies and Health in Society

Louise Haagh

Introduction

Attention to basic human freedoms as an imperative in development policy design was first brought into social policy debates in the 1990s through the human development approach linked with Sen (1987, 1998, 2002) and Nussbaum (2006). In the same period, egalitarian political theory was also more directly applied to debates about freedom-orientated welfare state reform (van Parijs 1995). Revival in the 2010s of the proposal for a universal basic income (UBI)—a universal cash grant to individuals without conditions—in the context of a deepening universal welfare crisis (Haagh 2019a, 2019b) drew attention to the question of what universality of rights means for institution design.

The new freedom-orientated welfare perspectives, however, have been relatively detached from macro-configurational concerns and trends in development that have reshaped institutions and the role of the state. I argue with Sen (1998) in this context that political sensitivity to human development can be explanatory of development outcomes. I argue however that we need a better institutional grasp of the pathways of this sensitivity at a macro-configurational level.

Freedom-Orientated Perspectives and the Development Debate

Conceptual challenges in welfare debate

Following on the heels of post-war humanistic approaches to welfare in the school of historical sociology of Marshall (1949) and Titmuss (2019 [1958]), Esping-Andersen's (1990) path-breaking work on welfare regimes introduced a systematic comparative approach to regimes or macro-configurations with a lasting legacy (Korpi and Palme 1998; Rothstein 1998). In the context of erosion of post-war welfare states and institutions after the 1980s, however, confidence in the ability of regime comparison approaches to explain and evaluate welfare outcomes began to fade. Concerns were raised that a strict regime comparison approach lays too much stress on historical path dependence (Kangas 2010). For instance, some argued that it is simply the generosity of earnings-related protection within the unemployment insurance systems in Sweden that explains how the unemployed do better (Lundberg et al 2015:52–58).

However, there are reasons to think that abandoning macro-configurational analysis is too hasty. In reality, global change in welfare design is filtered by capitalist system varieties (Haagh 2012, 2015, 2019a; Thelen 2014). In poor and middle-income countries, incomplete social service coverage to informal sectors (Lloyd-Sherlock 2019; Marx et al 2013) was used as a rationale to shift toward a less inclusive and more conditional model of "basic universalism". Basic universalism entailed the spread of targeted cash grants (Haagh 2007a; Lavinas 2013:7), alongside discretionary and risk-focused targeting, and short-term designs (Cecchini and Martínez 2012; Moore 2008).

In this context, it is relevant to reassess the post-war welfare state construct on a more critical basis, against a more general standard. I will hypothesize that rights are more stable and less punitively structured when linked with (i) more broad-based fiscal systems, and (ii) income, services and production. In other words, welfare state constructs should not be understood in terms of welfare services alone, but rather in terms of systems of rights connecting and differentiating persons' control in relation to core human development processes.

We can refer to the latter as *political security of welfare*, adapting Bates' (2006) concept of political security with which he refers to high levels of shared governance of risk through state-regulated institutions. The key point here is that security about *shared rules* in core spheres of human activity has implications not only for governance of developmental processes, but for individuals' motivation and well-being. The way the form of rights in and outside employment is systemically shaped in and by development paradigms justifies a new concept of human development state that acknowledges the key role of shared *human development risk* formations. Accordingly, I propose to rework emerging normative conceptions of welfare against a more objective standard as a way to inform our empirical analysis of the sustainability and effect of different designs. Rather than offer a comprehensive review, I discuss two approaches that have had a strong influence in reshaping thinking about standards of welfare, while also bringing to light underlying problems in welfare conceptualization linked with a tendency to exclusively focus on distributive polemics.

New normative approaches in welfare analysis

A new normativism is guided by a desire to evaluate or shape public policy according to standards that are independent of particular national histories. Two relevant fields of enquiry are the human development approach (HDA) and basic income advocacy (BIA). I argue their differences in terms of policy design can and ought to give way to a more overarching focus on the combination of egalitarian policies needed to promote overall equality in key development dimensions of well-being.

Both approaches are universalist and egalitarian in orientation. The object of valuation in both approaches is individual freedom: in BIA freedom is classically interpreted as a form of independence in terms of choice to do (van Parijs 1995:23), or a status to enjoy freedom through material independence (Widerquist 2013). HDA approaches emphasize well-being and agency (Sen 1998:74–76), and developmental integrity (Haagh 2019a), linked with basic human function.

While the HDA and its policy applications are established as core to the actions of global development agencies, BIA occupies a niche within the social sciences. Specifically, the UBI proposition has received new global traction in connection with a global rise in employment insecurity and income poverty (Haagh 2007a, 2011b; Standing 1999, 2008, 2009), and in rich countries revival of the poverty traps and stigma of post-war income assistance (De Wispelaere and Haagh 2019; Haagh 2019b). Since around 2017, the idea of a UBI has been received in increasingly positive terms by the global development institutions.

Here, however, it is important to understand how once analytical concepts and traditions become applied to policy, a dilution of the agenda, substance and applications often occurs. Both BIA and the HDA have been diluted in terms of a shift in focus from freedom to poverty. With respect to the HDA, the expansion of cash grants in middle-income countries in the end entailed a focus on income rather than agency, which contradicts Sen's concern to stress the merely instrumental role of income in relation to freedom (Sen 1985:110–111; 1998:24–25, 72–76).

The dilution and perversion of BIA and the HDA is, arguably, in part the inevitable consequence of bringing abstract ideas to bear on policies. However, it may also be argued that dilution reflects a tendency to underspecify the institutional dimensions and applications of each approach. The HDA as an analytical approach starts with tangible measures of human function, agency and well-being, and remains (deliberately) light on the *means* (Alkire 2002). On the other hand, BIA to prioritize difference in lifestyle choices is light on *common features* of human development. The upshot is a mono–institutional focus on basic income (BI) as an alternative to more strategic policy menus. In the study by Vanderborght and van Parijs (2017:99), which restates van

Parijs' (1995) classic work, this is grounded in Anglo-liberal egalitarian anti-perfectionism. In their later work, Vanderborght and van Parijs also prefer to justify BI as a scheme of distributive as distinct from cooperative justice (Vanderborght and van Parijs 2017:103). BI as a scheme of income distribution entails "not to equalise outcomes or achievements ... rather ... to make less unequal and distributive more fairly, real freedom, possibilities and opportunities" (Vanderborght and van Parijs 2017:107).

While the HDA in principle focuses on a range of policies to secure basic human functions and agency, BIA is concerned with the design of income security. This means in macro-configurational terms that prima facie BIA is at risk of assuming too much in the way of expected outcomes, in particular if or when not specifying wider governance conditions. HDA is at risk of assuming and explaining too little.

We can further gauge the dilution of both approaches in terms of their polemics about distributive principles by focusing on their approaches to evaluating freedom and health. Health equity concerns are commonly linked with an emphasis on social services. This is in line with the HDA's concern with targeting resources and provision to needs—as in the case of the debate around proportional universalism (Marmot et al 2010). A case for UBI appears to challenge the health equity agenda on at least three grounds: by making a case for a strict division of basic resources rather than targeting need; by thus individualizing the problem of social development; and by prioritizing money as a route to freedom while abandoning the novelty of the capabilities framework, which is to use resources to promote better outcomes in terms of basic common human functions and forms of agency rather than market choice.

Next, I examine how a humanist justice and governance framework addresses shortcomings of each approach, by spelling out how focus on developmental dimensions of freedom overcomes a too presentialist concern with freedom and relatedly a too distributively orientated policy design. Presentialist contracts represent the effort to simplify and magnify exchange, by reducing considerations in contract to the present. At stake is what Oliver Williamson identified as "presentiation" in classical (market) contract law intended to simplify exchange (Williamson, 1985: 69). Presentiation entailed eschewing the bigger and long-term picture surrounding the survival of contracts and social relations. In contrast with presentialist contracts, relational contracts encompass "the entire relation" as it evolves (Williamson, 1985: 70–72). I contend that the conception and experience of contracts as examined in Williamson, interact with conceptions of freedom which in turn has implications for the conception of governance. In regards to freedom conceptions, presentialist concerns reduce the focus to making choices in the present. In contrast, developmental conceptions of freedom acknowledge how relational and social factors shape choice sets and the process of making choices and carrying them out. In addition, developmental conceptions of freedom acknowledge relational aspects of human function and yearning (to learn to relate, to plan, Haagh 2019a, 2011b, 2007b). The conception of freedom "feeds back" into the conception of contract and how and what institutions should be purposely devised. Humanist governance embodies the developmental concept of freedom.

Humanist Governance

The humanist governance concept draws on but also modifies sociological theses in egalitarian thought about features and determinants of well-being. For example, a humanist governance concept has antecedents in Rawls' (1971:369, 375–378) Aristotelian principle of developmental motivation, which suggests plan-rational features of human cognition lead individuals to seek and benefit from stability in activities and relations (Haagh 2007b, 2019a). The concept also speaks to and builds on biological and behavioural research on well-being determinants that look at patterned interactions between mental and physical health (Fredrickson et al 2013), and studies that find more stable sources of economic security tend to upscale planning behaviours and longer-term employment attachments (Haagh 2011b; Tatsiramos 2014), whereas insecurity in work has the opposite effect (Sharif 2003).

The humanist governance concept extends to examine a range of policies relevant to developmentally composite psychological states such as motivation. As such it can also be applied to examination of combined and indirect effects of policies. For example, it can answer such questions as how policies designed to improve education or health may fail to do so if other policies fail to support learning processes or psychological health states.

Relatedly, the concept of humanist governance can be useful for the HDA, since it is concerned with *patterned* human functioning, and can be applied to evaluate policies and construct designs of policies to improve functioning and agency. Although it can be hard to distinguish between basic and patterned functions, the example of eating, which Sen has used to distinguish functions and capabilities, is insightful. Being able or not able to be fed involves a basic human function—eating. Fasting, on the other hand, involves a choice not to eat, and thus involves a capability, a choice to deny oneself the exercise of a basic human function. A patterned function refers instead to the ability to secure food and eat on a permanent social basis. A patterned capability is then an existential condition and well-being state linked with having confidence in institutions, socially and politically, for example, enjoying political security of welfare. Humanist governance in this context recognizes the connection between physical and mental health as governed by confidence in shared institutions. From the standpoint of humanist governance, stability and unconditionality of security are of normative importance in hypothesis testing and when explaining and evaluating policy design and systems of governance.

As such, the humanist governance concept pinpoints underlying human ecology constraints on welfare policies' effectiveness. Human ecology constraints refer to features of human life that bound agency and cognition within a set of developmental needs and social realities to which the formation of both formal and informal institutions and public policies must adapt more or less effectively in all social formations (Haagh 2019a, 2021). The core human ecology constraints are the need for security of care, time-bound features of learning and regularities linked with the reproductive cycle (Haagh 2019a). These needs have been documented separately in studies of mental well-being (Haagh 2001, 2007b, 2019a:69–79). Human economy refers to the way these features of the human lifecycle and social relations set constraints within human function and social relations, ultimately begging and creating forms of regulation, formal or informal, the form of which—I contend—become defining features of sets of institutions within national polities and economies. The effectiveness of policies can be determined by how well they respond to needs and capacities arising in human economy.

One way to understand the meaning of well-being in terms of functions of human ecology and demands of institutions involves conceiving dimensions of control of time as indicators of states of doing and being—revealing how mental well-being relates to confidence in our condition. Dynamic control of time refers to stability in core activities. Static control of time entails combining and maintaining core activities and relations. Cooperative control of time comprises equal standing in core relations. Finally, enjoying constant control of time requires access to underlying existential security (such as in income or place) (Haagh 2007b, 2011b, 2019a:62).

These forms of control of time can be further interpreted to have specific institutional ramifications in modern economies. In theory, dynamic control requires stability in occupation, including through long-term employment. Static control demands feasible combinations of time for leisure, occupation and care—relating to workloads and abating competitive pressures in schools and workplaces. Cooperative control demands enjoying a continuing fellowship structure through regulated hours of work and time for leisure and free childcare. Constant control requires an unconditional form of access to underlying security, such as through access at least to basic unconditional and permanent income, services and housing.

A core hypothesis is that the arrangements listed are mutually constitutive. This in turn implies that political security of welfare is a systemic condition both of *effective development* and *sustainability* of the listed institutions, and of the constitution of states of well-being. Examples of use in micro-studies include surveys of how combined sources of stable employment and external income security change motivation in work toward a more intrinsic form (Haagh 2011b). Counterfactually, use in macro-studies of time-use and control in relation to underlying institutional conditions, indicates control and well-being in workplaces and the home are overall greater where labour market institutions are governed by a range of shared regulatory norms and provisions (Haagh 2011a, 2015, 2019a).

Finally, a humanist governance concept, and its framework, can be applied to understand the role and structure of the state, in terms of how far governance is embedded in or disembedded from human economy. Before I examine applications of this human economy focus, I consider how the humanist governance concept helps take normative welfare debates beyond the consideration of distributive foci in favour of consideration of foundational questions concerning the design of institutions of welfare and the economy.

Humanist Governance and Distributive Debates: Equity, Equality, or Both?

The humanist governance concept intervenes in polemical debates about distributive justice by highlighting the deeper institutional conditions at stake. Sen made his case for health equity precisely against strict egalitarian reasoning on grounds it is ultimately unkind (2002). According to the logic Sen claims of the "fair innings" approach of Alan Williams (1998:330, cited in Sen 2002:664), we may end up arguing for limiting health care for women on the grounds women normally live longer lives (Sen 2002:664). An argument for strict rationing of a similar kind occurs frequently in the BI defence too. The left libertarian argument for BI has involved reference to the justifiability of limiting health spending for costly operations later in life (van Parijs 1995). Instead, a BI can be defended on the grounds of constant control of time, but this challenges the strictly egalitarian account and justification as applied *over time* (Haagh 2019a). Then, this suggests that we should not uphold the principle of strict equality as a justification for BI, or see the (strictly equal) format of the BI as sufficient for freedom or welfare.

Comparing with other theories that take a critical approach to distributive reasoning, for example, recognition theory, further brings out the distinctiveness of the humanist governance perspective. Two schools of recognition theory (as summarized in Jugov and Ypi 2019) are distinct in terms of the form of recognition that is privilege. Fraser's (2003) prioritises "participatory parity." Honneth (2003:179–184) emphasizes opportunity for the development of personality through social recognition of need (family), polity (legal equality) and merit through culture or work (achievement). Fraser's focus implies restoring justice through removing both cultural and economic exclusions of groups. Honneth's main point is that each level of recognition he identifies has "internal normative principles" that create "different forms of mutual recognition" (2003:143). Needs recognition is situated in the family.

Two relevant differences between recognition theory and the humanist governance framework concern the framing of well-being, and the character of different systems of liberal modernity. First, humanist governance is a way to gauge general, structural conditions for justice. Such conditions are ex ante to, as well as go beyond, the concern with recognition through differentiating rights and comparing the status of groups in particular historical settings.

Second, the humanist governance frame does not assume that relations of love or neediness are morally to be specified in the home or family relation distinctly or separately (as in Honneth 2003:181), nor that this is indeed a general pattern *of* liberal modernity. For instance, some modern liberal societies (such as Nordic societies) recognize obligations to neediness at more levels of governance, as a consequence of how public norms and institutions developed. These points become important when considering the contemporary challenge of reconstruction of shared security structures.

Specifically, with the transition to a global competition framework we saw a breakdown of the coordination among Honneth's recognition spheres from the perspective of governance that has disempowered agents and society as a whole at all levels. Hence, I maintain that congruence rests on a broader recognition of human vulnerability at all levels, which is precisely what a humanist governance perspective acknowledges, and the modern global competition economy threatens.

As revealed in the earlier discussion, at stake in humanist governance is a question of what informs the value and what governs the viability of solidarity in terms of humanist norms and practices in society.

We can now apply this to the question of institutional design, as I argue a humanist—developmental—perspective combines different egalitarian distributive principles.

For instance, a principal concern proponents of health equity might have with BI is that it will prevent differential distributions required to support people with different levels of physical need attaining similar valuable outcomes or opportunities. Suppose individual members with different heights within a family are standing on equal-sized boxes to try to view a football match that is occurring behind a fence. The equal size of the boxes indicates the unequal opportunity outcomes of institutions and policies based on the principle of strict egalitarian justice: in this picture, only the tallest person (the father) can watch the football match (Figure 4.1).

To counter this, health equity advocates argue we ought to defend a form of distribution that can guarantee equal opportunity to view a football match for all the family members with different-sized boxes. We can call this form of distribution "proportional universalism": those who need more resources

Figure 4.1: Basic income, equality and health equity—the 'problem'

Critics of UBI from a capabilities and health equity perspective; contrast bare or strict equality with strict equity

Bare equity can create status insecurity through re-evaluation of entitlement, making both the better and less resourced in society status insecure

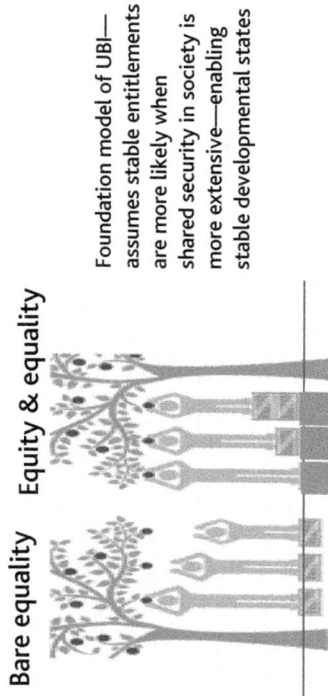

Foundation model of UBI—assumes stable entitlements are more likely when shared security in society is more extensive—enabling stable developmental states

Bare equality   Strict equity

Bare equality   Equity & equality

——— Line under which resources are always shared equally

Universal Basic Income—represents unconditionality of entitlement (individually based, independent of civil or household status, age, needs or means-testing and work-requirement

Source: Haagh (2019c)

get them on the assumption that all persons will need universal access to a smaller portion of resources. If we care about real inequalities, then we must side with the capabilities perspective at least in the distributional sense.

However, I argue it is wrong to only compare the HDA and BIA from a distributional perspective, because ultimately both perspectives appeal to freedom. What needs to be clarified is why we need to think about freedom in terms of stable (developmental) states.

As already noted, my claim is that agency and well-being states are connected through human experience and anticipation of humanist justice in time. It is, then, only when we realize, with Sen, that resources are not our real concern, but beyond Sen that understanding institutions is essential to get at what we want, namely a form of sustained empowerment to develop and exercise relevant (patterned) capabilities, that progress can be made.

When conceiving of BI as a foundation for stable entitlements, which is known as the foundation model (Haagh 2019a; Haagh and Rohregger 2019), a BI could be argued to help strengthen two dimensions of political security emphasized in the welfare state literature—horizontal and vertical. In terms of the horizontal structure or foundation, BI extends the political logic of institutions such as the basic citizen pension and universal child grants (Downes and Lansley 2018; Haagh 2007b, 2011b, 2012, 2017; Jordan 2008). In addition, it strengthens at least the foundations for vertical integration—defined as cross-class insurance arrangements—that are recognized to improve funding for universal welfare by avoiding defection by higher earners (Haagh 2012; Hills 2014; Kangas and Blomgren 2014; Korpi and Palme 1998; Rothstein 1998). On some accounts, the problem of the welfare state in middle-income countries is that it never managed to achieve both dimensions of social and financial integration. In both middle- and high-income countries, membership of unemployment insurance has fallen, alongside efforts to curb universal entitlements (Atkinson 2015).

Finally, it can be argued that failure to implement a BI (as *institution*) enabled austerity by making cuts to income assistance an available moral and financial option. It also enabled a qualitative shift in attitude toward the poor and vulnerability in general, which, when evidenced in the changed form of state policy, enables us to speak about a form of embedding of discrimination against vulnerable states.

Accordingly, next, to appraise institutional change processes linked with corrosion of political security of welfare, a comparative analysis is presented of ways dynamic features of contemporary globalization intercede within the fiscal nexus behind human development within different political economy systems.

Figure 4.2: Political security of well-being, the state and human economy

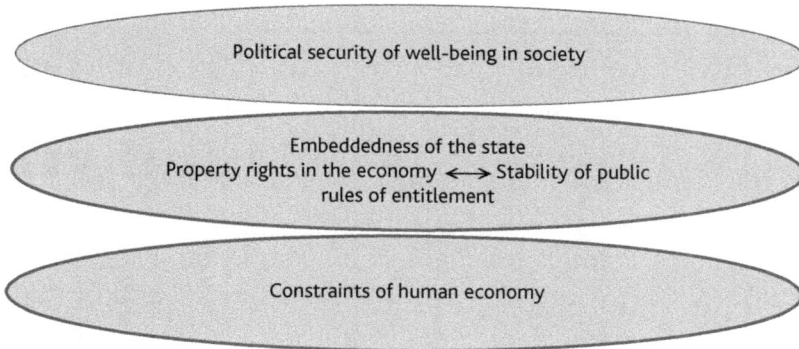

Universalism Revisited—Cooperative Public Finance and the Human Development State

Several welfare scholars have linked sustainable welfare programmes to a scale effect, whereby commitments to welfare are tied to the inclusion in public insurance schemes such as pensions, or core services like health provision of different social classes or interest groups in society (Haagh 2002, 2012; Hills 2014; Kangas and Blomgren 2014; Korpi and Palme 1998; Rothstein 1998; Steinmo 2018). I argue that to explain higher social equality and its effects on well-being, more attention needs to be paid to how risk socialization across society interacts with the form of entitlement to welfare, and with inclusion and coverage (political security of well-being—Figure 4.2).

Weak risk socialization has contrary adverse effects by fragmenting institutions and generating more punitive governance of access to welfare. *Effectiveness* is compromised as these processes generate exclusion of both the middle class and the most vulnerable, while *sustainability* is compromised as the political security of welfare which depends on shared legitimacy is eroded.

I surmise Korpi and Palme's (1998) distinction between comprehensive versus targeted welfare state institutions and structures remains valid. However, I ground such differences in the level of socialization of risk as a whole in public finance and a shape of rules that prioritize access through demand and need over targeting and control.

As a representation of the relationship between more redistributive and more egalitarian welfare state constructs, Figures 4.3 and 4.4 feature composite indices of tax structures and human development spending in Organisation for Economic Co-operation and Development (OECD) states where the relevant statistics are reliably comparable. They give a descriptive indicator of the cooperative structure of tax (based on levels in gross domestic product [GDP] and flatness of the structure) and a measure

Figure 4.3: Dimensions of human development states: early neoliberal globalization

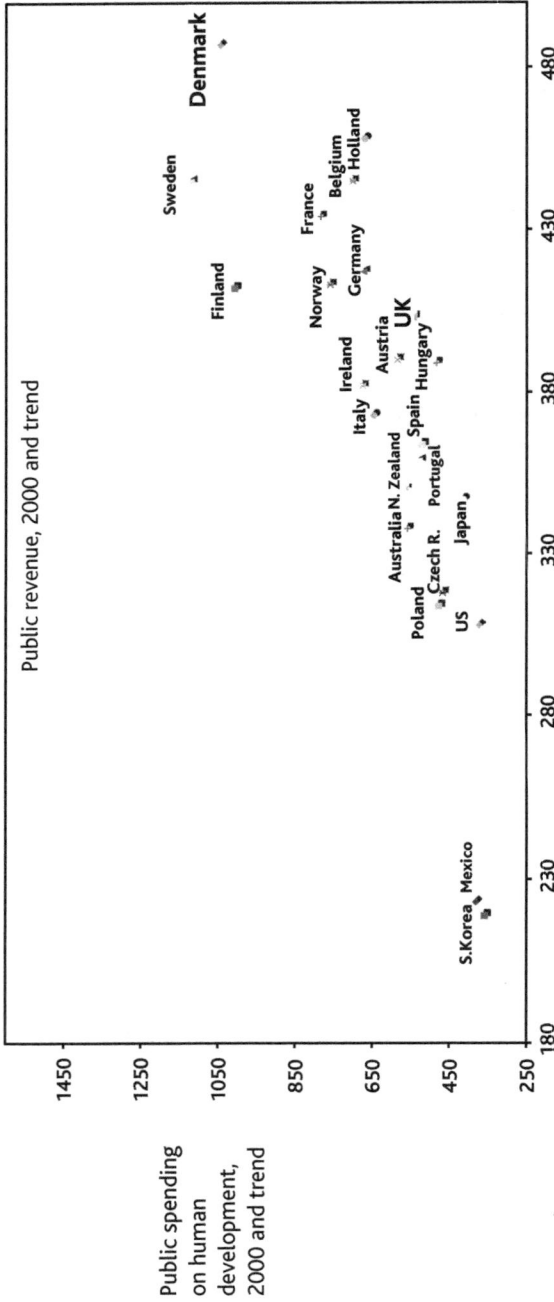

Public spending on human development, 2000 and trend

Public revenue, 2000 and trend

Note: Public revenue: Index of 1. Total tax revenue in GDP 2000 and trend 1975–2000, 2. Top marginal tax rate and multiple at which sets in, 2000 and trend. 3. Net statutory tax rates on dividend income (shareholder level), 2000. 4. Overall personal income tax and corporate income tax rates on dividend income, 2000. 5. Statutory corporate income tax rate, 2000. 6. Corporate tax revenue as % of GDP, 2000 and trend 1982–2000.

Public spending on human development: Index of 1. Public expenditure in GDP, 2000 and trend, 2000–2015. 2. Public social expenditure in GDP, 1990 and trend, 1990–2014. 3. Public expenditure on education in GDP, 1995 and trend, 1995/6–2011. 4. Public expenditure on education in public expenditure, 1995 and trend 1998–2005. 5. Public spending on training, job creation and supported employment 1995 and trend 1995–2006. 6. Public spending on child-care in GDP, 1998 and trend 1998–2005.

Sources and calculations: Tables 4A.1 and 4A.2 in Appendix.

Figure 4.4: Dimensions of human development states: late neoliberal globalization

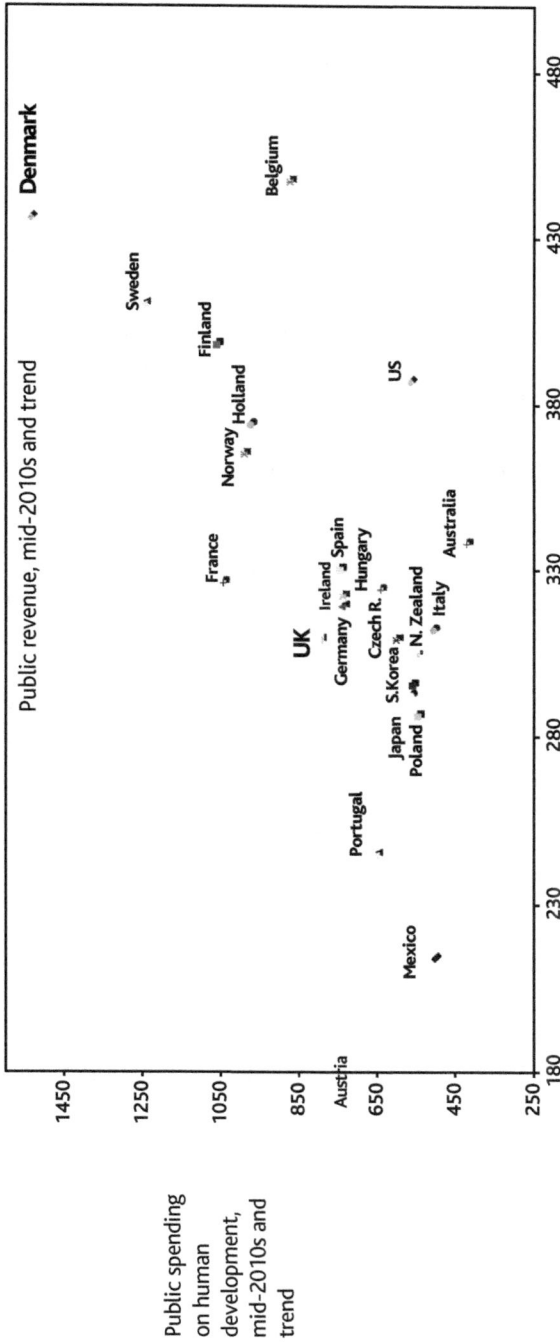

Public spending on human development, mid-2010s and trend

Public revenue, mid-2010s and trend

Denmark

Belgium

Sweden

Finland

Norway Holland

US

France

Ireland
Germany Spain
Hungary
Czech R.
Australia

UK

Japan S.Korea
Poland N. Zealand Italy

Portugal

Austria

Mexico

1450
1250
1050
850
650
450
250

180   230   280   330   380   430   480

Note: Public revenue: Index of 1. Total tax revenue in GDP 2015 and trend 2000–2015, 2. Top marginal tax rate and multiple at which sets in, 2016. 3. Net statutory tax rates on dividend income (shareholder level), 2009. 4. Overall personal income tax and corporate income tax rates on dividend income, 2009. 5. Statutory corporate income tax rate, 2016. 6. Corporate tax revenue as % of GDP, 2016 and trend 2000–2015.

Public spending on human development: Index of 1. Public expenditure in GDP, 2015 and trend 2000–2015. 2. Public social expenditure in GDP, 2014 and trend, 1990–2014. 3. Public expenditure on education in GDP, 2011 and trend, 1995–2011. 4. Public expenditure on education in public expenditure, 2011 and trend, 1995–2011. 5. Public spending on training, job creation and supported employment 2013 and trend, 2006–2013 and trend, 2006–2013. 6. Public spending on child-care in GDP, 2011 and trend, 2005–2011.

Sources and calculations: Tables 4A.1 and 4A.2 in Appendix.

of human development spending in GDP (level and allocation to strategic expenditure). They suggest a relationship between the cooperative structure of tax and strategic human development spending.

Cooperative public finance as an overarching concept offers a measure of inclusiveness of tax contributions and structure of spending, comprising Tables 4A.1 and 4A.2 (Appendix), which cover revenue and expenditure, respectively. The public revenue score (Table 4A.1) is an attempt to model the level of integration within the tax system of different income sources across groups, as an indication of the level of democratization of the economy. So, for example, it is important to have a measure both of the level of taxation in GDP and of how it is derived. In this regard, it is relevant to include both the level of top marginal tax rates and the multiple of income at which they set in. If the latter is very high, it means that only upper income groups pay those rates. This may be seen as fair from a distributive point of view, but is also often an indication of other factors, like the level of formalization of the wage economy and ability to pay of lower income groups. Counterintuitively, lower social integration often leads to more distribution from higher to lower income groups but not necessarily higher levels of equality (Haagh 2012, 2015). Redistribution from top to bottom in a hierarchical structure is a short-term way to deal with problems of social integration and lacking social equality. In the long run, a lower overall level of tax affects universal services, the latter of which shape the real value of income indirectly, including by washing out the effect of regional and income differentials to some extent.

On the other hand, the index of public spending on human development is a composition of overall capability and commitment to social spending in combination with measures that can be considered strategic for human development, even though they are relatively small posts in overall GDP. Here the use of weights is applied slightly differently. Again, there is no true or "right" way to select items of spend. The assumption I make is that there is not a proportionate relation between level of spending on a certain post and the explanatory significance of that post. So, for instance, although spending on public childcare in GDP may be a small item—less than 1 per cent—the explanatory value of this measure, in terms of opportunities for unbroken human development trajectories, and therefore differences between countries along this measure, is very high.

Hence, human development strategic measures are represented in the index for their social and developmental rather than (merely) their monetary value. These include measures such as level of spend on training, job creation and supported employment, and childcare. Higher public spending on said posts in GDP indicates commitment to human development within the economic process.

Figures 4.3 and 4.4 contrast two periods of recent (neoliberal) globalization. The scores within the indices that compare different periods in time are summarized under the headings of *Globalization 1* and *Globalization 2*, for ease of reference. The first refers to a time point around 2000 or the early 2000s, with inclusion of some trends up to this point, and the second to time points around the mid-2010s, and trends up to that point. Globalization 2 can be considered a period in which the distributive outcomes of market-permissive economic restructuring embed and is also the context for the deepening of austerity and fragmentation of public provision. In other words, if Globalization 1 was heavily focused on *private sector market extension* (disembedding), Globalization 2 included *public sector market* extensions (detachment).

From this perspective, it is interesting to observe those countries with the most cooperative systems of public finance also tend to have higher, albeit different, levels of strategic spending on human development. The trend is much stronger for the Nordic states, in particular Sweden and Denmark. In the post-austerity period, although there has been noticeable change. Overall, the countries with the highest levels of strategic human development spending are clearly discerned from the rest. This suggests that countries with historically higher levels of social equality and more cooperative systems of public finance tend to have more sustainable development commitments as well. A case in point is how—starting from a similar level—South Korea raised its level of taxation in GDP compared with Mexico. In the same period, Mexico exempted middle earners from higher levels of tax, as indicated in the much higher multiples of the average wage at which high rates set in. In the long run, the latter tax structure is more precarious because more rests on the ability to recoup tax from a smaller share of society. South Korea's level of tax not only grows significantly. It is also far less steep in terms of redistributive structures (highest rates set in at lower wage levels compared with Mexico's, which remains hierarchical in the extreme). In these cases, we can hypothesize that South Korea's historically lower market income inequality enables a more horizontal structure of tax and an overall broader push for raising the tax level.

The Distributive versus Institutional Case for BI Revisited

The implications of the macro-configurational trends discussed in the previous section are significant for the UBI debate. At stake is the question of conditions behind UBI, as well as the conditions in which UBI would be effective. We can surmise that UBI is much more likely and feasible in conditions of already higher levels of shared risk within the structure of tax and services. Hypothetically a UBI could also strengthen support for sharing of risk given that it is unconditional and paid to all.

The UBI debate needs to be set in the context of (i) very different systemic traits linked with more redistributive and more cooperative systems of public finance, and (ii) the multi-institutional character of support of well-being in society.

In the same vein, I argue that we can identify several risks in the recent debate in terms of the relationship between the systemic context and UBI.

First, with some exceptions, pilots in the South and experiments in the North run the risk of, respectively, extrapolating the local in the South, and flattening and thinning out the welfare debate in the North. For instance, one of the problematic aspects of localized pilots and surveys in especially the global South is that the implications of their findings can be hard to upscale systemically to the national level. Systemic factors or "inter-institutional" effects in BI impacts can be discerned in well-formulated pilots or surveys, for example, that contain control groups which adjust for differences in settings. The pilot scheme of BI in India found greater effects in villages with established solidarity networks, such as the Self-Employed Women's Association (SEWA) (Davala et al 2015). However, arguably, the "hidden" finance (human time and opportunity-facilitating cooperation) involved requires formal finance at a national level. This hidden finance does not just "emerge" without support.

The problem associated with underlying conditions in the UBI debate can be identified in the context of the idea versus reality of the so-called emergency temporary basic income schemes (TBIs). TBIs performing as alleviation programmes under COVID-19 inevitably presupposed a short-term intervention. The problem of generalization of high impacts of emergency measures can be seen, paradoxically, in the United Nations Development Programme's (UNDP) advocacy for TBI: "[h]ow to ensure a temporary scheme does not perpetuate itself beyond the emergency period?" (Gray Moline and Ortiz Juarez 2020:15).

A related analytical problem with regard to extrapolative risks is connected to the hidden presumption of economic formality. A move to embed BI security in the global market can be dated to the ideas of Friedman and the negative income tax (NIT) (Friedman and Friedman 1980:119–124; Friedman 1982 [1962] on the related flat tax:177–179, 192). This idea—known as a BI guarantee—differs from what we understand as BI in the current debate, since the form payments take is different from the forms the payment of BI schemes take. For instance, in the case of NIT, payments (in effect entitlements) are linked to an earnings threshold. This means the NIT is means-tested, whereas a BI is detached from earnings. Although a NIT sounds attractive and fair *and* cheaper(!), in fact it maintains the redistributive structure of the state that in political reality (as shown) lowers public finance for transfers and welfare. Therefore, the ostensible "fairness" is not fair from the perspective of the capability approach in so far as systemically it is linked with a low tax model of welfare. The "cheap" NIT is linked with reduced public finance for transfers and welfare. The NIT also therefore comes at a cost to sustainability and stability of entitlement. Although the proposition of the neoliberal case for a NIT is fairly clear in theory, namely to insure the market through a more permanent structure of minimum provision, the reality of implementation of neoliberal reforms shows us otherwise: *neoliberal reform increases informality.* This means a NIT could easily become an earned income supplement for a large share of the population.

A longer-term risk in the same context is a continuation of states acting as sources of wage subsidy while at the same time being subject to public austerity. In this context, notions of BI, no matter what forms it may take, insures the market but not in a sustainable way. In practice, a very patchy and gradual embedding of this kind has taken place in all states through a variety of channels as public subsidies have (partially) replaced wage incomes over several decades (Clasen 2020). As we have seen, this increasing state subsidization of production has contributed to destabilization, not a stabilization, of rights' *form.*

The market-insuring NIT in this sense draws two things together that do not in fact combine: labour market flexibility and productive formality. This contradiction sheds light on the cooperative logic at national level that I argue underpins realization of political security of welfare and rights in practice. Once a public finance structure is based on a low-budget redistributive structure—as in the United States and many middle-income countries—it is very hard to upscale. In part this is because a producer model based on precarious labour markets makes it difficult to raise tax from large segments of the population—rich and poor—reinforcing what can be termed an equity trap. This is whereby a moral logic to provide more sustained income support is reinforced by inequality and crises, but the same context makes this response unsustainable. In this context, the market-insuring NIT model cannot be sustainable.

The dynamics of the equity trap and the problems with Friedman's vision in practice are revealed in the sustained high spending in rich countries despite the rhetoric of austerity. Social protection spending continued to be high, but changed in structure to a more passive and ineffectual form, as indicated in low levels of investment in more active labour market policies linked with education and training. The problem with Friedman's vision is that, as it relies on deregulation, it produces informality and, in turn, greater need but less shared risk. Hyperglobalization created the pauper.

This helps explain why, despite austerity, government spending in rich countries is not necessarily falling, while its effectiveness is weak. In development aid, the same trend is reflected in the emergence of conditional cash transfer (CCT) schemes while employment is remaining or becoming precarious. Cynically, one could ask whether appropriating the term "basic income" to this trend is legitimate or even appropriate. Can BI really speak of anything new or transformative in a context where the trend is coinciding with deformalization of productive structures? The uptake of BI by core development institutions corroborates many of these points and concerns.

The main findings of the World Bank's report on UBI in terms of distributive issues are as follows (Rigolini et al 2020:147–148). First, replacing existing assistance schemes under budget neutrality would have significant distributive consequence, but this would generally tend to leave the poorest less well off (Gentilini et al 2020:8; Rigolini et al 2020:147). Second, in most countries, a UBI that has a significant impact on poverty is not possible under budget neutrality. This—third—is especially true in low-income countries. The costs to low-income countries look staggering, for example, in Mozambique with a per capita GDP of only USD 498 in 2018, a poverty-effective UBI is estimated to cost 48 per cent of GDP. The most important conclusion of the World Bank data refers to the tax base and follows from the above premise. Therefore, under budget neutrality, a poverty-effective UBI is unlikely to be sufficiently funded. Given the difficulty in raising consumption and resources taxes, most countries will need to raise direct taxes on the rich. "We find that in most cases, to finance UBI levels that have a meaningful impact on poverty, the burden of taxation on the top 10 percent would need to increase substantially" (Rigolini et al 2020:149). How politically likely is this?

Yet, while the World Bank's data on the cost of UBI in low and middle-income countries give us a measure of the equity trap, arguably the data does not fully explain it. For example, is the problem (as the World Bank report suggests) one about low income, or is it really a problem of low levels of sharing?

Highlighting country income level hides a number of factors at stake in the equity trap, namely income and asset concentration and their relations with taxation and labour formality.

On the face of it, higher levels of agriculture (lower urbanization) in countries such as Nepal, and similarly, India and Mozambique, help explain these countries' higher informality and lower levels of tax in GDP. However, this is only partially explanatory. India's very low level of tax in GDP (at 7.3 in 2020, Heritage Foundation 2020) (compared with 20.2 for Chile, 32.3 for Brazil, 20.3 for Nepal, 23.2 for Mozambique and 28.6 for South Africa) belies its higher level of urbanization compared with Nepal (34 per cent against 20.6 per cent), yet both with about the same level of informality, Nepal at 78 per cent and India at 80 per cent. Similarly, informality of the urban economy (categorical informality) is reflected in the relationship between Chile's and Brazil's high urbanization (87.7 per cent and 87.1 per cent; CIA 2022) yet high informality (Brazil at 38 per cent and Chile at 28 per cent). This raises a question: how come Chile's higher formality still generates lower levels of tax in GDP? This can be partly linked with the tax model adopted under neoliberal restructuring. Average earners pay lower rates of tax (above—the lowest in the OECD—at 7 per cent, below Mexico at 9.5 per cent; Carter 2014). This suggests Chile has a more "mature" or "qualitative" form of informality—or cheap formality—which means that the form of precarious, low-wage formality is distinct from the more clear-cut category of informality, and tax structures have been made to adapt to this.

On the other hand, despite a highly progressive structure, where top marginal rates set in at multiples of 7.6 of average income (Table 4A.1), the rich still pay less than in Brazil (Rigolini et al 2020:149). After Hungary, Chile has the lowest combined statutory Corporate Income Tax rates in the OECD (OECD 2022). Flexibility in how higher earners register income (such as through rules to exempt tax from reinvestment funds) also plays a role in reducing real tax intake despite higher marginal rates (Biehl et al 2019).

Viewed from this angle, the problem of low-income countries is a form of high inequality sustained by the linked problems of low formality and absence of strategic mobilization of resources for investment through shared-risk structures. The global South in this sense reflects the image of the North's future, in so far as Northern trends continue toward regressive redistribution and precarity.

The way finance is more achievable but still highly dependent on the rich in countries such as Brazil and South Africa is reflected in the World Bank's data, which suggest that to finance a poverty-effective UBI would raise the tax burdens (the share of income going to tax) on the richest decile from 7.2 per cent to 24.5 per cent in Brazil, and from 19.9 per cent to 40.3 per cent in South Africa. In countries where the rich already contribute less, such as Chile and India, at 5.4 per cent and 2.2 per cent, respectively, the share would need to rise at politically unimaginable levels, to 38.4 per cent and 68.4 per cent. These figures, combined with consideration of the tax proportion of GDP, suggest greater feasibility in Brazil compared with Chile since the former has a higher overall share of public finance in GDP while the latter has a less egalitarian tax structure. Therefore, formality of the labour market—both categorical and qualitative—is, at many levels, the main problem when considering fiscal challenges to UBI in the long-term.

Several concerns about the understanding or focus of the World Bank and also an International Monetary Fund (IMF) (2017) report on UBI are raised. In the case of the World Bank, it is its focus on the redistributive goals of a UBI that drives its analysis. Gentilini et al (2020:11) assume *"that coverage of the poor, which is already very high, is the primary goal of a UBI introduction"* (italics added).

The anti-poverty focus of the World Bank's interest in UBI is also revealed in its understanding of UBI as a replacement for unconditional cash transfers (UCTs). While acknowledging different paths and scenarios, the World Bank report privileges a transition from UCT to NIT, via UBI (Gentilini et al 2020:80). The IMF (2017) similarly implies a desirable transition to NIT or "back" to well-administered conditional schemes, which it argues now make a UBI needless in Europe (disregarding the health costs linked with sanctions policies [that a UBI would erase], as summarized in Haagh and Rohregger 2019).

How feasible or desirable is a transition from UBI to NIT? A conclusion that a UBI is relevant where state capacity is weak (IMF 2017) implies that UBI is understood as disconnected from a wider project of formalization, and other services. However in a context of low public capacity and high informality, the chances of inadequate coverage of a UBI would be greater. The foundation model of UBI, which rests the case on a UBI's political and institutional value, assumes a transition from UBI to NIT would be counterproductive by being seen as reserved for the poor. Counterfactually, once the stage is reached where NIT is feasible, at a higher level of formality of the economy and taxation in GDP, the levels of political security of welfare would also be very high, through shared systems of income security and services. In this case there would be no practical or, arguably, political sense to go "back" to a NIT, because a NIT entails less stable entitlements and less shared risk than a UBI. A good example of this is given in countries with well-funded two-tier income security systems, which comprise risk pooling through contributor savings combined with tax subsidy (in unemployment insurance systems) combined with assistance (Haagh 2006, 2012). The point here is that countries with higher levels and more horizontal contributions to tax do not choose a single level or targeted form of income support.

Income support tends to become more multifaceted and inclusive in contexts in which the welfare state configuration has attained the following conditions: a relatively high level of tax share in terms of GDP, a highly formalized labour market, and a diversified and high level of sharing of key economic and lifecycle risks (Haagh 2021). Besides the support of this premise already given earlier, Columbino (2009) has shown how only a few (Nordic) countries can sustainably finance a UBI, and that this capacity is strongly related to the formalization of the gender economy. In other words, in reality, NIT and UBI are only the same when good conditions of a sustainable UBI have been realized, through different means. Under these good conditions, the rationale for a NIT no longer exists.

We can, in this context, talk about three challenges to emerging UBI transitions—defined as relatively long-term moves to implement a universal, stable UBI system, in terms of institutional consolidation, shared-risk embedding and productive structural transformations. Proponents of UBI understandably want to push ahead as the moment seems opportune toward a full and even generous UBI, piggybacking on the COVID-19 crisis spending momentum. A valid argument is that once a population experiences a benefit—be it an emergency cheque paid to all or working from home—the experience will stick and generate a demand. I agree with this argument but think that its feasibility may be limited. There are two problems in practice with the assumption that an emergency-based transition to UBI will happen, or even that the proposition is positive. One problem is that the arguments for a short-term economic boost and for political security are entirely different. The latter as a more long-term argument may be lost in translation. In the same vein, paying incomes at the level of emergency payments will not be sustainable, and in that context paying to everyone equally will be seen as unfair (as governments have judged). Hence, rushing to a UBI could backfire. Tony Atkinson (2002) once (it seems rightly) argued that a UBI would be politically more realistic (in Britain) if introduced in a "silent" way through the back door of administrative reform, potentially at a very low level. I would add today—in view of the link between shared risk and attitudes to benefit design—we face not the back door but a long road to BI reform. A sustainable BI reform is predicated on larger fiscal states underpinned by shared-risk formations in institutions of state and society.

Conclusion

In this chapter I explored how new freedom-oriented perspectives in the welfare debate challenge development analysis, and in response I developed a more overarching institutionalist approach to the problem of human development and its political foundations. While new normative perspectives seem to go with the grain of global development transformations toward a focus on distributive foundations for choice-led development, I argued in fact the opposite is needed, namely a macro-configurational understanding of the institutional bases for freedom in society. How can we rescue freedom-orientated perspectives—an attractive feature of which is that they are by orientation universalist—from becoming part of the problem of contemporary development, in terms of a trend to adapt discourses and policy to the market and the associated trend towards passive and punitive income support?

Responding to these challenges, the chapter explored how a line of enquiry centred on the problem of political security of welfare allows us to evaluate factors that shape how systems of public policies affect well-being as a social condition. In this context, it was proposed that a new concept of human development state—and new criteria for humanist governance—can help encapsulate how state capacities built on shared-risk formations and economic formality contribute to formalization of human economy and society. This chapter also argued that more built-up shared security structures—larger human development states—are more likely to support humanist governance in practice, linked with sensitivity to human development needs through integration of principles of unconditional universal entitlement with principles of equity in institutional design. There are, therefore, two core constraints on BI today. The first is ideational, in terms of a lack of understanding of how principles of unconditional equality and capability-based equity are required in combination. The second is material, in terms of the constraints on governance effectiveness presented by contemporary trends to low taxation, low formality and low levels of risk-sharing in state and society.

Appendix

Table 4A.1: Structure of cooperative public finance: public revenue scores and levels

Total tax revenue as % of GDP 1:1975, 2: 2000, 3: 2009, 4: 2015				5 a.1975–2000 b.2000–2015 c.1975–2015			6a	6b	7a	7b	8a	8b		11 a 2000 b 2009 c 2016/7				
1	2	3	4	a	b	c	2000	2000	2009	2009	2016/7	2016/7	9	10a	10b	a	b	c
Den	37.0	46.9	45.2	46.6	127	99	120	62.7	1.0	62.1	1.0	55.8	1.2	89	496	492	32	25.0	22.0
Fin	36.1	45.8	40.9	44.0	127	91	122	59.8	2.1	55.0	1.8	58.9	1.8	96	491	485	29	26.0	20.0
Swe	38.9	49.0	44.1	43.3	126	88	111	55.4	1.5	56.5	1.5	60.1	1.5	103	491	487	28	26.3	22.0
No	38.8	41.9	41.2	38.1	109	91	98	55.3	2.6	47.8	1.6	46.9	1.6	85	432	427	28	28.0	25.0
Ger	34.3	36.2	36.1	36.9	105	102	108	53.8	1.8	47.5	6.3	47.5	5.5	88	443	427	43	30.2	30.2
Ho	38.2	37.2	35.4	37.8	97	103	99	60.0	1.8	50.2	1.2	52.7	1.4	87	459	456	35	25.5	25.0
Be	38.8	43.5	42.4	44.8	112	103	115	65.7	2.3	59.4	1.1	59.4	1.0	58	411	408	40	34.0	34.0
Swi	22.5	27.4	27.0	27.9	122	101	124	44.0	3.6	41.1	3.3	41.7	3.5	95	405	395	25	21.2	21.2
Aus	36.4	42.1	41.0	43.5	116	103	120	42.6	2.3	43.7	2.1	55.0	24.7	117	501	460	34	25.0	25.0
Fr	34.9	43.1	41.3	45.5	123	106	130	49.9	2.8	49.8	2.8	55.1	14.8	110	517	473	38	48.7	36.4
Sp	18.0	33.4	30.0	33.8	186	101	188	48.0	4.3	43.0	2.4	45.0	2.4	96	436	429	35	30.0	25.0
Por	18.9	31.1	29.9	34.5	164	111	183	46.6	3.4	48.4	4.6	61.3	16.0	132	530	481	35	26.5	29.5
It	24.5	40.6	42.1	43.3	166	107	177	46.4	3.6	50.7	3.2	48.8	9.8	105	488	460	37	27.5	27.5
Hu	44.8	38.6	39.2	39.4	86	102	n/a	68.5	0.9	62.0	0.8	33.5	0.0	50	374	374	18	20.0	19.0
Cze.	37.0	32.5	32.4	33.5	88	103	n/a	40.5	2.5	31.1	0.4	31.1	0.4	77	374	372	31	20.0	19.0
Pol	34.0	32.9	31.4	32.1	97	96	n/a	41.5	3.5	34.9	2.8	38.8	2.1	93	402	395	30	19.0	19.0
Sl R.	39.6	33.6	28.9	32.3	85	96	n/a	42.0	7.9	29.9	0.5	35.1	3.7	84	382	371	29	19.0	22.0
Ire	27.9	30.8	27.4	23.6	110	76	85	50.5	1.0	50.2	7.9	52.0	2.0	101	401	398	24	12.5	12.5
U.K	34.2	32.8	31.5	32.5	96	94	95	40.0	1.3	51.0	1.3	47.0	4.1	118	296	284	21	28.0	20.0
U.S.	24.6	28.2	23.0	26.4	115	94	107	48.0	8.8	43.2	8.6	48.6	8.0	80	369	344	39	39.1	38.9
Asr	25.4	30.4	25.8	27.8	120	91	109	48.5	1.2	46.5	2.8	49.0	2.2	101	423	416	34	30.0	30.0
N Z	27.5	32.5	30.3	32.8	118	101	119	49.0	1.7	38.0	1.5	33.0	1.2	67	366	362	33	30.0	28.0
Ja	20.4	26.6	27.0	32.0	130	120	157	49.5	4.5	47.7	4.6	56.1	8.7	114	498	472	41	39.5	30.0
S. K.	14.9	21.5	23.8	25.3	144	118	170	43.4	5.4	38.5	3.2	43.2	4.0	100	423	410	31	24.2	24.2
Mex.	14.5	13.6	3.6	7.4	94	105	n/a	42.9	48.6	29.7	4.7	35.0	26.6	82	344	259	35	28.0	30.0
Chile								15.1		15.5		10.9					15.0		

12 a 2000 b 2009 c2016/7			13 a 2000 b 2009 c 2016			(14) Statutory corporate income tax rate a 1982, b 1994, c 2000, d 2007, e 2010, f 2016/7						(15) Corporate tax revenue as a % of GDP a 1965, b 1982, c 1995, d 2000, e 2007, f 2010, g 2015							16 a 1982–2000, b 2000–2015		17 Public revenue score	
a	b	c	a	b	c	a	b	c	d	e	f	a	b	c	d	e	f	g	*		G1	G2
40.0	45.0	42.0	59.2	58.8	54.8	40.0	35	32	26	25.0	22.0	1.4	1.1	2.3	3.2	3.8	2.4	2.6	291	81	487	436
0.03	19.6	28.9	29.0	40.5	43.1	62.0	26	29	27	26.0	20.0	2.5	1.5	2.2	5.7	3.9	2.0	2.2	380	39	412	398
30.0	30.0	30.0	46.9	48.4	45.4	58.0	28	28	28	26.3	22.0	2.0	1.6	2.6	3.7	3.7	2.8	3.0	231	81	445	410
-0.1	28.0	28.8	28.0	48.2	46.6	51.0	28	28	28	28.0	24.0	1.1	7.2	3.7	8.8	11.4	8.2	4.5	122	51	413	365
31.1	26.4	26.4	60.9	48.6	48.6	60.0	52	42	39	39.0	15.8	2.5	1.8	1.0	1.8	2.2	1.3	1.7	100	94	417	319
60.0	25.0	25.0	74.0	44.1	43.8	48.0	35	35	26	25.5	25.0	2.6	2.9	3.1	4.0	3.2	n/a	2.7	138	68	458	374
15.0	15.0	27.0	49.1	43.9	51.8	50.0	40	39	35	33.9	33.0	1.9	2.0	2.3	3.1	3.5	2.5	3.4	155	110	445	447
42.1	20.0	21.1	56.5	36.9	37.8	33.0	28	9	21	8.5	8.5	1.3	1.7	2.2	2.4		3.1	3.4	3.0	141	125	429	266
26.0	25.0	25.0	50.5	43.8	43.8	47.0	34	34	32	25.0	25.0	1.8	1.1	1.4	2.0	2.4	1.7	2.3	182	115	390	170
40.8	30.1	44.0	63.2	55.9	64.4	50.0	35	38	37	34.4	34.4	1.8	2.2	2.0	3.0	3.0	1.4	2.1	136	70	434	326
27.2	18.0	23.0	52.7	42.6	42.3	34.0	37	35	33	30.0	25.0	1.4	1.2	1.7	3.0	4.7	2.2	2.4	250	80	364	330
25.0	20.0	28.0	51.4	41.2	49.2	50.0	40	32	28	25.0	28.0	n/a	1.2	2.3	3.7	n/a	n/a	3.2	308	86	359	245
12.5	12.5	26.0	44.9	36.6	46.4	40.0	53	37	32	27.5	27.5	1.8	2.9	3.3	2.8	3.8	3.1	2.1	97	75	373	312
35.0	25.0	15.0	46.7	40.0	31.2	n/a	na	18	na	19.0	19.0	n/a	4.5	1.8	2.2	2.8	2.2	1.9	49	86	389	324
15.0	15.0	15.0	41.4	32.0	31.2	n/a	na	31	na	19.0	19.0	n/a	6.1	4.3	3.2	5.0	3.7	3.6	52	360	318	309
20.0	19.0	19.0	44.0	34.4	34.4	n/a	na	3	na	19.0	19.0	n/a	6.6	2.7	2.4	2.8	n/a	1.7	36	71	314	286
15.0	0.0	0.0	39.7	19.0	22.0	n/a	na	39	na	19.0	22.0	n/a	5.9	5.9	2.6	3.0	2.8	3.5	44	135	274	252
44.0	41.0	51.0	57.4	48.4	57.1	50.0	40	24	12	12.5	12.5	2.3	1.6	2.7	3.6	3.4	2.4	2.7	225	75	382	322
30.0	25.0	38.6	45.1	46.0	44.5	52.0	34	30	30	28.0	19.0	1.3	3.7	2.4	3.5	3.4	2.8	2.5	95	71	403	309
43.3	19.7	28.5	65.6	49.4	56.3	50.0	40	35	39	35.0	32.9	4.0	2.0	2.4	2.2	3.0	2.1	2.2	110	100	308	387
22.0	23.6	27.1	48.5	46.5	49.0	47.0	34	34	32	30.0	30.0	3.3	2.7	4.2	6.2	6.8	n/a	4.7	230	76	374	338
8.9	11.4	6.9	39.0	38.0	33.0	46.0	34	33	34	30.0	28.0	5.0	2.6	4.2	4.0	5.0	3.3	4.4	154	110	350	304
43.6	10.0	20.3	66.7	45.6	44.2	n/a	50	30	40	30.0	23.4	4.0	5.2	4.2	3.5	4.8	2.4	4.3	67	123	347	292
20.0	29.3	35.4	44.0	46.4	51.0	n/a	na	28	na	22.0	22.0	n/a	1.9	2.2	3.0	4.0	3.7	3.2	158	107	219	295
0.0	0.0	17.1	35.0	28.0	42.0	n/a	na	35	na	30.0	30.0	n/a	1.7	1.7	1.7	n/a	2.0	3.3	100	194	223	214
35.3						15.0																

Notes: G1 Globalization 1: mid-1970s to 2000. G2 Globalization 2: 2000 to mid-2010s.

Column 5: Total tax revenue as % of GDP, earlier year as 100.

Columns 6–8: a: Top marginal tax rate, b: Multiple of average wage where sets in. Column 9: Top marginal tax rates 2000–2015, 2000 as 100.

Column 10: a: (4*3)+(5b)+(8a*3)+(9), b: (4*3)+(5b)+(8a*3)-(8b*3)+(9). Column 11: Corporate Income tax on distributed profits. Column 12: Net statutory tax rates on dividend.

Income (Shareholder). Column 13: Overall personal income tax and corporate income tax rates on dividend income. Column 16: Corporate tax rev – as % of GDP.

Public revenue score (column 17): G1 (2(*4)) + (5a/10) + (6a(*2)) - (6b*10)) + (13a*2) + (14c) + (15d*2) + (16a/20). G2 (4(*4)) + (5b/10) + (8a*2)) - (8b*10)) + (13c*2) + (14f) + (15f*2) + (16b/20).

Source: elaborated from OECD Tax revenue statistics

Table 4A.2: Public spending on human development

	(1A) General public expenditure in GDP, (a) 1970, (b) 1980, (c) 1990, (d) 2000, (e) 2005, (f) 2009, (g) 2015*, (h) Trend to 2015, 2000 as 100								(1B) Public social expenditure in GDP, (a) 1990, (b) 2007, (c) 2014*, (d) Trend to 2014, 1990 as 100				(1S) Score = G1, G2		(2A) Public expenditure on education in GDP, (a) 1995, (b) 2007, (c) 2011, (d) Trend to 2011, 1995 as 100			
	(a)	(b)	(c)	(d)	(e)	(f)	(g)	(h)	(a)	(b)	(c)	(d)			(a)	(b)	(c)	(d)
Den	42.9	53.6	57.0	52.7	51.2	58.6	55.7	106	25.0	26.1	30.1	120	283	306	7.3	7.8	8.7	119
Fin	31.9	40.6	48.6	48.1	49.3	56.1	57.7	120	23.8	24.9	31.0	130	266	318	6.8	5.9	6.8	100
Swe	n/a	n/a	n/a	53.6	52.7	46.3	50.4	94	28.5	20.8	28.1	98.6	291	277	7.1	6.7	6.8	96
Now	39.1	47.9	44.5	42.0	42.1	47.5	48.6	116	21.9	25.2	22.0	100	233	260	7.9	6.7	8.7	110
Ger	39.1	47.9	44.5	44.8	46.2	47.5	43.9	98	21.4	25.2	25.8	121	244	249	4.6	4.5	5.0	109
Hol	41.7	55.3	54.8	41.8	42.3	51.4	45.1	108	25.6	20.1	24.7	96.5	239	250	5.1	5.3	5.9	116
Bel	n/a	n/a	n/a	49.1	51.4	54.2	54.0	110	24.9	26.1	30.7	123	270	301	5.8	5.9	6.5	112
Swi	n/a	n/a	n/a	34.1	34	33.7	33.7	99	12.8	18.5	19.4	152	187	199	5.7	5.2	5.3	93
Aus	n/a	n/a	n/a	50.3	51	52.3	36.4	72	23.4	26.4	28.4	121	276	222	6.1	5.4	5.8	95
Fra	39.3	46.6	50.7	51.1	52.9	56	57.0	112	24.9	28.4	31.9	128	278	316	6.3	5.6	5.7	90
Spa	23.6	34.2	43.4	39.1	38.3	45.8	43.3	111	19.7	21.6	26.8	136	221	251	4.6	4.3	4.8	104
Por	n/a	n/a	n/a	42.6	46.7	48.3	48.3	113	12.4	22.5	25.2	203	227	275	5.1	5.3	5.3	104
Ita	33.5	41.7	54.4	45.5	47.1	51.9	50.0	110	21.4	24.9	28.6	134	250	282	4.7	4.3	4.3	91
Hun	n/a	n/a	n/a	47.2	49.6	50.5	50.7	107	12.9	23.6	22.1	171	242	275	5.2	5.2	4.7	90
Cze	n/a	n/a	n/a	40.4	41.8	45.9	41.8	103	14.6	18.8	20.6	141	215	233	4.8	4.2	4.5	94
Pol	n/a	n/a	n/a	42.0	44.5	44.4	41.5	99	14.9	20.0	20.6	138	222	231	5.2	4.9	4.9	94
Slo	n/a	n/a	n/a	52.0	39.6	41.5	45.6	88	18.6	15.7	18.4	98.9	264	238	4.6	3.6	6.8	148
Ire	n/a	n/a	n/a	30.9	33.4	48.9	35.1	114	17.2	16.3	21.0	122	182	206	5.0	4.9	6.2	124
UK	42.1	45.7	42.2	37.8	42.8	51.6	43.2	114	16.3	20.5	21.7	133	209	241	5.0	5.4	6.0	120
US	32.4	33.8	36.5	33.7	36.5	42.2	38.1	113	13.1	16.2	21.6	165	189	223	4.7	5.3	5.1	109
Aus	n/a	n/a	n/a	36.2	34.7	35.3	36.4	101	13.1	16.0	19.0	145	196	208	4.9	4.3	4.8	98
NZ	n/a	n/a	n/a	37.6	37.7	41.9	40.0	106	21.2	18.4	20.8	98.1	213	222	5.6	5.8	7.4	132
Jap	20.0	30.8	32.1	38.8	36.4	37.1	42.0	108	11.1	18.6	23.1	208	209	246	3.6	3.4	3.8	106
SK	n/a	n/a	n/a	24.7	29.5	30.5	32.4	131	2.8	7.5	10.4	371	155	201	n/a	4.2	5.0	n/a
Mex	n/a	n/a	n/a	n/a	19.5	5.5	24.5	126	3.2	7.2	7.9	247	122	149	4.2	4.8	5.2	124

(2B) Public expenditure on education in % of public expenditure, (a) 1995, (b) 2007, (c) 2011, (d) Trend to 2011, 1995 as 100				(2S) Score = G1 G2		(3) Training, job creation, and supported employment—public spending in GDP, (i) 1995/6 (ii) 2006, (iii) 2013, (vi) a Trend to 2006. 1995/6 as 100, b Trend to 2013, 2006 as 100, (S) Score = G1 (i*200)+(iva/10) G2 (iii*200)+(ibv/10)							(4) Public spending on child-care as % of GDP, (i) 1998, (ii) 2005, (iii) 2011, (iva) Trend to 2005 1998 as 100 (ivb) Trend to 2011, 2005 as 100, (S) Score = G1 (i*150)+(iva/20) G2 (iii*150)+(ivb/20)							Column 5 Score = 1S+ (2S*2)+3S+ (4S*2)	
(a)	(b)	(c)	(d)			(i)	(ii)	(iii)	(iva)	(ivb)	(S)G1	G2	(i)	(ii)	(iii)	(iva)	(ivb)	(S)G1	G2	G1	G2
12.2	15.4	15.2	125	97.4	114.4	1.67	1.57	1.82	93	116	343	376	0.7	0.8	2.0	114	250	111	313	1043	1537
11.0	12.5	12.2	111	89.6	90.7	1.54	0.76	1.01	49	133	313	215	0.8	0.7	1.1	86	157	124	173	1006	1060
10.7	12.7	13.2	123	92.7	92.2	2.10	1.32	1.35	63	102	426	280	0.7	0.6	1.6	86	267	109	253	1120	1247
15.5	16.4	14.9	96.1	105.8	112.2	1.01	0.58	0.56	57	97	208	122	0.3	0.5	1.2	167	240	53	192	759	990
8.5	10.3	11.0	129	71.4	72.9	1.20	0.60	0.67	50	112	245	145	0.0	0.1	0.5	100	500	20	100	672	740
9.1	11.7	11.9	131	72.5	83.2	1.12	1.20	0.94	107	78	235	196	n/a	0.1	0.9	100	900	25	180	669	974
12.1	12.4	12.2	101	80.8	87.9	1.16	1.06	0.72	91	68	219	151	0.1	0.2	0.7	200	350	25	123	701	874
13.5	12.2	15.7	116	81.0	79.2	1.52	0.77	0.56	51	73	309	119	0.1	0.1	0.1	100	100	20	20	698	516
10.8	11.1	11.4	106	81.9	79.4	0.25	0.58	0.76	232	131	73	165	0.2	0.3	0.5	150	167	36	83	585	712
11.6	11.5	10.2	87.9	83.5	76.1	1.14	0.75	0.87	66	116	235	186	0.3	0.4	1.2	133	300	52	195	784	1044
10.3	11.1	10.5	102	66.6	68.8	0.62	0.16	0.61	26	381	127	160	0.0	0.0	0.4	400	150	20	98	521	745
11.7	11.6	10.7	91.5	73.4	73.5	0.69	0.46	0.50	67	109	145	111	0.0	0.0	0.4	100	0	5	60	529	653
9.0	9.0	8.6	95.6	65.3	61.0	1.03	0.41	0.41	40	100	215	92	0.1	0.2	0.6	200	300	25	05	646	506
12.9	10.4	9.4	72.9	73.0	64.6	0.21	0.19	0.78	73	411	49	197	0.1	0.1	0.6	100	600	20	20	485	641
8.7	9.9	10.4	120	67.4	66.1	0.09	0.18	0.30	600	167	78	77	0.1	0.1	0.4	100	400	20	80	468	602
11.9	11.6	11.4	95.8	73.4	69.9	0.11	0.36	0.44	90	122	31	100	0.2	n/a	0.5	175	250	39	88	478	547
14.1	10.5	4.1	29.1	69.0	80.9	0.25	0.15	0.22	147	147	65	59	0.1	0.1	0.4	100	400	20	80	507	619
12.2	13.5	13.1	107	73.8	86.7	1.41	0.51	0.88	36	173	286	193	0.1	0.3	0.5	300	167	30	83	676	738
11.4	11.7	12.2	107	72.8	83.6	0.26	0.05	0.06	19	120	54	24	0.4	0.4	1.1	100	275	65	179	539	790
12.6	14.1	13.6	108	70.5	75.4	0.12	0.12	0.11	100	92	34	31	0.0	0.1	0.4	100	400	5	80	374	565
13.8	13.7	14.4	104	72.8	72.5	0.57	0.18	0.23	132	128	127	59	0.2	0.2	0.6	100	300	45	05	559	422
16.5	18.1	21.6	131	85.7	108.8	0.61	0.28	0.28	46	100	126	66	0.0	0.1	1.1	110	100	25	20	560	546
9.5	9.4	9.1	95.8	55.6	57.2	0.10	0.05	0.16	50	320	25	64	0.2	0.2	0.4	100	200	35	70	415	564
16.3	14.8	16.5	101	69.3	76.4	0.04	0.10	0.29	250	290	33	87	0.0	0.1	0.8	110	800	16	60	359	561
22.2	21.7	20.5	92.3	75.0	83.3	0.08	0.02	0.01	25	50	19	7	0.3	0.0	0.6	0	600	45	90	381	503

Notes: G1 Globalization 1: mid-1970s to 2000. Globalization 2: mid-2000 to mid-2010s.

1S score: G1: (Ad*4)+(Ah/10)+(Ba*2)+(Bd/10), G2: (Ag*4)+(Ah/10)+(Bc*2)+(Bd/10). Both G1 and G2 include the same figure for long-term trend in social expenditure (1990–2014), and in general public expenditure (2000–2015). The main difference in the two scores is therefore between the 2000 and 2015 figures for general public expenditure in GDP, and the 1990 and 2014 figures for public social expenditure in GDP. I used the 2000 data for general public expenditure because it is more complete. Had I used the 1990 figure, the trend evidenced in Table 4A.2 and Figures 1 and 2 of growing divergence between countries would have been even greater. Countries like Japan, France and Denmark see large increases in public spending between 1970 and 2000. Anglo-liberal countries see less change over the whole period. Public social spending continues to grow but more so in countries with historically high levels.

2S score: G1: (Aa*10)+(Ad/20)+(Ba)+(Bd/20), G2: (Ac*10)+Ad/20)+(Bc)+(Bd/20). On this score, G1 is indicated by 1995, and G2 by 2011. Both scores include the same indicator for trend, so the main difference is between the level of public expenditure in GDP, and the share of education in public expenditure in the two periods.

Source: elaborated from OECD National Accounts, Social Expenditure data, Family database, Education at a Glance, Employment Outlook.

References

Alkire, S. 2002. "Dimensions of Human Development." *World Development*, 30(2):181–205.

Atkinson, A. 2015. *Inequality*. Cambridge, MA: Harvard University Press.

Atkinson, T. 2002. "How Basic Income Is Moving up the Policy Agenda." Paper presented to the 9th International Congress of the Basic Income Earth Network, Geneva, 12–14 September. https://citeseerx.ist.psu.edu/viewdoc/download?doi=10.1.1.567.6370&rep=rep1&type=pdf.

Bates, R. 2006. "The Role of the State in Development." In *The Oxford Handbook of Political Economy*, edited by Barry R. Weingast and Donald A. Wittman, 708–722. Oxford: Oxford University Press.

Biehl, Andres, Jose Tomas Labarca and Jacinta Vela. 2019. "Impuestos sin Contribuyentes: la invisibilidad de los Impuestos en Chile." *Revista Mexicana de Ciencias Politicas y Sociales*, 64(236): 49–82.

Carter, B. 2014. "Which Country Has the Highest Tax Rate?" *BBC News Magazine*, 25 February. https://www.bbc.co.uk/news/magazine-26327114.

Cecchini, S. and R. Martínez. 2012. "Inclusive Social Protection in Latin America." *ECLAC: Libro de la CEPAL*, vol. 111.

CIA (Central Intelligence Agency). 2021. "Factbook." Accessed 29 June 2022. https://www.cia.gov/the-world-factbook/.

Clasen, J. 2020. "Subsidizing Wages or Supplementing Transfers? The Politics and Ambiguity of In-Work Benefits." *Social Policy and Administration*, 54(1):1–13.

Columbino, U. 2009. *Evaluating Alternative Basic Income Mechanisms*. Discussion Paper No. 578, February. Oslo: Statistics Norway Research Department.

Davala, S., J. Renana, G. Standing and S. Kapoor Mehta. 2015. *Basic Income: A Transformative Policy for India*. London: Bloomsbury Publishing.

De Wispelaere, J. and L. Haagh. 2019. "Introduction: Basic Income in European Welfare States." *Social Policy and Society*, 18(2):237–242.

Downes, A. and S. Lansley. 2018. *It's Basic Income*. Bristol: Policy Press.

Esping-Andersen, G. 1990. *The Three Worlds of Welfare Capitalism*. Cambridge: Polity Press.

Fraser, N. 2003. "Social Justice in the Age of Identity Politics." In *Redistribution of Recognition?*, edited by Nancy Fraser and Axel Honneth, 7–109. London: Verso.

Fredrickson, Barbara L., Karen M. Grewen, Kimberley A. Coffey, Sara B. Algoe, Ann M. Firestine, J. M. G. Arevalo, Jeffrey Ma and W. Cole. 2013. "A Functional Genomic Perspective on Human Well-being." *Proceedings of the National Academy of Sciences*, 110(33): 13684–13689. doi: 10.1073/pnas.1305419110.

Friedman, Milton. 1982 [1962]. *Capitalism and Freedom*. Chicago: University of Chicago Press.

Friedman, M. and R. Friedman. 1980. *Free to Choose*. San Diego: Harcourt.

Gentilini, U., M. Grosh and R. Yemtsov. 2020. "Overview: Exploring Universal Basic Income." In *Exploring Universal Basic Income*, edited by Ugo Gentilini, Margaret Grosh, Jamele Rigolini and Ruslan Yemtsov, 1–15. Washington, DC: World Bank.

Gray Moline, G. and Ortiz Juarez, E. 2000. *Temporary Basic Income: Protecting Poor and Vulnerable People in Developing Countries*. United Nations Development Programme,

Haagh, L. 2021. "Welfare-as-Freedom." In *Economic Policies for a Post Neoliberal World*, edited by Malcolm Sawyer and Philip Arestis, 269–344. London: Palgrave Macmillan.

Haagh, L. 2019a. *The Case for Universal Basic Income*. Cambridge: Polity.

Haagh, L. 2019b. "The Political Economy of Governance Capacity and Institutional Change." *Social Policy and Society*, 8(2):243–263.

Haagh, L. 2019c. "Basic Income, Health Constitution and Governance Coherence for Human Development." Plenary address at the inaugural policy strategy meeting of the Social Determinants of Health, WHO Geneva, 12 September. Accessed 4 January 2024. https://cdn.who.int/media/docs/default-source/documents/social-determinants-of-health/6_haagh_basic-income-health-constitution-governance-coherence.pdf?sfvrsn=c7588b1d_7.

Haagh, L. 2017. "The Basic Income Should Be Seen as a Democratic Right." *RSA Journal*. Accessed 29 June 2022. https://medium.com/rsa-journal/basic-income-should-be-seen-as-a-democratic-right-b249ab6078b0.

Haagh, L. 2015. "Alternative Social States and the Basic Income Debate." *Basic Income Studies*, 10(1): 45–81.

Haagh, L. 2012. "Democracy, Public Finance, and Property Rights in Stability." *Polity*, 44(4):542–587.

Haagh, L. 2011a. "Basic Income, Social Democracy and Control over Time." *Policy and Politics*, 39(1):41–64.

Haagh, L. 2011b. "Working Life, Well-Being and Welfare Reform." *World Development*, 39(3):450–573.

Haagh, L. 2007a. "Basic Income, Occupational Freedom and Anti-Poverty Policy." *Basic Income Studies*, 2(1):1–6.

Haagh, L. 2007b. "Developmental Freedom and Social Order." *Journal of Philosophical Economics*, 1(1):119–160.

Haagh, L. 2006. "Equality and Income Security in Market Economies." *Social Policy and Administration*, 40(4):385–424.

Haagh, L. 2002. "Introduction: Markets and Rights in the Governance of Welfare." In *Social Policy Reform and Market Governance in Latin America*, edited by Louise Haagh and Camilla Helgø, 1–44. Basingstoke: Palgrave Macmillan.

Haagh, L. 2001. "The Challenges of Labor Reform in Korea." In *Labor Market Reforms in Korea*, edited by F.-K. Park, Y.-B. Park, G. Betcherman and A. Dar, 386–419. Washington, DC: World Bank.

Haagh, L. and B. Rohregger. 2019. *Universal Basic Income Policies and Their Potential for Addressing Health Inequities*. Geneva: World Health Organization.

Heritage Foundation. 2020. "Explore the Data." Accessed 29 June 2022. https://www.heritage.org/index/explore.

Hills, J. 2014. *Good Times, Bad Times*. Bristol: Policy Press.

Honneth, A. 2003. "Redistribution as Recognition: A Response to Nancy Fraser." In *Redistribution of Recognition?*, edited by Nancy Fraser and Axel Honneth, 110–197. London: Verso.

IMF (International Monetary Fund). 2017. "Fiscal Monitor, Tracking Inequality." October. Accessed 29 June 2022. https://www.imf.org/en/Publications/FM/Issues/2017/10/05/fiscal-monitor-october-2017.

Jordan, B. 2008. *Welfare and Well-Being*, Bristol: Policy Press.

Jugov, T. and L. Ypi. 2019. "Structural Injustice, Epistemic Opacity, and the Responsibilities of the Oppressed." *Journal of Social Psychology*, 50(1):7–27.

Kangas, O. 2010. "One Hundred Years of Money, Welfare and Death." *International Journal of Social Welfare*, 19(Supplement s1):S42–S59.

Kangas, O. and J. Blomgren. 2014. "Socio-economic Differences in Health, Income Inequality, Unequal Access to Care and Spending on Health." *Research on Finnish Society*, 7:51–63.

Korpi, W. and J. Palme. 1998. "The Paradox of Redistribution and Strategies of Equality." *American Sociological Review*, 63(5):661–687.

Lavinas, L. 2013. "The Lost Road to Citizen's Income." In *Citizen's Income and Welfare Regimes in Latin America*, edited by R. Lo Vuolo, 29–49. Basingstoke: Palgrave Macmillan.

Lloyd-Sherlock, P. 2019. "Inequality, Social Spending and the State in Latin America." In *Routledge Handbook of the Welfare State*, edited by Bent Greve, 232–242. London: Routledge.

Lundberg, O., M. Yngwe, K. Bergquist and O. Sjöverg. 2015. "Welfare States and Health Inequalities." *Canadian Public Policy*, 41(2):S26–S33.

Marmot, Michael, Jessica Allen, Peter Goldblatt, Tammy Boyce, Di McNeish, Mike Grady and Ilaria Geddes. 2010. *Fair Society, Healthy Lives*. London: Marmot Review Team.

Marshall, T. H. 1949. *Citizenship and Social Class*. Cambridge: Cambridge University Press.

Marx, I., L. Salanauskaite and G. Verbist. 2013. "The Paradox of Redistribution Revisited," *IZA DP*, 7414(May). Accessed 29 June 2022. http://ftp.iza.org/dp7414.pdf.

Moore, C. 2008. *Assessing Honduras' CCT Programme PRAF, Programa de Asignación Familiar*. Research Report No. 15, April. Brasilia: International Policy Centre for Inclusive Growth.

Nussbaum, M. C. 2006. *Frontiers of Justice*. London: The Belknap Press.

OECD (Organisation for Economic Co-operation and Development). 2022. "Tax Database." Accessed 29 June 2022. https://www.oecd.org/ctp/tax-policy/tax-database/.

Rawls, John. 1971. *A Theory of Justice*. Oxford: Oxford University Press.

Rigolini, J., N. Lusig, U. Gentilini, E. Monsalve and S. Quan. 2020. 'Comparative Effects of Universal Basic Income." In *Exploring Universal Basic Income*, edited by Ugo Gentilini, Margaret Grosh, Jamele Rigolini and Ruslan Yemtsov, 123–152. Washington, DC: World Bank.

Rothstein, B. 1998. *Just Institutions Matter*. Cambridge: Cambridge University Press.

Sen, A. 2002. "Why Health Equity?" *Health Economics*, 11(8):659–666.

Sen, A. 1998. *Development as Freedom*. Oxford: Oxford University Press.

Sen, A. 1987. *Gender and Cooperative Conflicts*. Wider Working Paper No. 18, Worldwide Institute for Development Economics Research: Helsinki, July.

Sen, A. 1985. *The Standard of Living*. Cambridge: Cambridge University Press.

Sharif, M. 2003. *Work Behavior of the World's Poor*. London: Routledge.

Standing, G. 2009. *Work after Globalisation*. Cheltenham: Edward Elgar.

Standing, G. 2008. "How Cash Transfers Promote the Case for Basic Income." *Basic Income Studies*, 3(1):1–30.

Standing, G. 1999. *Global Labour Flexibility*. Basingstoke: Palgrave Macmillan.

Steinmo, S. 2018. *The Leap of Faith*. Oxford: Oxford University Press.

Tatsiramos, K. 2014. "Unemployment Benefits and Job Match Quality." *IZA World of Labor.*44.

Thelen, K. 2014. *Varieties of Liberalisation*. Cambridge: Cambridge University Press.

Titmuss, R. 2019 [1958]. *Essays on the Welfare States*. Bristol: Policy Press.

van Parijs, P. 1995. *Real Freedom for All*. Oxford: Oxford University Press.

Vanderborght, Y. and P. van Parijs. 2017. *Basic Income*. Harvard: Harvard University Press.

Widerquist, K. 2013. *Independence, Propertylessness, and Basic Income*, Basingstoke: Palgrave Macmillan.

Williams, A. 1998. "If We Are Going to Get Fair Innings, Someone Need to Keep the Score." In *Health, Health Care and Health Economics*, edited by M. L. Barer, T. E. Getzen and G. L. Stoddart, 319–330. New York: Wiley.

Williamson, O. 1985. *The Economic Institutions of Capitalism*, New York: The Free Press.

5

The South African Mining Sector: Exploring the Dynamics of the Social, Economic and Environmental Policy Nexus

Sophie Plagerson and Lauren Stuart

Introduction

The realization of Agenda 2030 for Sustainable Development requires social policy to transcend the confines of traditional "social" sectors (Yi, Kaasch and Stetter in this volume). Multisectoral policies and multilateral implementation strategies are essential for the pursuit of social policy goals. This chapter provides an analysis of social policies in the South African mining sector: how their trajectory, innovative at times, at other times regressive, has been variously forged at the dynamic intersection between social, economic and environmental policies. The role of different policy actors in expanding or seeking to restrict the scope of social policy within the mining sector is also examined.

For many decades, the mining sector in South Africa has formed the bedrock of the South African economy. It has also played a key role in shaping the contours of social policy and, in turn, has been transformed to some extent as social policies have been incorporated. The governance of the mining industry in South Africa provides an interesting case study of how social, economic and environmental policies and relationships between policy actors can intersect, and result in synergies as well as tensions. The analysis presented in this chapter builds on, and critically assesses, the premise that integrated policy is necessary to achieve national development goals and to address challenging issues that are core to social policy, such as poverty and inequality. Social policy (including gender as a cross-cutting theme) is taken as the starting point and is discussed in the context of its relationships to economic and environmental policies. It is argued that social outcomes are best achieved when complementarity between social, economic and environmental policy is pursued within the constraints posed by sectoral and intersectoral institutional capacity.

The analysis of the trajectory of social policies, and how they weave in and out of relationship with economic and environmental policies, transects with the deeply political context in which the policies are located. In post-apartheid South Africa, the Constitution and the National Development Plan 2030 represent clear mandates for policy making which pursues national goals and goes beyond the confines of sectoral policy making. Yet, as the mining sector illustrates, the formulation and enactment of policies in the past decade has occurred in a climate marked by political uncertainty, and manifestations of predatory collusion between state and capital, which has placed its democratic governance system under severe pressure. Nonetheless, since 2018, new leadership in the governing party has launched a series of investigations and judicial enquiries over misconduct by government officials and between government and private parties over the last decade. However, the direction of legislative and inter-stakeholder relationships remains unsettled.

The chapter examines the mining sector in terms both of the intersectoral linkages between policies, and of the relationships between policy actors. The case study illustrates the benefits of integrating social policy within multisectoral public policy strategies, as well as the persistent challenges of maintaining an integrated approach in the face of shifting sectoral and actor-centred agendas. The next section gives an overview of the mining sector. Then the chapter tracks the post-democracy development of policy and legislative frameworks in terms of their intersectoral nature. The fourth section maps key policy actors (the state, the private sector, labour and civil society) in the mining sector in relation to social, economic and environmental policy intersections. The chapter concludes by reflecting on policy complementarity as a new direction for social policy and identifying significant factors for its design and implementation: legislation and the role of the courts, multilateral stakeholder platforms and the retention of sectoral expertise within state departments.

The Mining Sector in South Africa

The contours of the mining sector relate to its size and scale, its economic contributions, its role in the labour market, its changing gender dynamics, public and political perceptions of the sector, and its environmental implications. Overall, the national backdrop is of declining mineral assets and an international context of mineral resource price volatility. Though now in decline, the mining sector has played and continues to play a significant role in the South African economy since minerals were first discovered in 1886. South Africa is still a leading producer and supplier of more than 50 different minerals including gold, platinum and coal. In 2017, there were 1,712 mines and quarries producing primary commodities (RSA 2017a). In 2017, mining contributed 6.8 per cent to GDP, down from 14.7 per cent in 1994 (CoM 2018). In 2017, the mining sector employed 3 per cent of the employed population (Stats SA 2017), down from 10 per cent in 1997 (Stats SA 1998:44). Despite increases in worker wages over the past decade, wage inequality in the sector remains acute.

From a gender perspective, the relative representation of women in mining has increased, but still remains low, rising from 11,400 women in 2002 to 53,179 in 2017. Women represent 12 per cent of the mining labour force (and 14.9 per cent of top management) (Minerals Council South Africa 2017). Under apartheid, the racialized and gendered nature of mining policy resulted in large-scale poverty, fragmented households, with exploitative and cheap migrant labour systems developed to produce high rates of profits. Few women were employed in the mines, and facilities were not provided for workers' families. Despite paradigmatic shifts in the democratic era to reverse these trends, current social protection systems provided by the state and the private sector still struggle to address the geographic and socioeconomic legacy of disparity produced by past discriminatory efforts to divorce responsibility for economic production from provision for social reproduction.

Politically, the mining sector holds a complex position. On one hand, it is still considered as an economic sector of comparative advantage in the South African economy, with expectation for the mining sector to support the achievement of social and economic goals (Jourdan 2014). On the other hand, the political establishment is also perceived as hostile to the mining sector, due to the mining sector's history, which is seen as a vestige of apartheid social and labour relations. The fragile space occupied by the mining sector, in terms of the unresolved and contested relationships between state actors, employers, trade unions and workers themselves came to a head in August 2012 with the lethal shooting by police of 34 miners at Lonmin's platinum mine in the Marikana area.

From an environmental perspective, the energy-intensive nature of mining and pressing demands for increased energy generation have clashed with water scarcity constraints, climate change commitments, detrimental environmental impacts to communities and farmers and the need for the industry to reduce its carbon footprint (RSA 2017b).

The policy frameworks and policy implementation actors create a complex milieu in which social, economic and environmental linkages are played out in the mining sector, in ways which we discuss in the sections that follow.

Social, Economic, and Environmental Linkages in Policy and Legislative Documents

The reform of the formerly exploitative mining sector was a major concern of the first democratic government, inaugurated in 1994. The timeline in Figure 5.1 summarizes several of the major public policy documents and

Figure 5.1: Public policy and mining legislation documents

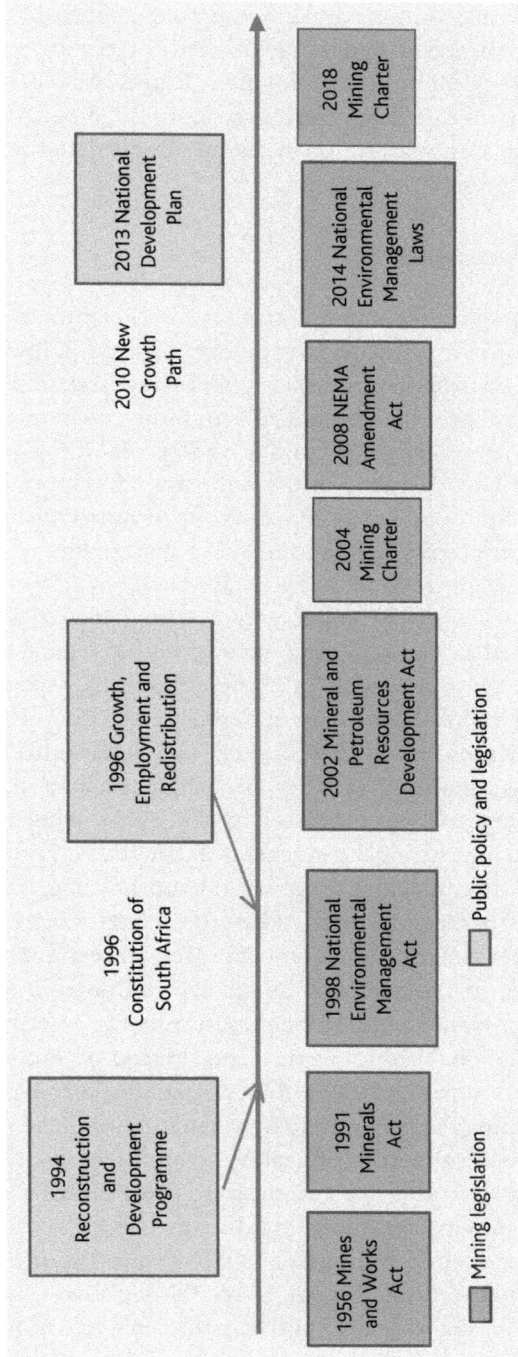

Source: adapted from RSA 2017b

mining legislation that have shaped the trajectory of social policy and its intersections with economic and environmental policies in mining. The list is not exhaustive since many other legislative documents, such as the Labour Relations Act of 1995, the Employment Equity Act of 1999, the Broad-Based Black Economic Empowerment Act of 2003 and other related Acts, have also played a significant role in giving substance to the policy mandates governing the mining sector.

Public policy documents

Legislative and policy documents formulated in the immediate post-apartheid era established a strong normative commitment to a holistic view of social, economic and environmental policy. This marked a definite departure from apartheid-era policy which propelled economic concerns to the fore, drove a mining-led process of industrialization and promoted discriminatory goals that advanced the well-being of the minority white population above that of the rest of the population. Similarly, environmental interests had very limited autonomous representation in apartheid policy.

The 1994 Reconstruction and Development Programme (RDP) policy framework was socially oriented with a strong redistributive remit. The RDP recognized that poverty and environmental degradation were closely related and that improvements in living conditions, access to services and access to land would all contribute to reducing negative human pressures on the natural environment in the country. The RDP introduced sustainable development as a guiding vision for ensuring participation, equitable use of natural resources, and protection of working and living environments, in alignment with international agreements (RSA 1997). The RDP recognized gender inequalities in access to jobs, land and housing, and supported the implementation of mechanisms to address the disempowerment of women and boost their role within the development process and economy (Section 3.2.7).

Furthermore, in order to redress the skewed distribution of social and economic opportunity and to begin the process of reintegrating South Africa into the global economy, the Constitution of South Africa affirmed the interconnectedness and indivisibility of social and economic rights (Patel 2015). Concerning the relationship between social and environmental policy, the Constitution outlined an obligation to ensure that nationally beneficial mineral exploitation did not compromise the health of the environment or its people, present and future, and made the connection between the environment, the economy and its people by entrenching "the right to have the environment protected through reasonable legislative and other measures that prevent pollution and ecological degradation while promoting justifiable economic and social development" (Section 24(b) of the Constitution of South Africa).

The introduction of the macroeconomic Growth, Employment and Redistribution (GEAR) policy in 1996, which coincided with the abandonment of the RDP, represented a decisive moment in the trajectory of South African public policy. GEAR did not mention the need to accommodate environmental considerations in central economic and social planning and rather focused on rapid routes to economic growth, including areas that constituted a source of environmental degradation such as the expansion of heavy industries and an increase in the rate of natural resource exploitation. GEAR was widely criticized by trade unions and sectors of civil society as prioritizing a conservative economic policy in response to pressure from national and global business interests at the cost of its previous commitment to social goals (Seekings and Nattrass 2015). While GEAR still held to a redistributive agenda (social spending remained stable in this period), it privileged economic development and growth as a means to tackling poverty and unemployment (Patel 2015).

In 2011, the National Development Plan (NDP) reiterated the importance of national planning and envisaged a leading role for the state as coordinator and mediator of social, economic and environmental policy, channelled toward the elimination of poverty and inequality by 2030 (NPC 2011). However, its future vision was arguably more multisectoral than intersectoral, encompassing policies for economic growth, increased productivity, poverty reduction and the building of social cohesion without a coherent strategy to identify synergies and overcome intersectoral tensions (Patel 2015).

Similarly, the NDP takes multiple approaches in relation to mining. It promotes mining as an economic driver and identifies strategies for expanding mineral production and exports (NPC 2011). In terms of linking mining to social outcomes, the NDP encourages mining companies to invest in enterprises that are owned by historically disadvantaged South Africans and supports preferential procurement for these groups (Phaladi and Odeku 2015). The NDP emphasized the potential for labour-absorbing and local economic development by the mining sector through supplier industries (such as capital equipment, chemicals and engineering services) and beneficiation. Regarding the environment, the NDP proposed both mitigating measures, such as carbon-pricing, and a long-term shift toward a low-carbon future, requiring considerable investment in renewable energy sources to be funded by current revenue flows and through changes in the taxation regime.

Overall, despite the partial unfastening of the strategic ties between social, economic and environmental policy over the past 20 years, ongoing importance has been accorded to social goals (including gender equality) and their articulation within policy documents. While the nature of its relationship to economic and environmental policy remains contested, its importance has not been questioned and remains pivotal to current policy frameworks. A growing level of autonomy in the conception of the environmental sector within policy mandates has developed, yet environmental concerns have tended to be subordinated to social objectives and thus have not been mainstreamed to the extent envisaged in the earliest democratic policy documents, such as the Constitution and the RDP.

Mining legislation in the democratic era

Mining policy development has mirrored the broader policy milieu described in the previous section. The post-1994 legislative landscape has reflected a growing awareness of the need to regulate and protect the autonomy of social and environmental rights. Yet the twists and turns in legislation highlight the real challenges in achieving a cohesive approach. Sectoral hierarchies continue to be in flux with a lack of consensus around social, economic and environmental priorities. These are reflective of instability in the sector and point to the influence of different interests in shaping the policy iterations, which will be discussed in the next section.

A new democratic mineral dispensation was introduced with the Mineral and Petroleum Resources Development Act (MPRDA) of 2002 which repealed the Minerals Act and divested custodianship of all South Africa's mineral rights from the private sector to the government and its citizens (RSA 2016). The MPRDA reflected national and international trends, including both a renewed recognition of mining as an economic driver and the need to balance the pursuit of profit with the needs of society and of the environment. The MPRDA was a clear move toward creating legislation aimed at improving mining companies' social responsibility, cementing South Africa's role as a regional policy leader in maximizing the social benefits of resource extraction (Corrigan 2019). The Act adopted principles of sustainable development and promoted the integration of social, economic and environmental factors into the planning, implementation, closure and post-closure management of prospecting and mining operations. The Act made provision for small-scale mining, which had been recognized by the RDP as a vehicle to foster broad social and economic growth, though legal and financial barriers to entry for artisanal and small-scale miners (including a high proportion of women) were high (Ledwaba 2017).

The MPRDA's commitment to a non-racial South Africa and to promoting equitable access to the nation's mineral and petroleum resources was taken further in the 2004 Broad-Based Socio-Economic Empowerment Charter for the Mining Industry. This Mining Charter aimed to realize the policy of socioeconomic responsibility and to bring historically disadvantaged South Africans into the mainstream of mining. The Mining Charter was intended to direct the mining industry toward substantial and meaningful transformation and redistribution through human resource development and employment equity; support to migrant labour, mining communities and rural development; improvement of housing and living conditions; preferential procurement, ownership and joint ventures; and beneficiation (Harvey 2015). For example, mining companies are required to draw up Social and Labour Plans (SLPs) in order to secure mining rights. The SLP system was introduced to ensure that local communities benefit from the mineral resources in their area either through job creation, training and the development of local infrastructure (CALS 2016). The Act and Charter originally stipulated that 10 per cent of those employed in core mining activity were to be women. The revised 2010 Charter increased the required share of women-held positions in core mining activity to 40 per cent (Botha and Cronje 2016), raised again to between 50–60 per cent in the Charter of 2018. A "Mining Scorecard" was developed to track progress toward these aims (Sorensen 2011a; Jourdan 2014).

In addition to the MPRDA, the 1998 National Environmental Management Act (NEMA) defines the environmental management approach that should be integrated across all sectors, including mining. It incorporates many key principles of international environmental law and establishes a regulatory framework for the conducting of environmental impact assessments (RSA 2017b).

In the past decade, the MPRDA, NEMA and the Mining Charter, and the linkages between them, have undergone repeated reviews and proposed amendments. Several considerations are noted here which relate to the complementarity of economic, social and environmental policies.

The impasse in mining legislation reform that has characterized the past decade indicates that a lack of trust between stakeholders has thwarted the drafting and implementation of integrated policy. The MPRDA was amended in 2008, but the amended Act was never passed. Further amendments were proposed in 2012, but remained contentious among investors, for example with regard to the proposed degree of ministerial discretion in the awarding of mining licences. Progress stalled until the end of 2018 when the Amendment Bill was withdrawn (RSA 2018). The Mining Charter was reviewed in 2010 and a third review was published in June 2017 but was immediately rejected by the Chamber of Mines (now the Minerals Council). In 2018, the Charter came under review once again, and by September 2018, a final version came into circulation. This breakthrough coincided with a ministerial appointment perceived to embrace multi-stakeholder engagement and sought to strike a balance between improving transformation and ensuring the industry's viability (Nicholson 2018).

Moreover, the shifting prioritization of economic and environmental interests and jurisdiction has become associated with interdepartmental turf wars rather than with a coherent approach to achieving national development goals. This tension is demonstrated by the trajectory of environmental governance in the mining sector. The drafters of the MPRDA (in 2002) sought to position the mining environmental management framework within the ambit of the NEMA, but also carved out an environmental management regime specific to the mining sector, allowing space for equivocal interpretations in practice (Humby 2015). In 2008, proposed amendments to the MPRDA and NEMA acknowledged the tensions created by the Department of Mineral Resources' (DMR) dual role as both facilitator and promoter of mineral development, and as protector of the environment, and reaffirmed the Minister of Environmental Affairs as the "custodian" of the environment (Sorensen 2011b). The amendments made provision for a gradual transfer of authority to the Department of Environmental Affairs (DEA) as regulator for environmental purposes of the minerals industry. However, these provisions were overturned by the National Environmental Management Laws Amendment Act No. 25 of 2014, which assigned oversight for environmental authorizations to the DMR, with the DEA appointed as the final appeals authority.

Overall, the tumultuous and unpredictable policy and legislative progress have resulted in a situation of stalemate and disequilibrium. In addition, reforms to mining legislation have struggled to address the need to clarify, streamline and align the social and environmental legislative requirements, particularly for prospective mining companies. Definitional confusion, regulatory gaps, procedural duplications, ambiguities and delays have resulted (RSA 2017b).

Policy Actors in the Mining Sector in Relation to Social, Economic, and Environmental Policy Linkages

The previous section showed that the new democratic regime offered a remarkable opportunity for a redrawing of public policy frameworks, but also that the arena in which inter-stakeholder negotiation is occurring has broadened well beyond policy implementation to drafting the contours of policy itself. In the sections that follow, some ways in which different policy stakeholders (the state, the private sector, labour and civil society) have positioned themselves with regard to social, economic and environmental policy intersections are highlighted. The analysis is not exhaustive but contributes to an overall picture of how social policies thrive or falter, as intersectoral complementarities and frictions are negotiated within the South African public policy arena.

The state

The state has multiple roles in relation to mining, as a player and a referee in the industry. First, the government is responsible for creating an enabling and transparent regulatory environment to ensure the availability of minerals, prospecting and mining technology, and to facilitate access to energy and water. More directly the state is an active participant in the sector through state-owned mining companies (RSA 2015). Second, the state promotes the well-being and representation of the labour force. The state's role in the pursuit of citizens' welfare is prominent given the constitutionally backed rights-based approach to social policy (see Ruparelia in this volume). Third, the state has a remit to preserve the environment and to ensure that mining communities reap economic and social benefits from mining activity. These three roles broadly represent economic, social and environmental sector interests, respectively. Importantly, the state also plays a coordinating role, enacted through the presidency, multilateral platforms, and the cumulative actions of its departments and levels of government.

Over the past two decades, the state has overseen seismic shifts in the promotion of an integrated agenda, including social and environmental aims in the mining sector, to counterbalance the dominance of economic interests. The achievement of social goals has been pursued through several channels, including changing patterns of ownership, training programmes, tax collection and redistribution, and compliance with the Mining Charter (Webster 2013). The state has increased its capacity to collect taxes and efficiently expanded its ability to spend revenues on pro-poor social assistance programmes (NPC 2011; World Bank 2014). Effective regulation and compliance of the labour market has increased. Active labour-market policies have been instituted to remove discrimination based on race, gender and disability, and to nurture opportunities and access to employment, with tax incentives for companies to invest in skills development (Patel 2015).

Over time, the central location for intersectoral coordination within government has shifted. The RDP office was an early attempt to establish an institution with responsibility for centralized coordination of economic and social transformation. After the closure of the RDP office, under the presidency of Thabo Mbeki, the Treasury and Vice Presidency became the central coordination hubs, supported by interdepartmental "clusters" of ministers.

Inter-stakeholder platforms include the National Economic Development and Labour Council (NEDLAC) which was established in 1995 as a statutory tripartite institution for social dialogue on economic, labour and development policy between government, labour and organized business (NEDLAC 2005). In the years after it was established, NEDLAC played a major role in the development of labour-related legislation and, more recently, in negotiating minimum wage legislation (Valodia 2018). However its influence has waned (Budlender 2011) and the state's ambivalence was already evident in 1996 when the GEAR strategy deliberations bypassed NEDLAC and outcomes were declared non-negotiable. Though it remains an important forum for bringing together a broad spectrum of interests, bilateral negotiations between labour and business with the state have frequently occurred outside its boundaries (Nattrass 2013).

The Mining Industry Growth and Development Task Team established by the DMR in 2008 in response to the global economic downturn, brought together representatives of several state departments, labour and business. The task team's aim was to pursue the sustainable growth of the mining industry together with a transformation agenda. This platform was initially viewed as increasing communication, cooperation and consensus between parties (CoM 2018; Leon 2013). However, commenting on the process of the 2017 Mining Charter review, the Chamber of Mines observed that the DMR had opted for a series of meetings with one set of stakeholders at a time, leaving business feeling excluded from consultation processes, in contrast with the consultative processes of the 2004 and 2010 reviews (CoM 2018).

Several coordination functions have been pursued by the Department of Performance Monitoring and Evaluation (DPME) unit within the presidency. Adopting the NDP as the country's socioeconomic development blueprint, the DPME has applied the recommendations of the National Planning Commission to align sector plans and policies, programmes, projects and operations, as well as budget and skills investment and resource allocation with the NDP. As part of this project, Operation Phakisa ("hurry up" in Sesotho) was launched in 2014 with the ultimate goal of boosting economic growth and creating jobs. At a meeting of the Phakisa project, in the wake of extended strikes in the platinum mines, the DPME minister summarized the functions of government in the sector as having the "holistic objective of unlocking investment in exploration and mining activities while optimizing the developmental impact on the sector on the economy, the workforce and on surrounding communities" and acknowledged the need to address the issues underlying the upsurge in adversarial industrial relations (Radebe 2015:1).

However, the state's credibility in hosting inter-stakeholder deliberative fora has been severely compromised in recent years (Bhorat et al 2017). Bhorat and colleagues document "concerted efforts underway that undermine collective political institutions in the Executive, including Cabinet" and the role played by "handpicked groups, masked as Inter-Ministerial Committees, that are able to function in an unaccountable manner" (2017:16). These points of concern have clear implications for the role of the state as coordinator of its economic, social and environmental roles, and its responsibility to direct the sector toward more equitable sharing of the value created by mining activities through transformation of ownership structures inherent to the mining sector and redistribution of the resources accruing through revenue collection from the mineral sector.

Overall, the state's adherence to multilateral platforms for policy implementation has been inconsistent and centralized planning functions have coexisted alongside independent departmental agendas. While Treasury has argued for greater workplace flexibility, the Department of Labour has supported the expansion of the number and coverage of bargaining councils (Webster 2013). The long-standing dispute between the DMR and the DEA regarding where the power of environmental authorization should lie, also highlights the tensions in the state's dual roles as regulator and promoter of the mining industry (Humby 2015). The tendency of state entities to bypass collegial forums in preference for bilateral channels has historical roots. An "active" relationship with labour has led to an implicit bargaining arrangement whereby the union movement has a veto over labour law but does not interfere on macroeconomic policy. This combined with a more ambivalent and "passive" relationship with business (particularly domestic), has resulted in an economic trajectory that has adopted a capital-intensive, relatively jobless growth path, characterized by high labour costs (Seekings and Nattrass 2015). By pursuing economic and labour interests separately, the state has fallen short of achieving the integrated policy vision set out in its founding democratic documents. Within the state, environmental priorities have remained ancillary and have struggled to break out of narrow institutional confines to influence the direction of the mining sector as a whole.

Two further factors emerge as significant constraints to the state's coordinating role, namely gaps in technical and administrative expertise and a lack of insulation from patronage-type relationships. Technical expertise lacunae in the DMR, the DEA and the Department of Water and Sanitation have limited the state's ability to direct economic strategy, to effectively review applications and oversee the awarding of licences, and to monitor and adequately enforce prevailing standards across the sector. This has resulted in onerous, delayed and conflicting assessment processes, and fragmented communication across national, regional and local government spheres. These issues have been compounded by high staff turnover resulting in limited institutional memory (Cronje et al 2014; RSA 2017b).

High-profile cases of collusion between local and international mining magnates and politicians in the ruling party have led to questions about the state's ability to maintain political and administrative impartiality and even implicated the Minister of Mineral Resources in the awarding of irregular mining deals (Madonsela 2016; Seekings and Nattrass 2015; van Wyk et al 2008). While women, youth, people with disabilities and people in rural areas have benefited to some extent from the implementation of the affirmative Broad-Based Black Economic Empowerment (BBBEE) policies, and representation at managerial level has increased (CoM 2016), reviews have shown that individuals with political and economic connections have disproportionately benefited from the policy (Patel and Graham 2012).

The private sector

As in the case of the state, an analysis of how the private sector has contributed to implementing complementary social, economic and environmental linkages in practice is complex since the sector is varied and far from monolithic. The private sector has historically controlled the mining landscape, with economic interests paramount. The capital- and skill-intensive mining industry is dominated by large companies against which small and medium-sized firms struggle to compete (Ledwaba 2017).

The corporate mining sector's relationship with intersectional policy is mixed and straddles different views regarding how social goals should be achieved. There is a broad understanding within mining houses that their primary contribution to the nation's developmental mandate is through employment creation and tax revenues, which the government is then responsible for redistributing in line with its social goals of poverty and inequality alleviation (Cronje et al 2014). Because of this perspective, the private mining sector typically views itself as overburdened with responsibility for transformative socioeconomic outcomes, that it sees as falling under the state's remit (CoM 2016, 2018; Cronje et al 2014). Additionally, the industry has been outspoken toward the state regarding constraints to growth in the mining sector including labour, electricity and regulatory challenges, local authority management of infrastructure development and discretionary practices in the allocation of mining rights (Cronje et al 2014:5).

Nonetheless, pressure on business to move toward responsible social and environmental practice has come from several places, including global shareholder and consumer activism, adherence to regulation and codes of conduct, media coverage and civil society campaigns (Fig 2007). The Minerals Council (previously Chamber of Mines), which acts as the principal advocate of the major policy positions endorsed by mining employers, argues that it has embraced a holistic and sustainable approach to mining (CoM 2018; RSA 2015) and strived to demonstrate the sector's progress against set targets, including housing of employees and their families, employment of women, investing in skills development, antiretroviral treatment and measures to limit risks to health and safety (CoM 2018; Cronje et al 2014; Kane-Berman 2017). The Minerals Council also claims to spend more on social programmes than any other sector of the economy, contributing a quarter of total corporate social investment (CSI) spending in 2017 (Trialogue 2017). Yet these interventions have not been sufficient to reverse levels of social disadvantage and degradation in off-mine communities, and views vary regarding whether CSI has overall played an integrated and transformative role or a compensatory and conscience-appeasing role in the practices of mining houses (van Wyk et al 2008). Critics note that despite significant pockets of CSI innovation with holistic social and environmental approaches, typically social and environmental concerns have not substantially redirected the business modus operandi and consumer-led demand for socially, and even more so for environmentally, responsible business (Rockey 2013).

Thus, the mining industry's approach to policy complementarity is shaped by competing perspectives regarding who should be responsible for the implementation of social (and environmental) policy, and weak levels of trust in multilateral platforms. Frustrated at the lack of institutional representation, established South African business has been largely reactive and sought to operate profitably within the constrained environment shaped by the state (Seekings and Nattrass 2015), generally opposing interventionist approaches by the state, preferring voluntary agreements, for example by engaging in litigation to contain the implications of BBBEE requirements (CoM 2018). Mining houses have also come under criticism for channelling technical and legal expertise toward avoidance rather than compliance with environmental standards (WWF 2012). Lacking political influence beyond personal ties to political leaders, the business sector has, nonetheless, held considerable economic power through the threat of retrenchments, firm closures, capital flight, investment strikes and entrepreneurial exit. In response to demands for better pay and working conditions on mines, intransigent companies have tended to increase their reliance on subcontractors and mechanization, creating situations where the casualization of labour has led to wage reduction and increased insecurity, contradicting the social gains achieved through other channels (Jourdan 2014; MacMillan 2012).

Mining corporations have increasingly acknowledged the importance of involving unions and civil society in their operations but have been unable to overcome the fault lines of discontent (see the following section). In response to protests about excessive wage gaps and the living conditions of mineworkers, unilateral employer actions around retrenchment have fuelled growing tensions. The preference by the mining industry for centralized industrial bargaining, for example around wages, has excluded small businesses, smaller union and business players, and ignored the concerns of mineworkers, fuelling discontent and violence (Harvey 2016; Webster 2013).

Labour

Labour interests in South Africa have played a unique role in brokering the relationships that affect the coordination of social and economic policy, and environmental policy to some extent. In the post-apartheid years, the Congress of South African Trade Unions and its affiliate organizations developed strong workplace institutions and comprised "a very substantial set of organizations, with more than 1,800 full-time officials, a dedicated parliamentary office and a research wing" (Webster and Buhlungu 2004).

Given their historical trajectory as partners with the state, there has been a natural alignment of trade unions with public policy mandates, even to the extent of holding the government to account when it was perceived to be straying from its original vision, for example in its GEAR framework. Trade unions have had less autonomy on matters of macroeconomic policy, but have been generally supportive of greater state intervention (Seekings and Nattrass 2015). Relying on its political power derived from its closeness to state structures and the state's dependence on the major trade unions for electoral support, organized labour has overseen tangible improvements in wages and living conditions of workers. Unions have taken up issues related to asbestos, mercury, uranium and cyanide poisoning due to industrial pollution, and action on health and safety and other environmental matters. They have also created civil society organizations, such as the Mineworkers Development Agency, established by the National Union of Mineworkers to mitigate retrenchments and retrain migrant miners who returned to rural bases (Bezuidenhout et al 2007). Also, in line with a broad vision of poverty and inequality alleviation, trade unions have frequently promoted the interests of the poor, transcending the confines of their membership. For example, trade unions have been strong supporters of the campaigns to introduce a basic income grant and to extend free medical treatment to people living with HIV/AIDS, social grant policies and the National Health Insurance programme. Their support for environmental policies has been more nuanced, as evidenced by their response to the "green jobs" government initiative in 2011 where moderate support was made conditional on the prioritization of the creation of jobs and the reduction of poverty and inequality, ahead of environmental goals (Sikhakhane 2011).

In recent years however, as in many developing countries, rather than representing a broad-based labour movement, established South African unions have tended to represent more privileged working-class groups (López-Cariboni and Cao 2015). As the gap between established trade unions and their constituencies has widened, emergent groups have formed causing a fragmentation of the labour movement. For example, the Association of Mineworkers and Construction Union, which very rapidly positioned itself to represent the interests of disenfranchised workers and challenged the National Union of Mineworkers for dominance, particularly in the platinum sector (Foudraine 2014). The shootings of 34 miners at the Lonmin mine at Marikana in 2012 and the prolonged platinum mines strikes in 2013 and 2014 drew worldwide attention to the growing discontent of unskilled workers. Inter-union competition raised the lid on a working class still divided by race, gender, class and access to skills. The persistence of the racial and hierarchical organization of labour (with a predominantly white management and a black workforce) has contributed to a workplace culture characterized by low trust, low skills and an adversarial nature (Webster 2013).

Despite overlap between the interests of labour and business for stability in the industry, the established channels for mutual cooperation and dispute resolution have proved inadequate to manage the widespread discontent that has emerged in the mines. The establishment of the Commission for Conciliation, Mediation and Arbitration under the Labour Relations Act of 1995, to resolve workplace disputes, was significant in arbitrating between employers and employees. Though initially effective in reducing conflict, strike action has increased, revealing social and economic divisions that the institution was unable to administer. Alienated by the loss of representation, workers have at times justified violence as a necessary element in maintaining worker solidarity (Webster 2013).

Civil Society: Balancing Legitimacy and Sustainability

A vibrant civil society has played a crucial role in achieving the progressive realization of social, economic and environmental rights through both collaborative and adversarial means in the mining sector as well as many others.

The role of civil society has changed considerably. In the early 1990s, civil society had a mainstream role in the realization of national development goals. Given its origins in the liberation movement there was a natural alliance between the newly formed government and progressive think tanks, non-governmental organizations (NGOs) and community organizations in which "ministerial and bureaucratic appointments were closely aligned with civil society and drew from this base for intellectual support" (Bezuidenhout et al 2007:17). Advocacy organizations include international, regional and national organizations established to represent women in the mining industry and affected by mining operations (UN Women 2016).

As the natural overlap between state, labour and civil society interests has gradually receded, and spaces for multilateral policy making such as NEDLAC have been sidestepped, civil society has drawn on other inter-stakeholder relationships to further their goals in several different ways: through the courts, with business through CSI and by affiliating with broader populist protest movements.

Although civil society has moved toward more adversarial positions and become more vocal in its criticism of the state (and of business), the state's legal courts (particularly the Constitutional Court) have been viewed as allies. National civil society coalitions, including prominent organizations such as the Mining-Affected Communities United in Action, supported by public interest legal firms have been instrumental in highlighting: industrial malpractices; the differential power of stakeholders and the lack of agency of mineworkers; the health, safety, working and living conditions of workers; levels of unhealthy cooperation between mining corporations and the government; the lack of representation of workers by trade unions; and the detrimental social and environmental impacts of mining, in terms of land and water availability and quality, on local farmers and traditional communities on whose land minerals are found (Theart 2017; van Wyk et al 2008). Particularly in the face of private (and state) interests which sought to argue for narrow and separate interpretations of social and environmental legislation, civic organizations and coalitions have, in many instances, resorted to the courts to defend the broad boundaries of social and environmental rights against encroachment from other interests. In one such case the courts affirmed that "by elevating the environment to a fundamental justiciable human right, South Africa has irreversibly embarked on a road, which will lead to the goal of attaining a protected environment by an integrated approach, which takes into consideration, inter alia, socioeconomic concerns and principles."[1]

New trends in cooperation have developed between some sections of the voluntary and business sectors in response to NGOs' need for sustainable funding sources and mounting pressure on mining houses to embrace social responsibility strategies (Bezuidenhout et al 2007). On one hand, in tandem with global organizations and certain investor groups, South African organizations have initiated public campaigns that utilized evidence of environmental and social damage to counter the notion that economic benefits accrued (unequally) through mining could justify allowances that compromised the health and environment of many mining communities (Adler et al 2007; Humby 2015; Mushonga 2012). Combined with bad press and production delays these campaigns have fuelled consumer-led demand for socially and environmentally responsible practices. On the other hand, the voluntary sector has developed income-generating strategies which range from small-scale economic enterprises to deliver social service functions, to partnerships with private business to implement CSI programmes, to innovative empowerment partnerships with other commercial consortia bidding for large public contracts and the licensing of public services (Patel 2015). Overall, these developments have started to blur the lines between for-profit and not-for-profit stakeholders and interests.

Reacting to the perception that the state has moved away from its focus on national development goals, some civil society groups have supported nationalization of the mines as "the only possible response that could meet the socioeconomic expectations of people working in the mining industry" (Cronje et al 2014:13). More broadly, civic organizations have identified with widespread protests which have become a channel for public

---

[1] *18 BP Southern Africa (Pty) Ltd v MEC for Agriculture, Conservation, Environment and Land Affairs* 2004 (5) SA 124 (W).

discontent, triggered by local struggles around service delivery failures and labour disputes (including in mining and off-mine communities) but also representing common demands for greater levels of redistribution and a shift from a mixed economy to a more statist, transparent and participatory regime (Seekings and Nattrass 2015).

Social Policy and Policy Complementarity: Analysis and Conclusions

South Africa presents a wealth of insight into the processes of integrated policy making and implementation, and the implications for social policies. As in many other countries, South Africa continues to grapple with the challenges of social, economic and environmental rights as both a normative and substantive reality.

A mixed picture has emerged regarding the direction of the mining sector toward the achievement of integrated policy making and implementation. Within the broad policy mandate established in the Constitution, despite notoriously antipathetic inter-stakeholder dynamics, there has been a slow rapprochement between different interests: painstaking and by no means linear or enthusiastic but in the direction of greater alignment nonetheless. There is broad agreement between stakeholders that the use of mining resources should accomplish social, economic and environmental aims, despite extensive disagreement regarding which institutions are responsible for the achievement of each of these aims.

Yet serious impediments challenge progress toward the realization of sustainable development goals. Legislative reform stalled for many years. Responsibility for the well-being of the mining workforce, mining communities, for social redistribution and for environmental preservation is reluctantly juggled between employers and the state, with civil society acting as both a vocal advocate and compliant implementer. Trade unions have been weakened by internal divisions. In the past few years, the mining sector has stuttered forward accompanied by strike protests, environmental court cases and economic volatility.

In conclusion, we note that the future direction of social policy is deeply intertwined with the course of economic trends and policies, and with the increasingly urgent implications of environmental and climate-related policies. Understanding how social policies develop beyond the realm of the social sector, and how sectoral policies can be directed toward greater levels of policy complementarity is, therefore, key for the achievement of social aims such as the reduction of poverty and inequality. Against a backdrop of political and economic turbulence, the South African example of the mining sector highlights three aspects which can promote a more cohesive alignment between cross-departmental policies and between policy actors.

Multilateral platforms

A range of institutional arrangements are needed to accommodate dialogue and negotiation between representatives of the state (central and departmental), business (including large, medium and small enterprises), established and emerging labour, and civil society. Such multi-stakeholder institutions importantly require representatives with decision-making authority, political will to contain both elite and popular expectations and capacity-building for partners (such as civil society representatives) to overcome power differentials between stakeholders.

Despite the painstaking and time-consuming nature of multilateral deliberations, the South African example suggests that bilateral negotiations between public, private and voluntary stakeholders based around pragmatic and expedient overlap of interests are primarily limited to the achievement of short-term aims and fall short of establishing sustainable goals such as environmental sustainability and community development, leaving large constituencies excluded from accruing benefits.

Retention of sectoral expertise within state structures

The mining sector represents a complex intersection between social, economic and environmental policies that require both sectoral and intersectoral technical expertise. The interface between sectoral and intersectoral policy mandates and actors is key to effective drafting and implementation of complementary policies. In the first decade post-apartheid, the state's role in legislative and institutional reform nurtured the growing autonomy, voice and administrative expertise of social and environmental interests (historically less powerful than economic interests) to shape the industry toward more equitable outcomes. The retention of technical and bureaucratic expertise within vertical departments and central planning institutions of the state is a key element for ongoing legislative reform and regulatory oversight, in line with national development priorities.

Legislation and the courts

The South African case shows how the Constitution helped to contain policy implementation within the broad remit of national development goals, as well as protecting the confines of social and environmental jurisdiction. Legislation can also provide a robust basis for an independent and informed court system to elucidate the intersections between social, economic and environmental policies, to widen the scope of their application, and to rule in the direction of equalizing power imbalances. The case study, however, has also highlighted the real threat posed even to robust democracies by practices of corruption, which may place disproportionate pressure on core legislative and judiciary institutions.

Despite the challenges that clearly emerge from this chapter's analysis, the evidence from the case study suggests that the pursuit of the transformative Agenda 2030, requires context-sensitive social policies to be carefully developed and implemented within the context of integrated public policies. Among other factors, this requires persistent and tenacious effort to maintain multisectoral and multi-stakeholder platforms of dialogue and negotiation, investment in sectoral and cross-sectoral expertise and unwavering support for independent courts whose remit is aligned with national development goals.

References

Adler, R., M. Claassen, L. Godfrey and A. Turton. 2007. "Water, Mining and Waste: An Historical Economic Perspective on Conflict Management in South Africa." *The Economics of Peace and Security Journal*, 2(2):32–41.

Bezuidenhout, A., D. Fig, R. Hamann and R. Omar. 2007. "Political Economy." In *Staking Their Claims: Corporate Social and Environmental Responsibility in South Africa*, edited by D. Fig, 13–94. Scottsville: University of KwaZulu-Natal Press.

Bhorat, H., M. Buthelezi, I. Chipkin, S. Duma, L. Mondi, C. Peter, M. Qobo and M. Swilling. 2017. *Betrayal of the Promise: How South Africa Is Being Stolen*. Stellenbosch: Centre for Complex Systems in Transition.

Botha, D. and F. Cronje. 2016. "Women in Mining: A Conceptual Framework for Gender Issues in the South African Mining Sector." *The South African Journal of Labour Relations*, 39(1):10–37.

Budlender, D. 2011. *Gender Equality and Social Dialogue in South Africa*. Geneva: Industrial and Employment Relations Department, Bureau for Gender Equality and the International Labour Office.

CALS (Centre for Applied Legal Studies). 2016. *The Social and Labour Plan Series, Phase 1: System Design Trends Analysis Report*. Accessed 27 May 2023. https://l1nq.com/Y9UDh.

CoM (Chamber of Mines of South Africa). 2018. *Integrated Annual Review 2017. Making Mining Matter*. Johannesburg: Chamber of Mines of South Africa. Accessed 25 January 2019. http://www.chamberofmines.org.za/industry- news/publications/annual-reports.

CoM (Chamber of Mines of South Africa). 2016. *Integrated Annual Review 2015. Repositioning the South African Mining Industry*. Johannesburg: Chamber of Mines of South Africa. Accessed 25 May 2017. http://www.chamberofmines.org.za/industry-news/publications/annual-reports.

Corrigan, C. 2019. "Deriving Social Benefits from Mining through Regulation: Lessons Learned in South Africa." *The Extractive Industries and Society*, 6(3):940–947. https://doi.org/10.1016/j.exis.2019.05.017.

Cronje, F., J. Kane-Berman, L. Moloi, T. Dimant, C. Schulze and B. Sethlatswe. 2014. *Digging for Development: The Mining Industry in South Africa and Its Role in Socio-Economic Development*. Johannesburg: Institute of Race Relations.

Fig, D. 2007. "The Context of Corporate Social and Environmental Responsibility." In *Staking Their Claims. Corporate Social and Environmental Responsibility in South Africa*, edited by D. Fig, 1–12. Scottsville: University of KwaZulu Natal.

Foudraine, J. 2014. *Mortal Men: The Rise of the Association of Mineworkers and Construction Union Under the Leadership of Joseph Mathunjwa and the Union's Move to the Political Left, 1998–2014*. Master's thesis, University of Leiden.

Harvey, R. 2016. "Why Is Labour Strife So Persistent in South Africa's Mining Industry?" *The Extractive Industries and Society*, 3(3):832–842.

Harvey, R. 2015. *Mineral Rights, Rents and Resources in South Africa's Development Narrative*. Occasional Paper No. 224. Johannesburg: South African Institute of International Affairs.

Humby, T. 2015. "'One Environmental System': Aligning the Laws on the Environmental Management of Mining South Africa." *Journal of Energy and Natural Resources Law*, 33(2):110–130.

Jourdan, P. 2014. "The Optimisation of the Developmental Impact of South Africa's Mineral Assets for Building a Democratic Developmental State." *Mineral Economics*, 26:107–126.

Kane-Berman, J. 2017. *Diamonds and All That: The Contribution of Mining to South Africa*. Johannesburg: South African Institute of Race Relations.

Ledwaba, P. F. 2017. "The Status of Artisanal and Small-Scale Mining Sector in South Africa: Tracking Progress." *The Journal of the Southern African Institute of Mining and Metallurgy*, 117:33–40.

Leon, P. 2013. "Marikana, Mangaung and the Future of the South African Mining Industry." *Journal of Energy and Natural Resource Law*, 31(2):171–203.

López-Cariboni, S. and X. Cao. 2015. "Import Competition and Policy Diffusion." *Politics and Society*, 43(4):471–502.

MacMillan, H. 2012. "Mining, Housing and Welfare in South Africa and Zambia: An Historical Perspective." *Journal of Contemporary African Studies*, 30(4):539–550.

Madonsela, T. 2016. *State of Capture*. Pretoria: Public Protector South Africa.

Minerals Council South Africa. 2017. "Women in Mining in South Africa." Fact Sheet. Johannesburg: Minerals Council South Africa.

Mushonga, H. 2012. *An Analysis of Corporate Social and Environmental Responsibility (CSER) and Sustainable Development in South Africa*. Johannesburg: University of Johannesburg.

Nattrass, N. 2013. *South Africa: Post-Apartheid Democracy and Growth*. Johannesburg: Centre for Development and Enterprise.

NEDLAC (National Economic Development and Labour Council). 2005. *Founding Declaration of NEDLAC.* Johannesburg: National Economic Development and Labour Council.

Nicholson, G. 2018. "Mining Charter III: A Compromise, Mantashe Style." Daily Maverick, 28 September. Accessed 15 January 2019. https://www.dailymaverick.co.za/article/2018-09-28-mining-charter-iii-a-compromise-mantashe-style/.

NPC (National Planning Commission). 2011. *National Development Plan 2030: Our Future – Make It Work.* Pretoria: National Planning Commission.

Patel, L. 2015. *Social Welfare & Social Development in South Africa* (2nd edition). Cape Town: Oxford University Press.

Patel, L. and L. Graham. 2012. "How Broad Based Is Broad-Based Black Economic Empowerment?" *Development Southern Africa*, 29(2):193–207.

Phaladi, H. N. and K. O. Odeku. 2015. "Challenges of Post-Apartheid Mining Transformation in South Africa." *Socioeconomica – the Scientific Journal for Theory and Practice of Socio-economic Development*, 4(8):419–428.

Radebe, J. 2015. "Launch of Government Phakisa Workshop." Opening remarks by Minister in the Presidency for Planning, Monitoring and Evaluation Mr Jeff Radebe, 20 July.

Rockey, N. 2013. "CSI in Mining Communities: A Complex Terrain." In *The CSI Handbook* (16th edition), edited by C. Duff and N. Rockey, 80–85. Cape Town: Trialogue.

RSA (Republic of South Africa). 2018. *Minister Gwede Mantashe on release of the Mining Charter 2018.* 27 September 2018, Department of Mineral Resources.

RSA (Republic of South Africa). 2017a. "Mineral Resources." In *Yearbook 2017/18*, 1–9. Pretoria: Government Communication and Information System.

RSA (Republic of South Africa). 2017b. *Report on the Implementation Evaluation of the Effectiveness of Environmental Governance in the Mining Sector.* Pretoria: The Presidency; Department of Planning, Monitoring and Evaluation; Department of Environmental Affairs and Tourism; Department of Mineral Resources.

RSA (Republic of South Africa). 2016. "Mineral Resources." In *Yearbook 2015/16*, 317–328. Pretoria: Government Communication and Information System.

RSA (Republic of South Africa). 2015. *Annual Report 2014/15.* Pretoria: Department of Environmental Affairs, Government Printer.

RSA (Republic of South Africa). 1997. *White Paper on Environmental Management Policy.* Pretoria: Department of Environmental Affairs and Tourism, Government Printer.

Seekings, J. and N. Nattrass. 2015. *Policy, Politics and Poverty in South Africa.* Basingstoke: Palgrave Macmillan.

Sikhakhane, J. 2011. "Green Economy Mustn't Cost Jobs: Cosatu." *Independent Online*, 26 August. Accessed 7 May 2018. http://www.iol. co.za/dailynews/news/green- economy-mustnt-cost-jobs-cosatu-1125349.

Sorensen, P. 2011a. "Mining in South Africa: A Mature Industry?" *International Journal of Environmental Studies*, 68(5):625–649.

Sorensen, P. 2011b. "Legislative Transformation of South African Mining Since 1994: What Progress?" *International Journal of Environmental Studies*, 68(2):171–190.

StatsSA. 2017. *P0211 – Quarterly Labour Force Survey (QLFS), 3rd Quarter 2017*. Accessed 29 November 2023. http://www.statssa.gov.za/?Page_id=1854.

StatsSA. 1998. *Unemployment and Employment in South Africa*. Pretoria: Statistics South Africa.

Theart, M. 2017. *Submissions by the Centre for Environmental Rights to the National Council of Provinces on the Mineral and Petroleum Resources Development Amendment Bill [B15D-2013]*. Cape Town: Centre for Environmental Rights.

Trialogue. 2017. *The Business in Society Handbook*. Cape Town: Trialogue.

UN Women. 2016. *Promoting Women's Participation in the Extractive Industries Sector: Examples of Emerging Good Practices*. Nairobi: UN Women Eastern and Southern Africa.

Valodia, I. 2018. "A Minimum Wage for South Africa: Challenging Labour Market Inequalities." Draft paper prepared for the UNRISD conference Overcoming Inequalities in a Fractured World, 8–9 November 2018, Geneva.

van Wyk, D., L. Segwe, F. Cronje, J. van Wyk and C. Chenga. 2008. *Corporate Social Responsibility and the Mining Sector in Southern Africa*. Johannesburg: Bench Marks Foundation.

Webster, E. 2013. "The Promise and the Possibility: South Africa's Contested Industrial Relations Path." *Transformation: Critical Perspectives on Southern Africa*, 81/82: 208–235.

Webster, E. and S. Buhlungu. 2004. "Between Marginalisation and Revitalisation? The State of Trade Unionism in South Africa." *Review of African Political Economy*, 100:229–245.

World Bank. 2014. *South Africa Economic Update: Fiscal Policy and Redistribution in an Unequal Society*. Washington, DC: The World Bank.

WWF (World Wide Fund for Nature). 2012. *Financial Provisions for Rehabilitation and Closure in South African Mining: Discussion Document on Challenges and Recommended Improvements (Summary)*. Cape Town: World Wide Fund For Nature.

6

The Rights-Based Approach to Social Policy in India: Innovations, Advances and Setbacks

Sanjay Ruparelia

Introduction

Since the 1990s, many Southern polities have changed the architecture and expanded the scope of their welfare regimes. The "social turn" in development strategy over the past two decades, an overarching theme of this volume, suggested the possibility of a post-neoliberal era.

This chapter explores one of the most striking cases of these changes in recent years: the establishment of a rights-based approach to social policy in the world's largest democracy. Starting in 2004, the United Progressive Alliance (UPA), led by the Indian National Congress, enacted a series of measures to expand the civil liberties and participatory opportunities as well as economic security and social entitlements of its most disempowered citizens. These ranged from a right to information, work and education to food and land. The UPA also introduced new digital technologies and cash transfer programmes in many realms in 2009, the footprint of which has expanded since 2014 under the auspices of the National Democratic Alliance (NDA). Yet the new ruling dispensation, dominated by the Bharatiya Janata Party (BJP), sought to restrict many rights-based entitlements.

What distinguishes India's new welfare regime? What have been its ramifications for absolute poverty and social inequality? Has the enactment of rights-based entitlements encouraged greater policy coherence and institutional complementarities in social welfare? Have they transformed underlying structures of power, wealth and status? Finally, have rights-based social policies survived following the transfer of power in New Delhi?

Given the spectrum and complexity of India's new social policy framework, this chapter synthesizes major trends. The first part examines its distinctiveness. I highlight the remarkable role of activist judges and social activists in legitimizing and formulating these new entitlements, the highly specific nature of legislation and the role of innovative governance mechanisms in many of them. The second part of the chapter analyses the implementation, performance and impact of these new social policies during the two parliamentary terms of the UPA (2004–2014). In general, India's rights-based approach enhanced the economic security of and infrastructural provisions for many vulnerable groups. Yet their impact on equalizing social opportunities and power relations was more limited. And innovative governance mechanisms proved difficult to operationalize. The third part examines the durability of rights-based welfare measures during the first parliamentary term of the NDA (2014–2019). On the one hand, their legislation made it hard for the BJP to abolish them, reflecting the foresight of their original architects. On the other hand, however, the party exploited its executive powers to undermine their scope and accessibility through official disparagement, budgetary constraints, rule amendments, political interference and administrative neglect. Moreover, the COVID-19 pandemic inflicted a severe toll upon India's most vulnerable citizens, exposing the inadequacy of the technocratic model of social welfare pushed by the BJP. I conclude by evaluating the advances and setbacks of rights-based welfare in India between 2004 and 2021.

The Formulation of India's Rights-Based Social Policies

The formal architect of India's rights-based social policies was the UPA, a diverse multiparty coalition led by the Congress Party, which ruled New Delhi from 2004 until 2014. The Right to Information Act (RTI) 2005, mandated all public authorities to release an array of information regarding their activities to individual citizens in a timely manner. The National Rural Employment Guarantee Act (NREGA) 2005 (subsequently renamed the Mahatma Gandhi National Rural Employment Guarantee Act (MGNREGA) in 2009), sought to protect the livelihoods of poor agricultural labourers during periods of distress. It granted every rural household the right to demand 100 days per year of unskilled work at stipulated minimum wages from the state, making it the largest work guarantee programme in the world. Finally, toward the end of its first parliamentary term, the UPA introduced the Right of Children to Free and Compulsory Education Act (RTE) 2009, making the enrolment, attendance and completion of schooling of every child between the ages of six and 14 the obligation of the state. It articulated minimum standards and infrastructural facilities for all schools to achieve, measures to increase equity and diversity, and provisions to enhance parental involvement and local participation in school management. The passage of these Acts signified the emergence of a new "welfare architecture" with a distinct "social contract" in modern Indian democracy (Mehta 2010).[1]

---

[1] Given word limits, I do not examine another key Act passed in these years, the Scheduled Tribes and Other Traditional Forest Dwellers (Recognition of Forest Rights) Act 2006.

The UPA began its second parliamentary term (2009–2014) by unveiling another flagship initiative. Aadhaar (Foundation) sought to give every resident of India a unique identification number (UID) on the grounds that many of its poorer citizens lacked official documents to prove their identity. Its primary developmental rationale was to ensure that social welfare benefits reached their intended beneficiaries, reducing the scope for corruption. Proponents of Aadhaar also claimed that precise social targeting would enable New Delhi and the states of the union gradually to transform many in-kind benefits and government subsidies for petroleum, food rations and other goods into direct cash transfers. These features, and the fact that Aadhaar lacked statutory authority, concerned many social activists. Independently, mass protests against mounting corruption scandals, beginning in the summer of 2010, paralysed the governing coalition.

Nonetheless, the UPA legislated two final social policy reforms before completing its second term. The National Food Security Act (NFSA) 2013, guaranteed 50 and 75 per cent of the urban and rural population highly subsidized food grains per month, respectively, allocating 5 kg for each individual and 35 kg for the poorest households. It also entitled all schoolchildren up to 14 years of age to free cooked meals, and pregnant women and lactating mothers as well as children up to six years of age to subsidized food and cash benefits. All eligible persons had a right to claim a food security allowance, to be paid within a month, if they failed to receive their entitlements (Puri 2017:8). Last, the UPA introduced the Right to Fair Compensation and Transparency in Land Acquisition, Rehabilitation and Resettlement Act (LARRA) 2013. The new law enjoined the state to gain the consent of local communities whose land it sought to designate for compulsory acquisition, compensate landowners beyond conventional market valuations, and ensure the rehabilitation and resettlement of every person whose livelihood had been affected.

As the preceding summary reveals, India's rights-based Acts vary tremendously in terms of their aims, character and scope. Nonetheless, they share a number of characteristics that mark significant innovations in Indian social policy.

Its principal architects, and the genesis and locus of the formulation of these laws, was the first. The surprising election of the UPA in 2004 under the leadership of Congress President Sonia Gandhi, and the extra-parliamentary support of the communist Left Front, provided a critical political opening. Yet the key driver was a remarkable coalition of progressive activists, intellectuals and bureaucrats that spearheaded various rights campaigns in the courts and civil society. These campaigns used public interest litigation to secure many landmark rulings by activist judges in the Supreme Court from the 1980s until the early 2000s. The apex judiciary was unable to enforce many progressive judgments. Many were limited in scope too. Yet these judicial victories dramatized public concerns (see Jayal 2013). Following the capture of power by the UPA, Sonia Gandhi invited many leading rights activists to join her newly created National Advisory Council. Many of India's new social policies were drafted by this extra-constitutional body and then submitted to the Council of Ministers. Extra-parliamentary campaigns subsequently pressured the UPA to deliver (Nilsen 2018:654). Put differently, the making of these rights-based laws relied on networks that transgressed the traditional state–society divide (see Chopra 2011).

The second major innovation concerns the form of India's new social policies, which had substantive as well as procedural dimensions (see Ruparelia 2013). The UPA extended social welfare benefits to poorer citizens through Acts of Parliament, creating a set of legally enforceable rights. Historically, successive governments in New Delhi pursued an extraordinary range of social welfare initiatives from community development projects, area-based initiatives and resettlement programmes to food distribution schemes, targeted anti-poverty schemes and policy interventions in health and education (Chandhoke 2007; Corbridge et al 2005; Ghosh 2004). The state justified these interventions via the Directive Principles of State Policy, which enumerated a series of social and economic aspirations in Part IV of the 1950 Constitution, unenforceable and non-justiciable, vis-à-vis the civil and political fundamental rights codified in Part III. Yet the residual basis of many of these schemes, offering minimal protection, constituted an "informal security regime" that compelled most citizens to rely on various informal networks too (Wood and Gough 2006). Major constitutional reforms in the early 1990s, decentralizing political authority and economic resources to and mandating reservations for women in local village *panchayats*, enhanced the possibility of greater civic participation in poverty-alleviation schemes. Yet these major efforts to restructure the design of the state retained the distinction between civil and political rights and social and economic entitlements in the Constitution. India's rights-based social welfare laws contested the principle underlying these distinctions.

In contrast, the operationalization of most of these rights built upon extant social policies and welfare programmes. The MGNREGA and RTE sought to consolidate gains made through the Employment Assurance Scheme set up in 1993, and the Sarva Shiksha Abhiyan (SSA) established in 2001, respectively. But the benefits of these government schemes never fully reached their intended beneficiaries. Thus, many of the new welfare Acts passed after 2004 conferred legal rights to social entitlements. And they stipulated procedural obligations in a meticulously detailed manner to ensure that front-line public officials implemented these Acts properly (Manor and Jenkins 2017).

Finally, the third major innovation that distinguished India's post-2004 social welfare architecture was perhaps its most unusual. It introduced a set of provisions to enhance political transparency, responsiveness and accountability, which sought to fuse a novel civil right and hybrid form of "governance rights" (Jenkins 2013:607) with a range of more conventional socioeconomic rights. The overt purpose of the RTI was to reduce the opacity, unresponsiveness and secrecy of public authorities. Yet the desire to promote greater transparency reflected the hard-won insights of many social activists into why welfare schemes failed. Practices of corruption and patronage often enabled relatively privileged groups to capture government benefits. Indeed, many "social" Acts in India's new welfare regime contain novel governance mechanisms. Inevitably, the latter varied across the Acts in terms of their specificity and ambition. Nonetheless, the desire to ensure that intended beneficiaries could participate in important decision-making processes and receive their legal entitlements is clear.

At one end of the spectrum were the MGNREGA and LARRA. The MGNREGA devolved the responsibility for planning, implementing and monitoring work projects to the Gram Sabha (village assembly), and encouraged the latter to disclose information proactively through wall writing, information boards and management information systems. The Act empowered villagers to hold and participate in social audits of local public officials. It also sanctioned trained volunteer auditors from local organizations to examine the records of development projects for irregularities and inconsistencies, and call public meetings to scrutinize the official accounts vis-à-vis oral testimonies. Hence the MGNREGA was designed to enhance the political awareness, connections and skills of poor citizens, and even mobilize popular discontent (Manor and Jenkins 2017:178–185). Similarly, the LARRA obliged local state officials to consult affected village assemblies of their intent to acquire land prior to notification, conduct a social impact assessment with the participation of village assembly representatives and non-governmental experts, and gain the consent of 80 per cent or more of project-affected persons in order to proceed. The Act then required the establishment of a project-specific committee, whose composition had to include women, Dalits and Adivasis, to monitor rehabilitation and resettlement. Last, the LARRA enjoined all state governments to create a Land Acquisition, Rehabilitation and Resettlement Authority, headed by High Court judges with the power to call witnesses, summon records and impose a schedule of penalties (Jenkins 2013:594–598).

At the other end of the spectrum, however, was the NFSA. This Act required state governments to appoint grievance redressal officers in each district, constituted a state-level food commission to monitor its implementation and empowered the latter to fine any public official up to INR 5,000 if they failed to comply with a remedy issued by any grievance officer (Puri 2017:9). Yet the law left the criteria for selecting beneficiaries and grievance officers to state-level governments, making individuals vulnerable to possible exclusion (Dreze 2017).

Whether the intended beneficiaries of these various Acts grasped these elaborate governance mechanisms, could avail themselves of their powers and overcome the resistance of local power holders, bureaucrats and politicians, and whether the courts would ensure their compliance, remained outstanding questions. Nonetheless, the codification of these new governance rights was a novel development in Indian social policy, which aimed to transform the hierarchical power relations and systems of patronage that characterized the delivery of many social entitlements.

The Implementation of India's Rights-Based Social Policies, 2005–2014

The implementation of India's new welfare regime varied tremendously across policy domains as well as the states of the union. The performance and impact of each social policy among the latter revealed complex patterns too.

RTI

The RTI captured public imagination. The number of petitions more than quadrupled from 2006–2007 to 2014–2015. In addition, citizens, activists and journalists used the Act to unearth many scams, from the enquiry into the allocation of spectrum in the 2G telecoms scandal to misappropriated funds, illegal evictions and labour violations during the 2010 Commonwealth Games. Attempts to constrain the power of the RTI grew during the second term of the UPA, including a rule to prohibit petitioners from gaining access to bureaucratic "file notings" (handwritten remarks on administrative files), except regarding developmental matters and ongoing executive decisions. But expectations that it would cause a public backlash reportedly convinced the UPA to shelve the proposal (*The Hindu* 2012).

Yet the use of the RTI over its first decade exposed various shortcomings. The vast majority of petitioners comprised men living in towns and cities (RTI Assessment and Advocacy Group and Samya-Centre for Equity Studies 2014:45). In addition, the popularity of the RTI, the only rights-based law that empowered citizens to make a complaint and receive a time-bound reply, paradoxically created its own problem: a rising backlog of petitions. Consequently, the work rate of many information commissioners began to deteriorate during the second term of the UPA (Rangan 2015). Inadequate staffing limited its early good work. Finally, the architects of the RTI expected bureaucratic resistance, but hoped the filing of petitions would slowly change the culture of administration. Section 4 of the Act enjoined proactive disclosure of "all relevant facts" by officials "while formulating important policies" and "announcing decisions that affect the public" (Venkatesan 2010). Yet more than two-thirds of the petitions filed by citizens nearly eight years after its legislation comprised requests for a response to a prior query, to know whether an action had been taken regarding an issue and for information that should have been proactively disclosed by the authority in question. Studies estimated that demands to see the "file notings" constituted merely 3 per cent of the total. Indeed, more than half of the orders issued by various information commissions failed to elucidate the facts, rationale or outcome demanded in a given petition, and thus comprised "non-speaking" orders. Moreover, many public information officers violated some rule of the Act. Yet the vast majority were neither censured nor penalized as prescribed in Section 20 (see RAAG and Satark Nagrik Sanghathan 2017:88). Despite these failures, petitioners were rarely compensated for delays (see RTI Assessment and Advocacy Group and Samya-Centre for Equity Studies 2014), undermining the detailed accountability mechanisms that had been devised to enforce the RTI.

Nevertheless, most political parties sought to exclude their activities from the purview of the RTI, claiming they were not public entities. The Supreme Court sought to protect itself from scrutiny too, stipulating that demands for information regarding the workings of the judiciary required "good cause"; that the Court could take as long as it wanted to respond, and faced no penalties for non-compliance; and that petitioners could not appeal any action taken by the Court in response to a petition because no mechanism existed (Aga 2015). In *Union of India v. Namit Sharma*, 2013, the apex judiciary ruled that information commissions were administrative tribunals. Hence any appeals process would terminate if its appellant died (see Bhardwaj et al 2015). The decision created ominous incentives to target social activists seeking to expose corruption. Many RTI activists experienced intimidation and violence, leading to fatalities in the worst cases. Limiting the purview of the Act over the judiciary, and failing to adequately protect citizens from retaliation, betrayed its spirit. Yet these developments simultaneously underscored its significance.

MGNREGA

The implementation of the MGNREGA registered many advances. Aggregate public funding for the programme quadrupled between 2006–2007 and 2014–2015. Women, Dalits and Adivasis, who generally constituted the poorest inhabitants, disproportionately benefited. The provision of work also helped to lessen rural poverty and distress migration. Apart from the pay directly received, MGNREGA increased rural wages by 5–10 per cent, cutting absolute poverty among the poorest third of the population by roughly 50 per cent (Mookherjee 2014). The programme also reduced child labour in many districts, improving test scores and grade progression rates (Mookherjee 2014). It also generated some productive assets, especially rural sanitation, water harvesting structures and flood control mechanisms (Vijayabaskar and Balagopal 2018). Finally, the programme provided opportunities for traditionally marginalized communities to engage the state and develop greater political awareness, confidence and skills (Manor and Jenkins 2017) and social dignity (Roy 2014), weakening traditional power relations in many regions. Voter satisfaction with the MGNREGA helped the UPA return to office in 2009 (Manor 2011).

More ambitious goals, however, proved elusive. Participation in the programme never reached its guaranteed 100 days per year. The number of person-days worked, as well as project completion rates, fell precipitously in most states over time. Higher agricultural wages and alternative opportunities explained some of this pattern in better-off states. But less than 50 per cent of beneficiaries were aware of their right to demand work, and only 20 per cent knew they could claim extra payment for inadequate work or delayed wages (Mookherjee 2014). Deliberate political interference and slow bureaucratic processes, especially in poorer states, combined with delays in wage payments and unemployment insurance, deterred many labourers from seeking work. These practices belied the rights-based premise of the Act. Some poor states performed relatively better. The commitment of their state-level politicians, seeking electoral dividends, were usually the most important. Finally, the innovative governance mechanisms enshrined in the MGNREGA, social audits to see whether public funds were spent correctly and legal entitlements to claim penalties for unpaid or delayed wages, occurred very irregularly. Low awareness or social reluctance to activate these institutions owing to cumbersome legal rules, inadequate judicial capacity and the lack of local civic organizations to mediate the process were important factors (Vijayabaskar and Balagopal 2018). These deficits allowed corruption to persist: "leakages" ran close to 30 per cent. Yet they were higher in many other programmes (Mookherjee 2014).

RTE

Finally, the performance of the RTE provided the most sobering lesson of the limitations of rights-based social policies in India. Public spending on primary education more than doubled from 2009–2010 to 2014–2015. The number of state primary schools increased dramatically (Kazmin 2015). Infrastructural facilities, such as girls' toilets, drinking water facilities and especially the number of classrooms, as well as student–teacher ratios, improved over these years (Kapur and Iyer 2016:8). Disparities in the enrolment of girls and children from Dalit, Adivasi and Muslim communities, which had lessened considerably post-2000, continued to decline. And the Supreme

Court rebuffed attempts by private schools to skirt the 25 per cent quota for children from disadvantaged backgrounds in all schools. Private school enrolment among the latter began to increase (Kapur and Iyer 2016:8).

But the impact of the RTE upon learning outcomes was disheartening. India had already nearly achieved universal student enrolment before its passage. Rates of attendance and retention—roughly 75 per cent across the country on average—were significantly lower than enrolment ratios. Moreover, teacher absenteeism in public schools was a serious problem in many parts of the country: up to 25 per cent were absent on any given day (Kazmin 2015). And the quality of education "remains abysmal for a vast majority of children" (De et al 2019: 132). Five years after the passage of the RTE, no district in the country had fully met its minimal school norms, while national measures of student attendance and teacher absenteeism showed little improvement (Harriss 2017:14). Most alarmingly, basic indicators of literacy and numeracy had generally worsened from a distressingly low base. The RTE failed to prioritize retention and learning (Harriss 2017:14). Private school enrolment consequently rose.

The drivers of these complex outcomes were manifold, but three factors stood out. First, public spending on primary education in India remained below international norms, and teachers' salaries consumed a significant portion (Kapur and Iyer 2016:5). Yet roughly one-third of all primary schools failed to have the requisite number of teachers in 2015–2016 (Dwivedi 2018). Second, inadequate government expenditure reflected a lack of sufficient political interest in improving the quality of education for all students. Practices of patronage and politicization continue to plague the selection, promotion and transfer of staff (Aiyar 2018). Finally (summarizing Harriss 2017), a centralized bureaucratic paradigm granted teachers insufficient autonomy to experiment with how best to meet differential student needs and imposed rigid financial allocation mechanisms upon states and village education committees, while the creation of parallel "mission-oriented" structures generated confusion and worsened accountability. Many claimed the legalistic rules-based foundation of the RTE exacerbated this problem. Such a framework was more suitable for measuring inputs such as infrastructure provisioning or student–teacher ratios. Without deeper bureaucratic reforms, however, it encouraged mindless rule adherence and arguably impeded learning. In contrast, deliberative bureaucratic practices that empowered front-line officials, and encouraged parental involvement, enabled flexible problem-solving that produced greater accountability and better results (see Mangla 2015). Paradoxically, despite constituting a legal right and being part of a wider architectural project to enhance political accountability in social policy, the RTE lacked any mechanism to allow families to file grievances, impose penalties or seek remedies for poor school performance.

The Decline of India's Rights-Based Social Policies, 2014–2019

The victory of the BJP-led NDA in the 2014 general elections put the future of India's rights-based welfare Acts into question. The new prime minister, Narendra Modi, attacked the UPA for pursuing a "welfarist" agenda. Touting the slogan "minimum government, maximum governance," the party vowed to pursue greater private investment, infrastructural development and market reforms that would ostensibly lead to "empowerment" rather than "entitlement" (Panagariya 2016). Misgivings toward specific provisions of various rights-based measures had grown during the UPA. Their implementation was clearly mixed. Indeed, some observers had foreseen how the electoral benefits won by the UPA for enacting these laws would become a political liability as problems of implementation became evident (Mookherjee 2014). But the resounding electoral defeat of the UPA called into question their political sustainability.

In general, the NDA pursued a two-fold strategy. On the one hand, it championed Aadhaar, claiming its digital technology provided a platform to enhance social protection through direct cash transfers and new insurance schemes. The Pradhanmantri Jan Dhan Yojana (PMJDY) was a National Mission for Financial Inclusion to provide 150 million families with debit cards linked to Aadhaar-seeded bank accounts, reducing their vulnerability to informal money lenders. The JAM (Jan Dhan Yojana, Aadhaar and Mobile) Number Trinity programme converted many in-kind subsidies to cash transfers, lowering the scope of officials and middlemen to extort bribes. And a series of accident, life and health insurance schemes sought to provide greater economic security to informal sector workers. Proponents of the new welfare reforms praised its effort to improve ministerial coordination and policy coherence. They also believed Aadhaar would bolster administrative capacity and expenditure performance by improving social targeting and reducing financial corruption, while cash transfers would ensure greater choice in social provisioning (Asher 2017:8–10).

Yet targeting had well-known problems. Moreover, to access many social entitlements, beneficiaries now had to confirm their identities through Aadhaar biometric authentication. Despite widely publicized technical deficiencies and concerns regarding individual privacy and data security, the NDA rapidly expanded its use. Finally, none of these policies granted legal entitlement to their intended beneficiaries.

On the other hand, the NDA embraced the technocratic vision embodied by Aadhaar to undercut India's rights-based Acts. Attempts to legislate their demise proved unsuccessful. Social activists had presciently demanded their legislation to make such policy reversals harder. All of them, *de jure*, continue to operate. But all of them grew weaker de facto, in some cases crippled through budgetary constraints, rule amendments and executive neglect.

The NDA targeted mechanisms to promote transparency, community participation and social accountability in particular.

RTI

The NDA set its sights on the RTI given its centrality in India's rights-based welfare architecture. The government delayed appointing a new chief information commissioner. Thus, petitions concerning national political offices and government ministries could neither be submitted nor adjudicated. Similarly, many posts at the state level were left vacant. In addition, the government undermined the autonomy of the central information commission, delegating its financial powers to a government-appointed secretary (Rangan 2015). In 2017, the NDA issued new draft rules. Some required appellants to submit advance copies of all documents pertaining to their petition, as well as evidence of their submission. Others terminated any complaint upon the withdrawal of a petition or the death of a petitioner, heightening the likelihood that powerful interests would impose pressure, intimidation or worse (Bhatnagar 2017). The passage of the Right to Information (Amendment) Bill 2019, undermined the autonomy of the information commissions in New Delhi and in the states by allowing the government to set their terms of appointment and salary (PRS Legislative Research 2019). The NDA claimed that its greater proactive disclosure of information reduced the need for the RTI (*Indian Express* 2019). The Act survived. But these various measures strangulated its powers. The rate of rejected petitions and non-speaking orders and the backlog of cases rose significantly.

MGNREGA

In 2015, Prime Minister Modi called the MGNREGA a "living monument" to the Congress's historic failure to eliminate rural poverty, but vowed to keep it alive. Central budgetary allocations roughly doubled between 2014–2015 and 2018–2019. The release of funds was also consistently high (Kapur and Paul 2019:2). Some observers credited the NDA for improving the scheme: "geo-tagging" all physical assets built through the programme to improve transparency; transferring wages directly into newly created bank accounts to improve efficiency; and integrating the MGNREGA with other asset-creation schemes to encourage policy convergence. The proportion of wage pay orders made within the stipulated 15-day period increased from roughly 27 per cent in 2014–2015 to more than 80 per cent in 2018–2019 (Kapur and Paul 2019:4).

Yet the average number of days worked per household generally remained below 50 per year. Wage payments fell below stipulated minimum rates in the majority of states. The main reason was underfunding: New Delhi imposed caps on expenditure after its efforts to limit the programme to the country's poorest districts provoked resistance (Dreze 2017). The big increase in formal outlays masked real declines. The approved labour budget fell short of state governments' demands. Thus, pending liabilities, reflecting additional state-level expenditure owing to greater demand for work, rose significantly after 2014–2015. The vast majority of these liabilities comprised material costs in 2018–2019 (Kapur and Paul 2019:3). Last, the index used to adjust minimum wage rates for inflation was based on an outdated consumption basket (Nair 2017). Indeed, the government declared that MGNREGA wages should be held constant over time in real terms (Dreze 2017). The share of compensation paid to workers for either lack of work upon demand or unpaid wages declined from 93 per cent in 2014–2015 to 65 per cent in 2018–2019 (Kapur and Paul 2019:5).

Social activists petitioned the apex judiciary to intervene in 2016. The Supreme Court ordered state governments to disburse compensation for delayed wage payments, but in vain. Programme officers manipulated the management information system to reduce the number of days labourers claimed to be seeking work, thereby reducing the amount of compensation owed to them, while the amount of compensation itself, which the Act had set at a maximum of INR 3,000, was drastically lowered (Narayanan and Dhorajiwala 2017). These changes turned a demand-driven bottom-up right to work into a top-down supply-driven process, depriving labourers of their legal entitlement (Narayanan and Dhorajiwala 2017).

NFSA

The NDA adopted a similar approach toward the NFSA, restricting its coverage and accessibility. It appointed a high-level committee to consider reforms to the Food Corporation of India (FCI), the body in charge of procuring, storing and distributing subsidized foodgrains to ration shops. The committee recommended outsourcing the procurement and storage to private companies; limiting the NFSA to cover only 40 per cent of the population; and replacing the Public Distribution System (PDS) with direct cash transfers, to reduce "leakages," over the long run. Food security activists had proposed decentralizing the workings of the FCI, but they opposed reducing the scope and form of coverage provided by the NFSA (Jakobsen 2018:9–10). In 2015, New Delhi notified the states not to add new households to the Antyodaya Anna Yojana (which targeted the poorest households) after they dropped out of the programme, to use decadal census figures to determine the number of beneficiaries and to require proof of citizenship (Patnaik 2015). Similarly, the government used a pre-existing cash-based maternity programme, the Indira Gandhi Matritva Sahyog

Yojana, to deliver the INR 6,000 entitlement to all new mothers. Yet the programme had been set up for only 53 pilot districts. The NDA expanded its apparatus to 200 high-burden districts in 2015–2016 but failed to provide adequate funding. And it restricted the maternity entitlements guaranteed by the NFSA to the first two live births (see Puri 2017:12), violating the rights of women regarding family planning.

In the end, few states rolled out the NFSA within a year of its passage, as legally mandated (Puri 2017:11–13). The Act became fully operational after three years. Many state governments failed to complete, and the central government did not release, the Socio-Economic Caste Census, which provided the most accurate basis for identifying all eligible persons and households. In the interim, the NDA drastically cut funding for three NSFA-related programmes—Mid-Day Meals, Integrated Child Development Services and Maternity Benefit—given the recommendations of the Fourteenth Finance Commission to devolve 42 per cent of tax revenue to the states. It argued that states would pick up their share, set at 40 per cent of total expenditure, to make up the shortfall. Yet the constrained fiscal situation of many states, especially poorer regions with worse social development indicators, lowered spending on these programmes. Finally, the NDA required claimants to provide their Aadhaar card to purchase subsidized food grains. Thousands of individuals lost their entitlement to subsidized food grains due to errors of omission and poor connectivity, technological failures that critics of Aadhaar had foreseen (Dreze 2017). In 2018, the Supreme Court intervened, saying the government should not deny benefits to citizens lacking an Aadhaar card. But the apex judiciary upheld its general constitutionality for delivering welfare entitlements. In sum, the delays and partialities of implementation, a new fiscal compact between the New Delhi and the states, and the de facto imposition of Aadhaar undermined the universality of the NFSA.

RTE

The fate of the RTE under the NDA was more deleterious. The government promised to introduce a new National Education Policy, last introduced in 1992. It took three years to do so. Central budgetary allocations for education declined each year, falling below 4 per cent of total government expenditure after 2015–2016 (Roy Chowdhury 2019). The expenditure performance of the SSA, which remained the largest component of the newly integrated policy, remained sub-par. Indeed, it declined from 70 per cent of the total approved budget in 2015–2016 to 59 per cent by 2017–2018 (Bordoloi and Kapur 2019:4).

In 2017, the NDA amended the RTE, permitting states to hold exams in Classes 5 and 8, which children were to repeat if they failed. Proponents claimed the amendment would introduce necessary standards and teacher accountability. However, critics believed it undermined continuous evaluation and age-appropriate classes, would compel marginalized children to drop out and failed to tackle the reasons why public schools were failing (Mody 2019). In 2018, the government launched the Samagra Shiksha Abhiyan, integrating primary school education with pre-school and secondary education to improve resource allocation and policy coherence. Education activists had campaigned for a similar comprehensive approach in the RTE. Yet the severe budgetary cuts to primary education by New Delhi raised obvious questions about the viability of the new policy framework. Learning outcomes for primary school students remained very poor in the country at large.

LARRA

Last, the NDA sought to amend the LARRA to enable rapid land acquisition for infrastructure and industrial development. In 2014, it passed an ordinance that exempted claims of eminent domain for industrial corridors, social and rural infrastructure and national defence from social impact assessments, lowered the consent threshold of all stakeholders and expanded the definition of public purpose to cover various private entities. It also annulled various provisions that protected the rights of dispossessed landholders (Rajalakshmi 2015). Lacking a majority in the upper house of parliament and facing internal dissension, the NDA let the ordinance lapse, devolving the matter to the states. Many targeted provisions of LARRA that required state officials to earn widespread consent and conduct social impact assessments before claiming eminent domain, and generous terms of rehabilitation and resettlement. Social activists petitioned the apex judiciary in 2018 to intervene. In 2020, the Supreme Court ruled that states had five years to compensate landowners and take possession of land acquired through compulsory acquisition. Yet landowners then had to accept compensation (Das Gupta 2020), legalizing social dispossession rather than preventing it, as some foresaw (see Nielsen and Nilsen 2015).

The Performance of India's Welfare Regime During the COVID-19 Pandemic

The NDA won a larger parliamentary majority in India's 2019 general election. Declining economic growth and rising absolute poverty (Subramanian 2019) failed to damage its fortunes. A focus on political leadership and national security, and the government's effective delivery of various social goods, from toilets, housing and bank accounts to power connections and cooking gas cylinders, paid electoral dividends. The BJP had previously decried such populist measures, but the subsidized public distribution of essential private goods, branded as prime ministerial largesse, represented its new welfare model (Anand, Dimble and Subramanian 2020). It galvanized the government to advance its technocratic welfare model at the expense of rights-based social policies.

The COVID-19 pandemic exposed the limitations of the former and significance of the latter. The NDA government imposed the most severe lockdown in the world during the first wave. It established the Prime Minister's Citizen Assistance and Relief in Emergency Situations (PM-CARES) Fund. And it announced new measures under the Pradhan Mantri Garib Kalyan Yojana (PMGKY, Prime Minister's Welfare Scheme for the Poor): free provision of an additional 5 kg of wheat/rice and 1 kg of pulses per family, covering roughly 800 million individuals, and free cooking gas cylinders to families below the poverty line; a 10 per cent increase in MGNREGA daily wages as well as cash transfers ranging from IND 1,000 to IND 2,000 for senior citizens, widows and the disabled, women and farmers; and medical insurance coverage worth IND 5 million for health care workers. All these measures were to be disbursed within three months (Venkataramakrishnan 2020).

An estimated 30 million seasonal urban migrants, completely dependent on daily wages in the informal labour market and given four hours' notice, however, were forced to undertake a perilous journey to their rural homes (Harriss 2020). Exhaustion, hunger and accidents took many lives. Cast as objects of charity, their plight exposed their lack of rights (Hensman 2020).

The relief measures, moreover, proved severely inadequate. The PMGKY largely accelerated the disbursement of pre-budgeted expenditures. Moreover, only beneficiaries registered in the PDS could receive additional rations. Stranded migrant workers and unregistered families comprised more than 100 million individuals. State governments could not grant new cards because the NFSA had pre-set ratios based on the 2011 census (Agarwal 2020a). Finally, the PMGKY was poorly implemented. Roughly 145 million eligible beneficiaries did not receive their additional 5 kg of grain (Agarwal 2020b). And direct cash transfers revealed clear drawbacks. Less than half of roughly 325 million poor women received their entitlement of IND 500 per month because they lacked a Jan Dhan bank account (Pande et al 2020). Of the latter, almost 40 per cent could not access these funds owing to authentication failures (Raghavan and Shah 2020).

Efforts to uncover the process of decision making ignited resistance. The prime minister's office rebuffed petitions by rights activists to clarify how PM-CARES funds were being spent, saying it did not fall under the purview of the RTI, and that such petitions were a distraction amid the pandemic, citing a controversial Supreme Court judgment (Mishra 2020).

Given mounting distress, the NDA changed the eligibility rules of the PDS to cover 80 million migrants, promising to issue a "One Nation, One Ration" card within 10 months to make food entitlements portable, and then extended free additional rations until the end of 2020. But it resisted universalizing the NFSA, as rights activists proposed, to eliminate errors of exclusion (Khera 2020). Similarly, the government allocated an additional IND 40,000 crores to the MGNREGA, to generate 300 million days of work in total. Rights activists proposed to double the number of workdays to 200 per year and give all migrants temporary job cards proactively (PTI 2020).

The first wave of the pandemic peaked in September 2020, with the official number of cases and deaths reaching almost 100,000 and 1,000 per day, respectively, making India one of the three worst-hit countries in the world. Approximately 140 million workers lost their jobs (Kazmin 2020). The MGNREGA had provided a crucial safety net through the first wave. Yet the demand for work consumed almost half of the annual budget within the first third of the fiscal year (*Deccan Herald* 2020). By January 2021, funds for labour were almost spent. The NDA refused to invoke an emergency provision in the Act to allow 150 work days per year (Dey 2021). Despite mounting food stocks and persistently high levels of malnutrition and stunting, the government proposed to reduce the coverage of the NFSA (Himanshu 2021).

As the first wave subsided, New Delhi declared that India had defeated the pandemic, allowing daily life and mass gatherings to resume. But its national vaccination drive had only just begun. The result was a catastrophic second wave, setting new global records for infections and deaths per day, which hit the urban middle classes to a greater extent. The actual toll, given the exponential spread of new variants, poor surveillance capacity and suppression of information, was many orders of magnitude worse.

Conclusion

The three major innovations that distinguished India's new social welfare architecture drew praise. Yet each raised critical questions.

First, how radical were these rights-based demands? Some observers stressed that highly educated urban middle classes, with relatively privileged access to official state power, led many of these campaigns. A key demand of many Acts, to improve the transparency of the state, fit easily with a neoliberal understanding of good governance in the 1990s (Sharma 2015). Others contended that few of these rights campaigns envisioned a fundamental restructuring of political institutions and social relations (Chandhoke 2007:186). For proponents of radical social transformation, the introduction of India's rights-based welfare architecture was an attempt to legitimize deeper capitalist accumulation: "'progressive social policies'

... are more likely to result in poverty management than in social alliances creating structural change" (Shah and Lerche 2015:36).

To be sure, many of India's rights-based campaigns resembled progressive lobby groups, comprising local non-governmental organizations and advocacy networks, which engineered a countermovement against liberalization from above rather than below (Harriss 2011:11). Their political ascendance at the start of the twenty-first century reflected the relative decline of mass grassroots movements demanding radical social change (Nilsen 2018:655).

Nonetheless, most of the preceding criticisms represented the disappointment of progressive voices, hoping these new rights might be more transformational. And the claim that India's rights-based social policy represents an attempt to legitimize greater capital accumulation and social dispossession is perhaps too neat. The pursuit of "[economic] reforms with a human face" revealed the "curious political weakness" of capitalist forces (Gopalakrishnan 2017:73). The meaning, scope and ramifications of particular rights claims, even when narrowly articulated in specific Acts, were rarely stable and final. They often contained fundamental ambiguities that could be radicalized through social mobilization (Nilsen 2018:663).

Second, were these new social rights comprehensive or residual? They inevitably varied. Some were targeted, others were universal. Yet these standard terms of categorizing social policies obscure important complexities.

The RTI was universal in scope. Yet the Act excluded public–private partnerships, which had expanded greatly in India, from its purview at the start. Similarly, the RTE obliged the state to ensure that all children completed primary schooling, directing private schools to reserve 25 per cent of their spaces for disadvantaged children. However, it failed to encompass children in pre-school and secondary education. The MGNREGA limited the provision of work to 100 days per year. Granting poor households the right to demand hard physical work might be construed as workfare. Unlike traditional vertical mechanisms of selecting beneficiaries, however, the MGNREGA introduced a form of self-targeting, seeking to empower citizens to demand work. Consequently, it lessened the possibility that errors of exclusion would penalize families in distress (Manor and Jenkins 2017). The final version of the NFSA abandoned its original universal aspirations. The use of a fixed predetermined formula to allocate subsidized food grains to specific population ratios maintained an apparatus of targeting with a residual character (see Jakobsen 2018). Nonetheless, the Act expanded coverage, which since the late 1990s had been restricted to individuals below the official poverty line (Puri 2017:7). Put differently, both the MGNREGA and NFSA provided a residual safety net for vulnerable rural workers and poor households facing the constant threat of severe deprivation. Yet the self-targeting principle of the former was far superior to the predetermined non-universal coverage of the latter.

Finally, did the elaborately detailed provisions of these rights-based Acts empower relatively marginalized citizens? On the one hand, the establishment of explicit norms, rules and procedures created measurable performance criteria in many policy domains and sought to limit the scope for arbitrary clientelist practices. It also created minimum national standards, an important norm of equal citizenship given the wide disparities in social development that marked India's federal political economy. The failure of local public officials to deliver entitlements as prescribed by social welfare programmes could encourage greater claim-making by citizens in their encounters with the state (Kruks-Wisner 2018).

On the other hand, though, highly detailed laws could also compel relatively poor citizens to learn, adopt and master the language and logic of governmentality (Webb 2013). They also exacerbated the proliferation of paperwork that bedevilled local bureaucratic administration. Explicit transparency protocols to reduce corruption could, paradoxically, hobble programme implementation (Mathur 2016). The uniform, input-driven, rule-bound design of some programmes, imposed from above, could make it difficult for states to be more creative in expanding social welfare. This was particularly true for services that required multiple interactions and great discretion (Aiyar 2019). Such complex tasks required giving front-line officials and service providers greater autonomy, and reforming the incentives and culture of bureaucracy to be more participatory, deliberative and responsive to genuine local needs (Mangla 2015).

Indeed, the legal entitlements and public accountability measures that distinguished the RTI, MGNREGA and LARRA proved difficult to enforce. The RTE improved infrastructural amenities and teacher–student ratios at many schools. But its uniform, input-driven, rule-bound design proved counterproductive for student learning. The reasons for these varied outcomes ranged from poor legislation and inadequate political mobilization to limited state capacity and a persistent mistrust in state–society relations. Yet the absence of such governance mechanisms in the RTE and NFSA made it harder formally to redress grievances.

Ultimately, the economic security and social opportunities provided by these Acts improved the lives of many poor citizens. Specific flaws in their design as well as implementation limited their potential. Yet the struggle to legislate these rights at the start, and contestation over their implementation over time, testifies to their genuinely reformist character. The concerted attempt by opponents of India's rights-based social welfare Acts to formally amend and practically stymie these Acts underscores how they destabilized traditional power structures in state and society. The technocratic model of social welfare pushed in recent years, dispensed as charity rather than entitlement, has gained popular electoral consent and offered some important benefits. Yet it fails to satisfy many pressing welfare needs. The retention of many rights-based Acts in India underscores their continuing significance.

References

Aga, Aniket. 2015. "The Supreme Court Still Adamantly Refuses to Yield to RTI." *The Wire*, 3 September. Accessed 29 June 2022. https://thewire. in/law/the-supreme-court-still-adamantly-refuses-to-yield-to-rti.

Agarwal, Kabir. 2020a. "As Hunger Grows, the Fear of Starvation Is Real." *The Wire*, 16 April. Accessed 29 June 2022. https://thewire.in/rights/ covid-19-100-million-hunger-pds-universal.

Agarwal, Kabir. 2020b. "144 Million Ration Card Holders Not Provided Grain in May." *The Wire*, 4 June. Accessed 29 June 2022. https://thewire.in/rights/ pm-garib-kalyan-144-million-ration-card-holders-not-provided-grain-in-may.

Aiyar, Yamini. 2019. "Solutions When the 'Solution' Is the Problem." *Seminar*, #713 (January). Accessed 29 June 2022. https://www.india-semi nar.com/2019/713/713_yamini_aiyar.htm.

Aiyar, Yamini. 2018. "The Politicization of Transfers Has Undermined Teacher Accountability." *Hindustan Times*, 10 July. Accessed 29 June 2022. https://www.hindustantimes.com/columns/the-politicisation-of-transf ers-has-undermined-teacher-accountability/story-y7YUwcECJK00Niu TcVBONN.html.

Anand, Abhishek, Vikas Dimble and Arvind Subramanian. 2020. "New Welfarism of Modi Govt Represents Distinctive Approach to Redistribution and Inclusion." *The Indian Express*, 22 December. Accessed 30 June 2023. https://indianexpress.com/article/opinion/columns/national-family-hea lth-survey-new-welfarism-of-indias-right-7114104/.

Asher, Mukul. 2017. "An Analysis of Post-2014 Social Protection Initiatives in India." Lee Kuan Yew School of Public Policy, National University of Singapore, Working Paper No. 17–12:1–13.

Bhardwaj, Anjali, Amrita Johri and Shekhar Singh. 2015. "R Stands for … ." *Outlook*, 30 March. Accessed 25 July 2022. https://magazine.outlookin dia.com/story/amp/r-stands-for/293775.

Bhatnagar, Gaurav Vivek. 2017. "New Draft RTI Rules Could Mean Greater Threats for Applicants." *The Wire*, 3 April. Accessed 25 July 2022. https:// thewire.in/government/rti-draft-rules-threats.

Bordoloi, Mridusmrita and Avani Kapur. 2019. "Samagra Shiksha, GoI, 2019–20." *Accountability Initiative Budget Briefs*, 11(1):1–10. New Delhi: Centre for Policy Research.

Chandhoke, Neera. 2007. "Democracy and Well-being in India." In *Democracy and Social Policy*, edited by Yusuf Bangura, 164–188. New York: Palgrave Macmillan.

Chopra, D. 2011. "Policy Making in India: A Dynamic Process of Statecraft." *Pacific Affairs*, 84(1):89–107.

Corbridge, Stuart, Glyn Williams, Manoj Srivastava and Rene Veron. 2005. *Seeing the State: Governance and Governmentality in Rural India.* Cambridge: Cambridge University Press.

Das Gupta, Moushumi. 2020. "Let States Do It." *The Print*, 18 May. Accessed 29 June 2022. https://theprint.in/india/governance/let-states-do-it-modi-govt-could-take-same-route-for-land-reforms-like-it-did-for-labour/423536/.

De, A., J. Dreze, M. Samson and A. K. Shiva Kumar. 2019. "Struggling to Learn." *The Hindu*, 18 February. Reprinted in Jean Dreze, *Sense and Sensibility: Jholawala Economics for Everyone.* New Delhi: Oxford University Press.

Deccan Herald. 2020. "45% MGNREGA Fund Spent in 4 Months of Covid-19 Lockdown." Accessed 29 June 2022. https://www.deccanherald.com/national/45-mgnrega-fund-spent-in-4-months-of-covid-19-lockdown-871644.html.

Dey, Nikhil. 2021. "Budget 2021 Is a Chance to Undo the COVID-induced Inequality That Has Surged Across India." *The Wire*, 26 January. Accessed 29 June 2022. https://thewire.in/economy/budget-2021-labour-employment-nrega.

Dreze, Jean. 2017. "Modi Government Gives Shock Treatment to Social Policy." NDTV, 11 September. Accessed 29 June 2022. https://www.ndtv.com/opinion/modi-government-gives-shock-treatment-to-social-policy-1747767.

Dwivedi, Maninder Kaur. 2018. "The ABC of RTE." *The Hindu*, 12 January. Accessed 25 July 2022. https://www.thehindu.com/opinion/op-ed/the-abc-of-the-rte/article22422870.ece.

Ghosh, Jayati. 2004. "Social Policy in Indian Development." In *Social Policy in a Development Context*, edited by Thandika Mkandawire, 284–307. London: Palgrave Macmillan.

Gopalakrishnan, S. 2017. "The Forest Rights Act–Political Economy of 'Environmental' Questions." *Economic & Political Weekly*, 52(31):71–76.

Harriss, John. 2020. "'Responding to an Epidemic Requires a Compassionate State': How Has the Indian State Been Doing in the Time of COVID-19?" *Journal of Asian Studies*, 79(3):609–620.

Harriss, John. 2017. *Universalizing Elementary Education in India: Achievements and Challenges.* UNRISD Working Paper No. 2017–3, February. Geneva: United Nations Research Institute for Social Development.

Harriss, John. 2011. "How Far Have India's Social Reforms Been 'Guided by Compassion and Justice?'" In *Understanding India's New Political Economy*, edited by Sanjay Ruparelia, Sanjay Reddy, John Harriss and Stuart Corbridge, 127–140. New York: Routledge.

Hensman, Rohini. 2020. "The COVID-19 Lockdown in India: A Predictable Catastrophe for Informal Labour," *Global Labour Journal*, 11(3).

Himanshu. 2021. "Let's Strengthen and Not Dilute the National Food Security Act." *Livemint*, 25 March. Accessed 29 June 2022. https://www.livemint.com/opinion/columns/lets-strengthen-and-not-dilute-the-national-food-security-act-11616687800051.html.

Hindu, The. 2012. "Power of RTI." 5 November. Accessed 25 July 2022. https://www.thehindu.com/opinion/editorial/The-power-of-RTI/article12496098.ece.

Indian Express. 2019. "Less RTI Use Shows Modi Govt More Open." 13 October. Accessed 29 June 2022. https://indianexpress.com/article/india/amit-shah-right-to-information-rti-modi-government-6066475/.

Jakobsen, Jostein. 2018. "Neoliberalising the Food Regime 'Amongst Its Others': The Right to Food and the State in India." *Journal of Peasant Studies*, 46(6):1–21.

Jayal, Niraja Gopal. 2013. *Citizenship and its Discontents: An Indian History*. New Delhi: Permanent Black.

Jenkins, Rob. 2013. "Land, Rights and Reform in India." *Pacific Affairs*, 86(3):591–612.

Kapur, Avani and Meghna Paul. 2019. "Mahatma Gandhi National Rural Employment Guarantee Scheme (MGNREGS), GoI, 2019–2020." *Accountability Initiative Budget Briefs*, 11(10). New Delhi: Centre for Policy Research.

Kapur, Avani and Smriti Iyer. 2016. "Sarva Shiksha Abhiyan (SSA), GoI, 2015–2016." *Accountability Initiative Budget Briefs*, 7(1). New Delhi: Centre for Policy Research.

Kazmin, Amy. 2020. "India's Exporters Face Crunch as Coronavirus Pummels Economy." *Financial Times*, 8 April. Accessed 29 June 2022. https://www.ft.com/content/bbbfec9f-6880-4f7e-9d38-497f34788037.

Kazmin, Amy. 2015. "Learning a Hard Lesson." *Financial Times*, 8 May. Accessed 25 July 2022. https://www.ft.com/content/96c189a4-ef58-11e4-a6d2-00144feab7de.

Khera, Reetika. 2020. "Modi Government's 'One Nation, One Ration' Is an Attempt to Deflect Attention from Actual Solutions." *Scroll.in*, 17 June. Accessed 29 June 2022. https://scroll.in/article/964761/modi-governments-one-nation-one-ration-is-an-attempt-to-deflect-attention-from-actual-solutions.

Kruks-Wisner, Gabrielle. 2018. "The Pursuit of Social Welfare: Citizen Claim-making in Rural India." *World Politics*, 70(1):122–163.

Mangla, Akshay. 2015. "Bureaucratic Norms and State Capacity in India: Implementing Primary Education in the Himalayan Region." *Asian Survey*, 55(5): 882–908.

Manor, James. 2011. "Did the Central Government's Policy Initiatives Help to Re-elect It?" In New Dimensions of Politics in India, edited by Lawrence Saez and Gurharpul Singh, 13–25. London: Routledge.

Manor, James and Rob Jenkins. 2017. *Politics and the Right to Work: India's National Rural Employment Guarantee Act*. London: Hurst.

Mathur, Nayanika. 2016. *Paper Tiger: Law, Bureaucracy and the Developmental State in Himalayan India*. Cambridge: Cambridge University Press.

Mehta, Pratap Bhanu. 2010. "Public Advisory." *The Indian Express*, 6 April. Accessed 25 July 2022. https://indianexpress.com/article/opinion/colu mns/public-advisory/.

Mishra, Dheeraj. 2020. "PMO Refuses to Give Details on PM-CARES." *The Wire*, 30 April. Accessed 29 June 2022. https://thewire.in/governm ent/pmo-rti-pm-cares-supreme-court.

Mody, Anjali. 2019. "Scrapping of No-Detention Policy in Schools Is an Admission of Failure by the Modi Government." *Scroll.in*, 20 January. Accessed 29 June 2022. https://scroll.in/article/909881/scrapping-of-no-detention-pol icy-in-schools-is-an-admission-of-failure-by-the-modi-government.

Mookherjee, Dilip. 2014. "The Other Side of Populism." *Indian Express*, 3 May. Accessed 25 July 2022. https://indianexpress.com/article/opinion/ columns/the-other-side-of-populism/.

Nair, Shalini. 2017. "Ten Years of MGNREGA." *Indian Express*, 4 May. Accessed 25 July 2022. https://indianexpress.com/article/india/10-years-of-mgnrega-upa-flagship-chugs-along-with-implementation-refo rms-under-modi-govt-4639585/.

Narayan, Rajendran and Sakina Dhorajiwala. 2017. "A Guarantee, an Illusion." *Indian Express*, 14 February. Accessed 25 July 2022. https://indian express.com/article/opinion/columns/mgnrega-provisions-on-right-to-work-and-timely-wages-are-being-violated-4523324/.

Nielsen, Kenneth Bo and Alf Gunvald Nilsen. 2015. "Law Struggles and Hegemonic Processes in Neoliberal India: Gramscian Reflections on Land Acquisition Legislation." *Globalizations*, 12(2):203–216.

Nilsen, Alf Gunvald. 2018. "India's Turn to Rights-Based Legislation (2004–2014): A Critical Review of the Literature." *Social Change*, 48(4):653–665.

Panagariya, Arvind. 2016. "Taking Stock, Two Years On." *The Hindu*, 23 May. Accessed 25 July 2022. https://www.thehindu.com/opinion/lead/Soc ial-Programs-under-2-years-rule-of-Narendra-Modi/article62116357.ece.

Pande, Rohini, Simone Schaner, Charity Troyer Moore and Elena Stacy. 2020. "A Majority of India's Poor Women May Miss COVID-19 PMJDY Cash Transfers." Yale Economic Growth Center. Accessed 29 June 2022. https://egc.yale.edu/sites/default/files/COVID%20Brief.pdf.

Patnaik, Biraj. 2015. "Cutting the Food Act to the Bone." *The Hindu*, 24 June. Accessed 25 July 2022. https://www.thehindu.com/opinion/lead/ article62119795.ece.

PRS Legislative Research. 2019. "The Right to Information (Amendment) Bill, 2019." Accessed 29 June 2022. https://prsindia.org/billtrack/the-right-to-information-amendment-bill-2019.

PTI (Press Trust of India). 2020. "In Final Tranche of Economic Package, Govt Allocates Rs 40,000 cr More for MGNREGA." *Outlook*, 17 May. Accessed 29 June 2022. https://www.outlookindia.com/website/story/business-news-in-final-tranche-of-economic-package-govt-allocates-rs-40000-crore-more-for-mgnrega/352960.

Puri, Raghav. 2017. *India's National Food Security Act (NFSA): Early Experiences*. LANSA Working Paper No. 14. Institute of Development Studies, Sussex. Accessed 25 July 2022. https://ims.ids.ac.uk/sites/ims.ids.ac.uk/files/documents/NFSA-LWP.pdf.

RAAG (Research, Assessment and Analysis Group) and Satark Nagrik Sanghathan. 2017. *Tilting the Balance of Power: Adjudicating the RTI Act*. Accessed 25 July 2022. https://snsindia.org/wp-content/uploads/2017/07/Adjudicating-the-RTI-Act-2nd-edition-2017.pdf.

Raghavan, Malavika and Samir Shah. 2020. "Fix the Problems in Aadhaar-Based Cash Transfers." *Livemint*, 8 May. Accessed 29 June 2022. https://www.livemint.com/opinion/columns/fix-the-problems-in-aadhaar-based-cash-transactions-11588930862806.html.

Rajalakshmi, T. K. 2015. "Land Bill Hits a Wall." *Frontline*, 4 March. Accessed 25 July 2022. https://frontline.thehindu.com/the-nation/land-bill-hits-a-wall/article6951358.ece.

Rangan, Pavithra S. 2015. "When the Haze Takes Over." *Outlook*, 30 March. Accessed 25 July 2022. https://www.outlookindia.com/magazine/story/when-the-haze-takes-over/293766.

Roy, Indrajit. 2014. "Reserve Labor, Unreserved Politics: Dignified Encroachments under India's National Rural Employment Guarantee Act." *Journal of Peasant Studies*, 41(4):517–545.

Roy Chowdhury, Shreya. 2019. "What Have School Children Gained in the Last Five Years?" *Scroll.in*, 26 January. Accessed 29 June 2022. https://scroll.in/article/909667/the-modi-years-what-have-school-children-gained-in-the-last-five-years.

RTI Assessment and Advocacy Group and Samya-Centre for Equity Studies. 2014. "People's Monitoring of the RTI Regime in India, 2011–2013." Accessed 25 July 2022. https://snsindia.org/rti-assessments/#people.

Ruparelia, Sanjay. 2013. "India's New Rights Agenda: Genesis, Promises, Risks." *Pacific Affairs*, 86(3):569–590.

Shah, Alpa and Jens Lerche. 2015. "India's Democracy: Illusion of Inclusion." *Economic & Political Weekly*, 50(41):33–36.

Sharma, Prashant. 2015. *Democracy and Transparency in the Indian State: The Making of the Right to Information Act*. London: Routledge.

Subramanian, S. 2019. "What Is Happening to Rural Welfare, Poverty, and Inequality in India?" *India Forum*, 6 December. Accessed 29 June 2022. https://www.theindiaforum.in/article/what-happened-rural-welfare-poverty-and-inequality-india-between-2011-12-and-2017-18.

Venkataramakrishnan, Rohan. 2020. "Sitharaman's 'Quick Response' to Modi's Coronavirus Lockdown Is a Start." *Scroll.in*, 27 March. Accessed 29 June 2022. https://scroll.in/article/957392/sitharamans-quick-respo nse-to-modis-coronavirus-lockdown-is-a-start-but-much-more-is-needed.

Venkatesan, V. 2010. "Secrecy Around Bill." *Frontline*, 10 September 2010. Accessed 25 July 2022. https://frontline.thehindu.com/cover-story/arti cle30181628.ece.

Vijayabaskar, M. and Gayathri Balagopal. 2018. *Politics of Poverty Alleviation Strategies in India*. UNRISD Background Paper. Geneva: United Nations Research Institute for Social Development.

Webb, Martin. 2013. "Disciplining the Everyday State and Society? Anti-corruption and Right to Information Activism in Delhi." *Contributions to Indian Sociology*, 47(3):363–393.

Wood, Geof and Ian Gough. 2006. "A Comparative Welfare Regime Approach to Global Social Policy." *World Development*, 34(10):1696–1712.

7

Incorporating Informal Workers into Social Insurance in Tanzania

Roosa Lambin and Milla Nyyssölä

Introduction

Public social insurance is part of the broader social protection "toolbox," typically understood to comprise also social assistance measures (such as cash transfers, benefits in kind, fuel subsidies and so on), social services and public works (see, for example, Carter et al 2019). Until recently, formal insurance arrangements had attracted little attention as a policy instrument in the context of the global South, being limited to a small minority in formal employment. Instead, social protection for the informal sector has been largely sought through the introduction and expansion of parsimonious social assistance schemes targeting the poorest—such as the conditional cash transfer schemes promoted largely by the World Bank. There has since been a recognition that cash transfer programmes as "safety nets" remain insufficient in ensuring sustainable livelihoods or acting as a springboard out of poverty. Typically targeted, donor-driven and without institutional "guarantees," these social assistance schemes leave most people working in the informal sector without critical protections (Olivier 2019).

To foster sustainable and equitable social policy expansion and present an alternative to the social safety net approach, the International Labour Organization (ILO) initiated the *Social Protection Floors* agenda in 2012. The agenda promotes an ambitious and comprehensive policy package across four pillars.[1] The same year, the United Nations General Assembly endorsed a resolution prompting countries to press toward the provision of accessible, affordable and quality health care for all—in order to achieve Universal Health Coverage (UHC). Initially conceptualized by the World Health

---

[1] These include (i) access to essential health care, including maternity care; (ii) basic income security for children, providing access to nutrition, education, care and any other necessary goods and services; (iii) basic income security for persons in active age who are unable to earn sufficient income, in particular in cases of sickness, unemployment, maternity and disability; and (iv) basic income security for older persons. See https://www.ilo.org/dyn/normlex/en/f?p=NORMLEXPUB:12100:0::NO::P12100_INSTRUMENT_ID:3065524.

Organization, the UHC agenda has spurred the introduction of diverse health insurance arrangements to cover informal workers in the global South. It is noteworthy also that the World Bank Development Report "The Changing Nature of Work" from 2019 widely recognizes the challenges in protecting the large and persisting number of workers in the informal economy and proposes a state-subsidized universal social insurance as a complementary policy tool alongside social assistance programmes and increased formal sector employment (World Bank 2019a).

In a parallel motion with the shifting trend in social protection agendas at the supranational level, numerous countries of the global South have initiated new approaches to expand social insurance coverage among informal workers (see, UNDP 2021). This chapter takes a closer look at the case of Tanzania (excluding the semi-autonomous territory of Zanzibar), which has introduced pioneering legislative reforms in the realm of social protection and seeks to expand coverage further through several domestically led policy measures and plans (URT 2021a).

This chapter draws on a comprehensive review and analysis of diverse sources of material, comprising academic publications, policy and programme evaluations, government documents and plans, relevant media sources and quantitative datasets and indices. It builds on a series of research papers examining social policy trajectories in Tanzania in the new millennium, published by United Nations University World Institute for Development Economics Research (UNU-WIDER).[2] The chapter describes the characteristics of employment and social protection needs in the informal sector in the development context and examines the extant social protection framework in the Tanzanian context. More precisely, we will shed light on social insurance arrangements for the formal sector, key social assistance measures, and informal social insurance arrangements that have emerged at the kinship and community level. Importantly, the chapter also addresses the emergence of formal social insurance arrangements for informal sector workers through pioneering legislative reforms and constantly evolving insurance packages, together with the key successes and caveats of the evolving social insurance arrangements in the Tanzanian context. We conclude by drawing attention to the future of Tanzanian social policy expansion and its challenges.

Emergence of Social Insurance for Informal Workers in Sub-Saharan Africa

Sub-Saharan Africa represents the world region with the most significant informal economy—as much as 89 per cent of the total employment was

---

[2] See Lambin et al 2022a, 2022b; Lambin and Nyyssölä 2022.

in the informal sector before the COVID-19 pandemic (ILO 2018). The informal sector is highly heterogeneous in terms of represented sectors, income levels and work arrangements. It includes street vendors, domestic workers, agricultural workers and domestic workers among others. Around one-half (52 per cent) of the informal workforce in the region consists of self-employed "own-account workers," who do not have employees, while the others are employees without formal contracts (in formal or informal businesses or households) or contributors, often unpaid, to family businesses or farms (ILO 2018).

Chen (2012) underscores the stratification of the informal sector into various tiers, characterized by different levels of income, work quality and poverty risks. Informal work, particularly at the lowest levels, is afflicted by hazardous work environments, onerous work and irregular, unpredictable wages (RNSF 2017). Informal workers (including small-scale/subsistence farmers) are also more vulnerable to shocks, such as natural disasters and environmental issues, economic crises and conflicts. Additionally, they typically have restricted access to assets and markets with a low capacity to accumulate savings, rendering them particularly vulnerable to any type of shock (Olivier 2019; Rwegoshora 2014). As such, informal workers have exceptionally high and diverse social protection needs. Yet only 13 per cent of the population in sub-Saharan Africa are covered by some form of social protection measure such as social assistance as of 2020 (UNDESA 2021). Informal workers are particularly poorly covered, and especially women have limited access to any social protection. In 2019, only 3.9 per cent of women in Africa were covered by comprehensive social security arrangements,[3] compared with 10.8 per cent of men (ILO 2021a).

Furthermore, both internal and external labour market dynamics shape the size and type of the informal economy. A recent study by Danquah et al (2021), drawing on several sub-Saharan countries, shows that workers in the lower-tier segment are typically locked into low pay and poor working conditions owing to a lack of alternative employment opportunities. In Tanzania, over 80 per cent of those engaged in lower-tier informal self-employment or family farm work typically remain in this category or shift to even lower quality informal wage employment (while also some upward mobility shifts workers from the upper-tier segment toward formal employment) (Danquah et al 2021). At the same time, informal sector and casual work arrangements tend to expand as part of the overall economy in times of economic crises. For instance, the informal sector grew during

---

[3] Referring to legal social security coverage in eight areas (sickness, unemployment, old age, employment injury, child/family benefit, maternity, invalidity and survivors), as specified in the ILO Convention No. 102.

the Asian economic crisis in the 1990s. Informal employment arrangements have expanded further in the context of the 2008–2009 global financial crisis and, most recently, the SARS-CoV-2 pandemic (see, for example, Jütting and Laiglesia 2009; King and Sweetman 2010; Nguimkeu and Okou 2020; Stavropoulou and Jones 2013). The experience from the global South also shows that there is no direct causality between economic and social development and the growing formalization of the economy, as the informal economy persists as the dominant share of labour markets in diverse contexts (Lam and Elsayed 2021).

The existing diversity within the informal sector and the constant "flexing" of the informal economy in the changing global economic trends pose a series of questions for social protection expansion for informal workers. Do all workers have the same social protection needs? Can informal workers participate in contributory schemes, and on what basis? What measures are needed to provide adequate protection for those in the lowest quality informal work? Does informal work need to be formalized to expand access to social protection, and is this a realistic option?

The ILO has promoted the formalization of the informal sector as an avenue to expand the key social protections provided through formal social insurance schemes to informal workers.[4] However, there are caveats and limitations in the approach prioritizing the formalization of the informal sector. First, formal jobs do not always provide superior incomes and working conditions, and consequently, many workers—particularly in the development context—may have to work in the informal sector or combine both formal and informal jobs to secure livelihoods. Second, informal jobs, in some cases, offer greater flexibility and control over working times, location and other arrangements, facilitating workers' survival. Third, employers of informal workers, when facing the formalization pressure, may not be capable of offering legal benefits and protections to workers at the current levels of operation, which may reduce the number of jobs or lead to the relocalization of production sites (see Lam and Elsayed 2021; Rosaldo 2021). Fourth, formalization schemes often force informal workers relying on street trading to relocate their worksites. Without complementary schemes providing safe and viable workspaces, the formalization process can produce perverse outcomes such as unsatisfactory or commercially impractical working conditions (Hunt 2009; Rosaldo 2021). Fifth, social security arrangements for the formal sector do not fully account for the extant social protection needs of informal workers, which will not automatically diminish in the

---

[4] See, for example, the 2015 "Transition from the Informal to the Formal Economy" Recommendation 204; see https://www.ilo.org/dyn/normlex/en/f?p=NORMLEX PUB:12100:0::NO::P12100_ILO_CODE:R204.

formalization process. Sixth, formal jobs are difficult to access for many, and job seekers may have to bear significant costs upfront, such as expenses related to signalling through education/training or even direct bribing to get a job. As mentioned earlier, informal workers face important challenges of economic security (related to loss of assets, market access and risks, among others) (Sankaran 2012), not covered in most public social insurance systems. And finally, in the context of the global South, women typically combine reproductive and care roles with productive activities (Sabates-Wheeler and Kabeer 2003). This could leave women at the margins of the formalization process, without access to any social protection. Given the aforementioned challenges, many have promoted informal sector-focused social protection approaches.

While the debates concerning the future direction of social policy delivery for the informal sector are ongoing, several countries of the global South have increased access of informal workers to formal social insurance schemes that had evolved as contributory schemes in the context of industrialized economies characterized by nearly full (formal) employment, to act as a mechanism for income protection during adverse lifecycle events. Therefore, formal social insurance schemes typically provide protection for health care, sickness, old age, unemployment, employment injury, family and child support, maternity, disability, and widowhood and orphanhood (ILO 2017). In the context of sub-Saharan Africa, several governments have introduced legislative reforms in the pursuit of expanding informal sector coverage in the 2010s, and the following public sector-operated policy arrangements stand out (see Table 7.1). Additionally, social security legislation in several countries has been reformed to enable voluntary, contributory access to "traditional" social security provisions for the formal sector (ISSA 2019). Such approaches have also been promoted by the African Union's *Social Protection Plan for the Informal Economy and Rural Workers* (SPIREWORK), reflecting a novel trend in "world-regional" social policy in the African context (see Chapter 1, this volume). The remainder of this chapter examines the policy developments in Tanzania.

Social Protection in Tanzania

Social insurance for the formal sector

In recent years, Tanzania has strengthened its compulsory social insurance arrangements for those in formal employment. Formal employment refers to all those types of employment which offer a work contract with agreed wages and hours, which carry with them employment rights and on which income tax is paid. In the Tanzanian context, this means coverage of around 21 per cent of the total population (59.7 million), concentrated in urban areas (Danquah et al 2021).

Table 7.1: Examples of social insurance arrangements for the informal sector in sub-Saharan Africa

Country	Key legislative reforms	Introduced policy measures/programmes	Target populations	Benefit packages
Zambia	2019: Statutory Instrument No. 72 enabled the extension of formal social protection provision to informal workers through the National Pension Authority (NAPSA)	Social insurance provisions by the NAPSA were extended to informal workers in 2019	Formal and informal workers	Old-age pension, early retirement, invalidity and survivor's pension, maternity and family benefits, funeral grants
Togo	2012: Legislation allowing informal workers to access formal social security provision by the Caisse Nationale de Sécurité Sociale (National Social Security Fund—CNSS)	2014: MUCTAM, mutual for motorbike taxi drivers 2015: MUAJ, mutual for artists and journalists; MUAPE, mutual for agricultural workers, fishermen and livestock breeders; MUCAT, mutual for artisans and traders	Four different occupational groups within the informal economy	Health insurance, pension scheme, capacity building and training services, a loan scheme for productive inputs
Kenya	2011: Kenya national social protection policy. 2013: National Security Fund Act (no. 45) extends coverage to workers in the informal economy	2009: Mbao pension plan (a voluntary retirement savings scheme run privately by the Kenya National Federation of Jua Kali Associations) 2013: Provident fund for the self-employed	Informal workers (but universal access) Self-employed	Pension/savings scheme (contributions can be withdrawn after three years) Old-age benefit, survivor's benefit, invalidity benefit, migration benefit
Rwanda	2010 Law no. 45 merged the Social Security Fund of Rwanda and the Rwanda Health Insurance Fund into the Rwanda Social Security Board. This administers the Ejo Heza	December 2018: Ejo Heza (a brighter tomorrow) pension plan	Informal workers	Pensions, health insurance, life and funeral insurance, low-interest loans (depending on saving levels and Ubudehe-category defining the household income level)
Cameroon	2014: Decree no. 2014/23/77/PM set up the National Voluntary Social Security Scheme under the National Social Insurance Fund (Caisse Nationale de Protection Social, CNPS)	2014: National Voluntary Social Security Scheme	Workers in the informal sector and self-employed	Old age, invalidity and death

Source: authors' compilation using several sources (Beri 2018; DOSI nd; ISSA 2019; Masabo 2019; Miti et al 2021; Phe Goursat and Pellerano 2016; the Republic of Cameroon 1967); ILO NATLEX (https://www.ilo.org/dyn/natlex/natlex4.home?p_lang=en); ISSA country profiles (https://ww1.issa.int/country-profiles); the Republic of Cameroon index. php/fr/assure-e/assurance-volontaire/assurance-volontaire; https://ejoheza.gov.rw/ltss-registration-ui/landing.xhtml;jsessionid=358CC7156 2DE822BF6C87A1FB684E34F; https://www.nssf.or.ke/M; https://mbaopension.com/.

To begin with, the Public Service Social Security Fund Act of 2018[5] rearranged Tanzania's previously fragmented social insurance schemes into two large programmes: the *Public Service Social Security Fund* (PSSSF) represents the primary insurer for the country's almost 700,000 public servants, and the *National Social Security Fund* (NSSF; established in 1997 and operationalized in 2014) is for other workers with formal employment contracts (247,000 members in 2020, yet only 11,000 were active; Riisgaard et al 2022). These schemes contain provisions dictated by the Employment and Labour Relations Act (ELRA) 2004 (amended in 2017). These include 12 weeks of fully paid maternity leave (with three days of paternity leave), six months of unemployment benefits paid at a 33 per cent wage rate, old-age pensions, survivor's pensions and health insurance covering the enrolled individual as well as his or her household.

The legal basis of Tanzania's social insurance system fares well in regional comparison. While maternity protection is mainly in line with provisions in other countries in sub-Saharan Africa, the availability of unemployment benefits makes Tanzania stand out from other countries in the region (ILO 2021a)—even though access to the benefit necessitates a minimum of 18 months of contributions and the replacement rate remains fairly low. Another important addition to Tanzania's social insurance system is the establishment of the *Workers' Compensation Fund* in 2015/2016, providing mandatory protection against work-related injury, disability and death. This represents a progressive step in the African context, where a high proportion of legal arrangements for employment injury consists of voluntary coverage (meaning that employers can compensate employees directly or buy private insurance) (ILO 2021a). Moreover, from the perspective of informal workers, one noteworthy specificity of the legal provisions introduced by the 2004 ELRA is the inclusion of domestic servants[6] in the legislation, despite them being typically considered informal workers.

Development of social assistance for informal workers

Informal workers make a significant contribution to the Tanzanian economy; 47 per cent of the gross domestic product is produced within the informal economy (Medina and Schneider 2019). Unsurprisingly, the share of

---

[5] Available at: https://www.ilo.org/dyn/natlex/natlex4.detail?p_lang=en&p_isn=109618&p_count=2&p_classification=22.10.

[6] Defined as "any person employed wholly or partially as a cook, house servant, waiter, butler, maidservant, valet, bar attendant, groom, gardener, washman or watchman" in the Regulation of Wages and Terms of Employment Order of 2010 (Mainland Tanzania) (see ILO 2014).

informal employment in total employment reached almost 80 per cent in 2014 (Danquah et al 2021).[7] However, regional, sectoral and demographic differences exist. According to ILO (2018), nearly all employment in rural areas is informal (97 per cent) and 78 per cent of total urban employment is informal. The largest sectors within the informal economy include the wholesale and retail trade (accounting for 48 per cent of informal employment), followed by accommodation and food services (15 per cent), manufacturing (10 per cent), construction (6 per cent) and transportation (6 per cent) (ILO 2018). Moreover, 93 per cent of women work in the informal economy compared with 88 per cent of men (ILO 2018).

The most important social assistance scheme offering social protection for informal workers in the Tanzanian context is the *Productive Social Safety Net* (PSSN) programme. The World Bank-backed PSSN was initially launched in 2012 and has secured external funding until 2024. Supporting around 1.29 million households in 2020 (World Bank 2022), the PSSN is the only scheme providing cash transfers for impoverished households in the country.[8] It includes several other subprogrammes such as Public Works (PW), Livelihoods Enhancement (LE) and Savings Groups (SG). The PSSN is operated by the *Tanzania Social Action Fund* (TASAF), a domestic government body established in 2000 to support communities' different needs through diverse service delivery structures.

From the perspective of informal workers, the programme is a significant source of direct income support and increased savings opportunities. It provides households with up to TZS 38,000 (USD 18) per month (de Hoop et al 2020). Those with children are entitled to conditional cash transfers with a variable rate depending on the children's ages to encourage older children's school attendance through a higher financial incentive. These transfers and potential savings represent important cushioning for informal workers against potential climate and economic shocks. At the same time, the PW component acts as a type of "unemployment protection," by providing work for one adult per household during the annual lean season. Work is provided for 15 days a month for four months and has attracted particularly women, who represented 85 per cent of enrollees in 2019 (World Bank 2020). The PW component also accommodates women's needs by offering lighter tasks and flexible working arrangements for pregnant or lactating women. Crucially, while those with children under two years of age are not allowed to participate, households are permitted to assign another able-bodied adult from the household to participate in the works,

---

[7] The rate differs depending on the definition between 80 and 90 per cent.

[8] Other much smaller social assistance schemes in Tanzania include school feeding and transportation programmes and nutritional interventions (see, for example, Ajwad et al 2018).

and if no such person is available, women continue to receive salaries as usual (World Bank 2019b).

Nevertheless, the PSSN lacks many of the provisions provided by the formal sector social insurance schemes described earlier. Unlike social insurance under the NSSF, PSSSF or the Workers Compensation Fund (WCF), the programme's future remains volatile depending on political will and external funding. Moreover, the programme remains targeted at the "most vulnerable" and leaves the majority of the country's informal workers uncovered. Additionally, not all programme components are implemented across the 161 Project Area Authorities (PAAs; districts, towns, municipalities and city councils), as the PW was implemented only in 44 PAAs, and the LE component in eight PAAs in 2019 (World Bank 2020).

Emergence of organized informal social security systems

Across the sub-Saharan African region, numerous types of social security schemes that are "self-organized" or "structured by social relations"— commonly referred to as "informal social security arrangements"—respond to the social protection needs in the informal sector (Razavi and Staab 2018). Some of the common (and earliest forms of social insurance) arrangements include transfers through kinship networks and diaspora. Also, more organized contribution-based insurance systems have proliferated, such as rotational savings groups, community-based banking schemes and insurance provided by informal workers' associations (see Mumtaz 2022).

In many contexts, informal social security remains completely outside of any government regulation and monitoring. In others, previously fully informal arrangements are being incorporated into legislative instruments. In Tanzania, for instance, the 2018 Microfinance Act introduced an innovative, tiered system to regulate community-based banking and other informal financing services offering mechanisms for social protection against economic insecurity. This contributes to strengthening the social security of informal workers, since the evidence shows that village community banking (VICOBA), Rotating Savings and Credit Associations, and Saving Associations and Credit Co-operative Societies (SACCOS) are a significant and growing source of loans, savings and even some forms of social insurance in the event of death or health issues for informal workers in the Tanzanian context (see, for example, Andrew et al 2018; Shau 2022).

Furthermore, informal workers' associations have organized more comprehensive, "unregulated" social insurance systems to offer protection against health issues and death in the near family, by providing access to loans (Riisgaard 2020; see also Torm 2020). In some particularly hazardous professions, such as transportation and construction, workers' associations have become a significant source of organized social insurance against accidents, sickness and disability. They also provide loans for productive assets, among others (Gervas 2022; Kinyondo 2022). It is noteworthy that some associations are exclusively catering for women, and female petty traders, in particular, have sought to access social insurance through informal social insurance arrangements (Riisgaard 2020).

Interestingly, informal social protection arrangements are not only a complementary informal safety net in the context of weak social protection provisions for informal workers but compete with state-provided contributory schemes. Masanyiwa et al (2020) find that SACCOS and VICOBA represent popular social security systems among informal workers in the capital region, and highlight the limited payment capacity and awareness of informal workers hindering enrolment to formal schemes. Also Torm et al (2021b) report that in the context of Tanzania, workers may shift from public sector schemes to unregulated social insurance arrangements provided by informal workers' associations, if the benefits level and policy design are perceived as less attractive for the set level of contributions. However, access to social insurance provided by associations may be restricted to workers who are unable to cover potential association entry fees and regular insurance contributions (Riisgaard 2020).

Besides the increasingly organized informal social insurance arrangements, financial support and benefits in kind received from the broader family and community remain a typical form of social protection in Tanzania. In 2020 alone, remittances from the Tanzanian diaspora reportedly amounted to USD 189.13 million.[9] However, informal transfers are typically characterized by unbalanced power relationships while being easily affected by the changing financial situation within the kinship system. For women who are particularly dependent on outside support for access to cash, housing and childcare, their access may be often conditioned to their status as mothers or wives (Hassim and Razavi 2006). This overview of the extant formal and informal social protection arrangements highlights the progress and gaps in social protection arrangements, particularly from the perspective of informal workers.

Incorporating Informal Workers into Social Insurance in Tanzania

Innovative reforms to social protection law

The National Social Security Act of 1997 in Tanzania represented the first Social Security Law reform in Africa enabling access to formal social insurance for informal workers. The Act allowed the enrolment of

---

[9] See https://www.ippmedia.com/en/news/tanzanians-diaspora-contributed-18913mill ion-country-2020.

self-employed persons in the NSSF (Masabo 2019). However, it was the 2008 Social Security (Regulatory Agency) Act that denoted a clear legislative change in favour of all informal workers, mandating the labour minister to introduce regulations extending social insurance access to all citizens operating in the informal economy. This represented a pioneering reform in the region by referring to "workers" instead of "employees," to legally cover those who were not in a formal employment relationship (Masabo 2019; Olivier 2019). These developments were followed by reforms in the Social Security Law in 2012, which was extended to "apply to any person employed in the formal or informal sector or self-employed within mainland Tanzania" (The Social Security Laws (Amendments) Act 2012). The legal framework was developed further in 2017 when the NSSF was mandated to develop separate social insurance products for informal workers (see Figure 7.1 for an overview of policy developments).

Despite the significant legislative progress, it is noteworthy that the legal system does not require the NSSF or any other government body to offer social insurance access to informal workers. At the same time, the 2004 ELRA, which was significant in improving the job quality and social protection for workers in Tanzania, makes no specific mention of informal workers (except for domestic servants). Further institutionalization is required for informal workers to access social insurance as a citizen right.

The beginnings of social insurance for informal workers: the Voluntary Savings Retirement Scheme (VSRS, 2009–2018)

Launched in 2009, the Voluntary Savings Retirement Scheme (VSRS) represented one of the first attempts to provide a specific social insurance product to informal workers in Tanzania, and the sub-Saharan African region. Following the study of the needs of farmers, small traders and more generally self-employed persons, the Government Employees Provident Fund (GEPF, since replaced by the PSSSF) developed the VSRS as a pilot project providing pension coverage to all Tanzanians including informal employees, self-employed persons, farmers, fishermen, drivers, petty traders and food vendors. In addition, organized groups such as VIBINDO (the umbrella organization for small producer and business associations), and SACCOS were covered (Ackson and Masabo 2013).

The scheme's main innovations were the existence of two accounts (one for meeting short-term needs such as health care expenses, and one for financing retirement) and the highly flexible contribution system. Members could make contributions on a monthly, weekly or daily basis depending on their ability to pay. Furthermore, contributing was made easier by using mobile phone payments (GEPF nd; Masabo 2019; Riisgaard et al 2022). However, after the 2018 reform and cessation of the GEPF, the VSRS was

Figure 7.1: Main legislative reforms and formal insurance arrangements (1995 onwards)

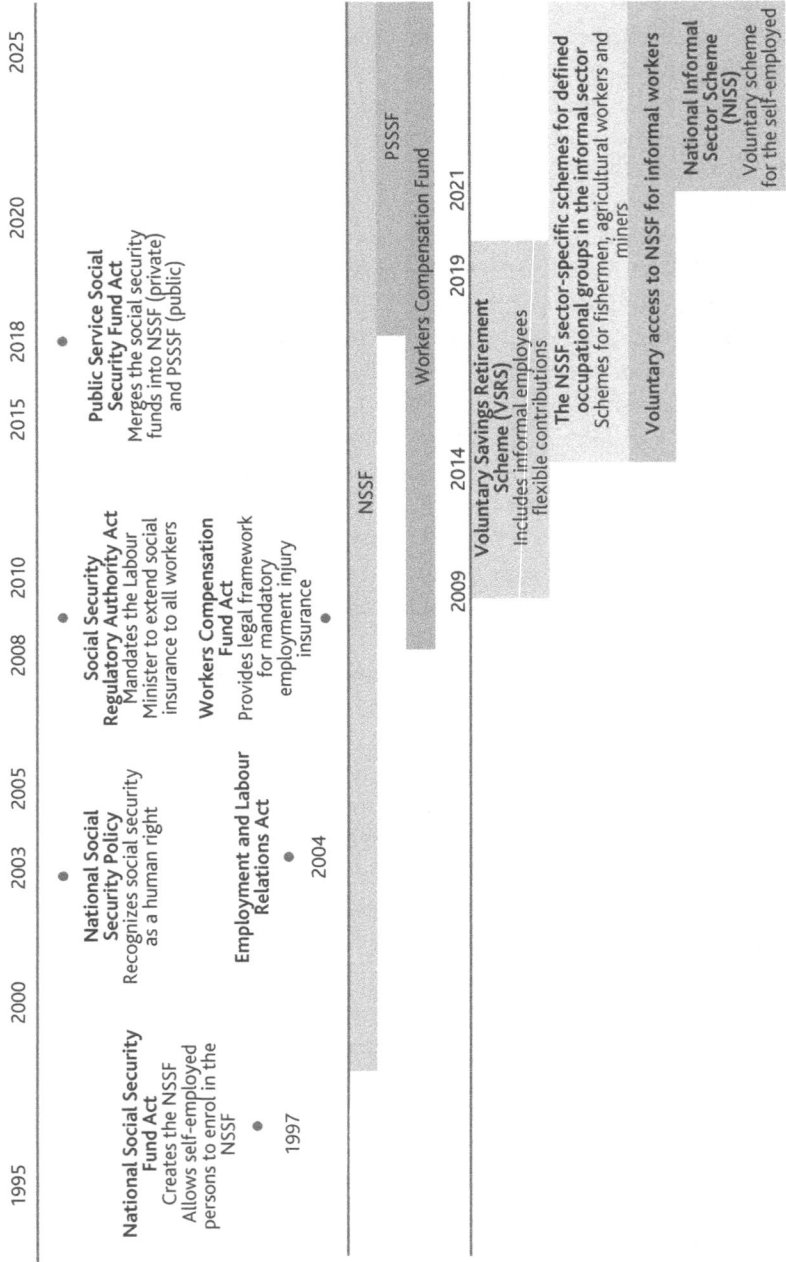

1995 2000 2003 2005 2008 2010 2015 2018 2020 2025

National Social Security Fund Act
Creates the NSSF
Allows self-employed persons to enrol in the NSSF
1997

National Social Security Policy
Recognizes social security as a human right

Employment and Labour Relations Act
2004

Social Security Regulatory Authority Act
Mandates the Labour Minister to extend social insurance to all workers

Workers Compensation Fund Act
Provides legal framework for mandatory employment injury insurance

Public Service Social Security Fund Act
Merges the social security funds into NSSF (private) and PSSSF (public)

NSSF

PSSSF

Workers Compensation Fund

2009 2014 2019 2021

Voluntary Savings Retirement Scheme (VSRS)
Includes informal employees flexible contributions

The NSSF sector-specific schemes for defined occupational groups in the informal sector
Schemes for fishermen, agricultural workers and miners

Voluntary access to NSSF for informal workers

National Informal Sector Scheme (NISS)
Voluntary scheme for the self-employed

Source: authors' compilation

172

ended following the policy plans for the National Informal Sector Scheme, discussed further in the text that follows.

Expanding social insurance: the NSSF sector-specific schemes (2014–present)

In 2014—six years after the 2008 reform—the NSSF introduced voluntary access (based on contribution) of informal workers to its social insurance scheme previously catering only to formal sector employees. However, accessing actual benefits is challenged by irregular and uncertain incomes among informal workers. Stringent contribution conditions (a minimum of three years of contributions, for instance) limit access to maternity and unemployment benefits, among others. To encourage continued membership among informal workers, the NSSF provides additional benefits upon satisfactory contributions on a yearly basis. This consists of a practical asset depending on the member's profession, such as cooking utensils for food vendors, or tyres for *boda boda* (motorbike taxi) drivers (Torm et al 2021b) (see Table 7.2 for an overview of current social insurance schemes).

In the same year, the NSSF also launched several social insurance schemes for "difficult to reach" populations within specific occupational groups. These included the *Wakulima Scheme* (Farmers' Scheme) and the *Madini Scheme* (Small Miners' Scheme), followed later by the *Wavuvi Scheme* (Fishermen's Scheme). In terms of benefit packages, the schemes are progressive as they include access to loans for productive investments in agro- and fishing inputs, access to savings groups, as well as loans for children's school fees (Masabo 2019).

An interesting element in the sector-specific schemes is the role of cooperative societies and workers' associations in policy design and promotion. For instance, coffee workers from the Kigoma region in the west of Tanzania reportedly pioneered the Wakulima Scheme in 2013.[10] After joining the NSSF through their cooperative society (*Rumako*), they accessed credit from NSSF to buy coffee beans at a lower interest rate than commercial banks, which positively impacted their production. Following this experience, all the coffee cooperative societies in Kigoma North registered, and the NSSF decided to roll out the scheme all over the country in 2014, targeting smallholder farmers in cooperatives. Since then, the schemes have enjoyed a high level of institutional support from the NSSF, which organizes village tours and local events (such as football matches) for

---

[10] See https://www.thecitizen.co.tz/tanzania/magazines/success/how-a-social-scheme-changed-lives-of-kigoma-coffee-farmers-2523794 and https://zittokabwe.wordpress.com/tag/nssf/.

Table 7.2: Social insurance schemes in Tanzania as of 2021

Scheme	NSSF	Wavuvi Scheme	Madini Scheme	Wakulima Scheme	National Informal Sector Scheme (NISS)
Target population	Formal sector (compulsory), informal sector (voluntary)	Fishermen (voluntary)	Artisan miners (voluntary)	Agricultural workers (voluntary)	Self-employed (voluntary)
Benefit coverage	Pensions (old-age pension, survivor's pension, and invalidity pension), unemployment benefit, health insurance, maternity benefit, and funeral grants	Cover for injury and disability; low-interest loans for fishing inputs; children's school fees; pensions; free "health treatment"	Credit and financial borrowing; free "health treatment"; cover for injury and disability; pensions	Cover for injury and disability; low-interest loans for agricultural inputs; children's school fees; pensions; free "health treatment"	Loans (under further development); health insurance; old-age pensions
Contribution level	*Formal sector:* 20% of wages shared between the employees (10%) and employers (10%) *Informal sector:* Minimum TZS 20,000 per month; benefits accrue depending on the contribution rate	Minimum TZS 20,000 per month	Minimum TZS 50,000 per month	Minimum TZS 20,000 per month	Minimum TZS 20,000 per month (contribution rate determines the level of available loans)
Other conditions	Tanzanian citizenship	Membership of a Beach Management Unit (BMU) or any other association	Must be a small-scale miner affiliated with regional miners' associations (REMAs) or any other association	Membership of basic crop associations (Agricultural Marketing Cooperative Societies, AMCOS) or any other association	

Source: authors' illustration using various sources (DTDA 2021; Lambin et al 2022; PwC 2022; UNDP 2021; PSSSF [Act No. 2 of 2018]; NSSF website, see https://www.nssf.or.tz/, https:// www.psssf.go.tz/benefits/)

awareness-raising.[11] At the same time, workers' associations have played a key role in facilitating member access to schemes, by offering subsidized contribution rates/loans covering fees for scheme enrolment (Verbrugge et al 2018).

The NSSF continues to collaborate with different well-organized groups and associations, offering valuable and fairly easy access to loans for informal workers who belong to such organizations. However, such arrangements are exclusive by nature and the covered occupational groups remain male-heavy.

A new attempt to achieve broad-based informal sector insurance: the National Informal Sector Scheme (2021 onwards)

The most recent, and potentially significant policy turn is the 2021 introduction of the *National Informal Sector Scheme* (NISS)[12]—inspired by the previous VSRS. The NISS represents a purpose-made programme for all self-employed workers in the informal sector (54.3 per cent of the total population; URT 2021b), while employers and employees who want to save for future may also enrol. While the benefits' range and level are still being developed, the scheme seeks to bolster informal workers' access to assets and savings schemes.

The scheme is planned to be piloted in three blocks. The first (current) step includes an old-age pension, a health insurance benefit for the contributing member only (provided through the National Health Insurance Fund, NHIF, which also runs the separate informal sector-targeted health insurance scheme "Iliyoboreshwa CHF"—an improved Community Health Fund) and access to two types of loans (Lambin and Nyyssölä 2022). These include: (i) loans for individuals or groups for purposes of establishing and developing enterprises, provided by the Azania Bank and government bodies such as the National Economic Empowerment Council, the Small Industries Development Organization and the Vocational Education and Training Authority; and (ii) loans for purchasing equipment and machinery to bolster productive activities.[13] After an evaluation of the first phase, the second phase is planned to include survivor, maternity, health, death and disability benefits, as well as health insurance for dependants. Finally, access

---

[11] Examples include participation in trade fairs (see https://www.mtaakwamtaa.co.tz/2018/08/nssf-yapeleka-elimu-kwa-wakulima-simiyu.html), village visits through the Kwanza Campaign (see https://jiachie1.rssing.com/chan-7007640/article13810.html?zx=814) and sponsoring football games (see https://gemmonetz.blogspot.com/2014/09/nssf-yadhamini-pambano-la-simba-na.html?m=0).

[12] See http://www.nssf.or.tz/schemes/saccos-sheme.

[13] Source: personal communication from NSSF. See also https://www.nssf.or.tz/schemes/saccos-sheme.

to soft loans to support economic activities and payments for school fees is envisaged for the third phase (UNDP 2021).

Moreover, payments to the NISS scheme can be made by utilizing mobile money as well as bank transfers and the NSSF representatives have reported practising flexibility in terms of contributions. In the case of enrollees failing to pay the minimum required contribution amount, their benefits will be pro-rated to the contributions made (UNDP 2021). While the actual mechanism determining benefit access remains unclear, this reflects an understanding of the issues and challenges related to payment ability among workers within the informal economy.

Discussion: Successes and Limitations of Social Insurance Expansion

This chapter has explored the notable progress in Tanzania's social protection landscape, spurred in part by the gradual expansion of social insurance arrangements to the informal sector. The presented overview highlights the pioneering legislative reforms and continuous expansion of policy instruments aimed at expanding social protection coverage among workers in the informal sector.

Nevertheless, the introduced policy measures have limitations in the dimensions of population coverage, benefit packages, contribution ability and financial viability. While the reach of the recently introduced NISS scheme is yet to be established, the coverage of the NSSF insurance schemes aimed at informal workers has remained limited. The level of membership among informal workers has varied on a yearly basis and went down from 47,780 in 2014/2015 to 29,149 in 2017/2018 (Torm et al 2021b:39). Some of the key drivers causing low enrolment include limited awareness, low levels of trust and low payment ability (UNDP 2021). Informal workers remain largely unaware of how social insurance schemes work and what benefits they provide (Torm et al 2021b). At the same time, those receiving low and irregular salaries often prefer to access their full wages rather than contributing to insurance schemes. The issue of regular contribution ability is particularly troublesome for informal sector self-employed workers, who are typically required to pay higher rates to cover both employee and employer contributions (Ackson and Masabo 2013).

Furthermore, it is also crucial to note that the emergent informal social security arrangements (such as those provided by community banks or workers' associations) have been hugely attractive to informal workers in the Tanzanian context, representing a competitive parallel social insurance system. This calls for further innovation and community-driven, bottom-up approaches to policy design in formal social insurance provision. Moreover, to fully benefit from Tanzania's innovative legal frameworks and policy ambition around social insurance, expanding coverage of informal workers could be sought through greater flexibility regarding both contribution rates and periods, which would ease payment ability among informal workers (see Olivier 2019; Ulrichs 2016). One way of easing the contribution burden among informal worker-members consists of subsidy mechanisms. In the Tanzanian context, the United Record of Beneficiaries developed for the PSSN offers an existing mechanism enabling the identification of the most vulnerable populations and could be deployed as a tool to offer subsidized contribution rates.

Moreover, the introduced informal sector-specific schemes lack some key protections, such as maternity and disability cover (at least until the second phase of the NISS is implemented). Also, other integrated and innovative policy components are relevant for consideration, given the social protection needs generated by global pandemics and climate crisis (see Introduction in this volume). In Tanzania, high-poverty areas are the most affected by drought and other natural disasters, with impacts on increased food poverty, infectious diseases, and crop and livestock loss (Akeel et al 2021). As such, insurance against climate-related shocks affecting productive activities remains key for protecting livelihoods in the informal sector.

It is also worth considering the social insurance measures at the system level. The described policy developments largely represent an approach characterized by separate layers in an existing social insurance structure. Different levels of targeting can be observed within the introduced policy measures; while there is voluntary, universal access to the "traditional" NSSF scheme initially developed for the formal sector, the NISS targets a defined but large group of self-employed workers, but the sector-specific schemes remain highly exclusive by nature. Such an approach differs from an "integrated model" seeking to include members from both the formal and informal sectors under one shared system (see, for example, Palacios and Robalino 2020). Besides the resulting issues of inclusion and exclusion, the extant approach bears a financial challenge, since integrated systems can foster larger risk pools, reinforcing financial sustainability (ILO 2021b). Additionally, integrated approaches can provide continuous social protection for workers changing professions and shifting status between formal and informal employment.

Conclusions

Since 2010, several sub-Saharan African countries have introduced significant policy reforms and expansion to enable greater inclusion in social protection arrangements. These domestically led and designed social insurance arrangements are yet to capture the attention they deserve, while debates and analyses around social safety nets and health insurance arrangements have dominated the scholarship on social protection evolution in the region. The visible interest in offering public social insurance services to informal workers also suggests that governments of the global South are increasingly recognizing the important and pressing social protection needs experienced by informal workers that cannot be met (at least solely) by lengthy "formalization" approaches.

In many contexts, social insurance schemes represent a politically and financially viable domestic policy initiative expanding social protection coverage, since contribution-based insurance mechanisms are not entirely dependent on state resources or external funding. In contexts where the government tax base for redistributive policies remains limited, social insurance schemes pooling funds through member contributions enable social protection expansion without full dependence on government resources (public expenses vary according to different elements in policy design, such as subsidized contributions for the lowest income earners).

Moreover, reluctance toward universalist ideas and social policy measures is common in many African countries, which view norms of universalism and individual rights as "alien and inappropriate" owing to traditional values related to work, family and dependency rooted in the (somewhat past) agrarian nature of society (Seekings 2019). Against this background, "productivist views" of social policy delivery that underscore the reciprocal responsibility between citizens (to engage in productive activities) and the government (who invests in skills, loans and other measures bolstering the productive activities of the population) have flourished.

Tanzania has adopted such a productivist view in its broader development strategy (Ulriksen 2016). This is demonstrated in the social protection targets under the Five Year Development Plan (FYDP) III, stipulating that the "possibility of scaling up social protection in terms of coverage and packages shall reasonably be matched with the promise and possibilities of the beneficiaries taking part in the productive activities" (URT 2021a:71).[14] As evidenced in this chapter, this ideological climate has offered a favourable environment for social protection expansion through social insurance arrangements with connections to productive activities. In addition to offering access to "traditional" social insurance arrangements through voluntary access, the NSSF has developed specific insurance services for informal workers incorporating loans for productive investments and activities. Such benefit packages can be seen to respond to the particular needs of economic security experienced by those operating in the informal sector.

---

[14] Also the 2010 National Social Protection Framework (NSPF) aims to be "a means of building the capabilities of the poor to engage in production so that they become effective participants in and beneficiaries of the growth process" (Torm et al 2021a:37–38; URT 2008).

At the same time, the resistance to universalist, non-contributory forms of social protection means that those excluded from social insurance arrangements and targeted social assistance measures (namely, the PSSN) remain dependent on informal sources of social security. It is also noteworthy that considerable fragmentation exists between the different social protection measures and their responsible agencies (for example, Ministry of Labour, Office of the Prime Minister, Ministry of Finance, TASAF, the NSSF, and others). Their differing interests have led to internal competition between different social protection measures, such as universal social pension and targeted social assistance through the PSSN (Ulriksen 2016). Consequently, the overall approach to social protection lacks a holistic vision of how to improve informal workers' livelihoods and well-being through synergetic measures across the different realms of social policy, including social assistance, employment and care policies, among others.

As Agarwala (Chapter 3, this volume) emphasizes, informal workers have held a key role in driving social policy expansion in various contexts of the global South, challenging conventional understandings of how social policies originate in the context of developing economies. Mounting evidence in the Tanzanian context shows that informal workers' associations across sectors have acted as a key promoter of workers' rights in the Tanzanian context (Torm 2022). However, informal workers' associations continue to face significant challenges in accessing authorities compared with formal workers' associations, which prevents these associations from contributing to the design of national schemes. Even if some national worker unions are represented on the board of the NSSF and include informal workers, their role in the policy processes leading to the creation of the NISS has reportedly been limited (see Riisgaard et al 2022; UNDP 2021). On the other hand, workers' associations continue to offer alternative and competing informal social insurance arrangements to NSSF insurances, being widely popular among informal workers in Tanzania. This points to the pivotal role of policy makers in raising awareness and developing formal social insurance arrangements that adequately respond to informal workers' needs.

Given these dynamics, it remains to be seen whether workers' associations can act as a bottom-up movement promoting holistic social policy expansion for informal workers in the Tanzanian context or whether future policy directions will be largely determined by governmental actors. Whatever the case, further integration of extant approaches within the social insurance arrangements—and at the level of the broader social protection system—would benefit the sustainability and equitable effects of social protection expansion between different population groups, and notably for those at the lowest tiers of the informal economy.

Acknowledgements

An earlier version of this chapter has been published as a WIDER Working Paper 84/2022. This study is also part of the UNU-WIDER project "Sustainable Development Solutions for Tanzania—Strengthening Research to Achieve SDGs," funded by the Ministry for Foreign Affairs of Finland.

References

Ackson, T. and J. Masabo. 2013. "Social Protection for the Informal Sector in Tanzania." Presented at the SASPEN & FES Conference, Johannesburg, South Africa, 16–17 September.

Ajwad, M. I., M. Abels, M. Novikova and M. A. Mohammed. 2018. *Financing Social Protection in Tanzania.* Washington, DC: World Bank.

Akeel, R., M. Bakanova, E. Mungunasi, C. Okou, M. Saldarriaga, R. Swinkels and G. Teri. 2021. *Tanzania Economic Update: Raising the Bar— Achieving Tanzania's Development Vision.* Tanzania Economic Update No. 15. Washington, DC: World Bank.

Andrew, D., J. George, L. Helgesson Sekei and P. Rippey. 2018. *Insights on the Preferences and Usage of Financial Services by Savings Groups in Tanzania (Savings at the Frontier (SatF) programme).* Dar es Salaam: Development Pioneer Consultants.

Beri, S. R. 2018. "Extending Social Security Coverage to the Informal Workers in Cameroon." Socialprotection.org blog. Accessed 20 September 2022. https://socialprotection.org/discover/blog/extending-social-security-coverage-informal-workers-cameroon.

Carter, B., K. Roelen, S. Enfield and W. Avis. 2019. *Social Protection Topic Guide (K4D Emerging Issues Report).* Brighton: Institute of Development Studies.

Chen, M. A. 2012. *The Informal Economy: Definitions, Theories and Policies.* WIEGO Working Paper No. 1. Manchester, Cambridge: Women in Informal Employment: Globalizing and Organizing.

Danquah, M., S. Schotte and K. Sen. 2021. "Informal Work in Sub-Saharan Africa: Dead End or Stepping-Stone?" *IZA Journal of Development and Migration,* 12. https://doi.org/10.2478/izajodm-2021-0015.

de Hoop, J., M. Gichane, V. Groppo and S. Simmons Zuilkowski. 2020. *Cash Transfers, Public Works and Child Activities. Mixed Methods Evidence from the United Republic of Tanzania.* Innocenti Working Paper No. WP-2020–03. Florence: United Nations Children's Fund.

DOSI (Délégation à l'Organisation du Secteur Informel). n.d. *De la mutualisation à la formalization: Les actions de la Délégation à l'Organisation du Secteur Informel (DOSI).* Lomé: DOSI.

DTDA (Danish Trade Union Development Agency). 2021. *Tanzania & Zanzibar Labour Market Profile 2021/2022.* Copenhagen: DTDA.

GEPF (Government Employees Provident Fund). n.d. "Government Employees Provident Fund's Voluntary Savings Retirement Scheme—A case of the Government Employees Provident Fund." Pretoria: GEPF.

Gervas, A. 2022. "Social Protection and Informal Construction Worker Organizations in Tanzania: How Informal Worker Organizations Strive to Provide Social Insurance to Their Members."

Hassim, S. and S. Razavi. 2006. "Gender and Social Policy in a Global Context: Uncovering the Gendered Structure of 'the Social'." In *Gender and Social Policy in a Global Context. Social Policy in a Development Context*, edited by S. Razavi and S. Hassim, 1–39. London: Palgrave Macmillan.

Hunt, S. 2009. "Citizenship's Place: The State's Creation of Public Space and Street Vendors' Culture of Informality in Bogotá, Colombia." *Environment and Planning D*, 27:331–351. https://doi.org/10.1068/d1806.

ILO (International Labour Organization). 2021a. *World Social Protection Report 2020–22: Social Protection at the Crossroads—In Pursuit of a Better Future*. Geneva: ILO.

ILO (International Labour Organization). 2021b. *Extending Social Security to Workers in the Informal Economy Lessons from International Experience* (second (revised) edition). Geneva: ILO.

ILO (International Labour Organization). 2018. *Women and Men in the Informal Economy: A Statistical Picture* (third edition). Geneva: ILO.

ILO (International Labour Organization). 2017. *World Social Protection Report 2017–19: Universal Social Protection to Achieve the Sustainable Development Goals*. Geneva: ILO.

ILO (International Labour Organization). 2014. *Domestic Workers in the United Republic of Tanzania: Summary of Findings of a Situational Analysis 2013*. Dar es Salaam: ILO Country Office for Kenya, Rwanda, Tanzania and Uganda.

ISSA (International Social Security Association). 2019. *Social Security Programs Throughout the World: Africa, 2019*. Social Security Administration Research, Statistics, and Policy Analysis. Accessed 17 May 2022. https://www.ssa.gov/policy/docs/progdesc/ssptw/2018-2019/africa/kenya.html.

Jütting, J. and J. R. Laiglesia. 2009. *Is Informal Normal? Towards More and Better Jobs in Developing Countries*. Paris: Organisation for Economic Co-operation and Development.

King, R. and C. Sweetman. 2010. *Gender Perspectives on the Global Economic Crisis*. Discussion Paper, Oxfam International. Accessed 20 September 2022. https://oi-files-d8-prod.s3.eu-west-2.amazonaws.com/s3fs-public/file_attachments/gender-perspectives-global-economic-crisis-feb10_9.pdf.

Kinyondo, G. 2022. "Self-regulating Informal Transport Workers and the Quest for Social Protection in Tanzania." In *Social Protection and Informal Workers in Sub-Saharan Africa: Lived Realities and Associational Experiences from Kenya and Tanzania*, edited by Lane Riisgaard, Winnie V. Mitullah and Nina Torm, 72–98. Abingdon: Routledge.

Lam, D. and A. Elsayed. 2021. *Labour Markets in Low-Income Countries: Challenges and Opportunities*. Oxford: Oxford University Press.

Lambin, R. and M. Nyyssölä. 2022. *Employment Policy in Mainland Tanzania – What's in It for Women?* UNU-WIDER Working Paper No. 67/2022. Helsinki: United Nations University World Institute for Development Economics Research.

Lambin, R., M. Nyyssölä and A. Bernigaud. 2022a. *Social Protection for Working-Age Women in Tanzania: Exploring Past Policy Trajectories and Simulating Future Paths.* UNU-WIDER Working Paper No. 82/2022. Helsinki: United Nations University World Institute for Development Economics Research.

Lambin, R. and M. Nyyssölä. 2022b. *Exploring Social Policy Trajectories in Mainland Tanzania: Driving for Gender-Inclusive Development?* WIDER Working Paper No. 38/2022. Helsinki: United Nations University World Institute for Development Economics Research. https://doi.org/10.35188/ UNU-WIDER/2022/169-3.

Masabo, J. 2019. "Informality and Social Insurance in East Africa: An Assessment of the Law and Practice." In *Social Security Outside the Realm of the Employment Contract: Informal Work and Employee-Like Workers*, edited by Mies Westerveld and Marious Oliver, 177–200. Cheltenham: Edward Elgar.

Masanyiwa, Z., E. Mosha and S. Mamboya. 2020. "Factors Influencing Participation of Informal Sector Workers in Formal Social Security Schemes in Dodoma City, Tanzania." *Open Journal of Social Sciences*, 8(6):229–242. https://doi.org/10.4236/jss.2020.86020.

Medina, Leandro and Schneider, Friedrich G. 2019. *Shedding Light on the Shadow Economy: A Global Database and the Interaction with the Official One.* CESifo Working Paper No. 7981. https://ssrn.com/abstract=3502028 or http://dx.doi.org/10.2139/ssrn.3502028.

Miti, J. J., M. Perkiö, A. Metteri and S. Atkins. 2021. "Pension Coverage Extension as Social Innovation in Zambia: Informal Economy Workers' Perceptions and Needs." *International Social Security Review*, 74:29–53. https://doi.org/10.1111/issr.12264.

Mumtaz, Z. (2022). "Informal Social Protection: A Conceptual Synthesis." *Social Policy & Administration*, 56(3):394–408. https://doi.org/10.1111/ spol.12772.

Nguimkeu, P. and C. Okou. 2020. *A Tale of Africa Today: Balancing the Lives and Livelihoods of Informal Workers during the COVID-19 Pandemic.* Washington, DC: World Bank.

Olivier, M. 2019. "Social Security Protection for Informal Economy Workers: Developing World Perspectives." In *Social Security Outside the Realm of the Employment Contract: Informal Work and Employee-Like Workers*, edited by Mies Westerveld and Marius Oliver, 2–29. Cheltenham: Edward Elgar.

Palacios, Robert J. and David A. Robalino. 2020. *Integrating Social Insurance and Social Assistance Programs for the Future World of Labor.* IZA Discussion Paper No. 13258. https://ssrn.com/abstract=3602434.

Phe Goursat, M. and L. Pellerano. 2016. *Extension of Social Protection to Workers in the Informal Economy in Zambia. Lessons Learnt from Field Research on Domestic Workers, Small Scale Farmers and Construction Workers.* Lusaka: International Labour Organization.

PwC (PricewaterhouseCoopers). 2022. *PricewaterhouseCoopers Tax Summaries.* Dar es Salaam:PwC.

Razavi, S. and S. Staab. 2018. "Rethinking Social Policy: A Gender Perspective from the Developing World." In *Handbook on Gender and Social Policy*, edited by Sheila Shaver, 74–89. Cheltenham: Edward Elgar.

Republic of Cameroon. 1967. "Loi no 67-LF-8 du 12 juin 1967 portant organisation de la prévoyance sociale." CMR-1967-L-18932. https://oi-files-d8-prod.s3.eu-west-2.amazonaws.com/s3fs-public/file_attachments/gender-perspectives-global-economic-crisis-feb10_9.pdf.

Riisgaard, L. 2020. *Worker Organisation and Social Protection amongst Informal Petty Traders in Tanzania.* Center for the Study of African Economies Working Paper No. 2020:4. Roskilde: Center for the Study of African Economies.

Riisgaard, L., W. Mitullah and N. Torm. 2022. *Social Protection and Informal Workers in Sub-Saharan Africa: Lived Realities and Associational Experiences from Kenya and Tanzania.* London: Routledge.

RNSF (Research, Network and Support Facility). 2017. *Extending Coverage: Social Protection and the Informal Economy. Experiences and Ideas from Researchers and Practitioners.* Rome, Milan and Brussels: RNSF, ARS Progetti, Lattanzio Advisory, AGRER.

Rosaldo, M. 2021. "Problematizing the 'Informal Sector': 50 Years of Critique, Clarification, Qualification, and More Critique." *Sociology Compass*, 15. https://doi.org/10.1111/soc4.12914.

Rwegoshora, H. M. M. 2014. *Social Security Challenges in Tanzania: Transforming the Present—Protecting the Future.* Dar es Salaam: Mkuki na Nyota Publishers Ltd.

Sabates-Wheeler, R. and N. Kabeer. 2003. *Gender Equality and the Extension of Social Protection.* Geneva: International Labour Organization.

Sankaran, K. 2012. "Flexibility and Informalisation of Employment Relationships." In *Challenging the Legal Boundaries of Work Regulation*, edited by Judy Fudge, Shae McCrystal and Kamala Sankaran, 29–47. Oxford: Hart Publishing.

Seekings, J. 2019. "The Limits to 'Global' Social Policy: The ILO, the Social Protection Floor and the Politics of Welfare in East and Southern Africa." *Global Social Policy*, 19:139–158. https://doi.org/10.1177/14680 18119846418.

Shau, I. 2022. "The Assessment of Challenges Facing the Growth of Informal Lending Groups in Tanzania: The Case of VICOBA." *African Journal of Applied Research*, 8(1):1–14.

Stavropoulou, M. and N. Jones. 2013. *Off the Balance Sheet: The Impact of the Economic Crisis on Girls and Young Women. A review of the evidence.* London: Plan & Overseas Development Institute.

Torm, N. 2022. "The Relationship between Associational Membership and Access to Formal Social Protection: A Cross-Sector Analysis of Informal Workers in Kenya and Tanzania." In *Social Protection and Informal Workers in Sub-Saharan Africa: Lived Realities and Associational Experiences from Kenya and Tanzania,* edited by Lane Riisgaard, Winnie V. Mitullah and Nina Torm, 48–70. Abingdon: Routledge.

Torm, N. 2020. *Social Protection and the Role of Informal Worker Associations: A Cross-Sector Analysis of Urban Sites in Kenya and Tanzania.* Center for the Study of African Economies Working Paper No. 2020:3. Roskilde: Center for the Study of African Economies.

Torm, N., G. Kinyondo, W. Mitullah and L. Riisgaard. 2021a. "Formal Social Protection and Informal Workers in Kenya and Tanzania." In *Social Protection and Informal Workers in Sub-Saharan Africa: Lived Realities and Associational Experiences from Kenya and Tanzania,* edited by Lane Riisgaard, Winnie V. Mitullah and Nina Torm, 31–47. Abingdon: Routledge. https://doi.org/10.4324/9781003173694-2.

Torm, N., G. Kinyondo and L. Riisgaard. 2021b. "Formal Social Protection and Informal Workers in Kenya and Tanzania: From Residual Towards Universal Models?" In *Social Protection and Informal Workers in Sub-Saharan Africa: Lived Realities and Associational Experiences from Kenya and Tanzania,* edited by Lane Riisgaard, Winnie V. Mitullah and Nina Torm, 31–47. Abingdon: Routledge.

Ulrichs, M. 2016. *Informality, Women and Social Protection: Identifying Barriers to Provide Effective Coverage.* Working Paper No. 435. London: Overseas Development Institute.

Ulriksen, M. 2016. *The Development of Social Protection Policies in Tanzania, 2000–2015.* CSSR Working Paper No. 377. Cape Town: University of Cape Town.

UNDESA (United Nations Department of Economic and Social Affairs). 2021. *Social Policy and Social Protection Measures to Build Africa Better Post-COVID-19.* Policy Brief No. 93. Geneva: UNDESA.

UNDP (United Nations Development Programme). 2021. *Informality and Social Protection in African Countries: A Forward-looking Assessment of Contributory Schemes.* New York: UNDP.

URT (United Republic of Tanzania). 2021a. *National Five Year Development Plan 2021/22–2025/26. Realising Competitiveness and Industrialisation for Human Development.* Dar es Salaam: URT, Ministry of Finance and Planning.

URT (United Republic of Tanzania). 2021b. *Integrated Labour Force Survey 2020/21.* Dar es Salaam: URT.

URT (United Republic of Tanzania). 2008. *National Social Protection Framework*. Dar es Salaam: URT, Ministry of Finance and Economic Affairs.

Verbrugge, Boris, Adeline Ajuaye and Jan Van Ongevalle. 2018. *Contributory Social Protection for the Informal Economy? Insights from Community-Based Health Insurance (CBHI) in Senegal and Tanzania*. Working Paper No. 26. BeFind, Belgian Policy Research Group on Financing for Development. HIVA, KU Leuven, Leuven.

World Bank. 2022. *Tanzania Productive Social Safety Net Project II— Implementation Status and Results Report*. Washington, DC: World Bank.

World Bank. 2020. *Implementation Completion and Results Report*. No. ICR00005010, Social Protection and Jobs Global Practice, Africa Region. Washington, DC: World Bank.

World Bank. 2019a. *World Development Report 2019: The Changing Nature of Work*. Washington, DC: World Bank. https://doi.org/10.1596/978-1-4648-1328-3.

World Bank. 2019b. *International Development Association Project Appraisal Document*. Tanzania Productive Social Safety Net Project II, No. PAD3139. Washington, DC: World Bank.

8

Economic Growth, Youth Unemployment and Political and Social Instability: A Study of Policies and Outcomes in Post-Arab Spring Egypt, Morocco, Jordan and Tunisia

Heath J. Prince, Amna Khan and Yara A. Halasa-Rappel

Introduction

As noted in the Sustainable Development Goals (SDGs), unemployment, particularly youth unemployment, is a major concern with respect to poverty reduction. Youth unemployment is referenced throughout the SDGs, including in SDG 4.4, which calls for substantially increasing the number of youth and adults with the skills needed for securing decent jobs by 2030. SDG 8.6 calls for substantial reductions in the percentage of youth who are neither employed, in education nor in training, so-called NEETS by 2020. Moreover, and in keeping with the direction we have taken with this study, SDG 17 calls for increased policy coherence, which, among other things, permits greater policy autonomy on the part of developing countries.

Our study focused on post-Arab Spring youth employment policies adopted in Egypt, Morocco, Jordan and Tunisia, and asked whether, after this series of massive social protests concluded, new policies have emerged to provide innovative solutions to address the problem. In particular, and for the purposes of this chapter, we examined guidance delivered to these countries prior to and post-Arab Spring by the International Monetary Fund (IMF) in the form of its Article IV Consultation documents.

Our review of the literature on youth employment policy in the region found that the topic is underrepresented among recent studies. Fieldwork conducted for this study suggests that the relative lack of publicly available information on youth employment policy and the lack of clearly identifiable national policies themselves have less to do with an absence of concern on the part of policy makers and more to do with external constraints on policy autonomy.[1] It is this line of argument that we chose to pursue with our study, including, and especially, our examination of the role that international financial institutions (IFIs), particularly the IMF, have in policy making in these countries.

The current COVID-19 pandemic and its impact on youth unemployment in the region cannot be overstated. Trends that were emerging prior to the outbreak of the pandemic, such as a reduction in employment opportunities in the oil-producing countries of the Gulf region and a general difficulty in producing sufficient employment opportunities for a rapidly growing youth population, have been greatly exacerbated since the Spring of 2020. Steep drop-offs in tourism, job losses from retail and manufacturing business closures, and reductions in foreign direct investment (FDI) related to COVID-19 contributed to a sharp increase in Jordan's overall unemployment rate, up to 35 per cent (Gavlak 2020). Egypt saw an additional 2.7 million workers lose employment between April and June of 2020, driving the unemployment rate up to 9.6 per cent from 7.7 per cent in the prior quarter (World Bank 2020), and the tourism-driven Tunisian economy saw unemployment rise from 15 per cent to 18 per cent in the months following the onset of the pandemic (Al-Arabiya News 2020). A similar story can be told about Morocco, where unemployment rose from 9.2 to 13 per cent over the summer of 2020, and where youth unemployment has topped 22.6 per cent (Asharq Al-Awsat 2020).[2]

The remainder of the chapter is structured as follows: the next section provides a brief literature review, focusing on the interaction between economic policy and youth unemployment in the region leading up to the Arab Spring. The chapter then analyses IMF Article IV Consultations delivered prior to the Arab Spring and after to determine if, through these documents, any indication is given that youth employment policy changed as a result of the revolts.

---

[1] Our focus with this study is youth employment *policies*. However, a more comprehensive understanding of the linkage between youth unemployment and social unrest in the region requires an examination of the programmes that result from these policies. While we briefly touch on programmes in this chapter, a richer description of youth employment programmes in the region can be found in Barsoum (2013) and Prince et al (2016).

[2] Data on youth unemployment since the outbreak of COVID-19, with the exception of Morocco, are not available as of this writing. However, given that youth unemployment generally exceeds unemployment for the population as a whole, it can be assumed that, as in Morocco, youth unemployment rates in Egypt, Jordan and Tunisia are substantially higher than the rates reported here.

Literature Review

Calls for "justice, freedom, and human dignity" heard throughout the Arab Spring uprisings were rooted in the failure of decades of market-led reforms to translate into significant improvements in the quality of life for the vast majority. Indeed, it might be said that the three central demands—justice, freedom and human dignity—are inherent in the demand for decent work: *justice*, in that many view employment and the means to earn a living as rights and their denial as an injustice; *freedom*, in that with decent work comes the freedom to fully engage in and contribute to society as a citizen; and *dignity*, in that through work comes self-actualization.

In her investigation of the Arab Spring's structural roots in Egypt, Bargawi (2014:219) concludes that "economic policy choices over the 2000s ... contributed to the economic and social outcomes witnessed in the run up to the 2011 uprisings," a diagnosis that can be extended to other countries in the region. Hanieh (2015) places IFI loans, their related debt, and their impact on economic and social questions such as unemployment at the heart of the uprising in Tunisia. Noueihed and Warren (2012) note that the job creation that did take place in the region prior to 2011 favoured older workers and expatriates, largely bypassing the region's youth.

As has been the case in sub-Saharan Africa (Prince 2014), economic growth as measured by increases in gross domestic product (GDP) per capita has not translated into improvement in well-being or in labour force participation rates for youth across the Middle East and North Africa (MENA) region. Yet despite the evidence (see, for example, Bayliss et al 2011), IFIs have continued to hew to neoliberal, market-oriented policies such as trade openness, low taxes, "flexible" labour markets and smaller governments. A review of IMF and World Bank policy recommendations (authors' database of IMF and World Bank public documents) indicates that these institutions still focus on "public sector consolidation" and "tightly managed" government budgets for each of the countries covered in this chapter. In each case, structural reform to promote economic growth is advised as a pre-condition for improvement in social outcomes, especially employment. Although large shares of the region's population remain excluded from the labour force after years of such reforms, these institutions maintain that market liberalization will generate the proverbial rising tide.

While the IMF has, in a post–Arab Spring moment, salted its policy recommendations with anti-poverty language, its guiding principles remain rooted in neoliberal economics—grow the economy and that growth will translate into higher demand for labour, despite, as Agarwala notes (Chapter 3, this volume), these policies' tendency to exacerbate poverty and swell the ranks of the precariat. At the same time, IFIs, including the IMF, have strongly encouraged the dismantling of state-owned enterprises, strongly discouraged public sector employment and promoted fiscal austerity, potentially resulting in the further eroding of the very institutions that are needed to assist in securing education, employment and individual agency.

Decades of improving education outcomes are not correlated with higher rates of youth employment, contrary to some of the main tenets of human capital theory. As shown in Tables 8.1 and 8.2, the high secondary and tertiary education rates in this cluster of countries have not translated into robust employment opportunities for youth. Low labour force participation rates for youth (Table 8.2),[3] assumed to be a key driver of political and social instability in the region, have declined steadily over most of the past decade. As of 2019, youth labour force participation rates ranged across the countries in our study from 23.0 per cent in Jordan to 28.7 per cent in Morocco, well below the already low global average of 41.0 per cent and MENA regional average of 42.2 per cent.[4] The United Nations' (UN)s' Economic and Social Commission for Western Asia reports:

[Even] with an educated labor force, opportunities for decent employment were curtailed after the implementation of structural adjustment programs and a general freeze on public sector recruitment in the 1990s. The private sector could not fill this void, leading to the proliferation of informal jobs, mainly in low value-added service sectors. ... Arab youth with higher education qualifications, in particular, became disenfranchised and increasingly sought to migrate, considering it their only employment option. (ESCWA 2014:21)

Potential explanations for this disconnect between heavy investment in improving primary and secondary education in these countries and low levels of labour force participation rates among youth are numerous, including population growth outpacing the ability to create employment opportunities,[5] the global economic downturn between 2008 and 2015/ 2016, the lack of comprehensive national policy frameworks, or some combination of these factors.

This observed disconnect between modest economic growth in the early and mid-2000s (Table 8.3) and youth employment may be attributed to weak public

---

[3] The ILO defines the labour force participation rate as: the proportion of the population that is economically active in supplying labour for the production of goods and services over a defined period.

[4] It is likely that these are conservative estimates given the modest capacity for collecting and reporting in several of these countries.

[5] Arab countries undoubtedly face demographic challenges. The MENA region has the most youthful population in the world, with 60 per cent of the population under the age of 25 and more than 28 per cent between the ages of 15 and 29.

Table 8.1: Secondary and tertiary school completion rates: 2003–2016

		2003 (%)	2004 (%)	2005 (%)	2006 (%)	2007 (%)	2008 (%)	2009 (%)	2010 (%)	2011 (%)	2012 (%)	2014 (%)	2015 (%)	2016 (%)
Egypt	Complete lower secondary	77	75.4					71.2				80.2		83.5
Egypt	Complete tertiary	13.2			16.4									17.4
Jordan	Complete lower secondary	85	83.5		80	82.5	84		74.1		77	68.8		
Jordan	Complete tertiary					15.4	15.9		16.1					
Morocco	Complete lower secondary	39.4	41.5		46.7	51	53.9		59.2	61.4	63.3	68.8	70.5	
Morocco	Complete tertiary													
Tunisia	Complete lower secondary		70.8	69.5	67.4		72.1	80.8	74.2	80.7			70.8	
Tunisia	Complete tertiary								12.5	13.2				

Source: World Development Indicators, Graduates of Lower Secondary, both sexes; United Nations Educational, Scientific and Cultural Organization Institute for Statistics, Graduates from Tertiary Education, both sexes.

Table 8.2: Youth labour force participation rates in Egypt, Jordan, Morocco and Tunisia: 1990–2019

	1990 (%)	2000 (%)	2010 (%)	2014 (%)	2017 (%)	2018 (%)	2019 (%)
Egypt	33.8	31.5	34.1	33.9	29.1	24.6	24.4
Jordan	28.3	28.1	26.6	25.3	23.1	23.1	23.0
Morocco	48	42.5	36	36.4	27.0	26.7	26.5
Tunisia	41.4	36.4	31.1	31.6	29.1	28.8	28.7

Source: World Development Indicators, labour force participation rates, youth total (percentage of total labour force ages 15–24) modelled International Labor Organization (ILO) estimate.

Table 8.3: GDP per capita in Egypt, Jordan, Morocco and Tunisia: 1991, 2000, 2010 and 2014 in USD

	1991	2000	2010	2014
Egypt	5,976	7,811	10,620	10,040
Jordan	6,425	7,695	11,253	11,490
Morocco	4,260	4,398	6,419	7,140
Tunisia	5,720	7,610	10,678	10,900

Source: World Development Indicators, GDP per capita, PPP (constant 2011 International USD).

institutions and the relative lack of persistent active labour market policies and programmes (ALMPs) that can translate economic growth into investment in the well-being of its citizenry and, ipso facto, future economic growth. However, certain prerequisites for sustainable programmes include policies that provide them with reliable funding, regulations that guide their implementation, and a system of monitoring and evaluation that can serve as a means of continuous improvement, each generally lacking in the region's ministries.

In their analysis of social policy in the region, Karshenas et al (2014) draw a line from budgetary imbalances in the 1980s to the Arab Spring. They argue that these historical budgetary imbalances led many countries to adopt market-oriented economic policies that diminished their state-led social safety net and ALMPs. A network of international non-governmental organizations (NGOs) arose to fulfil many of the core functions for which states had been responsible, potentially further weakening state capacity and authority by divesting the government of responsibility for training workers. Ultimately, state-guaranteed employment was dropped as governmental policy, allowing youth unemployment to reach the crisis levels that eventually contributed to the Arab Spring protests (El-Said and Harrigan 2014; Fergusson and Yeates 2013; Mossallem 2015).

Economic growth has long been asserted to be the vehicle through which well-being is improved when it is not presented as an end in itself.

It forms the core of the dominant, neoliberal paradigm in development economics and brings with it a limited set of tools that can affect growth. The application of these tools are often the quid for the quo of grants and loans to developing and middle-income countries, the acceptance of which tends to constrain individual states' ability to implement policies that are potentially more beneficial to their citizenry. Despite statements to the contrary, the IMF reportedly continues to chip away at policy autonomy in these four countries and promote fiscal and monetary policies that primarily serve to develop the economy, and only secondarily, if at all, to generate employment opportunities for youth or improve their well-being (DeMartino 1999; Kentikelenis et al 2016).

IFIs and their policy influence

A common denominator across most of the four countries in our study is the influence of IFIs in policy development, including those policies ostensibly aimed at youth employment. The World Bank and the IMF have long been active players in the macroeconomic policy-making decisions of these countries through the conditions placed on the receipt of grants and loans made by these institutions. Of particular interest to us in this study has been the influence of the IMF on pre- and post-Arab Spring policy (see, for example, El-Said and Harrigan 2014; Fergusson and Yeates 2013; Mossallem 2015; Stiglitz 2002).

The practice of "conditionality," or requiring the adoption or reform of policies in exchange for grants or loans from IFIs, is well established in the literature (see, for example, Babb and Buira 2005; Henisz et al 2005; Woods 2006). Kentikelenis et al (2016), in their study of IMF conditionality between 1985 and 2014, find little evidence supporting the notion that the IMF simply validates homegrown policy recommendations, but rather that the IMF continues to impose de facto conditions on countries that receive its assistance; conditions that often set real constraints on social policies and programmes.

Our working assumption for this study has been that, given the importance of youth unemployment in driving the Arab Spring revolts, policy recommendations coming from IFIs (and from bilateral aid agencies, to which we pay less attention in this chapter) would reflect the dramatically changed environment in the region after 2011. We find that this has not been the case.

In her article analysing economic policy in post-Arab Spring Egypt, Bargawi (2014) reports that IFI-initiated economic policies adopted by the Mubarak regime contributed to high levels of youth unemployment. Similarly, Hanieh (2015:123) cites recommendations from the World Bank that Tunisia would need "to engage in a series of comprehensive and politically sensitive reforms," which included terminating some ALMPs owing to the supposed burden it placed on the national budget. In each of the countries covered in our study, we found that policies to reduce public sector employment, a common IFI recommendation, were being pursued.

IFI influence over policy development in the region is better understood when the size of total grants and loans provided by IFIs is compared with annual budget expenditures. We have attempted to assess the degree of this influence by examining the national accounts data on both annual total expenditures of central government budgets and annual disbursements of International Bank for Reconstruction and Development (World Bank) loans, International Development Association (World Bank) credits and IMF credits.[6] In the years leading up to the Arab Spring, World Bank and IMF loans and credits have ranged in size from a low of only 4 per cent of the size of Jordan's annual budget expenditures in 2005, to 11 per cent as large as the total annual budget expenditures in both Morocco and Tunisia in 2010 and 2008, respectively, to over one-third the size, 35 per cent, of total annual budget expenditures in Egypt in 2006. It is our contention that World Bank and IMF policy recommendations are generally closely adhered to when grants and loans of this magnitude are in the balance.

Egypt's USD 12 billion loan from the IMF in 2016 provides a clear example of this dynamic. In order to receive the loan, Egypt agreed to the creation of a value-added tax, considered by many to be regressive, raised the price of gasoline, reduced electricity subsidies, floated its currency, "optimized" the public sector wage bill and reformed public sector management of state-owned enterprises (Hadid 2016; IMF 2016b; *New York Times* 2016). While then-IMF managing director Christine Lagarde averred that these are "homegrown" policies, they are also very similar to policies associated with IMF loans across the developing world since the 1980s (Henisz et al 2005).

Economic growth in most countries in the MENA region during the 1990s failed to fully address calls for more and higher quality employment opportunities for the vast majority in the region, particularly its youth. According to some analysts (see al-Nashif and Tzannatos 2013; Bellin 2013; El-Said and Harrigan 2014; UNDP and ILO 2012), the region's sharp focus on increasing privatization and trade openness, reducing debt and inflation,

---

[6] These figures were calculated with individual country data on World Bank and IMF grants and loans with data from the World Development Indicators and the IMF's International Financial Statistics (used to create a proxy variable for the size of World Bank and IMF grants and loans [and excluding grants and loans from other IFIs]); annual central government expenditures data in local currency were extracted from the IMF's International Financial Statistics database and converted to constant 2011 dollars; relative size of IFI influence was compared to total annual budget expenditures. We believe that presenting the size of World Bank and IMF influence in this fashion better reflects their relative magnitude to overall government investment in the economy and in social programmes than presenting grants and loans as a percentage of GDP, as is more commonly done.

and attracting FDI "glossed over two decades of skewed economic policies, a widening social protection deficit, and the absence of institutionalized social dialogue between governments, workers, employers, and other segments of society" (al-Nashif and Tzannatos 2013:18). The economic growth that did occur was not inclusive (Benar 2007), leaving out the growing numbers of well-educated and skilled Arab youth who had benefited from decades of state-level investment in improving education outcomes.

Others (Malik and Awadallah 2011) argue that not only was economic growth in the region not inclusive, the MENA region's difficulty in developing a private sector that is globally competitive was a major underpinning of the Arab Spring revolt. This, coupled with low levels of political accountability among elected officials and low levels of political voice among citizens, translated into a weakened ability of governments in the region to fully appreciate many of the social consequences of IFI-encouraged economic reforms.

Writing of Jordan, Assaad notes, "The employment challenges faced by these increasingly educated new entrants co-exist with an economy that is creating a large number of low-quality informal jobs in construction and services that are mostly being filled by a growing legion of foreign workers" (Assaad 2014:1). Salehi-Isfahani et al (2015) argue that a disappointing ability to translate relatively high educational achievement into employment opportunities (Table 8.4) has contributed to "[an] erosion of social trust in education as the path to social mobility that has been the hallmark of post-independence social and economic development in MENA countries."

In their largely qualitative study of economic reform and instability in the Middle East, El-Said and Harrigan (2014:100) ask whether "economic liberalization as promoted by the IMF and World Bank [has] had a negative impact on formal social welfare provisions in the Middle East." They answer that it has, noting that periods of economic growth have not been sustained, and as growth slows, poverty increases. The International Labour Organization (ILO) reports that the uncritical adoption of trade liberalization policies in the region since the 1990s has likely contributed to

Table 8.4: New labour market entrants, new postsecondary graduates and approximate jobs added 2014

	Egypt	Jordan	Morocco	Tunisia
New entrants ...	650,000	60,000	300,000	80,000
... of which, new postsec grads	344,000	9,365	88,000	69,000
Jobs created	435,000	10,000	160,000	75,000

Source: authors' calculations based on World Development Indicator data, and from ILO and SIDA (2015).

social unrest, in part through social exclusion and increasing unemployment rates for even well-educated youth (UNDP and ILO 2012). El-Said and Harrigan (2014) note that Tunisia's insistence on *maintaining* social spending during its structural adjustment period (but not until rioting resulted from implementing IFI-required cuts to food subsidies, which were soon restored) enabled it to implement reforms while also reducing poverty, making it the exception to the rule in the region.

For all of the hope for social, political and economic transformation engendered by the Arab Spring uprisings, the MENA region can hardly be said to have advanced economically, socially or politically as a result. Modest gains in these areas, particularly reductions in unemployment, eroded in the years immediately following the Arab Spring, although only partly because of it.

> Since 2011, most Arab economies have been dramatically impacted by social unrest, the surge in commodity and energy prices (for oil importers), recessionary impacts affecting private and public sectors, increased uncertainty for investors and greater demands for expansionary expenditure for economic recovery and social justice. The unrest has already had a huge direct cost, and has also contributed to a decline in economic activity and increased unemployment. Since 2010, the decline in regional unemployment rates has been reversed. (UNDP and ILO 2012:18)

A more thorough review of the literature on the causes and consequences of the Arab Spring is beyond the scope of this chapter. However, this selection of recent studies suggests two issues of critical importance to the topic of our study: first, a clear thread can be drawn from pre-Arab Spring economic policy through austerity and rising youth unemployment to growing social unrest; and, second, failing to fully address youth unemployment post-Arab Spring, through new policies and programmes, can only contribute to future unrest in the region.

Analysis of IMF Article IV reports

The IMF holds bilateral discussions with member countries on a near-annual basis, as called for in the Articles of Agreement that IMF loan recipients must accept. In these Article IV Consultations, as they are called, IMF and local economists survey a country's economic development needs and agenda, and offer policy recommendations that are meant to aid further growth. A common criticism directed at the IMF is that these Consultations are insufficiently attentive to the local context, needs and political exigencies of the countries they address, instead offering a set of policies uniformly structured around market liberalization and shrinking the public sector (Mossallem 2015; Ray and Schmitz 2016). The Arab Spring provides a recent opportunity to determine whether this criticism has any merit.

The Arab Spring protests were engendered by widely held concerns about jobs and the economy, and one would expect the IMF to modify its policy prescriptions in light of such a momentous shift in the domestic political climate. Accordingly, we have examined the Article IV Consultations for Egypt, Morocco, Jordan and Tunisia, both in the immediate run up to the events of Arab Spring and a few years afterward in order to determine whether any such change in the IMF's policy approach in fact occurred.[7] For the pre-Arab Spring reports, we reviewed Egypt's 2007 and 2010 Consultations, Morocco's 2009 Consultation, Jordan's 2009 and 2010 Consultations and Tunisia's 2010 Consultation. For the post-Arab Spring reports, we reviewed Egypt's 2014 Consultation, Morocco's 2012 and 2015 Consultations, Jordan's 2014 Consultation and Tunisia's 2012 and 2015 Consultations.

Persistently high unemployment is identified as a key economic issue in the pre-Arab Spring Consultations for Egypt (IMF 2007, 2010a), Morocco (IMF 2010b) and Tunisia (IMF 2010d, 2012), with the Morocco and Tunisia Consultations specifically referring to youth unemployment. Additionally, the Consultations for these three countries recognize the adverse macroeconomic impact of the global recession and grant that there is some room for state spending to act as a countercyclical stimulus. Jordan is somewhat of an outlier in both of these respects, however, as its Consultations (IMF 2014, 2015) focus much more narrowly on reducing public debt and current account deficits, with a strong emphasis on maintaining moderate monetary policy and ensuring the stability of the financial sector.

Despite the awareness evidenced in the reports that these countries' unemployment rates have not substantially improved in response to recent market reforms and that the global economic downturn could worsen them further, they conspicuously refrain from advocating robust ALMPs or expanding public sector employment. As the Egypt 2010 Article IV Consultation puts it, "Rather than containing the negative spillovers of the (global economic) crisis, the focus of policy should be addressing fiscal vulnerabilities and structural rigidities." Similar to its policy recommendations in Indonesia, as Kaasch and Wilmsen find in their study of the influence of

---

[7] A critical part of this component of our study is an analysis of 26 IMF Article IV memos, covering a range of years prior to and post 2011 for each of the four countries. In addition, we reviewed 289 IMF documents dating back to September 2010. These documents included press releases, speech transcripts, survey findings, policy papers, working papers, country reports and news articles published by the IMF. Our focus, however, was on IMF Article IV memos, given that they provide, among the publicly available documents, the clearest and most detailed guidance provided by the IMF.

global development actors on policy making in that country (Chapter 9, this volume), common IMF policy recommendations across the four countries' Consultations include replacing universal fuel and food subsidies with targeted cash transfers. Recommendations for further privatization of state-owned enterprises, instituting a value-added tax, taking preventative measures against possible inflationary pressures, and keeping public sector wages and pension costs down were also common policy recommendations found in each of the countries' Consultations.

Virtually the only solution to unemployment considered in the Consultations is growing the private sector by promoting competitiveness, making the regulatory environment more business friendly and signalling fiscal restraint. The concluding item in Tunisia's 2010 Consultation, which acknowledges the country's serious youth unemployment problem in its opening paragraph, is indicative of the basic tenor of this approach:

> [IMF staff] welcomes the new impetus to structural reforms to achieve higher growth. Plans to further enhance business climate and competitiveness, including through continued liberalization and openness, to develop high-value-added services, to make better use of the unemployed skilled labor force, and to diversify export markets, are key in developing new sources of growth. (IMF 2010d:18)

The events of the Arab Spring and the ensuing social unrest and political change feature prominently in the subsequent Article IV Consultation reports for these countries, with the exception of Morocco, which saw less internal instability brought on by the Arab Spring protests than did the other countries. The Consultation reports now all identify high unemployment, particularly among youth, as a severe problem facing these countries. Despite recognizing both of these situations and giving them a prominent place in the reports' narrative, only Tunisia's 2012 Article IV Consultation draws any connection between the two, and it finds the root of the problem lies in state intervention rather than market failure:

> The previous regime's state-centered development model delivered for several years high growth and stability but favored a few privileged, and left unemployment at a high level, substantial economic and social disparities across regions, and a sense of denied opportunities. In 2011, amid domestic and regional turmoil, Tunisia experienced a severe recession, its external position deteriorated and unemployment reached unprecedented levels. (IMF 2012:1)

From the rest of the Consultations, however, one would have little idea that frustration with widespread unemployment and recent economic policy was driving the protests across the region. Jordan's 2014 Consultation, for example, puts "corruption and political rights" at the center, while Egypt's 2014 Consultation cites vague "political tensions" against a backdrop of "chronic economic problems." While these were certainly factors feeding into popular discontent, the Consultations largely remain silent about the well-documented employment-related grievances expressed by the Arab Spring protestors in these countries (authors' analysis of Article IV Consultations; Mossallem 2015).

In general, the content of the post–Arab Spring Article IV Consultation reports is remarkably similar to that of the pre–Arab Spring reports. Beyond calling for continued investment in infrastructure and education, particularly vocational training in lieu of traditional university curricula, the IMF consistently warns against fiscal expansion and greater reliance on public sector employment, insisting that any solution to the unemployment crises must come from the private sector. The dilemma is stated especially clearly in Jordan's 2014 Consultation, which puts beyond question, as far as the IMF is concerned, the path that Jordanian policy makers must pursue:

> Jordan's key challenge is to create jobs amidst ongoing fiscal consolidation. … To absorb the new entrants to the labor force, Jordan will need to increase employment by an estimated 400 thousand full-time positions over 2013–20. These new jobs will need to be generated by the private sector, as employment in the public sector as well as emigration to the Gulf can no longer absorb as many Jordanians as they used to. Staff stressed that, in the absence of further reforms to labor and product markets, creating that many jobs would require an average annual real GDP growth to 6.1 percent – a tall order. Current growth forecasts would only generate 275 thousand jobs. (IMF 2014:18)

Although none of the other Consultation reports that we reviewed openly concedes how unlikely their neoliberal policy prescriptions are to achieve the necessary job growth, they all describe the policy terrain in roughly these terms: private sector growth is the only way these countries may realistically address unemployment, suggesting that policy makers in these countries must dedicate themselves to attracting FDI, further privatizing state-controlled industries, reducing hiring costs by loosening employee protections, and removing wage and price controls.

Inclusive growth and skills mismatch

While little changed following the Arab Spring in the specific policies that the Article IV Consultations recommend, two terms begin appearing in the language of the reports that warrant closer examination: "inclusive growth" and "skills mismatches." The reports admit that recent economic growth has had little effect on the countries' high rates of unemployment, but they insist that this growth be made more inclusive. These reports also frequently assert that the structural unemployment in these countries is due to a skills mismatch, which posits an unqualified youth workforce that lacks the skills that private sector employers need. The use of these terms is particularly striking, as they are invoked several times throughout the later Consultations, while they are largely absent from the Consultations issued before the Arab Spring. We address each of them in turn.

The word "inclusive" appears only once in the six pre–Arab Spring Article IV Consultations we surveyed, in Egypt's 2010 Consultation report. In contrast, "inclusive" and its cognates are used 65 times in the main text of the six post–Arab Spring Article IV Consultations we reviewed, not counting their appearances in the headings, tables of contents and accompanying press releases. Given the prevalence of "inclusive growth" and "inclusiveness" in these documents, one would expect the IMF to specify policies that should foster greater inclusion, but it is unclear what exactly about this growth is supposed to be inclusive and how it differs in substance from the previous growth–oriented policies that the IMF had been advocating. Presumably, the IMF in these Consultation reports is claiming that further promoting the private sector will deliver such inclusiveness, but the underlying mechanism by which this should occur is never clearly identified.

The "inclusion" invoked here seems to be a reference to greater absorption of women and currently unemployed youth into formal private sector labour markets. The actual labour market reforms they propose, however, are not ones that Arab Spring protesters or labour advocates would likely characterize as inclusive or equitable. Morocco's 2012 Consultation (IMF 2013:17), for example, claims that "given the limited space for macroeconomic policy to boost demand in the short term, the need for trade and financial liberalization, structural reforms in labor and product markets, and greater access to finance has arguably grown more urgent." Likewise, Egypt's 2014 Consultation (IMF 2015:17) advises that "structural reforms aimed at improving the business climate will support employment. ... Reforms to public service pay should also help by limiting reservation wages, thereby creating incentives towards private sector employment." Given that these are merely the standard neoliberal labour market reforms that the IMF has been promoting for decades, it is hard not to see this newfound emphasis on inclusiveness as anything other than a rebranding strategy.

Skills mismatch

The question of a possible "skills mismatch" behind youth unemployment is, fortunately, less vague and more amenable to empirical investigation. While

Figure 8.1: Real wage growth: 2000–2015

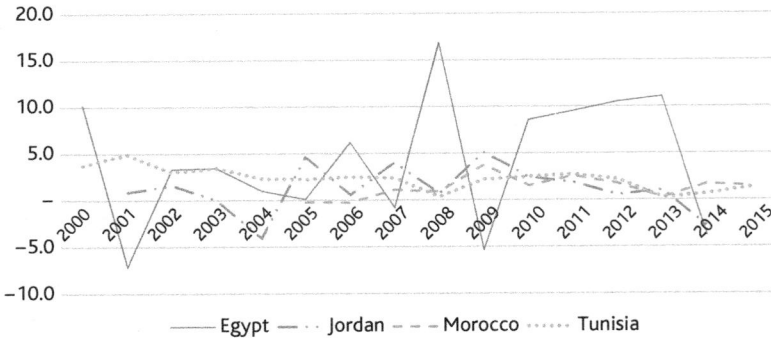

Source: author's calculations from dataset in ILO 2016.

there is some degree of skills mismatch in any economy, it is unlikely that it can account for more than a small percentage of the region's youth unemployment, despite the attention it has received in these reports. As Fergusson and Yeates (2013) found in their analysis of World Bank documents related to youth unemployment, we also find that the number of unemployed and annual new entrants to the labour market are simply much greater than current levels of job growth in all four of the study countries, and it is implausible that any level of skills improvement would create the private sector job growth needed to close this gap (see Table 8.3). Furthermore, we would expect to find workers' wages being bid upward if there were a regional shortage of skilled workers, as those with the requisite skills would become more valuable given the limited supply, but there is little evidence of this happening in these countries' labour markets. In fact, Figure 8.1 suggests that real wage growth among these countries has remained stagnant from 2000 through 2015, with Egypt demonstrating considerable volatility over this period.

Employer surveys from the region do not provide much evidence for this contention either. As shown in Table 8.5, employers in Egypt, Jordan, Morocco and Tunisia reported that political instability, low access to finance and corruption were the primary barriers to private sector growth. A skills shortage, as indicated by a poorly educated workforce, is considered by employers to be a less important obstacle to growth than political instability in Egypt and Tunisia, or corruption in Morocco, or tax rates in Jordan.

In their 2016 report on constraints on private sector growth in the MENA region, de Lima et al (2016) analysed the World Bank's "Enterprise Survey," a survey of over 6,000 manufacturing and service sector firms in eight countries from 2013 to 2014, and found that the average share of workers under 30 years old in the private sector across the region is 43 per cent. The

Table 8.5: Select obstacles to firm growth: percentage of employers indicating obstacle, 2013

Economy	Year	Access to finance	Corruption	Courts	Crime, theft and disorder	Electricity	Poorly educated workforce	Labor regulation	Political instability	Tax rates
Egypt	2013	10.4	5.5	0.2	4.4	9.2	1.8	2.4	48.8	3.9
Jordan	2013	31.2	4.6	1.4	0.6	1.8	4.8	6.0	10.6	23.2
Morocco	2013	9.8	20.6	4.6	1.2	2.4	12.9	2.6	7.7	8.8
Tunisia	2013	10.2	4.3	0.0	1.0	0.4	10.2	1.5	49.8	2.4

Source: adapted from 2013 World Bank Enterprise Survey data. Accessed 1 December 2007. https://www.enterprisesurveys.org/portal/index.aspx#/library?dataset=Enterprise%20Survey

Table 8.6: Labour market panel survey of youth, percentage indicating reason for unemployment

Reason unemployed Egypt, Jordan, Tunisia, youth 15–24, 2010–2014	
Absolutely no work	61.3
No work corresponding to qualifications	18.7
No work at acceptable pay	7.2
No work at suitable employer	6.3
No work at suitable location	2.5

Source: author analysis of Egypt, Jordan and Tunisia—Integrated Labor Market Panel Surveys, Egy-1988–1998–2006–2012, Jor-2010, and Tun-2014, Economic Research Forum.

survey results suggest that firms with higher percentages of young workers provide more training than other firms, which de Lima et al (2016) interpret as evidence of a skills deficit among younger workers. This practice, however, could be just as well explained by endogenous factors, such as a propensity for firms that hire a younger workforce to also be firms that have more progressive human resources policies and provide more incumbent worker training. The authors only speculate as to the cause behind the higher tendency for these employers to train, yet they go on to assert that graduates do not have the skills needed to compete in the private sector. Results from a recent survey of youth related to their labour force attachment (Table 8.6) would suggest that reasons for unemployment have less to do with inadequate skills than with too few employment opportunities.

Conclusion

We find little evidence that IMF policy recommendations for Egypt, Jordan, Morocco and Tunisia changed to reflect Arab Spring calls for significant improvements in employment opportunities for youth in the region. Instead, we find that the neoliberal policy prescriptions provided prior to 2011 remain largely in place. Indeed, in the years since 2011, new revolts have flared up, particularly in Jordan and Tunisia, which are a direct outgrowth in the absence of youth employment policy.

As noted earlier, the IMF's focus on skills mismatch appears to be a relatively new development, judging from our review of its Article IV Consultation memos. In pre-Arab Spring Consultations, skills and education are often mentioned but almost solely in terms of a general need for greater levels of support and then primarily to serve a broader population. After the Arab Spring, Article IV Consultations make frequent use of the specific term "skills mismatch," almost exclusively as an explanation for high levels of unemployment. As noted earlier, there is reason to doubt that youth unemployment can be explained, even partially, in terms of skills mismatch—education levels have been steadily on the rise, wages are not being bid up, job creation lags far behind the demand for jobs and little evidence has been provided to substantiate these claims of a mismatch.

At the heart of the youth unemployment in the region is the absence of sufficient numbers of decent-paying jobs that provide some level of benefits and security—the attraction of the very limited number of public sector jobs has to do precisely with these attributes. Conflict in the region, movements by the Gulf States away from accepting workers from poor countries in the region, remnants of post-Arab Spring-related political instability, and now setbacks related to the COVID-19 pandemic will likely mean that private sector investment in the region will remain inadequate compared to the growing supply of youth entering the labour market. This simple fact gives the lie to the victim-blaming notion, often promoted by IFIs and bilateral aid agencies as a fundamental cause of youth unemployment, that the region's youth lack the skills, whether technical or "soft" skills, to be employed. It is doubtful that increased numbers of educated and skilled youth will be enough to overcome the much larger structural impediments to increasing FDI and the willingness for employers to expand hiring in the region. Policies and programmes that take this idea of market-led solutions to unemployment as their reference point will likely do little more than increase the number of skilled, but still unemployed, youth in the region.

While the tourism industry and much of the service sector will likely rebound as the pandemic subsides, other sectors responsible for employing significant segments of the youth population, such as retail or manufacturing, may take longer to revive given the number of small- and medium-sized firms faced with bankruptcy (nearly one-third in Tunisia; see, for example, Al-Arabiya News 2020). Beyond presenting a temporary, albeit substantial, barrier to moving youth into formal employment in the immediate term, the COVID-19 pandemic has potentially fatally undermined growth-led solutions to youth unemployment for years to come.

A radically different approach to youth unemployment may be needed. One such example is emerging in Tunisia in the form of the solidarity economy work led by the Tunisian Center for Social Entrepreneurship (TCSE).[8] TCSE provides a useful model for focusing state, IFI and bilateral aid agency investment in employment projects that: (i) focus on meeting the most pressing human development needs in the country; (ii) build both technical and "soft" skills with applicability in either the public, non-profit or private sector; and (iii) address youth and female unemployment. With support from the European Union, United Nations Development Program (UNDP), Deutsche Gesellschaft für Internationale Zusammenarbeit (GIZ),

---

[8] See, for example, TCSE. https://tcse.network/.

in addition to the Tunisian Ministry of Women, Families, and Childhood and multiple international NGOs, TCSE has contributed to the formation of over 150 projects across the country, creating hundreds of jobs in the process.

There should be no illusions, though, about the ability of these types of solidarity economy projects to reach a scale soon enough to adequately address, in the near term, youth unemployment and the problems that come with it. The greatest advantage of pursuing these strategies, however, is that they decouple workers' ability to earn a living and live a fulfilling life from the impersonal demands of global trade and ever-changing skill needs required to remain "competitive" in a global economy. The example set by TCSE, as well as by other solidarity economy-oriented projects in the region, such as the Maghreb Social and Solidarity Network, suggest that human-centred alternatives to neoliberalism are possible.[9]

The IMF's emphasis on economic growth as a one-size-fits-all solution has contributed to an environment in which policy autonomy is limited and, through its continuing application of conditions in exchange for assistance, at the same time, public sector support, either through direct employment or through ALMPs, is drastically cut. This environment, in turn, contributes to undermining the foundations needed for economic growth by contributing directly to social instability. If investment from IFIs, instead, were focused on creating employment opportunities for youth, rather than leaving that role to the market, it is conceivable that the vicious cycle of unemployment and political and social strife that continues in the region to this day could be broken.

Acknowledgements

We would like to thank Charles Demakis, Caleb Seibert, Nina Guidice, Ghida Ismail and Leena Warsi for their invaluable assistance.

References

Al-Arabiya News. 2020. "Coronavirus: Tunisian Unemployment Soars as Economy Suffers under COVID-19." Al-Arabiya News, 10 October 2020. Accessed 30 June 2022. https://english.alarabiya.net/coronavirus/2020/10/10/Coronavirus-Tunisian-unemployment-soars-as-economy-suffers-under-COVID-19.

---

[9] This chapter summarizes a longer study that provides a fuller treatment of innovative active labour market policies that have emerged in post-Arab Spring Egypt, Jordan, Morocco and Tunisia, published by the United Nations Research Institute for Social Development (UNRISD). That paper details the policies, programmes and institutional infrastructure created in reaction to youth unemployment-led uprisings, ranging from the direct provisions of jobs by national governments, to solidarity economy-oriented projects, to multi-year national plans focused on youth unemployment. It can be found at https://cdn.unrisd.org/assets/library/papers/pdf-files/wp2018-12-prince-et-al.pdf.

al-Nashif, N. a. Z. T. 2013. "Only Fair: Social Justice Must Be at the Foundation of Arab Economic Reforms." *Finance and Development*, 50 (March):8–13.

Asharq Al-Awsat. 2020. "COVID-Driven Unemployment in Morocco." Asharq Al-Awsat, 29 September 2020. Accessed 30 June 2022. https://english.aawsat.com/home/article/2535721/covid-driven-unemployment-morocco.

Assaad, R. 2014. "The Structure and Evolution of Employment in Jordan." In *The Jordanian Labour Market in the New Millennium*, edited by R. Assaad, 1–38. Oxford: Oxford University Press.

Babb, S. L. and A. Buira. 2005. "Mission Creep, Mission Push and Discretion: The Case of IMF Conditionality." in *The IMF and the World Bank at Sixty*, edited by A. Buira, 59–84. London: Anthem.

Bayliss, K., Ben Fine and Elisa Van Waerenberge (eds). 2011. *The Political Economy of Development: The World Bank, Neoliberalism and Development Research*. London: Pluto Press.

Bargawi, H. 2014. "Economic Policies, Structural Change and the Roots of the 'Arab Spring' in Egypt." *Review of Middle East Economics and Finance*, 10(3):219–246.

Barsoum, G. 2013. "The Alignment of the Policy Objectives of Youth Inclusion and Population Regulation in Post Arab-Spring Egypt: A Discussion Paper." *International Journal of Sociology and Social Policy*, 33(7/8): 410–425.

Bellin, E. 2013. "From Authoritarianism to People Power in the MENA: Implications for Inclusion and Equity." In *Getting Development Right: Structural Transformation, Inclusion, and Sustainability in the Post-Crisis Era*, edited by Eva Paus, 137–152. New York: Palgrave Macmillan.

Benar, H. 2007. "Has Globalization Increased Income Inequality in the MENA Region?" *International Journal of Economic Perspectives*, 1(4):195–211.

de Lima, P., Debora Revoltella, Jorge Luis Rodriguez Meza and Helena Schweiger. 2016. *What's Holding Back the Private Sector in MENA: Lessons from the Enterprise Survey*. London, Luxembourg and Washington, DC: European Bank for Reconstruction and Development, European Investment Bank and World Bank Group.

DeMartino, G. 1999. "Global Neoliberalism, Policy Autonomy, and International Competitive Dynamics." *Journal of Economic Issues*, 33(2):343–349.

El-Said, H. and J. Harrigan. 2014. "Economic Reform, Social Welfare, and Instability: Jordan, Egypt, Morocco, and Tunisia, 1983–2004." *The Middle East Journal*, 68(1): 99–121.

ESCWA (Economic and Social Commission for Western Asia). 2014. *The Promises of Spring: Citizenship and Civic Engagement in Democratic Transitions*. Beirut: United Nations.

Fergusson, R. and N. Yeates. 2013. "Business, as Usual: The Policy Priorities of the World Bank's Discourses on Youth Unemployment, and the Global Financial Crisis." *Journal of International and Comparative Social Policy*, 29(1):64–78.

Gavlak, D. 2020. "Coronavirus Pandemic Adds Challenges to Jordan's Fragile Economy." Voice of America News, 7 October. Accessed 30 June 2022. https://www.voanews.com/middle-east/coronavirus-pandemic-adds-cha llenges-jordans-fragile-economy.

Hadid, N. 2016. "Painful Steps Help Egypt Secure $12 Billion I.M.F. Loan." *New York Times*, 11 November. Accessed 30 June 2022. https://www. nytimes.com/2016/11/12/world/middleeast/egypt-gets-final-imf-appro val-for-12-billion-loan.html?mcubz=1&_r=0.

Hanieh, A. 2015. "Shifting Priorities or Business as Usual? Continuity and Change in the Post-2011 IMF and World Bank Engagement with Tunisia, Morocco and Egypt." *British Journal of Middle Eastern Studies*, 42(1):119–134. doi:10.1080/13530194.2015.973199.

Henisz, W., B. Zelner and M. Guillen. 2005. "The Worldwide Diffusion of Market-Oriented Infrastructure Reform, 1977–1999." *American Sociological Review*, 70(December):871–897.

ILO (International Labor Organization). 2016. *Global Wage Report 2016/ 17: Wage Inequality in the Workplace.* Geneva: ILO.

ILO (International Labor Organization) and SIDA (Swedish International Development Agency). 2015. *SIDA-ILO Partnership Program 2014– 2017: Progress Report, Phase I 2014–2015.* Geneva: ILO and SIDA.

IMF (International Monetary Fund). 2016a. *Morocco: 2015 Article IV Consultation.* IMF Country Report No. 16/35, February. Washington, DC: IMF.

IMF (International Monetary Fund). 2016b. "IMF Executive Board Approves US$12 billion Extended Arrangement Under the Extended Fund Facility for Egypt." Press Release No. 16/501. Washington, DC: IMF.

IMF (International Monetary Fund). 2015a. *Tunisia: 2015 Article IV Consultation.* IMF Country Report No. 15/285, October. Washington, DC: IMF.

IMF (International Monetary Fund). 2015b. "Egypt: 2014 Article IV Consultation." IMF Country Report No. 15/33, February. Washington, DC: IMF.

IMF (International Monetary Fund). 2014. *Jordan: 2014 Article IV Consultation.* IMF Country Report No. 14/152, June. Washington, DC: IMF.

IMF (International Monetary Fund). 2013. *Morocco: 2012 Article IV Consultation.* IMF Country Report No. 13/96, September. Washington, DC: IMF.

IMF (International Monetary Fund). 2012. *Tunisia: 2012 Article IV Consultation*. IMF Country Report No. 12/255, September. Washington, DC: IMF.

IMF (International Monetary Fund). 2010a. *Egypt: 2010 Article IV Consultation*. IMF Country Report No. 10/94, April. Washington, DC: IMF.

IMF (International Monetary Fund). 2010b. *Morocco: 2009 Article IV Consultation*. IMF Country Report No. 10/58, March. Washington, DC: IMF.

IMF (International Monetary Fund). 2010c. *Jordan: 2010 Article IV Consultation*. IMF Country Report No. 10/297, September. Washington, DC: IMF.

IMF (International Monetary Fund). 2010d. *Tunisia: 2010 Article IV Consultation*. IMF Country Report No. 10/282, September. Washington, DC: IMF.

IMF (International Monetary Fund). 2009. *Jordan: 2009 Article IV Consultation*. IMF Country Report No. 09/159, May. Washington, DC: IMF.

IMF (International Monetary Fund). 2007. *Egypt: 2007 Article IV Consultation*. IMF Country Report No. 07/380, December. Washington, DC: IMF.

Karshenas, M., Moghadam, V. M. and Alami, R. 2014. "Social Policy after the Arab Spring: States and Social Rights in the MENA Region." *World Development*, 64: 726–739.

Kentikelenis, A., T. Stubbs and L. King. 2016. "IMF Conditionality and Development Policy Space, 1985–2014." Institute for New Economic Thinking, Cambridge Political Economy Society Trust and Center for Business Research at the University of Cambridge. Accessed 1 August 2016. http://www.tandfonline.com/doi/abs/10.1080/09692290.2016.1174953?journalCode=rrip20.

Malik, Adeel and Bassem Awadallah. 2011. *The Economics of the Arab Spring*. Centre for the Study of African Economies Working Paper No. WPS/2011–23. Oxford and Jeddah: Centre for the Study of African Economies.

Mossallem, Mohammed. 2015. *The IMF in the Arab World: Lessons Unlearnt*. London: Bretton Woods Project.

New York Times. 2016. "Egypt Averts Economic Collapse, for Now." Accessed 6 November 2016. https://www.nytimes.com/2016/11/06/opinion/sunday/egypt-averts-economic-collapse-for-now.html?mcubz=1.

Noueihed, Lin and Alex Warren. 2012. *The Battle for the Arab Spring: Revolution, Counter-Revolution, and the Making of a New Era*. New Haven: Yale University Press.

Prince, H.J. 2014. "Macro-Level Drivers of Multidimensional Poverty in Sub-Saharan Africa: Measuring Change in the Human Poverty Index." *African Evaluation Journal*, 2(1): 1–10.

Prince, H.J., Yara A. Halasa-Rappel and Amna Khan. 2016. *Economic Growth, Youth Unemployment, and Political and Social Instability: A Study of Policies and Outcomes in Post-Arab Spring Egypt, Morocco, Jordan, and Tunisia.* Working Paper No. 12 prepared for the UNRISD project on New Directions in Social Policy: Alternatives from and for the Global South. Geneva: United Nations Research Institute for Social Development.

Ray, N. and L. Schmitz. 2016. "The IMF and the Social Dimensions of Growth: A Content Analysis of Recent Article IV Surveillance Reports 2014–2015." Working Paper No. 202, Employment and Labour Market Policies Branch. Geneva: International Labour Organization.

Salehi-Isfahani, D., R. Assaad and R. Hendy (2015). *Inequality of Opportunity in Education and Youth Employment in Middle East and North Africa: Evidence from Household Surveys.* Giza: The Economic Research Forum (ERF).

Stiglitz, J. 2002. *Globalization and Its Discontents.* New York: W.W. Norton.

UNDP (United Nations Development Program) and ILO (International Labour Organization). 2012. "Rethinking Economic Growth: Towards Productive and Inclusive Arab Societies." Geneva: ILO.

Woods, N. 2006. *The Globalizers: The IMF, the World Bank, and Their Borrowers.* Ithaca: Cornell University Press.

World Bank. 2020. "The World Bank in Egypt." Accessed 1 October 2020. https://www.worldbank.org/en/country/egypt/overview.

9

Global Development Actors and Country Ownership in Indonesian Social Policy Making

Alexandra Kaasch and Brooke Wilmsen

Introduction

Social policy has become increasingly central in the development processes of low- and middle-income countries. At the same time, social protection has moved to the centre of global policy discourse and development aid agendas. This is, for example, featured in the recommendations and goals of global actors such as the International Labour Organization's (ILO) Recommendation 202 on social protection floors, the first Sustainable Development Goal (SDG) (see, for example, SDG 1.3) (UN 2017) and more broadly across international organizations that support universal social protection (such as, the recent United Nations Political Declaration of the High-Level Meeting on Universal Health Coverage; UN 2019). These broad recommendations, goals and aspirations are transposed into various development agreements at the bilateral and multilateral levels; however, the mechanisms designed to implement these agreements are often different between donor and recipient countries and can at times be contradictory.

Development aid generally comes with conditionalities or relationships of dependence that restrict the scope of national actors and policy makers to determine their national priorities. This is problematic in terms of democratic governance, as it undermines national competencies and processes, and often reflects the interests of the donor rather than those of the recipient of development aid. In the social policy space, this is even more problematic as it is the national and subnational levels of government that have the oversight and depth of understanding of the context of social policy institutions and arrangements. Social policy making is supposed to happen in response to the social needs of vulnerable groups that are specific to a particular society, culture and place. Macro players within a country (such as governments, parties, trade unions and civil society actors), in consultation with the meso- (subnational) and micro-level (community) stakeholders, need to determine what is needed and how this should be provided. In an attempt to strengthen social policy development, its origins and the drivers of institution building need to be critically examined against the potential and actual influence of external actors.

This research is positioned at the confluence of social policy and development studies scholarship. The former emphasizes the role of recipient nations in steering their political processes to formulate meaningful and legitimate social policy and practice. Similarly, since the endorsement of the Paris Principles on Aid Effectiveness in 2005 by the major bilateral donors and key multilateral organizations (such as the World Bank and the Organisation for Economic Co-operation and Development [OECD]) and subsequent agreements such as the Accra Agenda for Action (OECD 2008), the principle of *country ownership* has become a central guiding principle of development aid. The role of national actors is considered crucial in delivering beneficial and sustainable aid. Donors aim at supporting contextually relevant interventions that are determined by the recipient nation. While the notion of country ownership is just one pillar of a broader agenda for aid effectiveness, the other key principles are alignment, harmonization, managing for results and mutual accountability. In this chapter, we focus on country ownership as this is commonly recognized to be the most important of the five principles.[1] It implies countries have control over their own policies and that they are in the driving seat in policy-making processes (Dijkstra 2013).

As an emerging economy, Indonesia is a particularly interesting case for examining how social policy development is navigated by external actors that have endorsed the principles of aid effectiveness. Like other countries in Southeast Asia, Indonesia has made significant progress in expanding universal social protection in recent years. At the same time, numerous development actors continue to work actively in the country. Economic growth tends to strengthen the power of national governments to determine the conditions of development aid and the terms under which external actors can engage in domestic policy. However, the activities of international actors in the social protection sphere have also increased in recent years. It is in the context of this shifting power dynamics that this chapter investigates the engagement of key external agencies with Indonesia's social policy development. We are particularly concerned with how development relationships have been (re) shaped to reflect the principle of country ownership, while at the same time adhering to global or donor goals in social policy development.

Accordingly, this chapter is structured as follows: First, we introduce social policy development in Indonesia since the 1950s. Then, we present the case of Indonesia's health system development in order to demonstrate

---

[1] For a broader take on aid effectiveness, see another output of our project: Wilmsen et al (2019).

a successful, but also early test case of current social policy development in an emerging Southeast Asian economy. We then discuss the role of specific external agencies (donor countries and international organizations) that have been involved in this development, followed by an exploration of the relationships between agencies and actors in the development and reform of social and health policies in Indonesia. Finally, we reflect on the implications of what we observe for Indonesia for countries in the region and emerging economies in general.

Social Policy Development in Indonesia (1950s–2010s)

Formal social protection originated in Indonesia during the colonial period when the Dutch colonialists established a pension system that was accessible to a small and select group of military personnel and civil servants. A decade after independence, the Soekarno government expanded the colonial system it inherited from the Dutch and extended it with some additional benefits. It was not, however, made accessible to broader groups of the population, and instead only applied to public servants. In the mid-1960s, after the Soekarno administration ascended to power, the system was expanded to include both health and pension insurance for public sector workers. In the early 1990s, another extension saw the formal private sector included for the first time to provide accident, health, death and old-age benefits, based on employer and employee contributions (Pisani et al 2017). It is important to highlight that despite these progressions, informal sector workers, which accounted for the majority of Indonesians, remained outside the scope of these benefits.

Since the late 1990s, social policy development in Indonesia has occurred against a backdrop of significant economic advancement and deep crises. Considered to be part of the "East Asian miracle," Indonesia experienced rapid development from 1980, but then in 1997 the Asian financial crisis caused sharp economic contraction. This was followed by a period of imposed interventions from international actors such as the International Monetary Fund (IMF). Owing to a misinterpretation of the nature of the crisis, the IMF aggravated the economic crisis further by heightening internal and external public debt, resulting in a loss of Soekarno's trust in his economic advisers (Grenville 2004; Toussaint 2019). Post-crisis, social policy development was pulled in different directions by the IMF. It demanded that fuel and other subsidies be removed, which challenged the relationship between the government of Indonesia and external actors (Robinson and Rosser 1998) while also instigating some important developments in social policy—namely, the introduction of the Rice for Food programme (*Raskin*) (Neilson and Wright 2017).

From 1998 to 2004, social policy in Indonesia developed further with the introduction of public health insurance, which was the forerunner to a more comprehensive system of social protection. From 2011 onward, important institution building took place with the establishment of a new implementing agency devoted to social security. It had two sections that focused on health and employment (see, for example, Suryahadi et al 2017). The current system of social protection in Indonesia is broadly based on a rights–based approach to social security and pursues the aim of universal coverage of social protection. There is also an overarching aim of establishing a universal health system across Indonesia that would connect all the elements of social protection. In the next section, we focus more specifically on the development of the health system in Indonesia.

Health System Development

The development of Indonesia's health system can be described as following a gradualist approach with regard to the speed of inclusion of different groups of the population and the scope of expansion of provisions. This section provides a brief review of the most important steps of the past decades, in order to illustrate the role and potential impact of external actors in Indonesian social policy making.

Early health policy in Indonesia focused on the prevention of communicable disease; however, the introduction of a health insurance programme in the 1940s marked an important first step toward the gradual establishment of universal health care across Indonesia. Although it initially only covered formal sector workers, in the 1960s the Indonesian government introduced a more comprehensive health insurance programme that covered both private sector workers and civil servants (Sumarto 2017). This period marked the burgeoning of critical health care infrastructure in Indonesia.

During the 1980s and 1990s, significant institution building took place in Indonesia. By the end of the 1990s, as health became central to social policy development in Indonesia, the informal and poor sectors were prioritized. Of particular importance was the development of *Health Indonesia 2010*, an intersectoral programme that was established in 1998 with the aim to provide health insurance to the poor via a health card. This was followed by the 2010–2014 Strategic Plan, which was set up to guide the government of Indonesia to its ultimate aim of instituting a comprehensive health system based on the principles of self-reliance and equitable access. The government of Indonesia aimed to provide better health care, improve health outcomes for the population, and extend its reach to remote and poor populations (Kadar et al 2012).

The year 2014 was significant in the development of the Indonesian health system. It marked the first use of the term "universalization," which has remained a guiding principle ever since. The expressed aim of the government of Indonesia was to achieve universal coverage by 2019. While it is important for the government to have targets, in Indonesia there is still a way to go to achieve truly universal coverage. Major barriers remain in reaching remote areas of the large archipelago and providing adequate public funding to cover the costs of such an expansive health care system. Accordingly, at an IMF-JICA (Japan International Cooperation Agency) Conference in February 2017, Teguh Dartanto predicted that "with the current path (without any massive intervention), Universal Health Coverage (UHC) is difficult in 2019, but possible in 2030" (Dartanto 2017).

The Role of International Actors in the Development of Indonesia's Health System

The development of Indonesia's health care system has involved interventions by various international and bilateral donors. Given their number and diversity we cannot hope to give a complete description of the donor landscape over the past decades. Instead, we discuss the role of several key players in Indonesia's health policy—four international organizations (the World Bank, the World Health Organization [WHO], the ILO and the OECD) and four bilateral donors (Australia, Germany, the United States and Japan). Each of these agencies had specific contractual and funding agreements with the Indonesian government to assist in the development of the health system. We consider the activities of each of these organizations and consider to what extent they reflect notions of country ownership.

International organizations in Indonesia

In this section, we study four international organizations so as to understand their roles in the development of the Indonesian health system with a specific focus on if and how their notion of country ownership has changed during the time of their engagement with the government of Indonesia. For each of the organizations, we provide a general characterization, an account of their mechanisms of influence, and reflections on the changing relationships between them and the government of Indonesia.

The World Health Organization

The WHO has a long history of collaboration with the government of Indonesia and played a key role in extending Indonesia's system of social protection, going back at least to the 1950s. Early engagement saw the WHO focus on controlling communicable diseases, but it soon began providing technical, financial and coordinative support in developing the health system (WHO SEARO 1999). Over the past few decades, the WHO has been a strong supporter of the government of Indonesia's plans to universalize health care, and it has provided capacity building, monitoring and evaluation, training and the provision of guidelines for better quality of health care.

The main mechanism of support is the WHO's Country Cooperation Strategy (CCS), a medium-term vision for the WHO's technical cooperation with Indonesia. These CCSs are intended to support the national government's health policies and plans while aligning with national planning timeframes (WHO 2010). In 2001, Indonesia was one of the first countries to develop a CCS and since then it has had three successive CCSs (WHO 2016). These covered the periods 2001–2005, 2007–2011 and 2014–2019.

The CCSs marked a new and more reflective means of cooperation with countries for the WHO. This is particularly evident in the different framings of the second and third CCSs. Here we observe how the framing of the WHO's relationship with the government of Indonesia is more closely aligned with the principle of country ownership. At the same time, CCSs also provide a way of defining the continued role of WHO in health policy development in the country.

From the 2007–2011 strategy, we can identify a role of WHO that includes system assessments. These assessments are critical of the route taken, particularly the impact of decentralization on the health system. However, they also point the finger at other international organizations (particularly the IMF and World Bank) for questionable policy advice and conditionalities, rather than blaming the government of Indonesia. Nevertheless, there appears to be some contradiction in the role the WHO assumes in supporting the national government and its relationships with external partners. It states it will "support the Ministry of Health in coordinating health partners, in fostering intersectoral collaboration," and it will "strengthen partnerships among health actors as appropriate, for example, NGOs, UN and bilateral agencies, universities and development banks" (WHO 2008:31). By positioning itself between the government of Indonesia and other external actors, the principle of country ownership may be undermined.

Among the five priorities of cooperation between 2014 and 2019 was ensuring Indonesia achieved UHC (WHO 2016). The latest strategy shows more planning orientation along with national processes to achieve this aim. This is partly driven by the growth of Indonesia's economy, meaning that the government of Indonesia is increasingly able to self-fund its health services. However, the WHO still considers there to be a need for external agencies "in identifying key constraints in the health sector, along with innovations and solutions that can be expanded to country programmes and policies," and locates its own role there (WHO 2016:2). The criticisms levelled at decentralization are much more careful and reflect much more the actor role associated with the Indonesian government (rather than referring indirectly to the international financial institutions). In order to address some of the shortcomings identified in the health system, the WHO's aim is to have additional Country Office staff members.

With Indonesia's growing self-reliance for the provision of its health system, the WHO is becoming more careful about criticizing the policy directions taken by the government and instead is bolstering the number of in-country staff. This suggests the WHO is justifying its continued relevance to Indonesia by presenting a more engaged, embedded staff base that is attuned to the needs of the national government. However, there is a tension between this strategy and the WHO's continued promotion of the need for "external" assessment and actor coordination. The latter suggests a lack of confidence in Indonesia's institutions and capacity to undertake these roles, which ultimately undermines the principle of country ownership.

The World Bank

As an international financial institution, the World Bank has a different base and scope of influence in Indonesia than the WHO, but an equally long story of engagement. In the mid-1960s, the World Bank became the primary external actor in developing Indonesia's social policy programmes through financial support and technical advice. From the late 1990s onward, the World Bank supported the *jaring pengaman sosial* programme—a social safety net programme. And later, the World Bank provided technical assistance for the expansion of the health system, as part of a conditional cash transfer programme—Program Keluarga Harapan.

Among other things, World Bank influence was exerted by means of a structural adjustment programme, and through the mechanism of country partnership frameworks. In addition, the World Bank has assumed an increasingly powerful role in knowledge provision. Whereas the WHO's role has been to assess health problems, the World Bank's contribution has been to provide the technical solutions, that is, the "how to do" of health policy and reform (for example, the reports of the past few years demand more and better generation of taxes to go into the health system; Marzoeki et al 2014, World Bank 2015b, 2016).

In terms of the changing relationship between the World Bank and the government of Indonesia, there has been a clear shift from initiating the first social safety net to progressing universal health care to knowledge provision. Presently the World Bank provides advice on a range of issues from the generation of taxes to fund the health sector, to the coordination of the Indonesian ministries of health and finance, to making improvements in health spending (World Bank 2018). Equally telling is how former World Bank staff look back, comment and judge their previous ways of engagement. In documents from the 1970s they frankly speak about the need to place, more concretely: "resident staff ... so ... in relation to the structure of the Government of Indonesia that it is directly advising and has direct access to the top decision-making officers of that Government" (World Bank 1968:5). In the 1980s, apart from having a more comprehensive perspective on social development tasks, it is stressed that the Indonesian government approached the World Bank: "Both MOH and BAPPENAS expressed serious interest in Bank health sector assistance" (Liese 1980:no. 10). By the beginning of the 1990s, the World Bank was increasingly careful about the way in which it described its role in Indonesia, as can be evidenced by this statement made by Marianne Haug, a World Bank staffer between 1972 and 1999:

> So in many ways, for me, looking at what the World Bank has done in Indonesia, we only had a support role. We should NOT believe that we have been so terribly instrumental. We have been effective and often our advice has been implemented because there were people on the other end, in government and industry who listened. Despite the often difficult decisions, they were willing to adopt recommended solutions to pursue their fundamental objectives. Over 25-years the Indonesian government implemented pragmatic solutions always with these objectives in mind: equity, stability and growth. (Lewis and Webb 1991:2)

In more recent years, rather than focusing on the health sector in isolation, the World Bank is concerned more broadly with social issues and inequalities in the country. For example, in the 2015 World Bank Indonesia Country Partnership Framework, the World Bank focuses more specifically on children and the role of the water and sanitation programme (PAMSIMAS) in improving health outcomes rather than structural reforms to the health system (World Bank 2015a). However, the International Finance Corporation, the arm of the World Bank Group that supports the private sector in development, is more explicitly focused on the provision of health care services, for example, by supporting private sector health care providers to "complement the government to improve services for citizens" (World Bank 2015a:no. 78).

Overall, in terms of funding and the ability to impose conditionalities, the World Bank has been the most powerful external actor in Indonesia. This was at times beneficial for social policy development in Indonesia, for example, the initiation of the social safety net, but the World Bank's retreat from providing financial (and conditional) support to Indonesia has contributed to the growing independence of national institutions and policy-making processes. The rise of the World Bank as a knowledge provider and its support to the private sector may still have a significant impact, but is less likely to undermine the principle of country ownership. Whether such developments will improve the "social" side of the social policy system remains to be seen.

The International Labour Organization

While the ILO claims to play a role in the development of social and health policy in Indonesia, given its mandate, its role in the social policy space is more limited in terms of financial means, staff and perceived legitimation (Kaasch 2015).[2] The ILO's mechanism of influence is facilitating, rather than enforcing or providing accountability for, the international standards of labour rights and its labour conventions. To this end, the ILO has urged the government of Indonesia to adopt international labour standards (Caraway 2004; ILO 2015; Rupidara and McGraw 2010). It has also been involved in technical cooperation through several Decent Work Country Programmes (DWCPs) (ILO 2008).[3] The ILO has also been involved in social protection more broadly in Indonesia, in relation to its mandate: "Indonesia should have a core public social security scheme which provides adequate social security protection, broadly consistent with ILO standards, which should be part of a mixed system of social protection with three tiers or levels" (ILO 1999:1). As evidenced by this statement, in the 1990s the ILO was concerned with influencing the government's structure of social protection delivery. This culminated in a project entitled "Restructuring of the Social Security System in Indonesia" that lasted only a short time (from April 2001 to December 2002) and was funded by the government of the Netherlands (ILO 2003). Under this project, an ILO consultant was assigned (for one month) to prepare a national strategy for social security development in Indonesia, proposing reform of existing institutions, and developing an implementation plan. The objectives of the project included the establishment of an entire new institutional structure for the national social security scheme and the development of a national strategic plan for the restructuring of the social security system (ILO 2003). In the mid-2000s, the ILO again undertook an assessment of social protection developments in Indonesia and identified areas for additional ILO input, including improving the effectiveness of targeting

---

[2] The ILO engages with health policy development as part of its involvement in broader social security reform. The ILO also engages with health system development through the ILO social protection floor, which includes universal health care (see Social Protection Recommendation 202; ILO 2012).

[3] DWCPs are the ILO's mechanism to support countries, both in terms of a policy idea (decent work as a key component of national development strategies), and to organize its support (comprising knowledge provision, instruments, advocacy and cooperation). See https://www.ilo.org/global/about-the-ilo/how-the-ilo-works/departments-and-offices/program/dwcp/lang--en/index.htm (accessed 10 July 2022).

Health Cards for the Poor (ILO 2006). The third and current DWCP (2018–2022) has a minor health focus. The related activities are expected to contribute to the overall aim of social protection for all (ILO 2019).

When compared with the WHO or the World Bank, the ILO seems less concerned with the principle of country ownership and more concerned with creating or upholding its role in Indonesia. Overall, the ILO also provides limited budgetary support to the Indonesian health sector (Chowdhury et al 2016) and the scope of support is limited to those activities that fall within the purview of the ILO. The limited role of the ILO in the health sector is perhaps why the ILO is more forthright in emphasizing its function rather than taking a more reflective position in support of country ownership. Thus, unlike the World Bank and the WHO, the ILO has not demonstrated a clear change in its engagement with the government of Indonesia in response to the principle of country ownership.

The Organisation for Economic Co-operation and Development

Since 2007, Indonesia has been classified as one of the OECD's five key partners, which comes with specific cooperation agreements. However, the first consideration of social policy appeared in the second agreement (2017–2018), which discussed the notion of inclusive growth with the aim of assisting Indonesia in devising its response to the SDGs. In 2019, a new three-year Joint Work Programme was initiated that is less focused on social policy broadly, but more explicitly concerned with providing advice on how to measure health-related finances and services in the pursuit of UHC (OECD 2018:7).

In addition, the European Union–Finland–OECD Development Centre's Social Protection Programme is working toward improving the quality and coverage of social protection. In close cooperation with Indonesia's Ministry of National Development Planning (BAPPENAS) it produced a review of Indonesia's social protection system (OECD 2018). The report suggests that to improve the social protection system the Indonesian government needs to close the gaps in coverage with social assistance and social insurance provision and better coordinate the various social protection programmes, to improve coherence. It is recommended that higher allocations of funding and resources to social protection are needed, along with resource optimization and domestic resource mobilization. The report does not provide any specific recommendations with regard to health care, although in another report, the OECD acknowledges developments and successes in the field of social health insurance and beyond (OECD 2019:50).

Given that the role of the OECD is to provide knowledge and advice—not financial support—there is no evidence of a change in its engagement with Indonesia in response to the principle of country ownership. Nor is there evidence of imposing its role on the Indonesian government, as for example the ILO has done. The OECD is under less pressure to define its role in Indonesia as its mandate as an adviser to governments is to improve policies.

Bilateral relationships with Indonesia

The other key group of actors influencing social policy development in Indonesia is other national governments. Although they are not disconnected from the international organizations discussed previously, for example, many countries including Australia, Germany, Japan and the United States were members of the Intergovernmental Group on Indonesia (IGGI)/ Consultative Group on Indonesia (CGI),[4] they tend to be even more influential than their international counterparts. Here, the role of finance is stronger, but there is also evidence of powerful ideational influences. To explore how the principle of country ownership is observed, we consider the role of the United States Agency for International Development (USAID) (United States), former AusAid (Australia), the Deutsche Gesellschaft für Internationale Zusammenarbeit (GIZ) (Germany) and JICA (Japan) as four important bilateral partners that have influenced the development of the health sector in Indonesia.

Japan

The Japanese development relationship with Indonesia is the longest of those we explore. However, it is perhaps also Indonesia's most controversial relationship owing to Japan's occupation during the Second World War. Not to diminish the difficulties surrounding that period, presently Japan is one of Indonesia's largest bilateral donors. Japanese development work has had a focus on health, for example, JICA has supported health security projects such as Indonesia's public insurance system for health (JICA 2014) under its 2013 "Strategy on Global Health Diplomacy" and the global UHC initiative.[5] However, in recent years Japan's development aid has been directed to infrastructure projects (JICA 2016; OECD 2014) and it has reduced its interventions in the development of health care in Indonesia.

Though the shift in the development priorities of Japan in Indonesia is unlikely to be related to the principle of country ownership, JICA no longer considers the health sector to be a productive field to engage in. One explanation could be the ideology that underpins the provision of aid by

---

[4] Through the IGGI, and later CGI, lenders discussed and coordinated their aid between each other and in consultation with the government of Indonesia.

[5] http://www.mofa.go.jp/mofaj/files/000005946.pdf (accessed 10 July 2022).

Japan, that is, that aid should assist in "'graduating' recipient countries from aid dependence," or the "aid to end aid" principle (Kato et al 2016:347). Kato et al (2016) argue that long before any "country ownership" principle was invented, it was at the heart of Japan's aid to "work themselves out of the job" (Kato et al 2016:351), by linking aid and private investment. From such a perspective, it makes sense to move away from the health sector at the point when other sectors could benefit more. However, a more critical reading would suggest that the shift in Japan's activities in Indonesia was driven by an interest in maximizing the investment value of its aid rather than improving social outcomes.

The United States

Unlike Japan, through USAID, the United States has *explicitly* demonstrated a commitment to the principle of country ownership. This can be seen in the strategic document it released in 2018 called "Journey to Self-Reliance" (USAID 2018) that outlines USAID's aim to build capacity in its recipient countries so that those countries can address their own development challenges.

Health sector development features in USAID's new strategic approach, particularly to improve maternal and newborn health, and the eradication of specific communicable diseases by "working with the government of Indonesia to sustain and increase efficiency in financing for health to improve financial protection, equitable access to quality health services, and health outcomes" (USAID 2018:21). This suggests the US–Indonesia Strategic partnership is focused on strengthening Indonesia's health systems and increasing self-reliance of the country in preventing, detecting and responding to health challenges. However, the choice of health fields to engage in is fully oriented toward standard US development aid priorities, and neither developed out of an assessment of actual development needs in this specific country, nor was designed in an honest partnership mode.

The US approach, therefore, does not appear as a particularly nuanced or reflective one based on what country ownership might mean, even with the national government defining their own priorities.

Australia

Australia is presently Indonesia's second largest donor behind Japan. Through the aid arm of the Australian government (formerly AusAID but now part of the Department of Foreign Affairs and Trade), Indonesia's health policy development has been an important focus since 2009. Rather than imposing changes to Indonesia's existing health care system, Australia has worked with the Indonesian government to bridge the gaps in the current system. Australia has also had a particular interest in Indonesia's social development, including social protection. In 2007, this became a focus for the expansion of its aid activities in Indonesia. This coincided with the Indonesian president's declaration that poverty reduction was his highest development priority and the subsequent establishment of the Tim Nasional Percepatan Penanggulangan Kemiskinan (TNP2K)—or National Team for the Acceleration of Poverty Reduction (Wilmsen et al 2019). In 2009, the vice-president contacted AusAID for support with his endeavours and AusAID responded swiftly to set up the Poverty Reduction Support Facility (PRSF) (Wilmsen et al. 2019). The PRSF acted as an appendage to TNP2K that Indonesia could call on for research, special funding and expert advice to help inform the direction of social protection reform (Wilmsen et al 2019).

The Australian–Indonesian collaboration was explicitly framed as a "partnership" relationship, based on policy dialogue, rather than a traditional donor–recipient model. In terms of contributions, in the time from 2010 to 2015 Australia provided AUD 30 million per year to support social protection development in Indonesia, while the government of Indonesia invested more than AUD five billion annually (DFAT 2015). The Australian money was flexible and nimble to the needs of the Indonesian government and also allowed it to circumvent its own cumbersome bureaucracy. This example demonstrates the Australian government's commitment to the principle of country ownership and its careful engagement with the Indonesian government by providing an appendage institution to support the ministries. It provided knowledge and funding as requested rather than imposing structural changes or reforms.

Germany

The development agency of the German government, GIZ, is actively engaged in health sector development in Indonesia; however, rather than providing funding for particular projects, it provides knowledge and advice. In particular, GIZ focuses on providing expertise on social insurance models by running workshops with German and other experts in the field of social health insurance. They then provide technical advice to Indonesian policy makers and people working in public administration. GIZ claims that what has been emerging in Indonesia is "a statutory health insurance system based on the German model."[6] Given that the financial, social, cultural and political context of Indonesia is unlike that of Germany, the relevance and transferability of the German model to Indonesia is at best questionable. What's more, a factsheet (GIZ 2017) released by GIZ after the completion

---

[6] https://www.giz.de/en/worldwide/352.html (accessed 29 September 2019).

of its social protection project notes the continuing need for GIZ support. Such comments are reminiscent of the ILO's quest for a legitimate place in the changing architecture of aid in Indonesia. It seems unlikely that country ownership was at the foreground of the statements made by GIZ or its claims that there is an ongoing role for GIZ in the social protection programmes of Indonesia.

Accordingly, GIZ acts as a knowledge actor, providing support in terms of technical expertise to the Indonesian National Council on Social Welfare (INCSW) and the statutory health insurance company to extend the statutory health cover. It claims a role in the success of the INCSW in drawing up a national health insurance strategy coordinating with all the relevant institutions, and major achievements in increasing the number of recipients, among other things. The data available do not provide evidence of a reflection of country ownership principles, even in development cooperation based on knowledge provision.

Analysing Development Relationships

Based on the previous accounts of Indonesia's development relationships in the field of social and health policies, and the different roles played by various major donor agencies, this section explores what is driving the changing engagement of multilateral and bilateral partners in Indonesia, and its impact on the health sector. We explore the role of one of the Paris Principles for Aid Effectiveness, country ownership, in the changing nature of that engagement and how it is reflected in the activities that are being supported in social policy development.

First, global ideas about appropriate development relationships now emphasize "country ownership." While at a more abstract level, the change might have come about through a mix between recipient countries' claims and the changing mindset of donor countries (plus a more varied landscape of donors working with different principles of mutual national interests), looking at a concrete case, we see a more nuanced picture. In Indonesia, there are several common threads among national and international actors regarding social and health policy: (i) that the Indonesian government is directing policy developments and reforms; (ii) that universal social protection in the field of health has not yet been achieved but should be pursued further; and (iii) that continued development cooperation is in the best interest of Indonesia and the donor organizations and governments.

Second, the global emphasis on social policy as being an important cornerstone of development processes in general is visible in emerging economies such as Indonesia. The assumed benefits of improved social policy are now increasingly delinked from national economic gains, being a value of its own. The Indonesian example demonstrates that development relationships, though never free of hierarchies and power, can gradually also take the shape of more equal partnerships and greater independence of the recipient country in shaping its own national social policy institutions and arrangements. This is particularly true if social or health policy development is not too closely linked to economic development, and therefore delinked from donors' economic or financial interests.

Third, greater commitment in country ownership over the past years might have provided space for recipient countries to focus on the health sector in expanding social policy and universal social protection (and not so much following historical OECD development of welfare states). Weatherbee (2015:6) notes "efforts to apply Western-defined standards of civil and political rights as a benchmark for the quality of bilateral political relations have become the most visibly contentious part of the political agenda." The right to health might be easier to adopt, but the general challenges of dependencies remain.

Fourth, the latter is particularly relevant, as our examples suggest that the question of country ownership is much more prevalent to those development relationships that come with major projects and funding. Consider, for instance, the World Bank's careful consideration of its partnership with Indonesia compared with the ILO's clear statement of the necessity of its ongoing role in Indonesia. The small and more "ideational" external actors are less concerned with ideas of country ownership than those with larger programmes and investments in Indonesia.

Conclusions

In this chapter, we explored the role of international actors in Indonesia's social policy development, with a particular focus on health policy through the lens of country ownership. From the perspective of the international organizations, the picture is mixed. Those organizations with a long history and a broad mandate have changed their engagement in Indonesian health policy over time with greater adherence to principle of country ownership. A caveat here is that we have only studied the individual actors rather than their combined efforts as members of the IGGI. Future research might consider the role of the principle of country ownership in its different constellations whereby the leadership shifted from the Netherlands to the World Bank and then, in 2005, to the government of Indonesia (INFID 2007). Further studies could explore the role of collective action by international organizations and other donors in facilitating or hindering country ownership in social development processes.

Our research has found that some multilateral agencies are adjusting how they engage with Indonesia to provide aid, thus suggesting that the principle of country ownership, as laid down in the Paris Principles for

Aid Effectiveness, is having an impact. However, whether this is a genuine response to the Paris Principles or a reaction to general concerns of redundancy among the multilateral organizations as Indonesia increasingly self-funds its projects and programmes, is difficult to determine. It is probably at the confluence of those factors that the answer can be found. Even so, there is some apprehension about increasing country ownership and the impact this might have for long-standing donor-funded programmes. Recently, the World Bank raised concerns about Indonesia, as it is "losing access to donor aid threatening the financial and programmatic sustainability of traditionally donor-funded programs," and that the system might not yet be financially ready for that (World Bank 2019: iv).

With regard to bilateral donors, our accounts also showed varied adherence to the principle of country ownership. Therefore, also here in general, Indonesia is in the driving seat and diverse actors have had different influences and impacts on social policy making in Indonesia. While some countries, such as Japan, moved away from supporting social policy in favour of more lucrative investment in infrastructure in line with its own aid philosophy, Australia took a softer approach, by supporting the Indonesian government in its social policy reforms. In a sense, it appeared to be a legitimate partnership and, by all accounts, both the Indonesian government and their Australian counterparts reported that the feeling was mutual. The approaches of the other countries raise questions about whether development is most heavily driven by the aims of the donor without sufficient reflection on the transferability of policy models, as in the case of Germany.

Accordingly, for both types of actors we see a mixed picture both between donors and approaches over time. The language of country ownership is, however, much stronger now than it used to be, which certainly will also affect external engagement in the years to come.

Indonesia is not atypical of countries in Southeast Asia and so there is some value in discussing whether there are lessons that can be extended to other countries in the region. Indeed, there have been important advances in social policy throughout the region. Of particular note is the progress that the Thai government has made in its quest for UHC. Here, the WHO has been collaborating with the government of Thailand to universalize health care. In Tiantong and colleagues' (2019) examination of this case, they conclude that it is a positive example of a collaboration that demonstrates strong country ownership. They emphasize that Thailand (and the WHO) has found a way to unite the social, intellectual and financial capital of many domestic agencies and resources with the expertise and involvement of the WHO. In this sense, it is recipient driven but donor supported.

The similarity in the development paths of some of the countries in the region is partly related to their membership of the Association of

Southeast Asian Nations (ASEAN). ASEAN has a general commitment to social protection and accessible health care services and has worked across countries to provide health care coverage to labour migrants working between ASEAN countries (see also Guinto et al 2015). In addition, the free movement of professionals between ASEAN member states has mobilized ideas and expertise which has led to converging development strategies.

A couple of caveats remain: while this chapter has focused on the influence of "external actors" on Indonesia's national social and health policies, there are other powerful forms of impact at work that we have not been able to discuss. As Widiatmoko and Gani (2001) show, the World Trade Organization (WTO) agreements have paved the way for cross-border trade and provision in health services. The question of national interests or ownership requires greater exploration to understand how the WTO engages with Indonesia. Furthermore, there are other powerful health actors, namely the Global Fund for Aids, Tuberculosis and Malaria and the Gates Foundation. Their engagement should also be carefully studied, compared and related to the global and national actors and processes of health policy development, and discussed in relation to issues of country ownership.

Acknowledgements

The research for this chapter was completed in collaboration with the authors and Mulyadi Sumarto, who played an important role in designing the project and facilitating the interviews conducted in Indonesia. Unfortunately, he was not able to contribute to this chapter, but co-authored other publications from this project.

References

Caraway, Teri L. 2004. "Protective Repression, International Pressure, and Institutional Design: Explaining Labour Reform in Indonesia." *Studies in Comparative International Development*, 39(3):28–49.

Chowdhury, Anis, Isabel Ortiz, Jeronim Capaldo, Hiroshi Yamabana and Stefan Urban. 2016. *Indonesia: Financing Social Protection through Contributions and the Removal of Fuel Subsidy*. Geneva: ILO, Social Protection Department.

Dartanto, Teguh. 2017. "Universal Health Coverage in Indonesia: Informality, Fiscal Risks and Fiscal Space for Financing UHC." Presented at IMF-JICA Conference—Regional Development: Fiscal Risks, Fiscal Space and the Sustainable Development Goals, Tokyo.

DFAT. 2015. "Aid Investment Plan Indonesia". Barton: DFAT. https://www.dfat.gov.au/sites/default/files/indonesia-aid-investment-plan-2015-19.pdf.

Dijkstra, Geske. 2013. "The New Aid Paradigm: A Case of Policy Incoherence." DESA Working Paper No. 128. New York: United Nations Department of Economic and Social Affairs.

GIZ (Deutsche Gesellschaft für Internationale Zusammenarbeit). 2017. "Social Protection Programme (SPP): Expansion of the Innovative Approaches to Elevate the Economic Livelihoods." Bonn and Eschborn: GIZ.

Grenville, Stephen. 2004. "The IMF and the Indonesian Crisis." *Bulletin of Indonesian Economic Studies*, 40(1):77–94.

Guinto, Ramon Lorenzo Luis R., Ufara Zuwasti Curran, Rapeepong Suphanchaimat and Nicola S. Pocock. 2015. "Universal Health Coverage in 'One ASEAN': Are Migrants Included?" *Global Health Action*, 8(1): 2574.

ILO (International Labour Organization). 2019. *The ILO in Indonesia*. Jakarta: ILO.

ILO (International Labour Organization). 2015. *The ILO in Indonesia. Asia-Pacific Decent Work Decade 2006–2015*. Jakarta: ILO Country Office for Indonesia.

ILO (International Labour Organization). 2012. *R202 - Social Protection Floors Recommendation, 2012 (No. 202)*. Geneva: ILO.

ILO (International Labour Organization). 2008. *Social Security in Indonesia: Advancing the Development Agenda*. Jakarta: ILO.

ILO (International Labour Organization). 2006. *Social Protection in Indonesia. Issues and Options for Development*. Geneva: ILO.

ILO (International Labour Organization). 2003. *Social Security and Coverage for All. Restructuring the Social Security Scheme in Indonesia—Issues and Options*. Jakarta: ILO.

ILO (International Labour Organization). 1999. *Restructuring of the Social Security System in Indonesia*. Geneva: ILO.

INFID (International NGO Forum on Indonesian Development). 2007. "INFID Statement. Commemorating Two Years of the Dissolution of CGI. The 'Jakarta Commitment': A Reincarnation of CGI and a 'Commitment to Dependency.'" Jakarta: INFID.

JICA (Japan International Cooperation Agency). 2016. *JICA 2016 Annual Report*. Tokyo: JICA.

JICA (Japan International Cooperation Agency). 2014. *JICA Annual Report 2014*. Tokyo: JICA.

Kaasch, Alexandra. 2015. *Shaping Global Health Policy: Global Social Policy Actors and Ideas about Health Care Systems*. Basingstoke: Palgrave Macmillan.

Kadar, Kusrini S., Karen Francis and Kenneth Sellick. 2012. "Ageing in Indonesia—Health Status and Challenges for the Future." *Ageing International*, 38(4):261–270.

Kato, Hiroshi, John Page and Yasutami Shimomura. 2016. "Japan's Foreign Assistance at 60: Reflecting on the Past and Looking to the Future." In *Japan's Development Assistance*, edited by Hiroshi Kato, John Page and Yasutami Shimomura, 344–357. London: Palgrave Macmillan.

Lewis, John and Richard Webb. 1991. *Transcript of Interview with Marianne Haug with Amar Bhattacharya and Richard Calkins.* Washington, DC: Brookings Institution, World Bank History Project.

Liese, Bernhard H. 1980. *Letter to John Evans—INDONESIA—Briefing Notes for Discussion with Minister of Health, Dr. Soewardjono.* Washington, DC: World Bank.

Marzoeki, Puti, Ajay Tandon, Xiaolu Bi and Eko Setyo Pambudi. 2014. *Universal Health Coverage for Inclusive and Sustainable Development. Country Summary Report for Indonesia. Japan-World Bank Partnership. Program for Universal Health Coverage.* Washington, DC: World Bank.

Neilson, Jeff and Josephine Wright. 2017. "The State and Food Security Discourses of Indonesia: Feeding the Bangsa." *Geographical Research*, 55(2):131–143.

OECD (Organisation for Economic Co-operation and Development). 2019. *Towards Universal Social Protection: Lessons from the Universal Health Coverage Initiative.* OECD Development Policy Papers. Paris: OECD.

OECD (Organisation for Economic Co-operation and Development). 2018. *Active with Indonesia.* Paris: OECD.

OECD (Organisation for Economic Co-operation and Development). 2014. *OECD Development Co-operation Peer Reviews: Japan.* Paris: OECD.

OECD (Organisation for Economic Co-operation and Development). 2008. *Accra Agenda for Action.* Paris: OECD.

Pisani, Elizabeth, Maarten Olivier Kok and Kharisma Nugroho. 2017. "Indonesia's Road to Universal Health Coverage: A Political Journey." *Health Policy and Planning*, 32:267–276.

Robinson, Richard and Andrew Rosser. 1998. "Contesting Reform: Indonesia's New Order and the IMF." *World Development*, 26(8):1593–1609.

Rupidara, Neil Semuel and Peter McGraw. 2010. "Institutional Change, Continuity and Decoupling in the Indonesian Industrial Relations System." *Journal of Industrial Relations*, 52(5):613–630.

Sumarto, Mulyadi. 2017. "Welfare Regime Change in Developing Countries: Evidence from Indonesia." *Social Policy and Administration*, 51(6):940–959.

Suryahadi, Asep, Vita Febriany and Athia Yumna. 2017. "Expanding Social Security in Indonesia: The Current Processes and Challenges." In *Towards Universal Health Care in Emerging Economies. Opportunities and Challenges*, edited by I. Yi, 373–403. London: Palgrave Macmillan.

Tiantong, Sirinad, Attaya Limwattanayingyong, Suwit Wibulpolprasert, Liviu Vedrasco and Daniel Kertesz. 2019. "Towards Optimal Collaboration: Reforming the WHO Country Cooperation Strategy in Thailand." *Bulletin of the World Health Organization*, 97(9):642–644.

Toussaint, Eric. 2019. "The World Bank and the IMF in Indonesia—an emblematic interference." CADTM, 13 May, 2020. Accessed 1 July 2022. https://www.cadtm.org/spip.php?page=imprimer&id_article= 10860.

UN (United Nations). 2019. *Political Declaration of the High-Level Meeting on Universal Health Coverage "Universal Health Coverage: Moving Together to Build a Healthier World."* New York: UN.

UN (United Nations). 2017. "Social Protection Systems and Floors Partnerships for SDG 1.3." Accessed 1 July 2022. https://sustainabledeve lopment.un.org/partnership/?p=16346.

USAID (United States Agency for International Development). 2018. *Partners in Development. A Stronger U.S.-Indonesia Partnership Advancing Mutual Prosperity and Security. USAID Strategy for Indonesia.* Washington, DC: USAID.

Weatherbee, Donald E. 2015. *International Relations in Southeast Asia: The Struggle for Autonomy.* Lanham: Rowman & Littlefield.

WHO (World Health Organization). 2016. *WHO Country Cooperation Strategy 2014–2019.* New Delhi: WHO Country Office Indonesia.

WHO (World Health Organization). 2010. *WHO Country Cooperation Strategies. Guide 2010.* Geneva, WHO.

WHO (World Health Organization). 2008. *WHO Country Cooperation Strategy 2007–2011 Indonesia.* New Delhi: WHO.

WHO SEARO (World Health Organization South-East Asia Regional Office). 1999. *50 Years of WHO in South-East Asia. Highlights: 1948–1998.* New Delhi: WHO Regional Office for South-East Asia.

Widiatmoko, Dono and Ascobat Gani. 2001. *International Relations within Indonesia's Hospital Sector.* Depok: University of Indonesia.

Wilmsen, Brooke, Andrew van Hulten and Alexandra Kaasch. 2019. "Resolving the Tensions between the Principles of Aid Effectiveness: An Indonesia-Australia Technical Assistance Project." *Development in Practice,* 29(3):273–286.

World Bank. 2019. *Engaging with Civil Society in the Health Sector in Indonesia.* Washington DC: World Bank. https://documents1.worldbank.org/cura ted/en/637901568357782768/pdf/Engaging-with-Civil-Society-in-the-Health-Sector-in-Indonesia.pdf.

World Bank. 2018. *IBRD Program Appraisal Document on a Proposed Loan in the Amount of US$150 Millions to the Republic of Indonesia for Indonesia Supporting Primary Health Care Reform (i-sphere) Program/Indonesia Supporting Primary and Referral Health Care Reform (i-sphere) Program.* Jakarta: World Bank East Asia and Pacific Region.

World Bank. 2016. *Indonesia. Health Financing System Assessment. Spend More, Right and Better.* Washington, DC: World Bank.

World Bank. 2015a. *Country Partnership Framework for the Republic of Indonesia.* Jakarta: East Asia Pacific Region, World Bank.

World Bank. 2015b. *Taxes and Public Spending in Indonesia. Who Pays and Who Benefits?* Jakarta and Washington, DC: World Bank.

World Bank. 1968. *Terms of Reference for Bank Resident Staff in Indonesia.* Jakarta: World Bank.

10

New Actors and New Systems in Aged Care Services in China

Bingqin Li, Lijie Fang, Bo Hu and Jing Wang

Introduction

Due to population ageing, China is experiencing a rapid increase in demand for aged care and relevant services for older adults. According to the "2021 Social Service Development Statistical Communique" (Ministry of Civil Affairs 2016), by 1 November 2020, China's population aged 60 and over had reached 264 million—equivalent to 18.7 per cent of the total population. Further, the population aged 65 and over had reached 190.64 million—about 13.5 per cent of the total population. According to the *2013 Human Development Report of China* (UNDP China 2013), the proportion of the population aged 65+ will rise to 18.2 per cent by 2030—higher than in most industrialized countries. By 2020, the old-age dependency rate reached 19.7 per cent, 7.8 per cent higher than in 2010 (China Social Welfare and Elderly Service Association 2021).

In addition to demographic changes, China's aged care services are challenged by changing social and economic situations. As income increases, older people's lifestyles and demands for cultural activities differ from those of the past. Older people have begun to demand more convenient, varied and better quality services and facilities. The unmet need for essential aged care services and the unsatisfied demand for better quality services are becoming more serious as people's lifestyles change. As Chinese society became increasingly "Westernized" and experienced increased migration owing to urbanization and industrialization, the living arrangements of Chinese families also changed rapidly. A study by Lei et al (2015) found that in 2010 the proportion of older people living with their sons in rural and urban China was significantly lower than in the Fifth Census of China in 2005. This trend is expected to continue.

According to the *Chinese Family Development Report (2015)* (National Health and Family Planning Commission 2015), at the end of 2014, nearly 10 per cent of older people's households were single-person households, while only 41.9 per cent had two older people. Independent living requires supporting social services. A total of 32.4 per cent of people aged over 60 and living alone could not receive help when they encountered difficulties. The report indicated that among older people with partners, 65.3 per cent were cared for by their partners and 11.6 per cent by their children. By the end of 2014, on average, older people mainly relied on themselves and their families to meet their daily needs. They primarily used health care. Social care services in rural areas mainly involved health examination and consultation, with about 27 per cent of older people receiving these services. A total of 7.5 per cent of older people had received medical care, 6.8 per cent of older farmers had received some help on the farm, and 4.4 per cent visited doctors accompanied by younger people (National Health and Family Planning Commission 2015). Despite the improvement in services since 2015, the demand continued to grow. A survey conducted by Ke Research (2021) found that in 2020, 65.5 per cent of older people were not living with their children and even among the 80+ age group, 48 per cent lived separately from their children, showing a greater demand for aged care and the urgency with which these shortages must be addressed.

Reforms in several fields may have contributed to the changing patterns in the supply of aged care (Howell 2012):

- In 2000, the state started to emphasize the need to plan and provide social services in urban communities to deliver services close to where people live.
- In 2013, the state stopped providing social services directly and started contracting out social services to social organizations (SOs) and private providers.

These two changes mean that services will be increasingly delivered at the community level by non-government providers, including SOs, private providers and members of society. These changes have profound implications for aged care in China. Nearly ten years have passed, and it is time to review the change process, the new actors entering the system, and how the new actors have interacted with the existing actors.

The following areas are considered in this chapter:

- The changing core actors in the aged care service system in China. This analysis provides the historical background of the transition of China's aged service over time.
- The state of the system in terms of stakeholders' perception of the goals and roles of the new system, stakeholder trust, and coordination in implementation.
- The local variations in the new system are based on local case studies. For this part of the research, we used six cities in China as examples to examine the systematic change.

The conclusion discusses the key observations and lessons we can learn from China's attempt to address the challenges in delivering aged care to a rapidly ageing society. It is important to note that, as the system change is ongoing, there have been continued adaptations since this research was conducted. Also, field research took place before the COVID-19 outbreak. The disruption the pandemic has caused makes it difficult to tell whether what happened in the pre-COVID era will continue to be the case after the pandemic.

Background: An Aged Care Service System in Transition

Policies on old-age services in China have come a long way over the past three decades—from limited recognition of the needs of the ageing population in the 1980s, to a focus on legislating for older people's rights in the 1990s, to a deeper understanding of the need for better social services in the early 2000s, to the formal inclusion of addressing the care needs of the ageing population as a vitally important issue in the government agenda in 2015 and the growing efforts to embrace private sector providers since. This chapter focuses on the grassroots level and the restructuring of service delivery and finance.

Combining family care and state support (the 1950s–1990s)

In 1954, the first edition of the Constitution of the People's Republic of China (*zhonghua renmin gongheguo xianfa*) specified that sick and disabled older people were entitled to financial support from the state and society. The primary responsibilities of the state were to provide social protection to the retired people and to maintain the pensions and deliver very limited services to retirement employees of the state-owned enterprises, government agencies and public institutions (such as universities, schools, hospitals, and so on). For most older people, family members were expected to be the primary care providers. The policy required that children fulfil their duty of filial piety and not abuse their parents. After 1958, the traditional functions of the family were widely criticized. Women were not necessarily to be the only care givers in the family (Luo 1959). Since older people receive a pension from their employers, they could be financially independent. However, as financial independence could not address their physical needs, personal and domestic care remained the responsibility of their children.

In this period, the socialization of aged care was very limited, and public services were only accessible to those who could not take care of themselves and had no kinship support. The system in rural areas only targeted older people who suffered from the "Three No's" (no children, no income and no relatives). By 1964, there were 700 care homes nationwide serving

79,000 "Three No's" older people (Pei 2004). However, owing to funding shortages and poor management, this system stopped providing services in many regions in the early 1960s (Liu 2006).

On the whole, in the central planning era, family members were the primary providers of care.

Old-age care service network as a response to state enterprise reform (the 1990s–2000s)

In the 1990s, further changes to the family and social structure in urban areas took place in several respects.

First, the younger generations had a reduced ability to care for their older parents, especially as people became more mobile than in the past. Urbanization and rural–urban migration intensified, the speed and scale of housing demolition and relocation increased and the number of people seeking education and employment outside their hometowns increased. Consequently, the proportion of older people not living with their children also increased. Even adults living with their parents found it difficult to care for their declining parents because of higher work pressure and longer working hours.

Second, the average household size decreased from 4.41 in 1982 to 3.96 in 1990, then to 3.44 in 2000. This was partly caused by the One Child Policy. It was also related to the changing habits in people's living arrangements. As a result of improved housing, young couples are less likely to live with their parents. Nuclear families became more common than in the central planning era.

Third, the sense of community was eliminated. In the past, housing was distributed by state employers, and employees working for the same employer were geographically connected through this housing allocation system. Many large state enterprises provided accommodation for their employees in the same residential areas. In this case, older people living alone could receive some help from colleagues who lived nearby. However, following the privatization of housing and the higher mobility of the labour force, residential communities became communities of strangers. These changes challenged the traditional care model, which relied heavily on the informal help provided by family members and neighbours.

Despite the social changes, social welfare institutions for older people did not respond quickly. Bian et al (1998) observed that, at the beginning of the 1990s, aged care continued to rely heavily on family care, in stark contrast to other areas of society where the values of traditional society were seriously eroded. To address the care shortage, some urban communities started to bring female care workers in groups from rural villages to cities to conduct paid housework in Jiangsu and Zhejiang (Oxfam 2014). As the number of rural–urban migrants increased, a private housework market emerged. By the mid-1990s, paid domestic workers had spread across the country.

Combining the government, family and market in the caring system (2000–2010)

After 2000, the average household size declined, reaching 3.1 in 2010. Consequently, informal care struggled to cope, and there was a mounting demand for professional and accessible care and services for older people (Flaherty et al 2007; Hesketh et al 2005).

In the Eleventh Five-Year Plan (2006–2010), the government proposed to combine family-based care and social care. They also intended to foster a market that sold old-age friendly products to older people to meet their individual needs. Starting from 2008, home-based care became more common in urban communities.

SOs as service providers in the community 2015–now

In the Twelfth Five-Year Plan （2011–2015), the central government further proposed building an aged care system which would be "based on home care, dependent on the community and supported by care homes." The target was that there would be 30 care home beds per 1,000 older people. The state also introduced the national standards for care facilities at the community level (Wang and Xie 2013:156–157). In 2012, the central government published the *Revised Version of Older People's Rights Protection Law* (*laonianren quanyi baozhangfa xiuzhengan*), in which the basis of aged care shifted from family support to home-based social care. SOs (non-profit organizations and social enterprises) were allowed to contract services from the government.

The most apparent change in the service system during this period is the role of community service centres. In the past, these centres were *the* public service providers in the residential communities. After introducing SOs as service providers, the service centres were expected to be transformed into a platform that matches users with service providers and providers with fundholders. In this sense, a community service centre could become a grassroots service and finance coordinator. In this new system, SOs become service deliverers together with private providers.

Service providers in urban communities comprise several types, as follows:

1. Semi-privatized service providers, such as ex-public care homes. In the cities we visited, some government-funded care homes were converted into SOs that continued to receive funding from the local government. Their staff members were public servants but no longer part of the government system. The services were largely unchanged, providing

long-term care for the terminally ill. Some facilities that used to provide care to retired senior civil servants only also opened to the fee-paying general public.

2. Newly established SOs and social enterprises. They received in-kind support, such as office space and workshop space based in residential communities, and some startup funds or government subsidies (at different levels: provincial, municipal, district and street).

3. Private sector providers also pick up some subsidized services, such as assistance with domestic chores or food services.

Research Design and Data Collection

To understand the transition of the system, we looked at the following areas:

1. The stakeholder perception of the goals of the system and their roles. Implementing the new policies and establishing the new system will require a basic shared understanding of the need to make the changes and the acceptance that the new system will not be short-lived.

2. The stakeholders trust in each other. As the reform involves introducing new actors into the system, there is a need to establish trust between fundholders and service providers and new service providers and users.

3. Coordination between different policy priorities. This is a crucial facilitator or hindrance to the implementation of policies. As discussed earlier, aged care is a complex policy field that requires the joint efforts of multiple stakeholders.

To determine how stakeholders perceived and responded to the service system transition, we studied six cities in China: Shanghai, Hangzhou in Zhejiang Province, Chengdu in Sichuan Province, Guiyang in Guizhou Province, Haicang in Fujian Province, and Taicang in Jiangsu Province. These cities were selected because they were among the pilot cities covering coastal wealthier regions (Shanghai, Hangzhou, Haicang and Taicang) and inland poorer regions (Chengdu and Guiyang). It also included a metropolitan areas (Shanghai, Hangzhou, Chengdu and Guiyang), a satellite town to the metropolis (Haicang) and a small town (Taicang). The different experiences of these six cities and towns would give us a range of selections.

The data used in this paper include official government documents, official statistics, China Health and Retirement Longitudinal Survey (CHARLS) data and second-hand data reported in the national-level survey reports undertaken by government think tanks and relevant ministry research offices.

This research involves understanding stakeholder perceptions and interactions during the reform era. It needs a nuanced understanding of the interactions between the stakeholders; therefore, we needed to carry out in-depth interviews and focus groups with the stakeholders involved. Focus group discussions and interviews were conducted in residential communities with participants selected in consultation with local officials in charge of community-based care. Focus groups with government officials usually included 10–18 people from the government departments involved. After the discussions, in-depth interviews were conducted with some individual officials from each department. We also conducted interviews and organized focus groups with the government departments, including the Civil Affairs Office, Office of Ageing Affairs and commissioned service providers, including publicly and privately funded care homes and daycare centres, community service platforms, community managers, non-governmental organizations (NGOs) and volunteers. The interview questions focused on finance, service delivery and governance. The firsthand data were collected between August 2014 and May 2016.

Perceptions and Responses to Service System Transitions

Understanding the goals and roles of stakeholders

At the time of this research, have the stakeholders reached an agreement regarding the system's goals?

There is an overall supportive attitude to providing more services and diverse ones for older people in communities. From the government's perspective, SOs are expected to perform several functions: (i) mobilize different types of resources; (ii) deliver services as required and propose new services; and (iii) identify unsatisfied user needs and propose new services. In this sense, the purpose of the reform is to encourage SOs to be more involved in the service delivery and contribute additional resources to the services to better satisfy older people's needs. However, local governments interpreted this differently.

There were different understandings of local governments' roles in developing SOs. In the state–SO partnership structure, the government contributed in kind by providing venues, initial startup grants and annual cash input. The government rarely paid staff costs. Even when the government purchased services directly from non-profit organizations, it paid the minimum wage to the staff members, much lower than the wage paid to the professionals working for privately funded organizations. The government officials interviewed considered this partial funding model an incentive mechanism, as they did not wish SOs to become dependent on the government for too long. The SOs were expected to graduate from this stage and become financially independent. Therefore, the government adopted an incentive strategy even at the early stage by not fully funding the services. The SOs were expected to seek alternative funds to match government support to receive government funds.

However, SOs could have very different understandings of the relationship. They considered themselves to be providing social goods and, therefore, the government should be their primary source of funding. In the field research, we heard repeated complaints about insufficient government funding. The misunderstanding between the government and the SOs was highlighted in a focus group discussion involving district officials and the SOs. One SO proposed to set up an activity centre in a residential estate. The community office provided a room, yet the SO leader needed another CNY 100,000 to refurbish and furnish it. The government was reluctant to provide these funds; thus, the project did not move forward for a while. The manager of the SO was frustrated about the perceived lack of sincerity from the local government. However, the government officials believed that CNY 100,000 was a lot of support, and the SO should obtain extra resources or provide fee-based services to "earn" their way. As we observed in quite a few community-based services run by SOs, they would rather wait for the government to provide funding than charge fees for services, as they considered themselves non-profit organizations. This was a sign of what they considered to be "non-profit." Even in Shanghai, where SOs were highly active, our interviews showed that SOs expected the government to change their mind one day and preferred to "wait and see," which prevented them from seizing other opportunities.

As noted in our research, it would not be realistic to ask the government to provide full funding for all SOs, just because many new services and organizations did not exist in the past. Moreover, if SOs were all funded by the state, they would be unavoidably constrained by government budgeting exercises, which would likely further deprive the SOs of their autonomy. The government's intention to use seed funds to leverage private and charity funds is a more viable practice in the longer term. However, they have to provide more structured training and better communication with the SOs early on in the funding cycle to help the latter establish appropriate expectations.

Trust

Time is required to overcome the lack of trust between stakeholders. In the past, local officials only allocated funds to other government agencies according to the established budgets, which was a relatively simple administrative task. Now the government officials were required to decide which SOs to fund. They had to select projects proposed by people they had not previously worked with. This is very similar to the activities of a venture capitalist. In addition, they had to make sure that their "investment portfolio" performed well, ensuring that the SOs they had contracted would deliver good outcomes. As our study revealed, after making the investment, the government officials became restless. They worried about whether the SOs would fulfil their promises. They strove to monitor the SOs' activities closely.

In Guiyang, one community officer visited the social entrepreneurs in the local social entrepreneur incubator, a workspace which supports business development and knowledge sharing among new entrepreneurs. She was responsible for setting it up. Worrying that it might not function as planned, she went to the office every day and questioned the entrepreneurs and their employees on why they spent so much time in the offices, rather than visiting their prospective customers. In another case, the official interviewed said:

> "I had never worked with SOs in the past. The higher up [Shangbian] gave so much money to us, and we had to spend them. However, there were not many people that I could trust to give the money. After giving eight million to [A], I have to make sure that we can see some results. Otherwise … the government is now operating heavily in the anti-corruption campaign. I do not want to be viewed suspiciously by others."

In Taicang, the government introduced strict rules for the SOs—particularly those operated by people outside the province and those offering new services. To claim the costs, the SOs had to provide detailed financial reports daily. In a fiery exchange between an SO manager and a local official in a focus group session, the SO manager complained: "We received money from you, but I have to hire an extra staff member to write up what we have done and collect all the receipts every day to get the money. It is time-consuming and suffocating."

Users did not necessarily trust SOs' services—the legacy of the "strong government, strong market, and weak society" was difficult to change quickly. In the past, when the government prescribed social services, the users had high expectations of the services on offer. This was because the aged care services provided by the public sector were only accessible to high-ranking government officials or military retirees. When residents were invited to community-based facilities—which appeared to be less formal, smaller, cheaper to access and without a track record for good services—they were not what people would associate with "social services." As a result, new SOs found it difficult to attract customers, even with government subsidies. This was particularly problematic for domestic services.

This does not mean that the relationship between different parties in the system will remain unchanged. After completing the fieldwork for this project, which ran over a year, the overall attitude to community daycare centres had already changed. Event and activity services also improved over time.

Coordination

Within the community, the community service platform is coordinated and monitored by specialist agencies. Above the community level, the governing structure is organized by the government. However, each government department has its priorities and thus may not be willing or able to commit resources to aged care. In Shanghai, it is very difficult to find a place to provide services in the city centre. Even if one government department was willing to approve a new service for older people, the service provider could not obtain land/building space to house the service. When the departments offload responsibilities, a SO may have nowhere to operate. There are up to 20 government bodies at this level of government. A leading agency or an agency specializing in governance is needed to ensure effective decision making and network stability. At the time of this research, the Office for Ageing Affairs was in charge of coordinating at the local level. The Director of the Old Age Affairs Office (OAAO) in a district in Shanghai mentioned that the office did not enjoy the same power in different communities. It was influenced by the governing culture of each community.

There were also non-negotiable constraints. For example, the Environment Bureau could not allocate a quota for building green space. As one respondent said: "When it is about environmental constraint, nothing can be done, as it is the top priority of the central government." It would not be approved if the residents were opposed to the service. This was mainly a problem for long-term care services for the terminally ill, as it is considered inauspicious to have such a facility nearby.

Local variations in the system transition

By the end of 2015, the number of aged care services reached 116,000—23.4 per cent more than the previous year. Of these, 28,000 were registered in aged care institutions, and 26,000 were community-based aged care service organizations and facilities. Sixty-two thousand facilities offered mutual support services. There were 6.73 million care beds, of which 2.98 million were in community care homes and daycare centres (Ministry of Civil Affairs 2016). New types of services also boomed. By the end of 2015, there were 2,280 national-level aged service NGOs, 210,000 legal aid centres for older people, 71,000 organizations on protecting older people's rights, 53,000 older people's schools with 7.33 million older students, and 371,000 activity rooms (Ministry of Civil Affairs 2016). These figures indicate the shift from a government provision model to a mixed one, with the market, the SOs and home care providers, and a combination of government and market procurement. In this process, the government withdrew from being a service provider and let the SOs or the private sector take over service provision.

Locally, performance varies greatly. We categorize the six examined cities into two groups to report our findings. The first group comprises Shanghai, Hangzhou and Chengdu—cities more experienced in working with SOs, even though Hangzhou and Chengdu began this engagement later than Shanghai. The second group comprises Xiamen, Taicang and Guiyang—cities that have recently started SO development.

Shanghai, Hangzhou and Chengdu

These three cities encountered some changes owing to SO development, as follows.

First, the government's roles changed. The system used to be governed by the higher authorities. However, the management of service delivery was gradually assumed by professional organizations, such as service quality monitoring bodies or community service centres. The SOs took over some monitoring functions assumed by the government in the past. For example, since 2003, the Shanghai Social Welfare Association took on the role of governing members of the association. Members produced self-regulating rules and activities were evaluated by the association. The government continued to make long-term plans, formulate policies and standards, and approve applications.

Second, the government stood back from service provision and became service procurers. Various partnership models emerged, such as "public building and private/SO operating" (*gongjian minying*), "public-subsidizing and private/SO operating" (*gongzhu minying*), assignment of lease, private/SO–public partnership, co-investment and entrusted operation. In these models, the SOs and private businesses are service providers.

Third, the government was not the sole fundholder. The partnerships discussed earlier reflected the diversification of funding sources. The old-age services could be funded by the lottery, charity donations, private investment and in-kind contributions (such as volunteer services).

Fourth, the service coverage varied by type of services and new services were often better targeted. In the past, the government defined the administrative boundaries between communities and prescribed services for every 10,000 people. This planning model created standardized services. However, SOs were different from the government. They needed a catchment area larger than the administration-defined urban community.

A case in point is the community canteen. A canteen had to change its menu every day of the week and rotate the menus each week to avoid the older people becoming tired of the food. Even so, the older people soon became tired of the canteen food and demanded the canteens to change their menus more frequently. Why do people not make the same complaints about the repetitive of dishes sold in private restaurants? The difference is that the service users go to the same canteen daily, whereas restaurant customers can choose from different restaurants. This posed a challenge to the SOs, whose users were a fixed group of people. The same issue also arose among the scheduled activities for older people in daycare centres. Daycare centres in communities were popular initially but lost customers over time, even if the service quality remained the same. Some services even became unused. However, from the service providers' perspective, standardized services had lower requirements for staff training and facilities, reducing costs. Diversified services were not only more expensive but also more challenging to provide and manage.

Two solutions emerged in the communities in our research. The first was to develop inter-community cooperation. For example, meal service accessibility was jointly organized by several communities within the same subdistrict. In Shanghai, older people were given vouchers to go to different canteens in the subdistrict. Then even though the canteens did not change their menus frequently, older people could still enjoy varied menus by visiting different canteens.

Similarly, older people in Chengdu were entitled to participate in activities in a daycare centre in a different community. Such arrangements helped make better use of community space. Service providers that combined their operations were usually branches of the same SO, and redrawing the boundary improved the economy of scale. Service providers not affiliated with the same SOs might not be willing to cooperate, because joint operations also mean the risk of losing customers through competition. Further, this also complicated funding allocation by the government, as there was still no effective coordination for funding usage between communities. Thus, the second solution was to subsidize some privately funded services. For example, restaurants that were geographically close to a neighbourhood were subsidized for providing meals to older people, or older people could eat in these restaurants with vouchers. This was a win–win situation, with older people having more meal choices and catering services having more customers.

Fifth, the service system became increasingly multilayered. Above the community level, some networks started to emerge:

- Local government departments formed a policy network for stimulating aged care services, focusing on making policies. In a city, as many as 20 departments could be relevant to aged care services within a local government. The OAAO, affiliated with the Bureau of Civil Affairs, had been the central coordinating organization. Other organizations all established their plans for aged care services. For example:
  - The Bureau of Civil Affairs—community services for older people.
  - The Bureau of Health—geriatric and palliative care services through its hospital systems.

- The Bureau of Education—universities for older people.
- The Bureau of Transportation—offers a discounted rate on travel fares for older people.
- The Bureau of Finance—budget planning (in consultation with departments) and funding allocation.
- The Bureau of Construction and Bureau of Land Planning—building infrastructure.
- The Bureau of Commerce and Business—registration.
- The Bureau of Accounting—financial monitoring.
- A new specialized quality control network assessed, monitored and controlled the quality of services delivered by SOs. In the quality control network, local governments established professional evaluation standards and purchased evaluation services from independent organizations. The providers' performance could be assessed through expert inspection and user satisfaction tests. In some cases, an International Organization for Standardization quality control system was introduced to maintain the standard of services. Local governments contracted the quality control services, but the member organizations were not dependent on each other and had a clear division of labour.

Hangzhou and Chengdu started introducing SO services later than Shanghai. However, Hangzhou and Chengdu governments swiftly promoted the SOs, and the services in these two cities were similar to those provided in Shanghai. However, the Shanghai government played an important role in promoting and supporting the SOs. For example, new social entrepreneurs could enter government-funded business incubators to enjoy cheaper office space, receive training and build a social network. In contrast, in Hangzhou and Chengdu, the system's structures resembled those of the traditional bureaucracy. Helping SOs grow was not a priority for the local governments.

Hangzhou focused on services in institutionalized care and met the care home bed targets set by the government. As a result, Zhejiang Province had the country's second-largest number of care home beds per 1,000 older people. In urban communities, space for services was very limited. Even in wealthier communities, daycare facilities were not always available. At the same time, the occupancy rate of care homes in Hangzhou was lower than 50 per cent. Most of the care home residents were healthy older people, and only 25 per cent of the residents had care needs. A survey showed that the older people had low trust in the care homes because of the shortage of professionally trained care workers (Lv 2012). Privately funded care homes, in contrast, were much more popular.

The government strictly controlled staffing costs in the government-funded services, while the number of care homes kept increasing. This led to insufficient staffing, even in state-funded care homes with excellent facilities. The quality of services fell short of older people's expectations; thus, the government–owned care homes had a meagre occupancy rate. The largest care home in Hangzhou, which opened in September 2014, was no exception. The No. 3 Welfare Institute had 2,000 beds for older people. Before it was officially opened, more than 4,000 people came to register, and the institute had to choose the 2,000 people to live in the facility. However, only 290 people lived in the institute after one year. The price was considered the main issue, with the following costs incurred for accommodation:

- Nursing room (about 42 m^2): CHY 1,100 per month.
- Standard room (about 33 m^2, shared by two people): CHY 1,500 per month.
- Small single room (28 m^2): CHY 2,700 per month.
- Large single room (33 m^2): CHY 3,250 per month.
- En–suite for singles or couples: CHY 4,100 to 7,500 per month.

This price did not include care services. The extra care costs for people who could live independently were CHY 430, 530 or 630 per month, depending on the level of care needed. Care costs for people with special needs ranged from CHY 830 to 2,230 per month.

However, in wealthy cities like Hangzhou, there may have been many people who could afford these prices. In care homes run by private investors, the facilities and living conditions may not have been as good, but the prices were similar. This means there must have been other reasons for the institute's low occupancy rate. The reason lies in the quality of care. In most care homes, workers had not received professional training. Professionally trained care workers would not want to work in public or government-subsidized care homes, as the salaries were much lower than the market rates for private care workers and childcare nurses.

Since Chengdu is an old industrial city, state-owned enterprises allocated housing properties to their employees during the planning era. Residents in these communities tended to have known each other for many years. In these communities, party committees at the grassroots level were strong and active. Younger old people were encouraged to be volunteers to help older people. Some of these volunteers were appointed by the party committee or members of the party, while others wished to lead an active life after they retired. They provided light-touch home-based care. Meanwhile, the recipients highly trusted the volunteers, who were often their neighbours.

In contrast, at the time of this research, Hangzhou did not have as active an SO sector, either in terms of number of organizations or in terms of range of activities, as in Shanghai. The Hangzhou government mainly relied on private enterprises. Therefore, the community was not as much involved in coordinating and developing services as in the other two cities. There were some active SOs in the communities, but their presence was often small. The service systems in Hangzhou and Chengdu were still in their infancy.

Guizhou, Xiamen and Taicang

A serious problem faced by Guiyang was the shortage of qualified service providers. The city was more impoverished than all the other cities studied because of the lack of an overarching structure to start a community-based platform. Some SO members had previously worked in international organizations on poverty reduction and human rights protection. A few people with such experience became part of a professional organization to help subdistrict governments to establish the needed community service platform. As they had to serve multiple communities simultaneously, most platforms were still empty shells as we carried out this research. Local officials were unsure how to follow up and were anxious about the ability of the SOs to establish the service system. Each district had set up incubators for social entrepreneurs; however, the local government assumed the training responsibilities. As reported by staff members of the SOs, the local officials wanted to see visible results, as they wished to showcase their achievements.

Both Haicang in Xiamen City and Taicang in Jiangsu Province had powerful governments. However, their governments worked differently. Haicang's government introduced a "co-production" framework which treated SOs as part and parcel of the Communist Party's initiative to promote mass mobilization and improve social control. The government was dominant, and SOs were initially "imported" from other provinces, such as Shanghai and Guangdong. However, as discussed earlier, imported SOs found it even more difficult to be accepted by local communities. Xiamen City is geographically close to Taiwan and has many Taiwanese migrants. Taiwanese SOs were also active in Xiamen, initially to provide services to the Taiwanese population. They had a good experience and were trusted by users. The service spilled out to non-Taiwanese residents. In Haicang, aged care facilities were not well developed in urban communities; however, government-subsidized domestic help using private providers was active. As such, almost 92 types of services were available for older people in Haicang. In contrast, Taicang's government was cautious of SOs. The local government had introduced some professional care services to well-to-do employees in high-tech parks.

Discussion and Conclusion

This chapter has studied the transition of China's aged care system since 2010. The research project aimed to capture the interactions between stakeholders in the initial stage of system transformation. Introducing new actors to the system unavoidably has disruptive effects, but the system will continue to evolve or improve over time. We do not expect this research to capture the whole process. The research findings highlighted some important elements for the development of a new community-based care system from scratch. The multidimensional transformation includes several aspects:

1. The providers have moved from *adult children as the primary providers and the state as the residual provider* to multiple providers where households, the state, the market, SOs and civil society all play a part.
2. The foci of care have expanded *from medical care to a larger range of social care* where care may include non-medical support, such as household services, support for daily chores, community-based services, organization of social activities and daycare services.
3. The dominant form of care has shifted from *family member-provided home-based care to community-supported home-based care.*
4. The catchment area of services has shifted *from administratively defined to market defined.*

Despite the acceptance of the need for SOs in aged care services, trust and coordination between stakeholders were not consistent. Service providers and the state did not have high trust in each other and neither did users and SO service providers. Over time, as the state stopped being the service provider, people became more accepting that social and private providers deliver aged care with the state left out of direct provision. In this sense, government institutions and individuals could both impose control over SOs. The control could be either deliberate or unconscious. In the context of transition, these seemingly controlling behaviour could result from the reaction to changes. Relaxation of this control may be achieved once the stakeholders manage to find their new roles.

While coordination can be an important factor in defining the nature of a system, it does not mean that the system will be sustainable. A seemingly well-established system may still be fragile when not all stakeholders embrace the goals. Goal changes can occur at any stage of a system's lifecycle. As discussed earlier, when contractual relations shift to a bureaucratic relationship or the SOs cannot demonstrate their comparative advantages conclusively, actors in the system may become less cooperative, which may even lead to the collapse of the service system.

This research also shed light on the concept of transformation. As discussed in the introduction of this book, transformation is expected to address the root causes of vulnerability and inequality. The case of China represents only the initial phase of an attempt to bring about transformation. During this early stage, it was unclear whether the changes would ultimately be transformative. A seemingly profound change based on a different ideology at a given time did not necessarily lead to transformation along the same trajectory. As explored in this chapter, there are evident institutional barriers impeding progress.

At the time of publication, we can observe that China's community-based old-age care system has made significant progress toward a hybrid model, with the private sector assuming an increasingly prominent role compared to state organizations (SOs). This indicates that although the introduction of SOs did not succeed in transforming the system entirely, it has enabled practitioners to recognize the limitations of relying solely on SOs as service providers and further opened the care service sector to new actors. In this sense, the trajectory of transformation can be a windy path.

The limitations of this research should be given due attention. The fieldwork was in the pilot cities of the reform, which means they were ahead of other parts of the country in adopting the reform. The local governments were more eager to embrace the reform. Given the nature of the pilots, they were more open to suggestions and interactions with other stakeholders. In this sense, the government's willingness to implement the reform would be substantial. However, this may not be the case all over the country. As this research did not aim to comprehensively assess the aged care services across the country, but rather to understand the transition process, we did not consider it inappropriate to only study the pilot cities. Gathering information in cities with an active implementation meant we could investigate a wider range of services and contact many stakeholders. At the same time, we fully acknowledge that further research will be useful to enable a more representative sample.

References

Bian, Fuqian, John R. Logan and Yanjie Bian. 1998. "Intergenerational Relations in Urban China: Proximity, Contact, and Help to Parents." *Demography*, 35(1):115–124.

China Social Welfare and Elderly Service Association. 2021. *2020 National Aging Development Bulletin (2020 Niándù guójiā lǎolíng shìyè fāzhǎn gōngbào)*. Accessed 1 July 2022. https://www.sohu.com/a/495667186_121124546.

Flaherty, Joseph H., Mei Lin Liu, Li-liang Ding, Birong Dong, Qunfang Ding, Xia Li and Shifu Xiao. 2007. "China: The Aging Giant." *Journal of the American Geriatrics Society*, 55(8):1295–1300.

Hesketh, Therese, Li Lu and Zhu Wei Xing. 2005. "The Effect of China's One-Child Family Policy after 25 Years." *New England Journal of Medicine*, 353(11):1171–1176.

Howell, Jude. 2012. "Civil Society, Corporatism and Capitalism in China." *Journal of Comparative Asian Development*, 11(2):271–297.

Ke Research. 2021. *2021 Report on Aging and Elderly Living*. Accessed 1 July 2022. http://www.sohu.com/a/541712914_121222159.

Lei, X., J. Strauss, M. Tian and Y. Zhao. 2015. "Living Arrangements of the Elderly in China: Evidence from the CHARLS National Baseline." *China Economic Journal*, 8(3):191–214.

Liu, S. 2006. "The Old People's Social Participation and their Self-harmony." *Journal of Nanjing College for Population Programme Management*, 22(2):32–35.

Luo, Zhufeng. 1959. "People's Commune and Family Issues (*Rénmín gōngshè yǔ jiātíng wèntí*)." *Academic Monthly* (*Xuéshù yuèkān*), 2:25–28.

Lv, Jin. 2012. *A Survey of Institutionalised Old Age Care Services (Zhèjiāng shěng jīgòu yǎnglǎo fúwù xiànzhuàng de diàochá yánjiū)*. Master's thesis for Public Administration, Electronic Technology University.

Ministry of Civil Affairs, PRC. 2016. *2015 Social Service Development Statistical Communique (2015 Nián shèhuì fúwù fāzhǎn tǒngjì gōngbào)*. Accessed 1 July 2022. http://www.gov.cn/xinwen/2016-07/12/content_5090289.htm.

National Health and Family Planning Commission. 2015. *Chinese Family Development Report, 2015 (Zhōngguó jiātíng fāzhǎn bàogào, 2015)*. Beijing: China Population Publishing House.

Oxfam. 2014. *Chinese Rural Women in Poverty Reduction: Summary and Outlook (Zhōngguó nóngcūn fùnǚ jiǎn pín gàikuàng jí zhǎnwàng)*. China Development Brief. Accessed 1 July 2022. http://www.chinadevelopmentbrief.org.cn/news-16680.html.

Pei, Xiaomei. 2004. "The Development and Issues of Long-Term Care Services for Cities with Aging Population (*Lǎonián xíng chéngshì chángqí zhàohù fúwù de fāzhǎn jí qí wèntí*)." *Urban Management* (*Chéngshì guǎnlǐ*), 36:36–37.

UNDP (United Nations Development Programme) China. 2013. *China National Human Development Report 2013—Sustainable and Livable Cities: Toward Ecological Civilization*. Beijing: UNDP. Accessed 1 July 2022. https://hdr.undp.org/content/sustainable-and-liveable-cities-toward-ecological-civilization.

Wang, Dewen and Liangdi Xie. 2013. "Supply of Community Old Age Care (*Shèqū yǎnglǎo zhàohù de gōngjǐ*)." In *The Status Quo and Development Strategy of Old Age Care for Older People in Community (Shèqū lǎonián rénkǒu yǎnglǎo zhāohū xiànzhuàng yǔ fāzhǎn duìcè)*, edited by Dewen Wang and Liangdi Xie, 156–157. Xiamen: Xiamen University Press.

11

NGOs in the Context of the Reform of Social Services in Russia

Linda J. Cook and Elena Iarskaia-Smirnova

Introduction

This chapter addresses development and change in Russia's social policies since 2005. We focus on three areas that have undergone significant reform: policies toward people with disabilities, child welfare and outsourcing of social service delivery to SONPOs (socially oriented non-profit organizations). In these areas, the Russian government has adopted potentially transformative changes, moving away from Soviet-era practices of state monopoly and institutionalization toward a rights-based approach featuring deinstitutionalization, social inclusion and diversity of service providers. This chapter identifies the problems and pressures that motivated these policy shifts, the purposes and functions they are designed to fulfil, and how much each has changed Russia's social sector. Briefly, we find that changes in child welfare policy have been transformative; those in disability policy significant but more limited. Development of outsourcing has faltered, though its success varies across regions and policy areas.

These policy changes are dramatic, based on what Meri Kulmala (2017) characterizes as a "paradigm shift" in policy toward children in state care and people with disabilities.[1] Changes are based on the Russian government's adoption of international social policy norms and practices as codified, for example, in United Nations Conventions. But their adoption is selective, depending on the Putin administration's priorities, and does not extend to other areas of social policy. Chief among these priorities are demographic concerns, cost efficiency in the social sector and public satisfaction with services delivered. Civil society organizations, including non-governmental organizations (NGOs), do effectively promote and influence reforms, but the initiative for significant policy changes comes from the top. Implementing such reforms requires substantial changes in social sector organization,

---

[1] Kulmala applies the term "paradigm shift" to changes in child welfare policy, but it could equally be used to characterize changes in disability policy.

financing, skill sets and so on, and inevitably confronts structural and institutional barriers.

Reforms in disability, child welfare and outsourcing took place in the same timeframe, with initial steps introduced between 2005 and 2010 and full-blown reforms legislated between 2012 and 2015. The disability and child welfare reforms involved similar normative or ideological shifts: from beliefs that people with disabilities and orphaned children should be controlled, isolated from society and institutionalized, to fundamentally new commitments to deinstitutionalization, social inclusion and rights to have needs accommodated in communities. The outsourcing reform had some additional goals, but it was integrally connected with the first two: emptying institutions and integrating their former residents into society would require rapid expansion of smaller-scale community-based facilities and services. SONPOs that had experience working with children and those with disabilities were well positioned to help provide such services. For the research, we undertook 40 interviews with NGO leaders and activists, academic specialists and government representatives in Moscow and several Russian regions.

The chapter proceeds as follows: the next section gives a brief overview of the statist Soviet-era welfare system and tracks the early development of independent NGOs after the 1991 transition. We then describe the significant shifts in outsourcing of service provision, disability and child welfare policy, explaining why and how each was initiated and identifying sources of support as well as resistances. Next, we compare the outcomes of the three reforms, obstacles they confronted, and the possibilities and limits of SONPOs' influence in each case. The conclusion explains the differential success of the three reforms based on their "fit" with the Putin administration's priorities and the institutional space open for innovation.

The Statist Social Sector and Emergence of NGOs in Russia

Until the collapse of communism in the early 1990s, the state provided welfare and social services in Russia. The population's access to basic health, education and other services was nearly universal, though the quality was low. The welfare regime had been constructed not in response to demands or needs articulated by society but from the top down, by the communist political elite. It was heavily bureaucratized, centralized and standardized in its rules, norms and practices. The state held a virtual monopoly on welfare provision; with a few small exceptions, private services were illegal. Nor were independent civil society (non-state) organizations allowed to form. A significant part of the labour force, mainly women with professional qualifications, worked in the social sector. This statist system produced orthodoxies about social needs and deservedness, and professionals who were educated in and committed to these orthodoxies.

Rather than considering this welfare system generally, we concentrate on the two policy areas: policy toward people with disabilities and child welfare policy, especially toward children living in state orphanages. During the Soviet period, the government defined disabilities as conditions that required medical care. It established categories to determine what therapies should be provided to persons with disabilities and whether they should live in society or be isolated in institutions. Adults who had some capacity to work were given therapy and training, and the government required the management to accept an assigned number (quota) as employees. Children with mild disabilities attended separate schools, but most lived with their families. Both children and adults with severe disabilities lived in a Federation-wide system of specialized residential institutions, often from birth, and were excluded from the general society throughout their lives (Rasell and Iarskaia-Smirnova 2014). There was no concept of rights for those with disabilities, and little effort was made to provide facilities or services in communities.

This model of institutionalization extended to children who were orphaned, as well as the broader category of "social orphans"—those without parental or family supervision though they had a living parent. The orphanages had developed during the cataclysms of the revolutionary period and the Second World War, and the third wave of children entered during the decade-long recession of the 1990s.

While some of these children had been abandoned, the state took many from troubled families. They were placed in residential facilities, usually isolated from the general population, and provided with education but little nurture. Soviet society for the most part lacked systems of adoption, foster care or other programmes to integrate these children into society. Beginning in the 1970s, international social policy norms and practices moved toward deinstitutionalization, social integration and community-based care of children as well as people with disabilities. But for several decades, the Russian government continued to rely mainly on institutionalization. When its approach began to change, both international conventions and domestic NGOs would strongly influence the directions of reform.

The emergence of NGOs

NGOs and other civil society organizations were first legalized in Russia during the transitional decade of the 1990s. By 2000, the NGO sector included at least four distinct categories of organizations: socially oriented NGOs (SONPOs); political, civil rights and environmental advocacy organizations; "legacy" organizations; and government-organized NGOs (GONGOs). We will be concerned mainly with SONPOs, organizations that focused on social needs. Two types of SONPOs will concern us. The first and larger group were self-help grassroots organizations that emerged to serve children and adults with disabilities, chronic illnesses, HIV/AIDS and other vulnerable groups. Most were small, informal membership organizations that coordinated support and services for a network of families or neighbourhoods. While they coordinated and delivered services in communities, most lacked professional staff and funding (Cook and Vinogradova 2006).

Many smaller groups of SONPOs developed into professional staffed organizations that engaged in fund-raising. Some cooperated with and received grants from foreign counterparts and organized collaboration with international experts in various areas of social policy. Such professionalized organizations generally did not deliver services directly but engaged in education and advocacy. Some members became part of international epistemic social policy communities that promoted new norms and practices, including deinstitutionalization, social inclusion, rights of people with disabilities and integration of orphaned children into society through foster care and adoption (Yakimets 1999). SONPO activists became advocates for these global norms within Russian professional and NGO communities and later helped move them onto the policy agenda.

While the largest group of SONPOs was engaged in education, substantial numbers of them worked with orphans, mothers and children (vulnerable families), people with disabilities, as well as the elderly and marginalized groups. According to Russia's State Statistical Agency, in 2020, 6,194 SONPOs worked with people with disabilities and their families, 5,021 with social orphans, mothers and children, and another 117,000 in other spheres of activities (Rosstat 2021). The majority of their workers—about two-thirds nationally—were volunteers. SONPOs were unevenly spread throughout the Russian Federation, with concentrations in major cities and a few regions. Until the 2000s, few domestic sources of support were available to them. Some SONPOs received external funding or offered fee-based services, but most worked pro bono, remaining resource-poor, fragile organizations. Their greatest problem was inadequate and unstable funding.

Beginning in 2005 the Russian government increased its attention to the NGO sector. This attention was first motivated by the Putin administration's belief that Western-backed NGOs had triggered the recent democratizing "colour revolutions" that destabilized governments in neighbouring Georgia and Ukraine. In an effort to inoculate Russia against a similar threat, the government restricted activities of advocacy NGOs that promoted political, civil and environmental rights. NGOs receiving international funds were demonized as "foreign agents," and many closed. (Romanov and Iarskaia-Smirnova 2015). These repressive policies excluded advocacy NGOs from politics and generated public hostility and distrust toward the sector.

But Russia's government distinguished "socially useful" SONPOs from political and rights-advocacy organizations, and used this distinction to justify radically different treatment of the two categories. Officials came to see greater state cooperation with SONPOs as a way to address multiple problems in Russia's social sector: to introduce diversity and competition into service provision, increase cost efficiency, debureaucratize and modernize. Beginning in 2008, the presidential administration and central ministries sponsored expansive programmes of grants and competitions to improve SONPOs' organizational capacities and to subsidize their cooperation with regional governments. After several years of successful competitions in which the majority of Russian regions participated, the government scaled up these efforts. In 2013 it initiated a new system that required regional governments to contract out part of their social services to SONPOs and small commercial organizations.

Major Social Policy Shifts in the Russian Federation
Outsourcing delivery of social services

The first major outsourcing initiative, FZ (Federal Law) 44, "On the Contracting System in the Sphere of Goods, Works and Services for Ensuring State and Municipal Needs," was passed in 2012 (FZ-44 2012). It stipulated that 15 per cent of the total annual value of contracts for social service provision must go to SONPOs and small businesses in each of Russia's regions. This law proved difficult to implement because mechanisms for including small non-state organizations in tenders for contracts were undeveloped. It was soon followed by Federal Law 442 (FZ-442 2013) "On the Basis of Social Services for Citizens of the Russian Federation," which established a new process for integrating SONPOs into the system of social service provision. FZ-442, which came into effect in January 2015, provided that SONPOs and small businesses could register as official social service providers, contract with regional governments to deliver services and receive payment from regional social sector budgets. The law authorized SONPOs to provide eight types of services, including medical and psychological care (social-medical services), preventative measures against deviant behaviour (social-pedagogical services), help in employment (social-labour services), and protection of social and civic rights (social-judicial services). Up to this point state social service centres had always provided these services (Tarasenko 2018). FZ-442 paved the way for a major expansion in the role of non-governmental providers. According to projections of the Agency for Strategic Initiative, a non-profit think tank that advised the Russian government, the law was expected to lead to an increase by more than eight-fold in the financing of social protection programmes implemented by private, non-profits or small businesses by 2018 (Expert.ru 2014).

Why did Putin's government cede its near monopoly over social service provision? The reform had several motivations: Outsourcing was expected to make social services more responsive to the population and more cost effective than direct service provision by the state, helping to meet the goals of New Public Management in budget optimization and accountability. FZ-442 was designed to create an alternative market for social services outside of state institutions, in fewer institutional settings and in clients' homes. It was expected to create competition between state and SONPO providers and to reorient the system of service provision to individual needs and demands. NGOs were viewed internationally as better than state service providers because they were closer to their clients, more knowledgeable about local conditions and less bureaucratic. Promoters of FZ-442 anticipated that the law would increase the range and quality of social services, allow eligible service recipients choice of providers and provide a more tailored approach. It was hoped that SONPOs would address the deep popular dissatisfaction with social services that was revealed in public opinion polls. The reform envisioned citizens as clients who would take the initiative to find, compare and choose the best providers, and document their own eligibility, rather than as passive recipients of state services.

Bringing in SONPOs could, at the same time, allow the state to utilize a large pool of volunteer labour that socially oriented organizations had mobilized. Though Russian civil society remained weak in international comparison, Russian SONPOs had almost 2.5 million volunteers working in more than 140,000 organizations throughout the Federation in 2016 (see Table 11.1). Russia was also following international experience and practice. State–NGO partnerships were common in Europe and the United States, and research confirms they did generally provide services at a lower cost than purely state organizations (Cook 2015). Russia's government could benefit from activating this sector of civil society, and simultaneously increase incentives for political compliance by making SONPOs financially dependent on the state.

SONPOs were also important for the success of the disability and child welfare reforms adopted at this time. Successful deinstitutionalization of people with disabilities would require a rapid expansion of community-based services that were tailored to individual needs, outpatient facilities and individual assistance for those now living independently (Karelia NGO interview #1, 2015). SONPOs could establish new care models, such as daycare facilities and sheltered workshops (Kolpakova 2019). They were also needed to help establish programmes to care for children who were moved out of orphanages. Activists working on child welfare had learned about global norms and practices of foster care and preventative family services through earlier international collaborations, while existing state social sector staff had little experience placing children in homes or counselling troubled

Table 11.1: Socially oriented non-commercial organizations (SONPOs) in the Russian Federation and selected regions 2015–2016

Region	Number of SONPOs	Approx. no. of workers	Approx. no. of volunteers	No. of SONPOs in regional registry
Russian Federation	140,031	991,081	2,492,974	300 (approx.)
St Petersburg City	3,966	39,955	31,841	198
Republic of Bashkortostan	5,118	23,403	88,634	118
Perm Krai	3,093	15,882	35,058	34
Khanti-Mansiiski Auton Region	215	1,783	1,546	12
Moscow City	4,856	225,940	137,115	5
Republic of Karelia	1,104	3,063	25,424	4

Note: SONPOs may include some non-state commercial providers.

Source: Goskomstat Rossii cols 2, 3, 4; col. 5 MinTrud February 2016.

families. Dimitri Medvedev, who presided over new programmes of federal financing for SONPOs, stressed in a 2010 speech that, "We have to call the non-profits to social service provision more actively. They often know better about actual situations … participation of non-profit organizations may make social services more focused and better targeted, and decrease corruption in the state apparatus" (Poslanie Presidenta 2010).

Reforming disability policy

As noted earlier, in the 1970s, international norms and practices moved toward a rights-based approach to people with disabilities, including deinstitutionalization and social inclusion. However, Russia retained its established practices until 1995. The first significant reform legislation, the 1995 Federal Law "On Social Protection of People with Disabilities in the Russian Federation" (FZ-181 1995), mandated measures for the integration of those with disabilities into communities. Some urban social service centres began providing therapies and other resources on a modest scale, but for more than a decade there was no more significant change (Fröhlich 2012).

A major policy shift took place with the Russian government's ratification of the United Nations Convention "On the Rights of Persons with Disabilities" (CPRD) (UN 2006). Russia signed the Convention in 2008, and official ratification in 2012 was viewed as a watershed event. The Convention defined a broad set of rights for people with all types of disabilities. Ratification committed governments to make public spaces accessible, ensure equal opportunities for education, employment, the right to a family, and choice about the place and type of appropriate social services. Services should be available in communities and adapted to individual needs. By ratifying the Convention, the government implicitly recognized that Russia's existing practices of institutionalization and segregation were obsolete.

Three implementing reforms followed ratification. First was the State Programme of the Russian Federation "Accessible Environment 2011–2016," which mandated changes in physical structures such as building entrances, sidewalks, transportation and so on that would accommodate those with limited mobility. The second, a set of 2014 laws "On Education in the Russian Federation" and "Federal State Education Standards for Students with Disabilities," provided for "inclusive education," that is, integration of children with disabilities into mainstream schools and classrooms from which they had been excluded (Iarskaia-Smirnova and Romanov 2007). The third reform addressed employment rights. A 2013 Order of the Ministry of Labour and Social Protection confirmed the main requirements for equipping workplaces for citizens with disabilities, including people who use wheelchairs, have visual and/or hearing loss among others, with special technical means relevant to the individual capacities of a worker (Ministry of Labour 2014). Amendments to dozens of federal laws have been made to bring them into compliance with these reforms, and additional legislation prohibits discrimination against people with disabilities, affirms their right to form families, and enables adoption and foster parenting of children with disabilities.

Agents of change and resistance

The watershed decision to approve the UN Convention came "from above," promoted by then-President Medvedev as part of his Modernization Programme. Experts on disability, including academic researchers and those from SONPOs working in the disability field, favoured the reforms but were surprised by their rapidity. One disability expert we interviewed supported the adoption of the Convention in principle but thought it was too fast, imposing many binding obligations that Russia could not meet at that time (Moscow disability interview #1, 2015). While the political leadership strongly supported the reform, considerable resistance was reported in the ministries that would be responsible for implementing it. Ministry officials argued that they were not prepared to meet all the Convention's conditions.

There was also opposition from some mental health professionals. As Shek's research has shown, staff in both inpatient and outpatient facilities for those with intellectual and psychological disabilities were critical of the reforms (Shek 2018). One survey found that deinstitutionalized care was strongly contested even by the staff of outpatient facilities in a large Russian city (Shek and Pietila 2016). The majority of those surveyed argued that much in

Russia's traditional system was worth preserving and that any reforms should be based on Russian practice, not imported Western models. In their views, institutionalized care protects people with mental disabilities from ostracism in communities. Pointing to underfunding in the present, many expressed doubts that adequate community services would be provided for those leaving institutions. Some educators argued against mainstreaming children with disabilities in public schools, which did not have staff specialized in working with them. There were, in sum, problems with building consensus around the reform, and a widespread sense that it was approved without the necessary preparation. We will return to an evaluation of its effectiveness.

Reforms of child welfare: family services and foster care

The Soviet Union and its Russian successor state cared for a large number of children in residential "children's homes." While some had no living parents, an estimated 80 per cent were social orphans, either given up by parents who could not care for them or removed from troubled families. The proportion of children left without parental care in Russia ranks among the highest in international comparison, equalling 2.4 per cent of the child population (Kulmala et al 2021). Part of the problem was the lack of child protection and family reconciliation services. The state was quick to institutionalize children rather than trying to help their parents. According to one of our interviewees, the head of a Karelian NGO that assisted vulnerable families:

> "There were many cases of parents who lost their right to take care of their children. The system of care doesn't give a chance to those parents who happened to get into trouble [with alcohol abuse, loss of jobs, etc.]. These families suffer the most because nobody assists them. Centres of social work claim that citizens don't ask for assistance … they [families] are afraid to lose their right to take care of their children." (Karelia demography interview #1, 2015)

Most of these children remained in institutions throughout their childhoods. Volunteers from child welfare SONPOs who worked in these understaffed children's homes testified to the social and emotional deprivation of child residents.

The shift toward keeping more children in families began with Russia's 1990 ratification of the UN Convention on the Rights of the Child and the 1995 Family Code but, as with disability policy, little changed over the following decade. In 2006, after a major Presidential Address placed Russia's demographic crisis at the top of the government's social policy agendas, regions were required to reduce the number of children living in institutions

(Biryukova and Sinyavskaya 2017; Kulmala et al 2021). In a 2012 Presidential Order (No. 761), "On a National Strategy of Action for Children 2012–2017," Putin announced a major policy shift: Russia's welfare system would now focus on providing every child with a home and family. To this end, the system of social services would be reformed to help disadvantaged or "vulnerable families" so that more children could stay with their parents. Of those living in children's homes, 90 per cent were to be moved into foster or adoptive families within Russia (the government ended international adoptions at this time). For the remaining children, institutions would be reorganized into "family-like" structures. The government launched a campaign to promote fostering, established systems of support for new foster families including group "foster villages," and provided them with stipends and sometimes housing (Kulmala 2016–2018).

Agents of change

Deinstitutionalization of children became a high priority of Putin's government as part of a package of policies designed to address Russia's sharp decline in population since 1990. The motivations for the policy linked children's welfare with the state's need for productive citizens. Two slogans framed the deinstitutionalization policy: "Every child deserves a home" and "Russia needs all its children." Child welfare SONPOs campaigned for this policy shift, advocating international norms of children's welfare and rights, disseminating "attachment theory," which holds that every child needs a stable relationship with a primary caretaker to develop emotionally and socially, and promoting practices of fostering and adoption. There is a general consensus among scholars that child welfare SONPOs succeeded as "policy entrepreneurs," influencing the direction of policy development and practice in their area of expertise (Bogdanova and Bindman 2016; Kulmala et al 2021). But it is important to recognize that they succeeded in part because their agenda aligned closely with the executive's priorities.

In contrast to disability policy reforms, we found scant evidence of resistance to deinstitutionalizing children. There was broad normative acceptance. Some viewed these children as troubled, but no one argued that they would be better served by remaining in institutions, in contrast to mental health professionals' arguments for some people with disabilities. There was also more space for the development of new policies and practices and SONPOs' participation. Because Russia's social sector workers had very little experience with family reconciliation counselling or foster family placement, authorities turned to child welfare SONPOs for help in designing new institutions and implementing new practices (Kulmala et al 2021). These SONPOs, in turn, drew on past international collaborations to help develop similar policies in Russia.

Evaluating Outcomes

Outsourcing

We turn first to the contracting-out system, focusing on an evaluation of its outcomes, then to an analysis of the obstacles that limited its success (Council of the Federation 2015). The outcomes of FZ-442 have varied throughout the Russian Federation. Overall, though, in the years since the legislation came into effect, its implementation has proven quite disappointing. One key measure of success is the inclusion of SONPOs in regional registries of social service providers, a step that must precede their bidding for contracts. According to the Russian State Statistical Agency (Rosstat 2021) there were approximately 128,000 SONPOs in Russia at the end of 2020. In 2016, only 300–350 SONPOs had been approved for inclusion in regional registries. Moreover, these 300+ organizations were concentrated in a small number of regions, while many regions had one or none registered (see Table 11.1). State organizations continued to provide more than 90 per cent of all social services. In 2017 the numbers of the registered SONPOs had increased only to 468 (Tarasenko 2018). While numbers did later increase in some regions, the reform remained uneven and its implementation varied with regional resources and political support from their governors (Cook et al 2021).

Why, given initial expectations, has the outsourcing reform remained limited? Our research, as well as assessments by the Russian government and independent scholars, have identified several obstacles to its success. First were structural obstacles: some of Russia's regions had weak civil societies with few and small NGOs. They simply lacked the structural conditions for outsourcing. Some confronted bureaucratic obstacles in their efforts to register as service providers. Mechanisms for financing and compensation from public budgets were undeveloped. Social service clients, often from vulnerable groups—elderly, poor—were accustomed to relying on statist providers.

Barriers to entry into regional registries

In regions that had SONPOs interested in contracting, the local governments confronted different types of obstacles. Some SONPO representatives interviewed for our project described the process of applying for entry into regional registries as a "difficult quest." Problems arose because of inconsistencies in the law itself as well as actions of officials on the ground. In some regions, officials imposed additional requirements such as many years of continuous operation before an NGO could apply to the register. Some organizations confronted bureaucratic obstacles, including excessive paperwork, repeated requests for documents and long-delayed responses. Regional social sector officials had long benefited from their monopoly over service provision; some did not welcome sharing state funding with non–state competitors.

A related problem was the small scale and low level of professionalism of many SONPOs that had been engaged in pro bono direct service delivery. State providers were required to meet standards (professional specialists, facilities) in order to deliver particular types of services. Most SONPOs were too small and lacked the professional staff to qualify. According to a representative from one:

> "Certain amendments [to FZ-442] were adopted according to which the whole packet of services [mandated by the state for particular categories of recipients] should be provided by one organization. This is, of course, contrary to the spirit of the law, but it is specified in one of the law's Acts. This means that any organization that does not have the "full complex" of services has no chance to participate. As we understand, this is the majority of non–state organizations." (Moscow NGO interview #2, 2015)

According to another interviewee whose NGO was in the process of trying to register, "We have to change our director, staff, charter, to be included in the register" (Moscow NGO interview #3, 2015).

Even if they wanted to make these changes, most lacked adequate resources. The lack of resources and low level of professionalism, in turn, led regional authorities to reject SONPOs as unqualified to provide adequate services.

Nevertheless, SONPO representatives reported wanting to enter registries because they saw two potential benefits: stable financing and possibilities for dialogue with state institutions. Approval as a service provider opened the long-term possibility of regular payments for their services from the state budget, rather than grants which "you win one year and not the next" (Moscow NGO interview #2, 2015). Stable financing could, in turn, allow the SONPO to expand and develop its work. Some thought that state contracts might give them more influence on policy, or that they could provide services more effectively than state institutions.

Financing and compensation

Rules and mechanisms for compensation also presented obstacles. Payments for contracted services were made as reimbursements, but most SONPOs did not have the financial resources to finance delivery upfront. Compensation rates set by regions often underestimated SONPOs' costs. Calculation of reimbursement is based on the cost of providing similar services in state organizations, which do not pay taxes, rents and other expenses that should, however, be paid by NGOs. SONPOs often provided types of services that met their clients' needs, but that had no equivalents on state lists of social services and so could not qualify for compensation under FZ-442. Some SONPO representatives concluded that the financing system was rigged against them.

Difficulties finding clients

When they did succeed in entering the registries, SONPOs had difficulty finding clients. The entrenchment of the state system, refusal of its workers to refer people out, and clients' own lack of knowledge and habit of relying on state services, all contributed. Recipients of social services are, as a rule, elderly people and others from vulnerable groups of the population, who are accustomed to established routines. According to one interviewee:

> "He [the client] may choose, but they [state authorities] will say to him, 'Go to a certain place.' ... [O]ur clients are a specific category of people, they all go where they are told. There are not many among them who are active, able to find information independently, to compare, to make choices, to find alternatives. They [state authorities] will be interested in sending people to social organizations only when ... there is a deficit of internal [state] services." (Moscow NGO interview #2, 2015)

Even service recipients who know they now have a choice are often not prepared to make demands on the basis of the law (FZ-442). In addition, many people were reluctant to trust any NGOs because of the state's campaign of vilification against political organizations. In sum, the reform brought only modest changes, both in the status of SONPOs and in the delivery of social services to Russian citizens.

Disability reforms: outcomes

In 2018, the Russian government issued a report showing significant progress in meeting the conditions of the UN Convention on the Rights of Persons with Disabilities (Cook and Iarskaia-Smirnova 2018; Government of Russia 2018). According to the report, more than 18,000 (51.3 per cent of the total) priority sites providing health care, education, cultural and social services, sports and transportation had been made accessible. The "Accessible Spaces" programme was extended to 2025, with a projected budget of USD 7.6 billion (OHCHR 2018). The federal budget had funded the creation of more than 44,000 specially equipped workspaces. Still, according to one interviewee who worked for a SONPO that helped with job placement for those with disabilities, inaccessible transport and communication barriers continued to present the most serious problems for those seeking work

(Moscow disability interview #1, 2015). Russian employers remain resistant to hiring adults with disabilities, and any employment tends to be low-wage. Most adults remain dependent on benefits from the state rather than income from employment.

There have been advances in social and educational inclusion for children with disabilities. The number of those living with their families, as well as support for these families, have slowly increased. "Inclusive education" (mainstreaming) has been expanded; in 2011, there were only about 1,000 inclusive general education schools in Russia. By 2018 almost 10,000 schools, about 20 per cent of the total, enrolled more than 270,500 children with disabilities, and numbers increased in post-secondary schools (OHCHR 2018). However, most of the schools that can accommodate children with disabilities are concentrated in urban centres. There are problems in designing inclusive education, as practical measures are often not differentiated according to the needs of different children. Regional inequalities contribute to considerable differences in the availability of specialized schools and other facilities. As one interviewee emphasized, "It is impossible to evaluate the effectiveness of [disability reform] policies at the national level ... [because] outcomes differ on regional and even municipal bases, depending on available resources" (Moscow disability interview #2, 2015).

Especially for those with psychological and intellectual disabilities, care has remained predominantly institution-based. While there has been some increase in outpatient and daycare services and sheltered workshops, community-based facilities remain very limited. Parents struggle to find resources in their communities and still experience pressure to give up their children. Long-term residential care facilities are run by professional psychiatrists who remain committed to traditional practices and rarely cooperate with SONPOs or others promoting models of recovery and social inclusion. The author of a recent study assessing outcomes of the reform concludes that, while approaches to mental health care in Russia have changed on a discursive level, in practice, it seems that the network of psychiatric facilities has remained similar to that in the 1990s. SONPOs have virtually no opportunities to deliver psychiatric care because funding remains committed to established residential institutions (Kolpakova 2019).

Still, in contrast to the situation before the reform, the rights of people with disabilities are now recognized by Russia's government and society. The activism and agency of parents with disabled children have played a significant role in bringing public attention to disability issues (Iarskaia-Smirnova and Romanov 2015). Now public officials openly express concerns about the special needs and inadequacies of current approaches. Grassroots associations, NGOs and networks take part in discussions and contribute to overcoming stigmatization and exclusion in society. SONPOs, both registered and not, provide home care and assistance to children with disabilities and their families, including rehabilitation and counselling. Such services are rated (for reimbursement) in a straightforward way, and these organizations prevail in the registries.

Transforming child welfare

Child welfare reforms have been by far the most successful; indeed, they have transformed support services for families and substantially emptied Russia's orphanages. Priority is now given to family preservation, support and reconciliation services, and placements in foster homes. The share of children taken out of parental care fell by half from 2008 to 2015 (Kulmala 2016–2018), though courts more often turn to limiting rather than terminating parental rights. The number of children living in orphanages declined dramatically. In 2005–2015, the share of children placed with foster families grew from 2 to 24 per cent, while there was a ten-fold increase in the number of foster families (Biryukova and Sinyavskaya 2017). The number registered in the state databank of children left without parental care declined from 180,000 in 2006 to 71,200 in 2016 (see Figure 11.1). Those left in institutions are disproportionately children with disabilities, who are everywhere more difficult to place.

SONPOs have played a significant role in child welfare reform. As the work of Kulmala et al (2016–2018), Bogdanova and Bindman (2016), and others has shown, SONPOs provide support services for foster families as well as for children who remain in residential care. Some run programmes

Figure 11.1: Number registered in Russia's state databank of children left without parental care 2006–2016 (thousands)

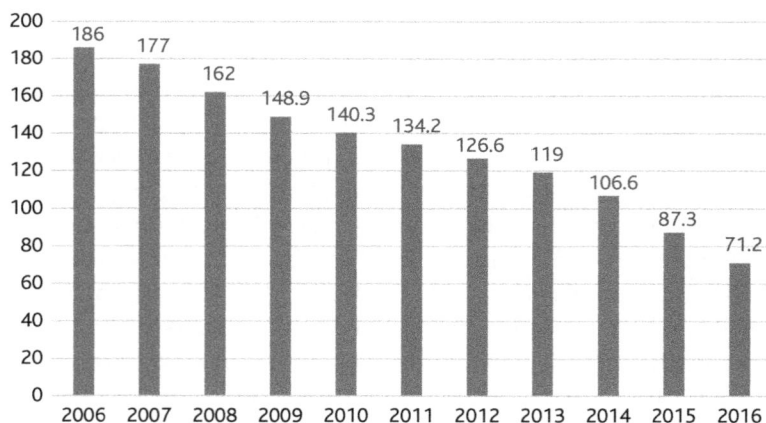

Source: http://www.usynovite.ru, УСЫНОВЛЕНИЕ В РОССИИ (Adoption in Russia), Internet Project of the Ministry of Education and Science of the Russian Federation, Department of State Policies in the Area of Defence of Children's Rights (accessed 28 August 2017).

to help prevent parents from losing custody of their children, and to counsel those whose children are already in state care. Government-funded family services, including orientation and education for foster parents, are often outsourced; this is one policy area in which the system of contracting-out seems to be working (Kulmala et al 2021; Tarasenko 2018). In sum, SONPOs provide, and are needed to provide, expertise in developing and implementing new and previously untried foster care and other child welfare programmes.

Discussion

Why have child welfare reforms been more successful than similar reforms in disability policy, and why have SONPOs that provide services for children and families been more successful in contracting with the state than those in other policy areas? In answer to the first question, we argue that Putin's administration prioritized child welfare policies above other areas because they help to address demographic issues. Halting the demographic decline stands near the top of the government's agenda. A broad package of policies, including pro-natalist incentives, family benefits, restrictions on reproductive rights, as well as child welfare reforms, are directed toward increasing the population. Supporting and nurturing all children in Russia, rather than offering them for international adoption or leaving them to languish in institutions, responds to the interests of children as well as complementary priorities of the state. Further, there appears to be consensus on this policy change. There is no evidence of normative challenges; no group advocating for institutional care. And there is more space for SONPOs because existing state institutions and staff have no experience with adoption or foster care.

While the policy outcome indicators—lower percentages of parents losing custody of their children, many more in foster homes—are very positive, the reform is by no means without problems. Some foster placements fail, sending children back to institutions. Reorienting child welfare services toward supporting family reconciliation is an ongoing struggle (Kulmala et al 2021) There is a concern that some families take foster children because they need the state payments that come with placement. Nevertheless, norms, attitudes and practices in Russia's child welfare policy have been transformed.

Conclusion

What are the needs and problems that have driven changes in the social policy sectors since the turn of the millennium? What are the newly emerging ideas and principles for distributing social services, and the consequences of new trends and innovations, their outcomes and beneficiaries? How have particular political, economic and social circumstances brought about these changes? Have they been transformative—addressing structural causes of poverty, inequality and social exclusion? This chapter has addressed these questions. The reforms on which this chapter has focused have the potential to transform the lives of many people who had been kept on the margins of Russian society, to include them in families, schools and public places, to give them more freedom and opportunities, and so to reduce structural inequalities.

We have shown that since 2005 the Russian government has adopted major reforms in three areas: policy toward people with disabilities, child welfare policy and outsourcing of social service delivery to SONPOs. These are potentially transformative changes, moving away from Soviet-era practices of state monopoly and institutionalization toward a rights-based approach to social policy featuring deinstitutionalization, social inclusion and diversity of service providers. Reforms have been directed toward a range of goals: to make social service delivery more flexible, responsive to people's needs and cost effective; to help troubled families and give every child a home; and to include people with disabilities in society and give them more opportunities. Together, they are designed to make Russia's social sector more modern, and to adopt international norms and practices, including rights-based norms that seem at odds with other aspects of the Russian state's ideology.

The responses of the SONPOs to the COVID-19 pandemic and their impacts have demonstrated benefits gained from this institutional reform. Although the SONPOs had difficulty in providing services owing to the limitations on movement during lockdowns and declines in funding, their roles in providing care services to vulnerable groups, including people with disabilities, children in need of care, the elderly and others, became more important during the COVID-19 pandemic. For instance, the SONPOs provided assistance to adults and children with disabilities, sponsoring a meal delivery service for the elderly and homeless, and offering shelter during the pandemic. They helped in fighting the pandemic by distributing face masks and antiseptic, food, and other assistance to the elderly and people who were in isolation. Those already listed in provider registries have provided a means for Russia's government, philanthropists and citizens to channel funds effectively for essential social services during the crisis. One of Russia's major newspapers, *Novaya Gazeta*, called NGOs part of a "rapid response" system that can in some situations be more effective than the government's Ministry for Emergencies and Disaster Relief. In sum, the reforms, especially the integration of SONPOs into social service delivery networks have, despite their limitations, proved to be very significant in responding to Russia's COVID-19 crisis (Rozhanovskaya 2020).

All three policy shifts described in the chapter have advocates in Russia's civil society, among experts and the NGO community, as well as among government advisers. Ultimately, though, given the centralization of Russia's political system, major initiatives for policy change have come from the top.

It is worth noting that these norms have been applied only in selected policy areas. In other areas, including gender equality, rights of migrants and their families, and treatment of people with addictions, for example—all of which are part of the same international rights discourse—these norms are ignored or explicitly rejected. In these areas, Russian policy has instead moved in conservative and exclusionary directions.

Acknowledgements

We would like to thank Ilcheong Yi and Kelly Setter from the United Nations Research Institute for Social Development (UNRISD) for detailed comments and suggestions on earlier drafts, and the Russian team of sociologists who helped to collect interviews, especially Daria Prisyazhnyuk and Nikita Bolshakov. Support from the Swedish International Development Cooperation Agency (SIDA) and the Basic Research Program of the National Research University Higher School of Economics is gratefully acknowledged. The authors take full responsibility for the chapter's contents.

References

Biryukova, Svetlana and Oxana Sinyavskaya. 2017. "Children Out of Parental Care in Russia: What Can We Learn from the Statistics?" *Journal of Social Policy Studies*, 15(3).

Bogdanova, Elena and Eleanor Bindman. 2016. "NGOs, Policy Entrepreneurship and Child Protection in Russia: Pitfalls and Prospects for Civil Society." *Demokratizatsiya*, 24(2):143–171.

Cook, Linda. 2015. "New Winds of Social Policy in the East." *Voluntas*, 26(6):2330–2350.

Cook, Linda and Elena Iarskaia-Smirnova. 2018. "Outsourcing of Social Service Provision to NGOs in the Russian Federation." Draft Paper, Project, "New Directions in Social Policy from and for the Global South." Geneva: United Nations Research Institute for Social Development.

Cook, Linda J. and Elena Vinogradova. 2006. "NGOs and Social Policy-Making in Russia's Regions." *Problems of Post-Communism*, 53(5):28–41.

Cook, Linda, Elena Iarskaia-Smirnova and Anna Tarasenko. 2021. "Outsourcing Social Services to NGOs in Russia: Federal Policy and Regional Responses." *Post-Soviet Affairs*, 37(2):119–136.

Council of the Federation. 2015. "The First Results of Implementation of 442-FZ, 6.06.2015." Accessed 1 July 2022. http://council.gov.ru/activity/activities/roundtables/56229/.

Expert.ru. 2014. " Business will open access to the social sphere " (in Russian). Accessed 1 July 2022. http://expert.ru/2014/06/25/biznesu-otkroyut-dostup-k-sotsialnoj-sfere/.

Fröhlich, Christian. 2012. "Civil Society and the State Intertwined: The Case of Disability NGOs in Russia." *East European Politics*, 28(4):371–389.

Government of Russia. 2018. "Disabled. Accessible Spaces: Several Important Decisions and Indicators for 6 Years" (in Russian). 11 April.

Iarskaia-Smirnova, Elena and Pavel Romanov. 2015. "Parenting Children with Disabilities: Institutions, Discourses and Identities." *Europe-Asia Studies*, 67(10):1606–1634.

Iarskaia-Smirnova, Elena and Pavel Romanov. 2007. "Perspectives of Inclusive Education in Russia." *European Journal of Social Work*, 10(1):89–105.

Kolpakova, Svetlana. 2019. "A Journey through Russian Mental Health Care: A Review and Evaluation." *International Journal of Mental Health*, 48(2):106–132.

Kulmala, Meri. 2017. "Paradigm Shift in Russian Child Welfare Policy." *Russian Analytical Digest*, No. 200, March 28.

Kulmala, Meri. 2016–2018. "A Child's Right to a Family: Deinstitutionalization of Child Welfare in Putin's Russia." Accessed 15 June 2017. http://blogs. helsinki.fi/childwelfare/about-the-project/.

Kulmala, Meri, Maija Jäppinen, Anna Tarasenki and Zhanna Chernova (eds). 2021. *Reforming Child Welfare in the Post-Soviet Space: Institutional Changes in Russia*. Abingdon: Routledge.

Ministry of Labour. 2014. *The Ministry of Labour Confirms Demands for Equipping Work Places for People with Disabilities* (in Russian). April 29. Accessed 14 June 2018. http://hrdocs.ru/novosti/trebovaniya-k-raboc him-mestam-invalidov/.

OHCHR (Office of the United Nations High Commissioner for Human Rights). 2018. "Committee on the Rights of Persons with Disabilities Examines the Report of Russia." 28 February, Geneva. Accessed 2 June 2018. http://www.ohchr.org/EN/NewsEvents/Pages/DisplayNews. aspx?NewsID=22733&.

Poslanie Presidenta. 2010. Poslanie Presidenta Federal'nomu sobraniu. 30 November. Accessed 4 January 2024. http://kremlin.ru/events/president/ news/9637.

Rasell, Michael and Elena Iarskaia-Smirnova (eds). 2014. *Disability in Eastern Europe and the Former Soviet Union: History, Policy and Everyday Life*. London: Routledge.

Romanov, P. and Iarskaia-Smirnova, E. 2015. "'Foreign Agents' in the Field of Social Policy Research: The Demise of Civil Liberties and Academic Freedom in Contemporary Russia." *European Journal of Social Policy*, 25(4):359–365.

Rosstat (Russian State Statistical Agency). 2021. *Svedenia o deyatelnosti SONKO [Information on the Activity of SONPOs]*. Accessed 24 November 2023. https://rosstat.gov.ru/storage/mediabank/1-sonko.html.

Rozhanovskaya, Nina. 2020. "Russian NGOs on the COVID-19 Front Lines." The Russia File, A blog of the Kennan Institute, 26 May. Accessed 1 July 2022. https://www.wilsoncenter.org/blog-post/russian-ngos-covid-19-front-lines.

Shek, Olga. 2018. *Mental Healthcare Reforms in Post-Soviet Russia: Negotiating New Ideas and Values.* PhD dissertation, University of Tampere, Finland.

Shek, Olga and Ilkka Pietila. 2016. "Limits of Deinstitutionalization of Psychiatry in Russia: Perspectives of Professionals Working in Outpatient Mental Health Services." *International Journal of Mental Health,* 45:118–134.

Tarasenko, Anna. 2018. "Russian Non-Profit Organizations in Service Delivery: Neo-liberal and Statist Policy Principles." *Europe-Asia Studies,* 70(4):514–530.

UN (United Nations). 2006. "Convention on the Rights of Persons with Disabilities" (CRPD). https://www.un.org/development/desa/disabilities/convention-on-the-rights-of-persons-with-disabilities.html#Fulltext.

Yakimets, V. N. 1999. Якимец В. Н. "Некоммерческие организации России: динамика роста, проблемы развития, место и роль в реформе социальной сферы, Гражданское общество: первые шаги /под ред" (Non-Profit Organizations in Russia: Dynamics of Growth of the Problem of Development: Place and Role in the Reform of the Social Sphere). Accessed 1 July 2022. https://www.civisbook.ru/files/File/Yakimez_N_org_R.pdf.

Interviews cited

Moscow disability interview #1. Disability specialist at a non-commercial (non-governmental) organization working on job placement for people with disabilities, Moscow, 3 November 2015.

Moscow NGO interview #2. Government expert on people and children with disabilities and social care, Moscow, 5 November 2015.

Moscow NGO interview #3. Leader of a social organization working on the rights of people with disabilities, Moscow, 5 November 2015.

Karelia demography interview #1. Leader of a regional social organization working on social rehabilitation and support, Petrozavodsk, 29 October 2015.

Karelia NGO interview #1. Leader of a project of a charitable foundation to help children without parental supervision, Petrozavodsk, 18 December 2015.

Conclusion: Toward New Social Policies for Transformation

Ilcheong Yi, Alexandra Kaasch and Kelly Stetter

Over the past few decades, there has been considerable dynamism in terms of discourse and practice in the social policy field. In the Introduction, we introduced six themes around which the discussions of the chapters in this volume have introduced new theoretical and analytical frameworks and the development of new social policies and programmes in non-Organisation for Economic Co-operation and Development (OECD) countries. These were: a rights-based approach to social welfare; integration of social policy into other public policies; the newly assumed role of civil society organizations (CSOs) in delivering social services in transition economies; the emergence of supranational-level social policy; informal workers shaping the system of social policy programmes; and national ownership of social policy in the context of development cooperation.

Rights-Based Approach to Social Welfare

The establishment of institutions guaranteeing economic and social rights, particularly regarding access to education, health and work, has been a prominent trend of reforms in many developing countries over the past two decades. Constitutional reforms and strengthened judicial power, political organization of hitherto marginalized persons in the newly opened democratic spaces and adopting international norms in service provisions have contributed to establishing and consolidating the rights-based approach to social policy. As Chapters 5 and 6 highlight, judicial institutions such as the constitutions and courts play an increasingly important role in creating the space for social policy advocacy and implementation of programmes, particularly those programmes based on the new articulation of human rights. There are still many obstacles to overcome in translating these newly established norms, values and principles within the context of a rights-based approach into a transformative result. The constitutional guarantee of health and education often meant thinly spread benefits and services. The court rulings to protect the rights to universal access to social service only ensure the bare minimum when the government provision of service is insufficient. The adoption of international norm is often applied to only certain sectors, as in the case of Russia (Chapter 11).

Integration of Social Policy into Other Public Policies

An integrated and balanced approach is central to realizing the visions and aspirations of the 2030 Agenda composed of economic growth, environmental sustainability and social inclusion. It is, in fact, an attempt to correct the siloed approach of different sectors, particularly the sectoral dominance of economic growth-related issues in the development of discourse and practice in the past. This requires policy makers and practitioners to build a process in which sectoral goals and targets are organized to mitigate the trade-offs and conflicts among themselves.

In Chapter 5 on the South African mining sector, Sophie Plagerson and Lauren Stuart offer an excellent example of emerging dynamics around the institutions and organizations facilitating the integration of policies for social development and environmental protection. Highlighting the roles of the constitution, the court and democratic participatory mechanisms, it offers lessons on how to establish and manage a democratic process of consensus-building among stakeholders with different sectoral interests, which is key to creating a synergistic integrated approach to different policy sectors.

One of the key areas of integration of sectoral policies highlighted by Smita Srinivas in Chapter 2 is the social and industrial policy interface. The chapter shows that innovations in health technology significantly affect the supply chains of health services. Innovations in pharmaceuticals, vaccines, medical services, diagnostics and surgical techniques affect the institutions and organizations of health service delivery, and consequently the health system as a whole, through cost to patient considerations, pricing, state procurement, reimbursements, generics availability, and prescription and treatment choices. The chapter also offers an explanatory and analytical framework of how policies of different sectors, in this case, technology and health, can create a virtuous or vicious cycle of production, exchange and consumption for health care at the national level.

Chapter 4 by Louise Haagh calls for an integrated perspective on the debates regarding the universal basic income, which has attracted the attention of policy makers and practitioners of social policy as a viable option to address a variety of social policy challenges. She warns that the recently (re)emerging freedom-oriented welfare state reform approach and its extension to universal basic income have been relatively detached from macro-configurational concerns, in particular the concerns about institutions and the role of the state. Arguing against the conceptual reduction of welfare to anti-poverty policy, Haagh emphasizes the importance of institutional arrangement or configuration for stable entitlements such as institutions for favourable fiscal conditions.

Civil Society Organizations in Transition Economies

The participation of CSOs in social service delivery is not new in development discourse and practice, but represents a new trend in transition economies such as Russia and China. The space for social organizations at the grassroots level has been created by top-down legislation, government subsidies and contracting out. This newly created space, however, is full of tensions between bureaucracy and civil society over political, economic and social dimensions. At the local level in both Russia (Chapter 11) and China (Chapter 10), the central governments' efforts to address the rigid, bureaucratic system of the social provision have met with resistance from local-level administrators, who may act as gatekeepers.

According to Bingqin Li and colleagues, local governments in China utilize specific administrative functions that the central government does not have in order to protect their inefficient public social service provision by preventing CSOs from entering into social provision contracts. There is also an emerging new relationship between bureaucracy and CSOs. In China, the gatekeeping of bureaucracy is sometimes accompanied by bureaucrats actively learning from the CSOs, which leads to improvements in the performance of public sector service provision. This points to the importance of creating incentives for the bureaucracy to adapt to a new system of social policy governance in which CSOs play a significant role in delivering social services.

In Chapter 11 Linda J. Cook and Elena Iarskaia-Smirnova describe Russian reform of care services delivered by CSOs known as SONPOs (socially oriented non-profit organizations) for people with disabilities and children as a paradigm shift in the social service delivery by the Russian Federation. However, this paradigm shift has had mixed results across the areas of services: relative success in the services for children and failure in those for people with disabilities. In both policy areas, various problems and obstacles have hindered the effective delivery of social services. One of the key obstacles to providing efficient services under this outsourcing service regime is the limited inclusion of SONPOs in the public service provision system, and their concentration in a small number of regions. Various structural and institutional factors have created these obstacles: weak development of civil society with few and small SONPOs in many regions; bureaucracy resisting reform and preventing the interested SONPOs from being registered as eligible contractees; and rules and mechanisms for compensation designed to disfavour SONPOs.

Emergence of Supranational-level Social Policy

One of the key questions for social policy research in the twenty-first century is whether social policy can be studied in isolation from its embeddedness in an international society of nations. As the world is increasingly interconnected through the increased mobility of information, capital and people, transborder social policy issues associated with communicable disease, cooperation, mobility of professional qualifications and food security demand global approaches to social policy. Regional social policy, broadly defined as cross-border public interventions on a regional scale that directly affect social welfare, social institutions and social relations, has developed particularly rapidly in the areas where trade and economic integration has accelerated, such as Latin America. As Nicola Yeates reports in Chapter 1, various regional social policy instruments, ranging from declaration to regional standard-setting and regulation, to resource mobilization and allocation at the regional level, have been established in many regions of the world. She emphasizes the importance of the transnational or regional perspective in the analysis of contemporary social policy by examining the cases of the emergence of regional social policies and the spread of cash transfer programmes.

Informal Workers Shaping the System of Social Policy Programmes

The focus of social policy research on the actors shaping the welfare state or the system of social protection has been biased toward welfare states in industrialized countries. The history of the welfare state in industrialized countries has often been framed as the development of a formal social security system based on a mandatory contribution system. The key actors in this process are the central government, who set the rules and regulations on the mandatory contribution system, and those who are the subjects of the regulations and rules and can afford the contribution. Scholars with this bias have paid attention to organized political power of employers and workers, and in some cases, coalitions between them such as the coalition of industrial and agricultural workers. Chapters 3 and 7 demonstrate the need to expand this analytical scope, which is currently biased toward the welfare state history of industrial countries and explain the new dynamic created by the organization of informal workers to understand the changes in social policy of the global South. In Chapter 3, Rina Agarwala explains how certain organizations of informal workers emerge as a new political driver of social policy, providing a new conceptual and theoretical framework of political analysis of informal workers as actors in social policy formation. In addition to their coalition with formal workers, informal workers create new coalitions with immigrant and Indigenous rights movements, which produce varieties and continuities of the twenty-first-century social policy in the global South and North. The exploration of the development of social insurance for informal workers in Tanzania by Roosa Lambin and

Milla Nyyssölä in Chapter 7 is a good example of how governments in the global South change the provision of goods and services to informal workers and how informal workers are shaping the welfare system. In Tanzania, in particular, this is through the expansion of the formal social security system, which is one of the emerging trends in sub-Saharan Africa. Although they face significant challenges in accessing authorities compared with formal workers' associations when contributing to the design of national social policy schemes, evidence shows that informal workers' associations across sectors have acted as a key promoter of worker's rights in securing social security for all in the Tanzanian context.

National Ownership of Social Policy in the Context of Development Cooperation

Emphasis on the importance of the global view for and of social policy is not new. In the early 1960s, concerns about the lack of international perspective on social policy had already been raised by many scholars, albeit without much resultant research. The international or global perspective of social policy also demands that we expand our analytical scope of welfare to include knowledge and material resources transferred through governmental and non-governmental agencies across borders. Since the social turn in the 1990s, multilateral and bilateral donors, particularly international financial institutions, have significantly affected the forms and content of national social policies. The results regarding indicators of poverty, education and health are mixed in aid-dependent developing countries. What those countries with sustainable social policy programmes have in common, however, is strengthened social policy ownership. How can these countries, even though they are dependent upon aid to implement social protection programmes, have strong policy ownership? What are the impacts of the social policy ownership on institutions, programmes and actors in the social policy sector? Chapter 9 by Alexandra Kaasch and Brooke Wilmsen on the Indonesian case explains the nature of the relations between donors and recipients, which can facilitate the generation of strong and sound social policy ownership with a positive impact on social policy design and implementation. In particular, the chapter's analysis of how both donor and recipient governments could create institutional and organizational environments that facilitate positive interactions between donors' policy intervention and the Indonesian government's actions, placing the latter in the driving seat in a genuine sense, offers various lessons for policy ownership in the context of development cooperation.

In Chapter 8 on four North African countries, Heath Prince and colleagues explain well the mechanisms of international financial institutions (IFIs) that have created and continue to produce negative impacts in the policy areas where the Arab Spring occurred in the early 2010s. In Tunisia and Morocco, for instance, IFIs, major donors to these countries, have shaped social policies along the lines of economic growth-centred development strategies through prescriptive policy interventions embedded in the donor–recipient relationship. Policy prescriptions have only accentuated inequality and increased unemployment rates. The way IFIs intervene in social policy making has not changed since the Arab Spring, which gave a strong policy signal for redistribution and job creation-centred policies. IFIs have been preoccupied with "sound" macroeconomic policies rather than industrial policies, while continuing to neglect productive investment in industries to absorb a large number of highly educated unemployed youth.

Toward New Agendas for Social Policy Research

Are we witnessing the emergence of new directions in terms of theories and practices of social policy in these evolving policies and programmes? The short answer is yes—a qualified yes, since we are lacking comprehensive explanatory and analytical frameworks, precise tools and robust analytical skills to understand or measure the force and impacts of these emerging social policies and programmes. Theoretical discourse still revolves around what we learn from OECD high-income countries, such as many in Europe and the United States, and delves less enthusiastically and directly into the realities of what is occurring elsewhere, in particular those new social policies and programmes that have emerged across the global South or non-OECD middle- or low-income countries, which comprise 82.4 per cent of the world population and account for 36.3 per cent of the world's gross domestic product.

Will these new social policies and programmes contribute to transformative changes in developing countries and beyond in the twenty-first century? Perhaps, but again, a qualified perhaps. The design and implementation of social policy is a fundamentally political process where diverse political ideologies and actions compete with each other over the distribution of resources and outcomes. It is too early to tell whether and how these new and innovative social policies are genuinely transformative in the sense that they can correct the structures and relationships that generate poverty and inequality. Various challenges and opportunities can already be found both within the social policy sector and within the interfaces and linkages with other policy sectors. Further, even if a government succeeds in establishing social policy programmes that are transformative, social gains from those transformative programmes may not be translated into political gains or be sustained if they need a period longer than an election cycle to produce impacts strong enough to affect voters. Recent political events unfolding in

Russia and China that have caused these countries to drift away from the routes to democracy and peace are notable.

We still live with "considerable uncertainties about how to frame and manage disparate social programmes, many of which—driven by the market-friendliness of earlier years—provide at best minimal benefits, overdependent on the social safety net model," as Srinivas describes in Chapter 2. Our research on emerging trends in social policy in the global South shows silver linings. New perspectives and approaches to social policy that integrate policies across sectors and different levels of governance and absorb lessons from the global South as well as the global North, are needed to change these silver linings into golden opportunities for transformation.

Index

References to footnotes show both the page number and the note number (231n3).